Explore THE UNITED STATES

History

History is the study of events that happened in the past.

The Freedom Trail
Boston, Massachusetts

You Are There You're following the Freedom Trail through the narrow streets of Boston. You have to really watch your step since the sidewalks are made of brick. Wow! Most of these buildings are really old! Many were built before the United States became a country. You can picture what life was like here more than 200 years ago. You pass by the Old South Meeting House, where colonists held protests. You find Paul Revere's home, where he began his famous journey. You stand where a battle began at Bunker Hill. You can almost hear the firing of the cannons.

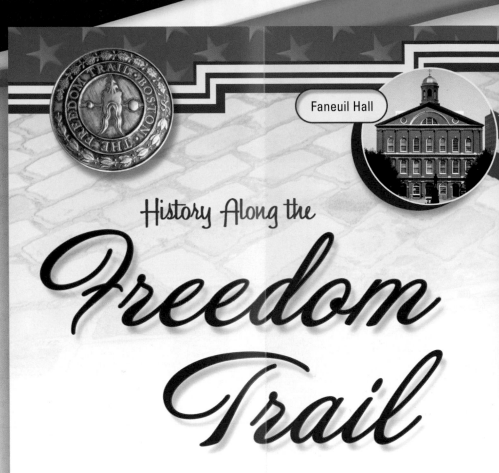

Faneuil Hall

History Along the

Freedom Trail

The Freedom Trail is a walking tour of sixteen historic places. Boston is one of the oldest cities in the United States. It was once part of a colony ruled by Great Britain. Many people in Boston fought for freedom from British rule. **Freedom** is the power to do, say, and think as you want. Each site on the Freedom Trail was important to the fight for freedom and the birth of our country.

The Freedom Trail

Boston ★

Bunker Hill Monument

A painted line connects the sixteen sites on the Freedom Trail.

USS *Constitution*

Paul Revere warned other colonists of a British attack the night before the American Revolution began. His house, the oldest wooden building in Boston, is a stop on the Freedom Trail.

Fast Facts:

- The Freedom Trail was created in 1958. It has helped preserve historic sites in Boston. **Preserve** means to keep something from being harmed or changed.

- The Freedom Trail starts at our country's oldest public park, called the Boston Common. Long ago the people of Boston used to graze sheep and cattle there.

Link to You

What historic buildings in your community have been preserved?

Economics

Economics is the study of how people produce, distribute, and use goods and services.

Georgia Peach Packinghouse

You Are There It's a hot summer day in Georgia. You're at a peach packinghouse. Hundreds of peaches roll past you. They were picked this morning and brought here by tractor. Each one is inspected. You watch as the peaches are washed, rinsed, and dried. They are inspected again. Peaches that are too small or bruised are removed. Then the good peaches are packed up in boxes. You know that once they are loaded into cold trucks, they will be on their way to stores.

E4

Get a taste of economics at work in the

Peach Packinghouse!

Years ago, the peaches **produced**, or grown, in Georgia could only be sold at nearby stores or stands. If peaches were shipped too far away or got too hot, they would spoil. Only people near the orchards could buy them fresh. The **profits**, or money made by the business, were small. Now peaches can be packed in refrigerated trucks. They are **transported**, or delivered, to places all over the country. Today, the state of Georgia earns about $35 million a year from the sale of peaches.

Peach Region

Peaches are used to make many other products such as peach preserves and peach pies.

Fast Facts:

• Georgia's nickname is "The Peach State."

• Fresh Georgia peaches are only available for about 16 weeks of the year.

Some forty different kinds of peaches are produced in Georgia's peach region.

75¢
Peaches

$1.75
Peaches

Link to You

What are some products produced in your state? What are some products that are transported to your state from other places?

Science and Technology

Science and technology change people's lives. These changes bring opportunities and challenges.

Windmill Tours
Palm Springs, California

You Are There The wind whips through your hair as you stand in the desert. A "sea of giants" surrounds you. Each one stands more than 100 feet tall with long powerful arms. As you gaze up at one of them, the sun reflects off the white metal. You squint. These "giants" are windmills, and they are using the wind to make electricity. As wind turns the blades, or arms, of the windmill, energy is produced. As you get ready to leave, you look behind you. The windmills are spinning almost silently. The wind rustles your hair again as you wave good-bye to the giants.

OBJECTS IN MIRROR ARE CLOSER THAN THEY APPEAR

Nature Meets Technology at

WINDMILL TOURS

Windmills are a good example of nature and technology working together. The windmill farm near Palm Springs, California, is in one of the windiest places in the state. More than 3,000 windmills line the valley. Wind power spins their blades. Engines inside these **modern**, or newer, windmills turn the wind's energy into electricity. An engine is a machine that uses movement to make power. **Electricity** is the kind of energy that can power a light bulb or TV.

Windmills have been used for hundreds of years. Modern windmills make more energy than older ones do.

Palm
Springs

More than 3,000 windmills line the valley.

Fast Facts:

- Wind must blow at least 14 miles per hour to spin the blades of a windmill. Wind farms are built in locations where it is windy most days of the year.

- The windmill farm near Palm Springs makes enough electricity to provide power for every house and business in the city.

Link to You

What are some things in your home that use electricity?

The vehicles used to give tours of the windmill farm do not use gasoline or cause pollution. They run on batteries charged by electricity made by wind power!

E7

Geography

Geography is the study of the relationship between Earth's physical features, climate, and people.

Mount Washington
New Hampshire

You Are There You're standing at the top of a snow-covered mountain. It's one of the windiest spots in the world! The wind howls against the windows of the observatory. You are safe and warm behind the thick glass of the building. Outside, you can see icicles that stick out sideways, straight off the building. You see people struggling to stand up straight against the wind. You take one last look out the window. Then you bundle up in your winter coat. You step outside, point the top of your head into the wind, and put one foot forward.

A Geography Getaway to

Mount

The unique physical geography of Mount Washington causes the cold and windy weather at its peak. **Weather** is the temperature and other conditions at a certain time and place. Mount Washington is located in the state of New Hampshire and is part of a **range**, or group of mountains. Cold winds blow upward from the mountains. Because Mount Washington is the tallest mountain in the range, it receives the coldest and fastest winds. Mount Washington's average **temperature**, or how hot or cold a place gets, is below freezing. One-hundred-mile per hour winds are common any time of the year.

Mount Washington is part of the Presidential Range in New Hampshire's White Mountains. Mountains in the range are named for United States Presidents.

BBRR

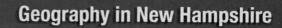

6,288 feet high!!!

Washington

Mount Washington is 6,288 feet high. You can see the weather station and observatory at the top.

Visitors to the observatory can see the Atlantic Ocean 60 miles away in good weather. The observatory is covered in snow, ice, and fog on most days.

RR!!!!

Fast Facts:

- The peak of Mount Washington is the highest, coldest, and windiest spot in the Northeast region of the United States.

- The world's fastest wind speed (231 miles per hour) was recorded on Mount Washington in 1934.

Link to You

How does the physical geography where you live affect the weather?

Culture

Culture includes the customs, traditions, behavior, and values of a group of people.

Let your friendships blossom...

Japanese Tea House and Friendship Garden
Saginaw, Michigan

You Are There The gong sounds and the tea ceremony, or "Way of Tea" begins. Taking off your shoes, you enter the tatami (tah TAH mee), or woven straw mat, tearoom. Then you walk toward the scroll and flowers and sit to admire them. You move next to your hostess, and wait as she prepares the tea in the traditional way, as it has long been done in Japan. While you watch, she adds boiling water to the tea and whisks it. When the tea is ready, you receive the tea bowl, then turn it twice and sip the tea. It is delicious!

Japanese Tea House
and Friendship Garden

The Friendship Garden is a traditional Japanese garden. The Garden and Tea House were built as symbols of friendship between the cities of Saginaw (SA-gi-naw), Michigan, and Tokushima (TOH-koo-shee-mah), Japan. A **symbol** is an object that represents an idea. People come here to learn about Japanese culture. Visitors can participate in an authentic Japanese tea ceremony in the Tea House. **Authentic** means done in a traditional way.

Saginaw

Fast Facts:

- No nails or paint are used in the construction of an authentic Japanese tea house.

- Japanese tea houses have very low doors. Guests must bend down to enter them.

Craftsmen from Japan helped build the Tea House in Saginaw. It looks like an authentic tea house from Japan.

Link to You

Have you ever seen or taken part in a cultural ceremony? What made it memorable?

Citizenship

Citizenship is the rights, privileges, and duties that a member of a nation has.

The Women's Museum
Dallas, Texas

You Are There You look into the eyes of Sojourner Truth's photograph. You remember learning that this brave woman fought hard for equal rights of citizenship. It was illegal for women to vote at the time this photograph was taken. Women were turned away from elections. Others were put in jail or even beaten for trying to vote. Sojourner Truth gave speeches about equality all over the country. You pause and look at her photograph again. You wonder if you could have been that brave.

Honor Citizenship and Equality at

The Women's Museum

WOMEN   HONOR   EQUALITY   CITIZENS

Dallas

The Women's Museum in Dallas, Texas, has exhibits that honor women who fought for equal rights of citizenship. **Rights** are things you are allowed to do. Although women have gained many rights over the years, some still fight for equality. **Equality** means having the same rights as others. The museum inspires visitors today to become responsible citizens and leaders by teaching about strong women.

Fast Facts:

- The Women's Museum in Dallas tells the stories of more than 3,000 American women.

- More than 100,000 people have visited the Women's Museum since it opened in 2000.

Companies and individual citizens donated money to open the museum.

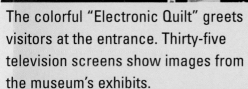

The colorful "Electronic Quilt" greets visitors at the entrance. Thirty-five television screens show images from the museum's exhibits.

Link to You

What rights do you have as a citizen? What responsibilities come along with those rights?

Government

A government is a system for ruling or running a city, state, or country.

State Capitol Complex
Honolulu, Hawaii

You Are There It is 9:55 A.M. on the third Wednesday in January. Today is Opening Day at Hawaii's State Capitol. You and your classmates have come to see how your state government works. You're curious to watch as lawmakers make big decisions. At 10:00 A.M., the doors will open and the year's first senate meeting will begin. You look up at the senate building. It is shaped like one of Hawaii's famous volcanoes. You can't wait to see what goes on inside!

Explore Government in the HAWAII STATE CAPITOL COMPLEX

Each island in Hawaii once had its own government. In 1810, Kamehameha (kah-MAY-ha-MAY-ha) united the Hawaiian Islands into one kingdom and became its first king. A monarchy (mahn-ARE-key) is a government ruled by a king or a **monarch**. Today, Hawaii is no longer a monarchy. It is a state of the United States of America. Like all states, Hawaii has a **constitution**, or a written plan of government. Hawaii's constitution is based on the constitution of the Kingdom of the Islands of Hawaii.

Hawaii's Capitol is in Honolulu, on one of the state's eight islands, Oahu (oh-AH-hoo). Hawaii is the only island state in our country.

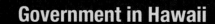

Honolulu

Visit the ONLY island state in our country!!!

Fast Facts:

- Hawaii became our fiftieth state in 1959.

- Hawaii is the only U.S. state that was once a monarchy.

Link to You

How does your state's government work for you?

King Kamehameha ruled the Kingdom of the Islands of Hawaii for many years. His palace was located in Honolulu.

KAMEHAMEHA I

National Symbols

Independence Hall
Philadelphia, Pennsylvania

◀ Many important events in United States history took place in Independence Hall. This stately, red brick building is a symbol of our nation's birth. Colonial leaders met here to plan the future of the new nation. The Declaration of Independence and the United States Constitution were both signed here.

The Declaration of Independence

▲

The Declaration of Independence is a document that declared the colonies free from British control. The document was signed in Independence Hall in 1776. It is a symbol of our nation's freedom.

Jefferson Memorial
Washington, D.C.

▲ The Jefferson Memorial honors Thomas Jefferson, an author of the Declaration of Independence and the third President of the United States. The memorial is a symbol of gratitude for Jefferson's contributions to our country.

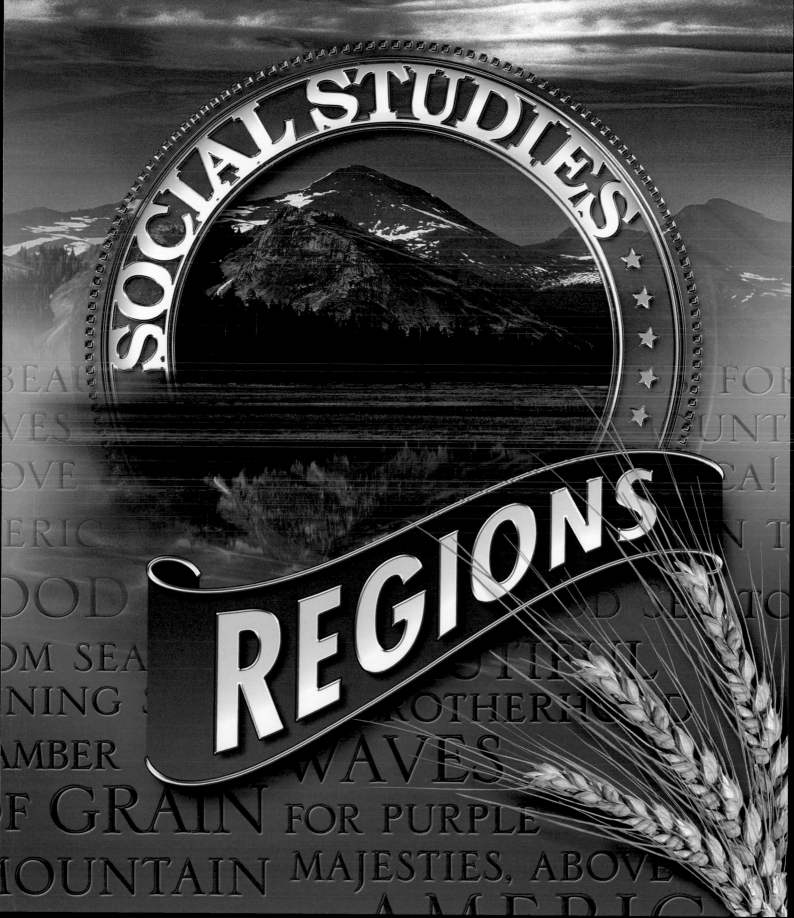

SCOTT FORESMAN

SOCIAL STUDIES

REGIONS

PROGRAM AUTHORS

Dr. Candy Dawson Boyd
Professor, School of Education
Director of Reading Programs
St. Mary's College
Moraga, California

Dr. Geneva Gay
Professor of Education
University of Washington
Seattle, Washington

Rita Geiger
Director of Social Studies and
Foreign Languages
Norman Public Schools
Norman, Oklahoma

Dr. James B. Kracht
Associate Dean for Undergraduate
Programs and Teacher Education
College of Education
Texas A&M University
College Station, Texas

Dr. Valerie Ooka Pang
Professor of Teacher Education
San Diego State University
San Diego, California

Dr. C. Frederick Risinger
Director, Professional Development
and Social Studies Education
Indiana University
Bloomington, Indiana

Sara Miranda Sanchez
Elementary and Early Childhood
Curriculum Coordinator
Albuquerque Public Schools
Albuquerque, New Mexico

CONTRIBUTING AUTHORS

Dr. Carol Berkin
Professor of History
Baruch College and the Graduate Center
The City University of New York
New York, New York

Lee A. Chase
Staff Development Specialist
Chesterfield County Public Schools
Chesterfield County, Virginia

Dr. Jim Cummins
Professor of Curriculum
Ontario Institute for Studies in Education
University of Toronto
Toronto, Canada

Dr. Allen D. Glenn
Professor and Dean Emeritus
Curriculum and Instruction
College of Education
University of Washington
Seattle, Washington

Dr. Carole L. Hahn
Professor, Educational Studies
Emory University
Atlanta, Georgia

Dr. M. Gail Hickey
Professor of Education
Indiana University-Purdue University
Fort Wayne, Indiana

Dr. Bonnie Meszaros
Associate Director
Center for Economic Education and
Entrepreneurship
University of Delaware
Newark, Delaware

CONTENT CONSULTANTS

Catherine Deans-Barrett
World History Specialist
Northbrook, Illinois

Dr. Michael Frassetto
Studies in Religions
Independent Scholar
Chicago, Illinois

Dr. Gerald Greenfield
Hispanic-Latino Studies
History Department
University of Wisconsin, Parkside
Kenosha, Wisconsin

Dr. Frederick Hoxie
Native American Studies
University of Illinois
Champaign, Illinois

Dr. Cheryl Johnson-Odim
Dean of Liberal Arts and Sciences and
Professor of History
African American History Specialist
Columbia College
Chicago, Illinois

Dr. Michael Khodarkovsky
Eastern European Studies
University of Chicago
Chicago, Illinois

Robert Moffet
U.S. History Specialist
Northbrook, Illinois

Dr. Ralph Nichols
East Asian History
University of Chicago
Chicago, Illinois

CLASSROOM REVIEWERS

Diana Vicknair Ard
Woodlake Elementary School
St. Tammany Parish
Mandeville, Louisiana

Sharon Berenson
Freehold Learning Center
Freehold, New Jersey

Betsy Blandford
Pocahontas Elementary School
Powhatan, Virginia

Nancy Neff Burgess
Upshur County Schools
Buckhannon-Upshur Middle School
Upshur County, West Virginia

Gloria Cantatore
Public School #5
West New York, New Jersey

Stephen Corsini
Content Specialist in Elementary Social Studies
School District 5 of Lexington
and Richland Counties
Ballentine, South Carolina

Deanna Crews
Millbrook Middle School
Elmore County
Millbrook, Alabama

LuAnn Curran
Westgate Elementary School
St. Petersburg, Florida

Kevin L. Curry
Social Studies Curriculum Chair
Hickory Flat Elementary School
Henry County, McDonough, Georgia

Sheila A. Czech
Sky Oaks Elementary School
Burnsville, Minnesota

Louis De Angelo
Office of Catholic Education
Archdiocese of Philadelphia
Philadelphia, Pennsylvania

Dr. Trish Dolasinski
Paradise Valley School District
Arrowhead Elementary School
Glendale, Arizona

Dr. John R. Doyle
Director of Social Studies Curriculum
Miami-Dade County Schools
Miami, Florida

Dr. Roceal Duke
District of Columbia Public Schools
Washington, D.C.

Peggy Flanagan
Roosevelt Elementary School
Community Consolidated School District #64
Park Ridge, Illinois

Mary Flynn
Arrowhead Elementary School
Glendale, Arizona

Sue Gendron
Spring Branch ISD
Houston, Texas

Su Hickenbottom
Totem Falls Elementary School
Snohomish School District
Snohomish, Washington

Allan Jones
North Branch Public Schools
North Branch, Minnesota

Brandy Bowers Kerbow
Bettye Haun Elementary School
Plano ISD
Plano, Texas

Martha Sutton Maple
Shreve Island School
Shreveport, Louisiana

Lyn Metzger
Carpenter Elementary School
Community Consolidated School District #64
Park Ridge, Illinois

Marsha Munsey
Riverbend Elementary School
West Monroe, Louisiana

Christine Nixon
Warrington Elementary School
Escambia County School District
Pensacola, Florida

Cynthia K. Reneau
Muscogee County School District
Columbus, Georgia

Brandon Dale Rice
Secondary Education Social Science
Mobile County Public School System
Mobile, Alabama

Liz Salinas
Supervisor
Edgewood ISD
San Antonio, Texas

Beverly Scaling
Desert Hills Elementary
Las Cruces, New Mexico

Madeleine Schmitt
St. Louis Public Schools
St. Louis, Missouri

Barbara Schwartz
Central Square Intermediate School
Central Square, New York

Editorial Offices:
• Glenview, Illinois
• Parsippany, New Jersey
• New York, New York

Sales Offices:
• Parsippany, New Jersey
• Duluth, Georgia
• Glenview, Illinois
• Coppell, Texas
• Ontario, California
• Mesa, Arizona

www.sfsocialstudies.com

ISBN: 0-328-07571-X

6 7 8 9 10 V057 13 12 11 10 09 08
07 06 05

Contents

UNIT 1

Continued

The Northeast

The Southeast

The Midwest

The Southwest

UNIT 6

The West

Reference Guide

★ BIOGRAPHY ★

Graphic Organizers

Charts, Graphs, Tables & Diagrams

Time Lines

Citizenship Skills

There are six ways to show good citizenship: through respect, fairness, caring, responsibility, courage, and honesty. In your textbook, you will learn about people who used these ways to help their community, state, and country.

Respect
Treat others as you would want to be treated. Welcome differences among people.

Fairness
Take turns and follow the rules. Listen to what other people have to say.

Caring
Think about what someone else needs.

Responsibility
Do what you are supposed to do and think before you act.

Courage
Do what is right even when the task is hard.

Honesty
Tell the truth and do what you say you will do.

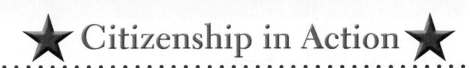

★ Citizenship in Action ★

Good citizens make careful decisions. They solve problems in a logical way. How will these students handle each situation as good citizens?

Decision Making

The students are choosing a pet for their classroom. The following steps will help them make a decision.

1. **Tell what decision you need to make.**

2. **Gather information.**

3. **List your choices.**

4. **Tell what might happen with each choice.**

5. **Act according to your decision.**

Problem Solving

Sometimes students argue at recess over whose turn it is to have a ball. The fourth-graders can use the following steps to help them solve the problem.

1. **Name the problem.**

2. **Find out more about the problem.**

3. **List ways to solve the problem.**

4. **Talk about the best way to solve the problem.**

5. **Solve the problem.**

6. **Then figure out how well the problem was solved.**

Living History from
Colonial Williamsburg
www.history.org

Think Like a Historian

Written records are a way for us to learn about the past. Historians search libraries for letters, diaries, and other records. Documents written by the people who saw the events, places, and people of the past are called primary sources. Primary sources help us understand what life was like long ago.

Nicholas Cresswell traveled in Virginia in 1777. This is how he described the city of Williamsburg.

"The Capitol is the place where all public business is done, the Colonial Assembly meets, &c . . . In the Capitol is a fine marble statue of the late Governor . . . "

"This is the finest town I have seen in Virginia . . . It consists of one principal street about a mile long, very wide and level with a number of good buildings, the Capitol at the end of the street and the College at the other . . . "

Capitol

Governor Botetourt

"The Governor's Palace is a good brick building, but it does not make a grand appearance."

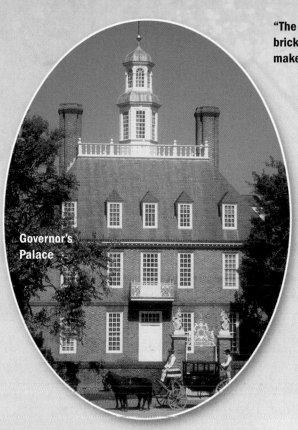

Governor's Palace

"Here is only one Church, none the grandest, and I suppose there may be about 250 houses in town."

Bruton Parish Church

College of William and Mary

Write a description of your neighborhood. Use details that will help people in the future understand what life was like there. What does it look like? Who lives there? What events take place there?

Research Skills

When you need to find information for a report or a project, you can use three main resources: **Print Resources**, **Technology Resources**, and **Community Resources**.

The information you find can be from either primary or secondary sources. Primary sources are documents that were written by people who lived at that time or who were at an event and saw it. Journals, diaries, letters, and photographs are all primary sources.

Secondary sources are descriptions of an event written by people who have researched the event. These people tell what they learned from reading about the event and looking at primary sources, but they were not there. Look for both kinds of sources when you do research.

Print Resources

A **reference tool** is any source of information. Books are reference tools. Libraries often have reference books such as atlases, almanacs, dictionaries, and encyclopedias. Usually, reference materials cannot be checked out of the library, but you can use them to look up information while you are at the library.

An **encyclopedia** is a collection of articles, listed alphabetically, on various topics. When you need information quickly, an encyclopedia is a good choice. Electronic encyclopedias, available on the Internet or CD-ROM, have sound and video clips in addition to text.

A **dictionary** is an alphabetical collection of words, their spellings, their meanings, and their pronunciations. If you find a word you don't understand, you can look it up in a dictionary. Many dictionaries also include abbreviations, names, and explanations of well-known people and places.

An **atlas** is a collection of maps. Some atlases have one particular kind of map. Others have a variety of maps showing elevation, crops, population, or natural resources.

An **almanac** is a book or computer resource that lists facts about a variety of topics. Almanacs are usually organized in sections by topic. Much information is given in charts, tables, and lists. Almanacs are usually updated every year, so they have the latest statistics on population, weather, and other topics.

A **nonfiction book** is a book on a topic that was researched and written by someone who knows about that topic. In a library, all nonfiction books are numbered and placed in order on the shelves. Books on the same subject are grouped together. You can search for a book in the library's catalog by title, subject, or author. The call number of the book will guide you to the area of the library where you will find the book. A librarian can help you.

A **periodical**, such as a newspaper or a magazine, is published on a regular basis, usually daily, weekly or monthly. Most libraries have a special periodical section. Many magazines and newspapers also have their own Web sites.

Technology Resources

You can use technology such as the Internet, CD-ROMs, databases, television programs, and radio programs as sources of information.

The Internet is a system of linked computers that can store information for others to find and use. The World Wide Web, which is part of the Internet, has a great deal of information.

Before you search for information on the Web, plan your research. If you want to research your community or neighborhood, write down some words or names of places you can use to search the Web. If you have not used the Internet before, you might want to ask a librarian, teacher, or parent for help.

To find a search engine to begin your research, click on SEARCH or NET SEARCH at the top of your screen. Type one of your subject words or terms into the search engine field. Then click SEARCH or GO. The computer will list Web sites about your topic. You can try different search engines for more complete results.

Web sites have Uniform Resource Locators, or URLs. A URL is like an address. If you already know the address of a site that might have information you need, type it in the LOCATION/GO TO box in the upper left corner of the screen. Here is an example of a URL: www.sfsocialstudies.com.

It is important to check all information you find on the Web to make sure it is accurate. Try to find at least three reliable sources that give similar information. Once you find a reliable Web site, you can mark it so that you can find it again. Click BOOKMARKS at the top of your screen and choose ADD BOOKMARK.

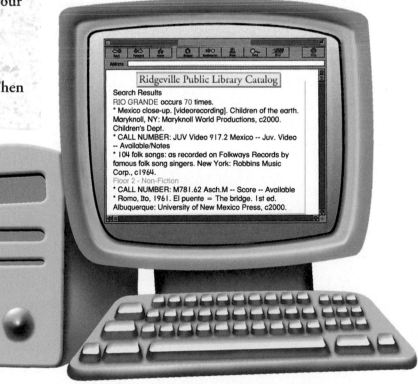

Community Resources

The people in your community are good sources of information.

Interviews

An interview is a good way to find out what people in your community know. This means asking them questions about the topic you are researching. Follow these steps:

Plan ahead
- List the people you want to interview.
- Call or write to ask if you can interview them. Let the person know who you are and why you need information.
- Agree on a time and place to meet.
- Find out about the topic.
- Write a list of questions to ask.

Ask/Listen/Record
- Ask questions clearly.
- Listen carefully. Be polite. Do not interrupt.
- Write notes so that you will remember what was said. If possible, use a tape recorder.

Wrap-up
- Thank the person when you are finished.
- Send a thank-you note.

Surveys

A survey is a list of questions that you ask people, recording everyone's answers. This gives you an idea about what people in your community know, think, or feel about a subject. You can use yes or no questions or short-answer questions. Make a tally sheet with a column for answers to each question. Follow these steps:
- Write down a list of questions.
- Decide where you want to conduct the survey and how many people you want to ask.
- Use a tally sheet to record answers.
- After the survey, look through the responses and write what you found out.

How long have you lived in the neighborhood?	What has changed the most?	What has changed the least?	What do you like most about living here?
30 years	There used to be cornfields at the end of the street.	People still feed ducks at the pond in the park.	People are still friendly.
12 years	There are several tall buildings now.	Our track team is still first in the district.	I have lots of friends here.

Write for Information

Another way to get information from people or organizations in your community is to e-mail or write a letter asking for information. Follow these steps:
- Plan what you want to say.
- Tell who you are and why you are writing.
- Thank the person.
- Be neat and careful about spelling and punctuation.

Writing a Research Report

Prewrite

- Decide on a topic for your report. Your teacher may tell you what kind of report to research and write, and how long it should be.
- Write down questions about the topic for which you want to find answers.
- Use different sources to find information and answers for your questions. Be sure to write down all your sources. This list of sources is called a bibliography.
- Take notes about what you learn from your sources.
- Review the notes you have taken from all your sources.
- Write down the main ideas you want to write about. Two or three main ideas are enough for most reports.
- Make an outline, listing each main idea and some details about each main idea.

Write a First Draft

- Using your outline, write what you have learned, using sentences and paragraphs. Each paragraph should be about a new idea.
- When you use exact words from your sources, give credit to that source. Write down the sources from which you got the information. This list of sources will become part of your bibliography.

Revise

- Read over your first draft. Does it make sense? Do you need more information about any main idea?
- Change any sentences or paragraphs that do not make sense. Add anything that will make your ideas clear.
- Check your quotations to make sure they are accurate.

Edit

- Proofread your report. Correct any errors in spelling, grammar, capitalization, sentence structure, and punctuation.

Publish

- Add pictures, maps, or other graphics that will help make your report interesting.
- Write or keyboard a final copy as neatly as possible.

Geography Skills

Five Themes of Geography

Geography is the study of Earth. This study can be divided into five themes that help you understand why Earth has such a wide variety of places. Each theme reveals something different about a spot, as the following example of Grand Teton National Park shows.

Location

Where is this park located? Grand Teton National Park is located in Wyoming at about 44°N, 111°W.

Place

How is this area different from others? Grand Teton National Park has steep mountains without foothills.

Human/Environment Interaction

How have people changed this place? The park's largest lake was partly created when people built a dam.

Movement

How has movement changed the region? Grand Teton National Park has an airport and is the only national park to have one.

Region

What is special about Grand Teton's region? The park is in a rugged area that is part of the Rocky Mountains.

Geography Skills

What Does a Globe Show?

This is an image of Earth. It lets you clearly see some of Earth's large landforms (continents) and bodies of water (oceans).

The image below shows Earth as it actually is.

Vocabulary

globe
equator
prime meridian
hemisphere

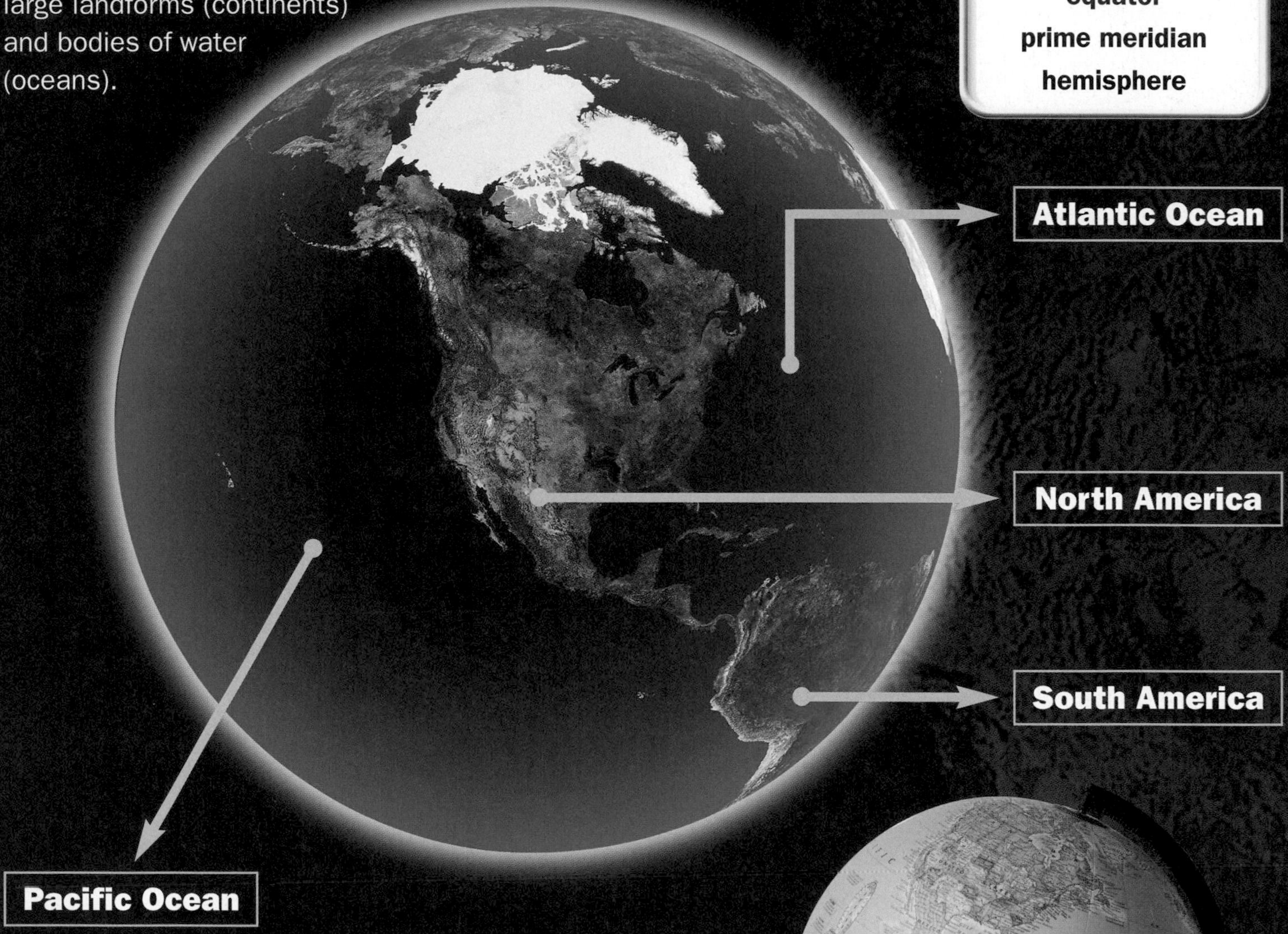

Atlantic Ocean

North America

South America

Pacific Ocean

At the right is a **globe,** a small copy of Earth you can hold in your hands. It has drawings of Earth's seven continents and four oceans. Can you name the continents and oceans not shown here?

Also, a globe shows the two imaginary lines that divide Earth into halves—the **equator** and the **prime meridian.**

Hemispheres: Northern and Southern

You can see only half of Earth or of a globe at a time. Half views of Earth have names—**hemispheres**—and the illustration at left below shows Earth separated into these views at the equator. The **Northern Hemisphere** is the half north of the equator, which circles Earth halfway between the poles. However, there is only one way to see the Northern Hemisphere all at once. You have to turn a globe until you are looking down directly at the North Pole. The picture at the top right shows that view.

What are the only continents not found, at least in part, in the Northern Hemisphere?

The **Southern Hemisphere** is the half of Earth south of the equator. The picture below turns the globe until you are looking down directly at the South Pole. You see all of the Southern Hemisphere. Which hemisphere—northern or southern—contains more land?

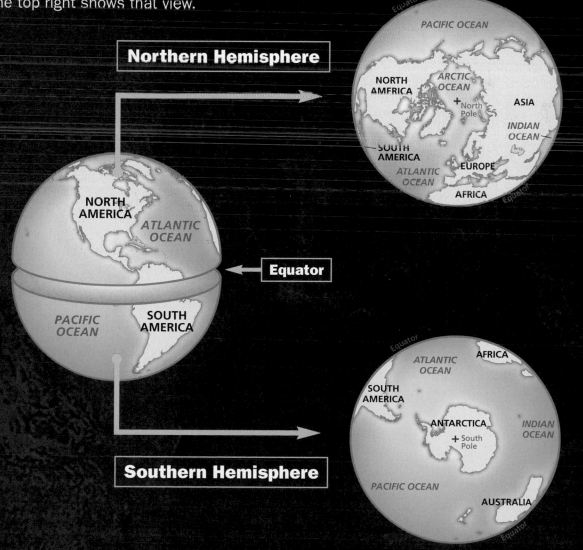

Geography Skills

Hemispheres: Western and Eastern

Earth has two other hemispheres. They are formed by dividing Earth into halves a different way, along the prime meridian. The prime meridian is an imaginary line that runs from the North Pole to the South Pole. It passes through Greenwich, England, an area of London. The **Eastern Hemisphere** is the half east of the prime meridian. The prime meridian passes through which continents?

The **Western Hemisphere** is the half of Earth west of the prime meridian. Which two continents are found entirely within this hemisphere? Which of the four oceans is not found in this hemisphere? In which two hemispheres is the United States found?

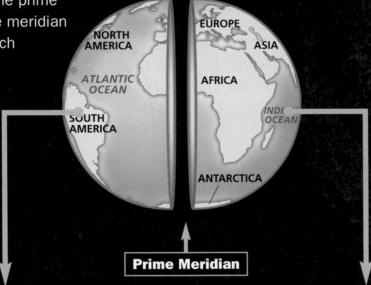

NORTH AMERICA
ATLANTIC OCEAN
SOUTH AMERICA
EUROPE
ASIA
AFRICA
INDIAN OCEAN
ANTARCTICA

Prime Meridian

North Pole
Prime Meridian
ARCTIC OCEAN
NORTH AMERICA
ATLANTIC OCEAN
AFRICA
Equator
PACIFIC OCEAN
SOUTH AMERICA
ANTARCTICA
Prime Meridian
South Pole

Western Hemisphere

North Pole
Prime Meridian
EUROPE
ARCTIC OCEAN
ASIA
PACIFIC OCEAN
AFRICA
Equator
INDIAN OCEAN
AUSTRALIA
ANTARCTICA
Prime Meridian
South Pole

Eastern Hemisphere

Understand Latitude and Longitude on a Globe

Mapmakers created a system for noting the exact location of places on Earth. The system uses two sets of imaginary circles crossing Earth. They are numbered in units called **degrees.**

Lines of **latitude** are the set of circles that go east and west. The equator is 0 degrees (0°) latitude. From there, the parallel circles go north and south. They get smaller and smaller until they end in dots at the North Pole (90°N) and the South Pole (90°S). The globe below at the left is tilted to show latitude lines 15° apart up to the North Pole. Most of the United States falls between which degrees of latitude?

Lines of **longitude** are the set of half-circles that go north and south. They are all the same size. The prime meridian is 0° longitude. However, from there, the degrees fan out between the North and South poles. They are not parallel and go east and west for 180°, not just 90°. The globe below at the right shows longitude lines 15° apart. They meet at 180° on the other side of Earth directly behind the prime meridian. Most of Africa falls between which degrees of longitude?

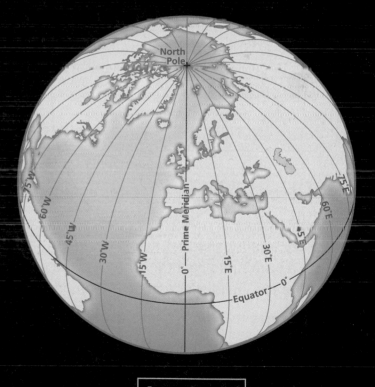

Longitude

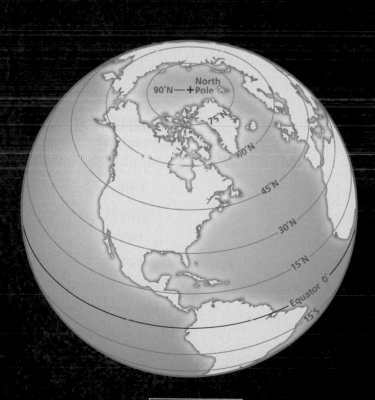

Latitude

Geography Skills

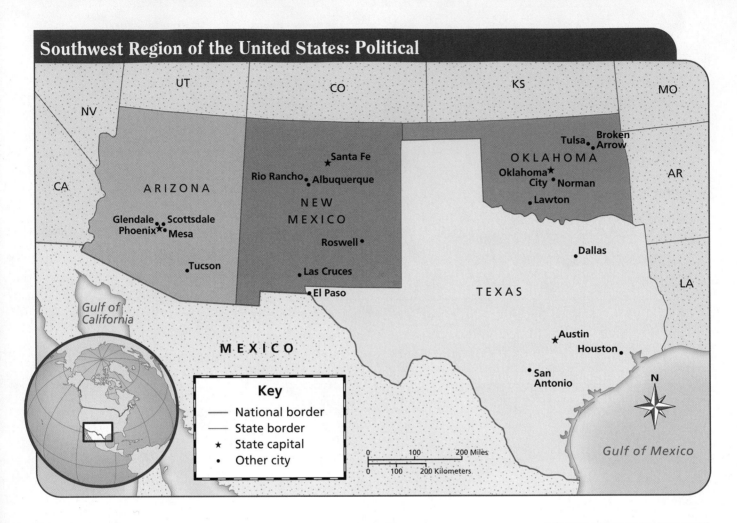

Southwest Region of the United States: Political

UT · NV · CO · KS · MO · CA · ARIZONA · NEW MEXICO · Santa Fe · Rio Rancho · Albuquerque · OKLAHOMA · Tulsa · Broken Arrow · Oklahoma City · Norman · AR · Glendale · Scottsdale · Phoenix · Mesa · Lawton · Tucson · Roswell · Dallas · Las Cruces · TEXAS · LA · El Paso · Gulf of California · MEXICO · Austin · Houston · San Antonio · Gulf of Mexico

Key
— National border
— State border
★ State capital
• Other city

0 100 200 Miles
0 100 200 Kilometers

N

Political Map

A **political map** shows what humans have created on Earth's surface. This means that a political map can show borders that divide an area into countries, states, and counties. It can also show cities, roads, buildings, and other human-made elements.

A map's **title** tells what a map is about. What is the title of this map?

A map's **symbols** are lines, small drawings, or fields of color that stand for something else. The map's **key,** or legend, is a small box that tells what each symbol stands for. What do the stars stand for on the map?

Sometimes a map has a **locator,** a small map in a box or circle. It locates the main map in a larger area such as a state, country, continent, or hemisphere. In what larger area is the Southwest region shown?

Vocabulary

political map
title
symbol
key
locator
physical map
compass rose
cardinal direction

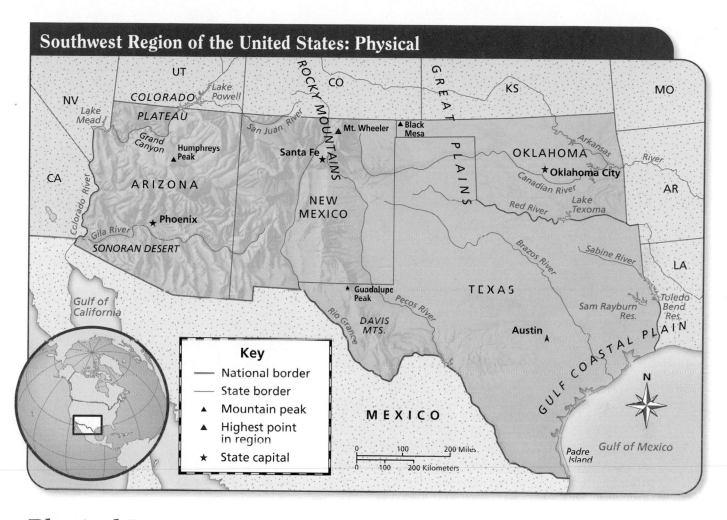

Southwest Region of the United States: Physical

Key

— National border
— State border
▲ Mountain peak
▲ Highest point in region
★ State capital

0   100   200 Miles
0   100   200 Kilometers

Physical Map

A **physical map** shows the major landforms and water on an area of Earth's surface. What are some examples of mountains, a desert, rivers, and gulfs on the physical map of the Southwest region on this page? Notice that a physical map can have a few elements of a political map.

A **compass rose** is a fancy design with four large pointers that show the **cardinal directions.** The north pointer, which points toward the North Pole, is marked with an **N**. East is to the right, south is opposite north, and west is to the left. What direction is the Gulf of Mexico from the Gulf of California?

Four other features common on maps are intermediate directions, scale, grid, and latitude and longitude. They are covered in detail on the following pages.

Geography Skills

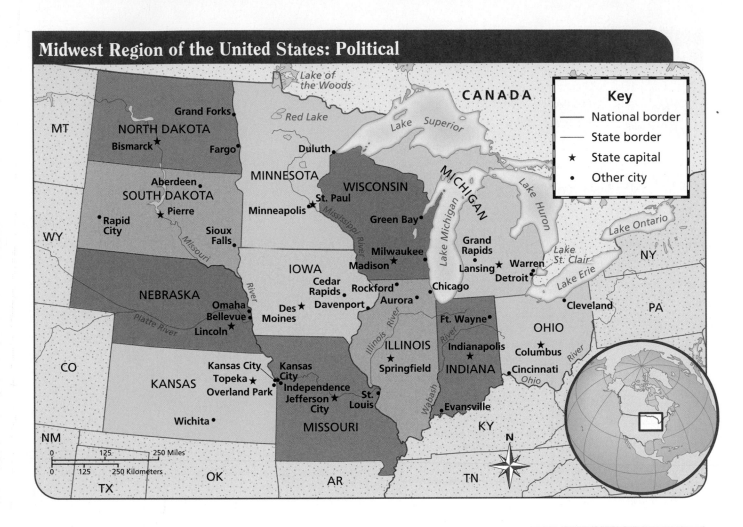

Midwest Region of the United States: Political

Key
— National border
— State border
★ State capital
• Other city

Lake of the Woods · Red Lake · Lake Superior · CANADA

MT

Grand Forks
NORTH DAKOTA
Bismarck ★   Fargo •   Duluth •

MINNESOTA
Aberdeen •
SOUTH DAKOTA
★ Pierre   St. Paul ★   WISCONSIN
Minneapolis •   Green Bay •
• Rapid City
WY
Sioux Falls •   Milwaukee •   Madison ★
Missouri
IOWA   Cedar Rapids •   Rockford •   Chicago •
NEBRASKA   Des ★ Davenport •   Aurora •
Omaha •   Moines
Bellevue •   Platte River   Illinois River
Lincoln ★

MICHIGAN
Lake Michigan   Lake Huron
Grand Rapids •   Lake St. Clair
Lansing ★ Warren •
Detroit •   Lake Erie
Lake Ontario   NY

Ft. Wayne •   Cleveland •   PA
OHIO
ILLINOIS   Indianapolis ★   Columbus ★
★ Springfield   INDIANA   • Cincinnati
Ohio River

CO
KANSAS
Kansas City •   Kansas City •
Topeka ★   Independence •
Overland Park   Jefferson ★   St. Louis •
City
Wichita •   MISSOURI   • Evansville   Wabash
KY

NM
0   125   250 Miles
0   125   250 Kilometers
TX   OK   AR   TN   N

Mississippi River

Intermediate Directions

As you just reviewed, a compass rose is a pointer that shows the four cardinal directions. Look at the compass rose on the map on this page. In addition to showing the large cardinal directions, it shows smaller points that are midway between them. These are the **intermediate directions.**

Each intermediate direction shares the names of the cardinal directions on either side of it. For example, the intermediate direction between north and east is called northeast. The intermediate directions are **northeast, southeast, southwest,** and **northwest.** Which state is southeast of Nebraska? Which is northeast of Iowa? What direction is Madison, Wisconsin, from Columbus, Ohio?

Vocabulary

intermediate direction

northeast

southeast

southwest

northwest

scale

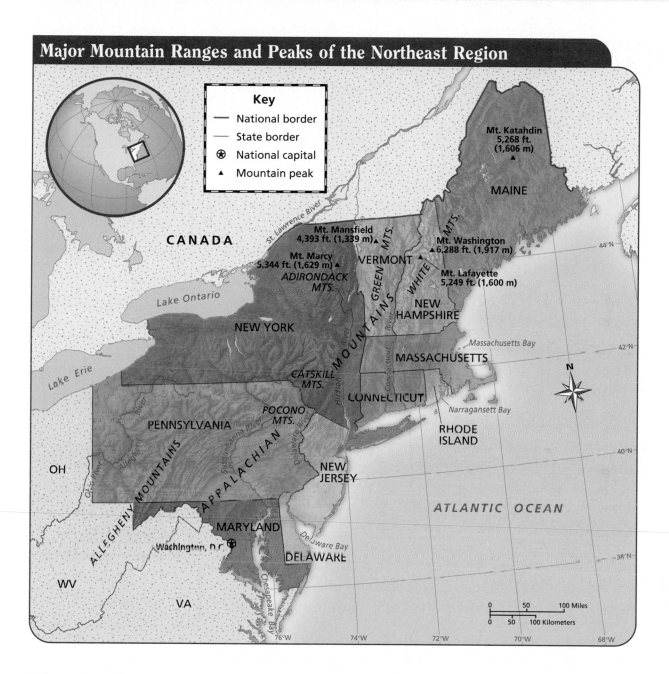

Major Mountain Ranges and Peaks of the Northeast Region

Key
— National border
— State border
⊗ National capital
▲ Mountain peak

Mt. Katahdin
5,268 ft.
(1,606 m)
▲

MAINE

CANADA

St. Lawrence River

Mt. Mansfield
4,393 ft. (1,339 m)▲

Mt. Marcy
5,344 ft. (1,629 m) ▲
ADIRONDACK
MTS.

VERMONT

Mt. Washington
▲6,288 ft. (1,917 m)

Mt. Lafayette
5,249 ft. (1,600 m)

WHITE MTS.

GREEN MTS.

Lake Ontario

NEW YORK

NEW
HAMPSHIRE

44°N

Massachusetts Bay

MASSACHUSETTS

42°N

Lake Erie

CATSKILL
MTS.

CONNECTICUT

N

POCONO
MTS.

PENNSYLVANIA

Narragansett Bay

RHODE
ISLAND

40°N

OH

APPALACHIAN

ALLEGHENY MOUNTAINS

NEW
JERSEY

ATLANTIC OCEAN

MARYLAND

Washington, D.C. ⊗

Delaware Bay

DELAWARE

38°N

WV

Chesapeake Bay

VA

0   50   100 Miles
0   50   100 Kilometers

76°W   74°W   72°W   70°W   68°W

Use Scale

A **scale** will help you figure out how far it is in real miles or kilometers from one point on a map to another. Starting at 0, a scale marks off tens, hundreds, or even thousands of miles. The measurement chosen depends on the size of the area shown. One way to use the scale is to hold the edge of a scrap of paper under the scale and copy the scale onto it. Then you can place your copy directly on the map and measure the distance between two points. Use the scale on the map above to help you find out about how far it is in miles from Mt. Katahdin to Mt. Washington. Is this a political or a physical map?

Geography Skills

Downtown Chicago, Illinois

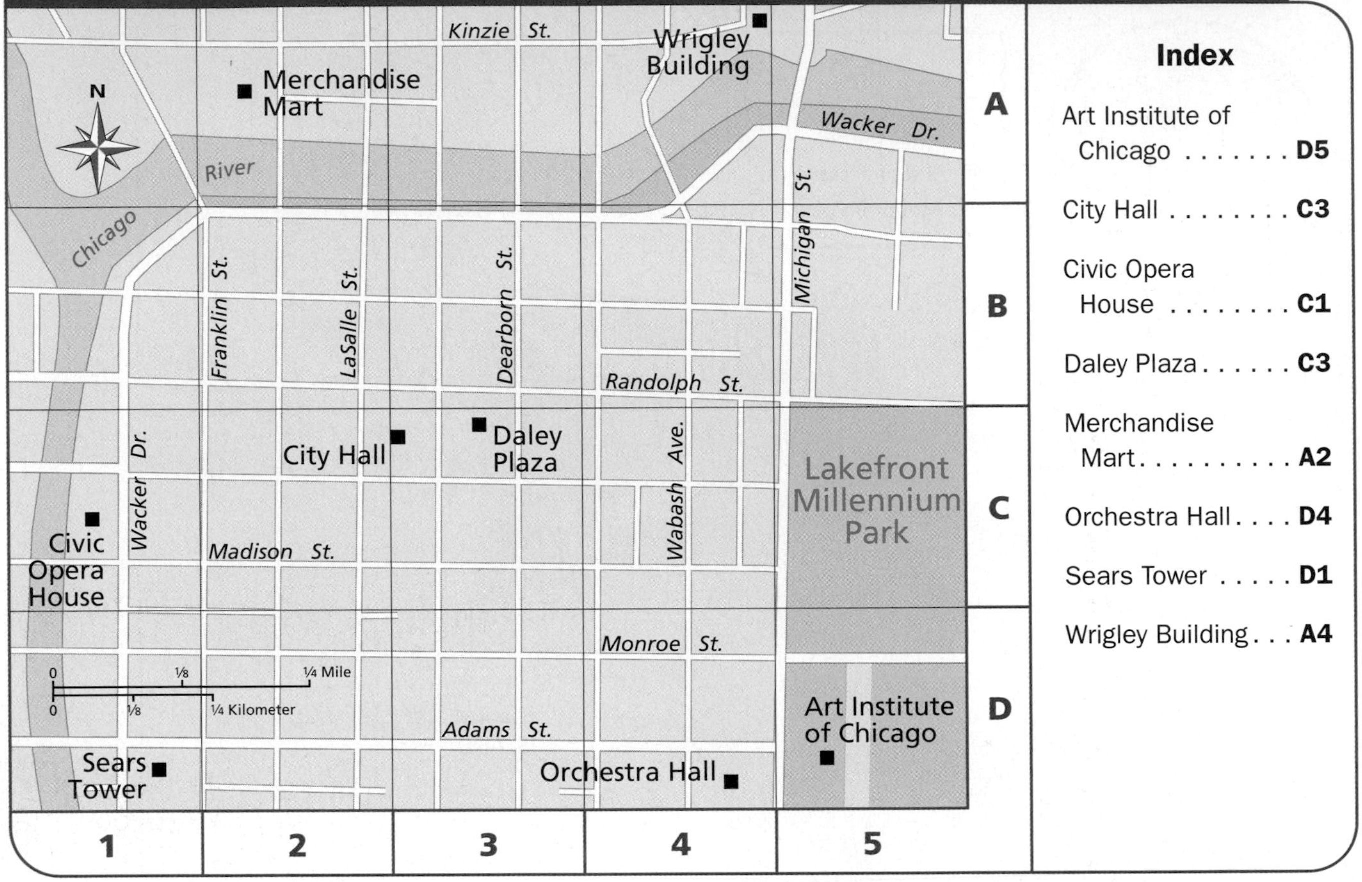

	Index
	Art Institute of Chicago **D5**
	City Hall **C3**
	Civic Opera House **C1**
	Daley Plaza **C3**
	Merchandise Mart **A2**
	Orchestra Hall **D4**
	Sears Tower **D1**
	Wrigley Building . . . **A4**

Map labels: Kinzie St., Wrigley Building, Wacker Dr., Merchandise Mart, River, Chicago, Franklin St., LaSalle St., Dearborn St., Michigan St., Randolph St., Wacker Dr., City Hall, Daley Plaza, Wabash Ave., Lakefront Millennium Park, Civic Opera House, Madison St., Monroe St., Art Institute of Chicago, Adams St., Sears Tower, Orchestra Hall

Scale: 0 ⅛ ¼ Mile / 0 ⅛ ¼ Kilometer

Grid rows: A, B, C, D — Columns: 1, 2, 3, 4, 5

Use a Grid

A city map shows the streets of a city. It might also show some points of interest or natural features. What natural feature do you see on this map? Point to and name a street in downtown Chicago.

This map also has a **grid.** A grid is a system of rows of imaginary squares on the map. The rows of squares are numbered and lettered along the edges of the map. You can use an index to find places where rows of numbers and letters cross. An **index** is an alphabetical listing of places. The number-letter combination attached to each place tells you where the two rows cross. Here you can find the place you are looking for.

Look down the index until you find "Sears Tower." It is located in grid square D1. Find the "D" row on the map and move your finger over to where the "1" row crosses it. Now find the City Hall in the same way.

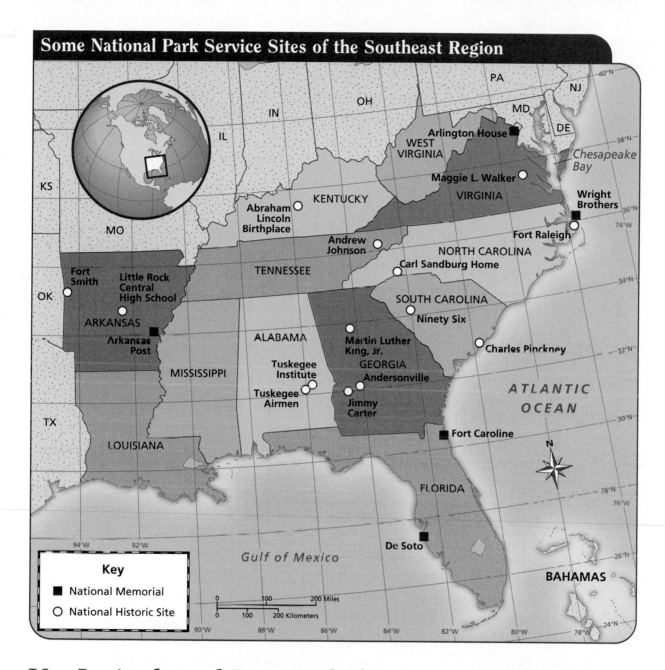

Some National Park Service Sites of the Southeast Region

Key

- ■ National Memorial
- ○ National Historic Site

Use Latitude and Longitude for Exact Location

Lines of latitude and longitude are like city-map grid rows. When they are used on a map, the lines are numbered in degrees along the edges. Each point where east-west latitude and north-south longitude cross is an exact location. If a place is found at or nearly at where latitude and longitude lines cross, the place takes those two numbers as its exact location.

In the map above the exact location of Tuskegee Airmen National Historic Site is almost 32°N, 86°W. The Andersonville site is nearly 32°N, 84°W. What two sites are found at nearly 36°N, 76°W?

Geography Skills

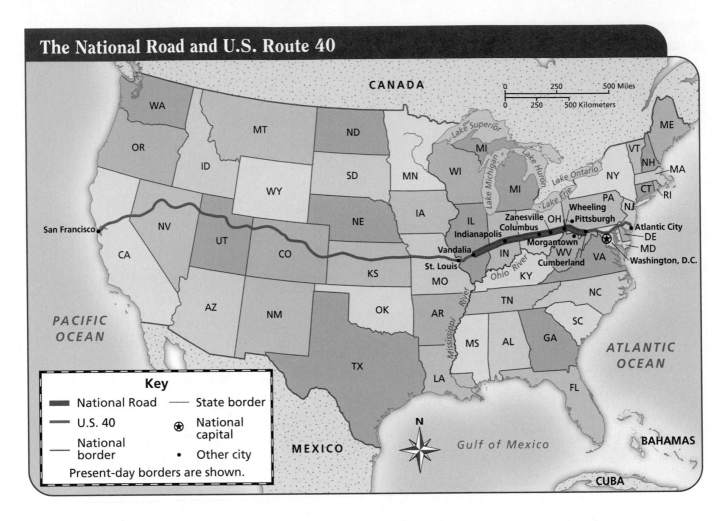

The National Road and U.S. Route 40

CANADA

WA
OR
ID
MT
ND
SD
MN
WI
MI
MI
Lake Superior
Lake Michigan
Lake Huron
Lake Ontario
Lake Erie
ME
VT
NH
MA
NY
CT
RI
PA
NJ

NV
UT
WY
CO
NE
IA
IL
Indianapolis
Vandalia
IN
OH
Columbus
Zanesville
Wheeling
Pittsburgh
Morgantown
WV
Cumberland
VA
MD
DE
Atlantic City
Washington, D.C.

San Francisco
CA
AZ
NM
KS
OK
St. Louis
MO
AR
Ohio River
KY
TN
NC
SC
GA

Mississippi River

MS
AL

TX
LA
FL

PACIFIC
OCEAN

ATLANTIC
OCEAN

MEXICO

N

Gulf of Mexico

BAHAMAS

CUBA

0   250   500 Miles
0   250   500 Kilometers

Key

— National Road
— U.S. 40
─ National border
— State border
⊛ National capital
• Other city

Present-day borders are shown.

Follow the Routes of a Historic Road

The map on this page shows the routes of the old National Road and U.S. Route 40. Federal funds for the National Road were approved when Thomas Jefferson was president. Construction began in Cumberland, Maryland, in 1811. By the 1830s, stagecoaches and wagons followed the National Road through several states. What city lay at the western end of the old National Road in the 1800s? Which states did the National Road pass through?

In the 1920s a new highway, U.S. Route 40, was built. This highway covered much of the same route as the old National Road in the eastern part of the United States. By the 1950s, U.S. Route 40 stretched 3,220 miles from coast to coast. Later, the Interstate highway system was created. About 800 miles of U.S. 40 were discontinued. Today U.S. 40 ends in the west in Utah.

Living in the United States

What unites people in the different regions of the United States?

Begin with a Primary Source

"This land is your land, this land is my land,
From California, to the New York island,
From the redwood forest to the Gulf Stream waters;
This land was made for you and me." —Woody Guthrie, from "This Land Is Your Land"©

Welcome to the United States

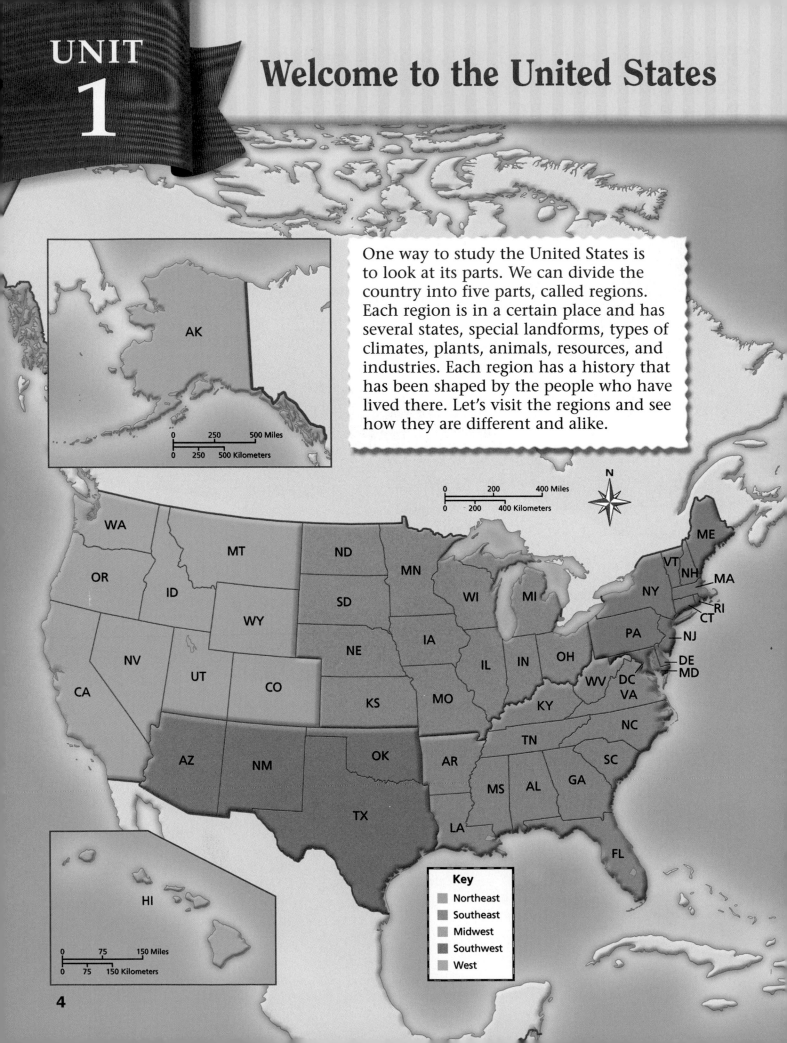

One way to study the United States is to look at its parts. We can divide the country into five parts, called regions. Each region is in a certain place and has several states, special landforms, types of climates, plants, animals, resources, and industries. Each region has a history that has been shaped by the people who have lived there. Let's visit the regions and see how they are different and alike.

AK

0   250   500 Miles
0   250   500 Kilometers

N

0   200   400 Miles
0   200   400 Kilometers

WA
OR
MT
ID
ND
MN
ME
VT
NH
MA
NY
WI
MI
NV
UT
WY
SD
IA
CA
CO
NE
IL
IN
OH
PA
NJ
DE
MD
WV
DC
VA
AZ
NM
KS
MO
KY
NC
TN
OK
AR
SC
GA
MS
AL
TX
LA
FL
RI
CT

HI

0   75   150 Miles
0   75   150 Kilometers

Key

Northeast
Southeast
Midwest
Southwest
West

Midwest

Northeast

West

Southeast

Southwest

For more information, go online to the *Atlas* at **www.sfsocialstudies.com.**

Living in the United States

Summarize

- Summarizing will help you recall and organize information.
- Choose important details or events as you read.
- Leave out unimportant details or events.
- Use only a sentence or two in a summary.

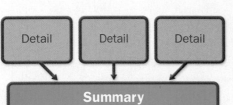

| Detail | Detail | Detail |

Summary
A summary is a short statement that tells the main ideas of an article or story.

Read the following paragraph. The most important ideas have been highlighted.

The United States is divided into five regions. The regions are the Northeast, the Southeast, the Midwest, the Southwest, and the West. These regions have many different landforms. They also have different climates. The five regions are surrounded by both land and water.

Summary: The five regions of the United States have different landforms and climates.

Word Exercise

Superlatives A **superlative** is a form of a word or a combination of words that shows the greatest something can be. *Best* is a superlative of *good*. *Fastest* is a superlative of *fast*. Sometimes a superlative is made by adding the *-est* ending to an adjective. The passage says that the hottest climates are found in the West. The word *hottest* is made by adding *-est* to the word *hot*.

| hot | + | -est | = | hottest |

The United States: Vast and Varied

The United States covers most of the southern part of the continent of North America. It is surrounded by both water and land. The Pacific Ocean is to the west and the Atlantic Ocean is to the east. Mexico and the Gulf of Mexico are to the south, and Canada and the Great Lakes are to the north. The United States is more than 3.5 million square miles in land area. It would take more than two days and nights of non-stop driving to cross this country from coast to coast. The main part of the country is so large that it crosses four different time zones. Alaska and Hawaii are in two additional time zones.

Across the five regions of the United States, landforms and climates can be very different. Farmlands stretch through the Midwest. Warm, sandy beaches line the Southeast, and tall, jagged mountains rise in the West. Climates range from freezing cold to dangerously hot. In one day it could be snowing in the Northeast, raining in the Southwest, and as hot as 100° F in the West. Even within each region, landscape and climate can be different. For example, the West region has the highest and lowest landforms in the United States as well as the hottest and coldest areas.

Use the reading strategy of summarizing to answer questions 1 and 2. Then answer the vocabulary question.

1 What is the most important idea in paragraph one?

2 Which sentence is the better summary of the passage?
   a. The United States is a big country, and the five regions have different landscapes and climates.
   b. The United States is so large that it has five regions.

3 The superlative form of the word *hot* is *hottest*. What other superlative words can you find in the passage? From what words are they formed?

CHAPTER 1

The Regions of the United States

Lesson 1

Regions and Landforms
Each region of the United States has a variety of landforms and boundaries.

1

Lesson 2

Climate
Many factors influence climate, which varies from region to region.

2

Lesson 3

Regional Resources
Each region has special resources.

3

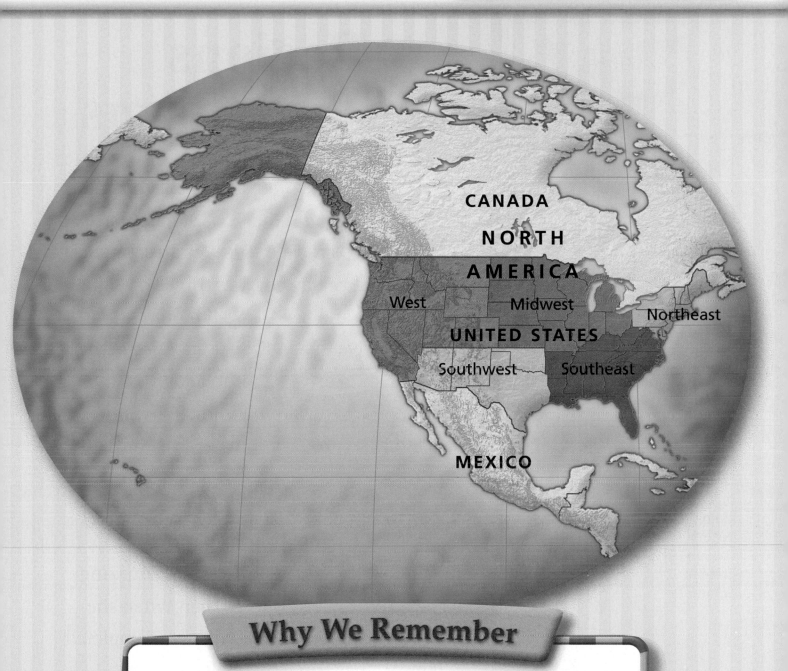

CANADA

NORTH

AMERICA

West   Midwest

Northeast

UNITED STATES

Southwest   Southeast

MEXICO

Why We Remember

From coast to coast, the United States is a vast and varied country. It is a land of fruitful plains, majestic mountains, rugged canyons, rocky coasts, and sandy beaches. Its resources range from the lobsters caught off the coast of Maine to the bright red cherries grown in Washington state. This vast land can be divided up into smaller areas, called regions. You will see that each region has its own unique landforms, climates, and resources.

PREVIEW

Focus on the Main Idea
The United States is divided into five regions.

PLACES
Northeast region
Southeast region
Midwest region
Southwest region
West region
Washington, D.C.

VOCABULARY
region
landform
mountain
plain
desert
canyon
plateau
boundary

▶ **A Maxwell motorcar like the one driven by Alice Ramsey**

Regions and Landforms

You Are There

It is August 6, 1909. You and your family are standing in a crowd on Market Street in San Francisco. Alice Ramsey, her three traveling companions, and her Maxwell motorcar are about to arrive in San Francisco. Alice is the first woman to drive a motorcar across the country. They are coming into town on the Oakland Ferry. You want to see this woman. Your mother has been reading newspaper accounts about Alice's trip to you. Nothing has stopped her, not bad roads, not bad directions, not flat tires. She is one amazing person! You can't wait to see her. When she gets here, she will have completed her trip in only 59 days—a record-breaking time!

Summarize As you read, pay attention to details that will help you summarize the lesson.

Regions of the United States

Alice Ramsey would be surprised to see the road system that now covers the United States and allows travelers to visit almost every part of this vast and varied country. To help us understand the United States, we can divide the country into five different regions. A **region** is an area in which places share similar characteristics. Places within a region may share certain landforms. A **landform** is a natural feature on Earth's surface, such as a mountain or a river.

Areas within a region also may be completely different from each other. For example, the West has snow-covered mountains, fertile valleys, shining lakes, and an island state. The Midwest has fertile plains and the Great Lakes. In the Southwest you will find deserts and the largest canyon in the United States.

Use the map below to find the states and landforms for each region. Find your state on the map.

REVIEW Summarize the differences in landforms among the West, the Midwest, and the Southwest regions.
◎ **Summarize**

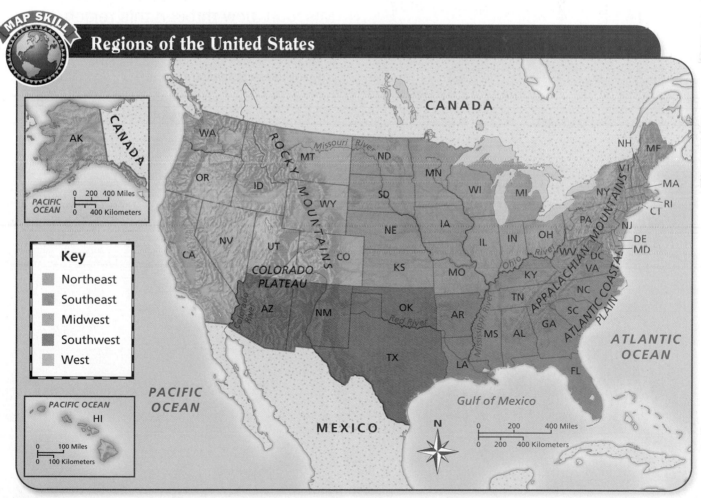

MAP SKILL

Regions of the United States

Key
- Northeast
- Southeast
- Midwest
- Southwest
- West

▶ This map of the United States is divided into five regions.

MAP SKILL Understand Cardinal Directions *What direction would you travel from the West to the Midwest?*

Landforms of the Regions

The **Northeast region** contains part of the oldest mountain range in the country—the Appalachian Mountains. A **mountain** is a very high landform, often with steep sides. The Appalachian Mountains run all the way from Georgia in the Southeast through Maine in the Northeast and into Canada. The Northeast region is mostly hilly and rocky along the Atlantic coast but has good farmland to the west.

In the **Southeast region** the Appalachian Mountains gradually flatten eastward into the Atlantic Coastal Plain. A **plain** is a large area of mostly flat land that is often covered with grass. West of the mountains, Louisiana and Mississippi have plains leading into the Gulf of Mexico. The Mississippi and Red Rivers flow through the region, creating rich farmland in states like Arkansas and Louisiana. The world's largest known cave system is the Mammoth Cave system in Kentucky. It's almost 350 miles long!

The **Midwest region** has flat, grassy plains and large areas of forest. There are some rolling hills, such as the Smoky Hills in Kansas. Big rivers, such as the Mississippi, Ohio, and Missouri, flow through this region.

▶ Regions across the United States have many different landforms.

12

Four of the five Great Lakes—Lake Erie, Lake Huron, Lake Michigan, and Lake Superior—border parts of the Midwest. They are large bodies of fresh (not salty) water.

The **Southwest region** has only four states in it. It is home to beautiful deserts and canyons. A **desert** is an area that gets very little rain. A **canyon** is a deep valley with steep rocky walls. Over time, the Colorado River has slowly carved the red land into canyons. Only about the thickness of a credit card is shaved from the walls of the Grand Canyon every five years. The depth of the Grand Canyon is equal to 80 four-story houses!

The canyons of the Southwest are found in an area called the Colorado Plateau. A **plateau** is a large, flat, raised area of land. The Rocky Mountains run from the West region into the Southwest, through New Mexico. To the east of these mountains are flat plains.

The **West region** is a region of extremes. The highest and lowest temperatures in the United States have been recorded in the West. The highest temperatures were recorded in Death Valley, California, and the lowest in Alaska.

The highest and lowest landforms in the United States are in the West. The highest landform is Mt. McKinley in Alaska, and the lowest is Death Valley in California. The coastal mountains border the Pacific coast, and white sandy beaches run along part of the Pacific Ocean. There are fertile, green valleys in Oregon and California. Other areas are heavily forested, such as western Oregon and Washington. The West region also includes Alaska and Hawaii.

REVIEW List five types of landforms found in the United States.

↪ **Summarize**

Boundaries

A **boundary** is a line or natural feature that divides one area from another or one state from another. For example, the boundaries of the state of Florida include two natural features—the Atlantic Ocean and the Gulf of Mexico. Florida's northern boundary line also includes the southern boundaries of Georgia and Alabama.

The lines that make boundaries around the states in the United States are found only on maps. If you rode to the border of your state, you would not actually see a line drawn in the ground. But you might see a sign welcoming people to your state.

State boundaries are legal borders with exact measurements around each state. These boundaries were set by the government. The United States is divided into fifty states plus the District of Columbia, which is land set aside for the nation's capital, **Washington, D.C.** Each state has a

▶ Marina on Kentucky side of the Ohio River near Louisville. The other side of the river is Indiana.

government that allows the state officials to make choices about state issues, such as education and laws.

Regional boundaries are not set by any rule or law. In fact, you may see regions named or marked in different ways than they are in this book. Regional boundaries are sometimes based on the major landforms of the area. For example, the Northeast is mostly hilly and rocky with farmland in the western part of the region. The Southeast is mostly rolling hills, mountains, and plains bordered by beaches. The Midwest is mostly plains and lakes while the Southwest is mostly plateaus and canyons.

▶ State-line sign welcoming visitors to Utah

WELCOME
Utah
~ Still the
right place
1896   CENTENNIAL   1996

14

▶ At the Four Corners Monument, you can put your feet in Utah and Colorado, and your hands in New Mexico and Arizona!

The West includes perhaps the greatest variety, from the desert of Death Valley in California to the snow-covered peaks of Mt. McKinley in Alaska.

Regardless of the way in which the regions may be divided, regional boundaries are different from state boundaries—they are not marked with signs.

REVIEW Describe the two different types of boundaries. ↺ Summarize

Summarize the Lesson

- There are five regions in the United States.
- Each region is made up of various landforms.
- Regional boundaries can be based on similar landforms. State boundaries are set by the government.

LESSON 1   REVIEW

Check Facts and Main Ideas

1. ↺ Summarize On a separate sheet of paper, summarize each of the other four regions into graphic organizers like the one below.

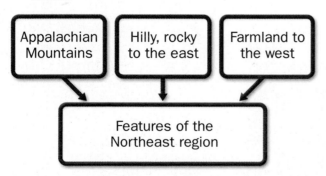

| Appalachian Mountains | Hilly, rocky to the east | Farmland to the west |

→ Features of the Northeast region

2. Name some of the landforms found in each region.

3. How do regional and state **boundaries** differ?

4. In which **region** or regions do you find each of the following: the Appalachian Mountains, the Mammoth Cave System, the Great Lakes, and the Rocky Mountains?

5. Critical Thinking: *Make Inferences* Choose one region and explain how the **landforms** of that region might affect how people work and play there.

Link to ⚭ Art

Draw a Landform Choose one landform discussed in this lesson and make a drawing of it. Tell why people might want to visit it.

Highest and Lowest

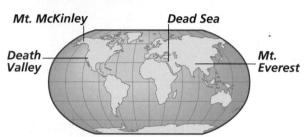

Mt. McKinley   Dead Sea

Death Valley

Mt. Everest

Mt. Everest is part of the Himalayan mountain system that runs across Asia. Did you know that the peak of this high mountain was once the floor of the sea? Long ago, India and the rest of Asia were two separate areas of land. An ocean lay between them. Then, millions of years ago, parts of Earth's crust on which India sat moved slowly toward the other part of what is now Asia. These two pieces of land collided. Slowly, the sea floor was pushed up, higher and higher. Over millions of years, the rock that was once the sea floor became the peaks of the Himalayan Mountains.

Earth has its low points too. Low points on land are actually below sea level! **Sea level** is the level of the ocean's surface. The shore of the Dead Sea in Israel is the lowest point in the world. Death Valley in California is the lowest point in the United States.

Death Valley (California)

200 feet

400 feet
282 feet (86 meters) below sea level

Lowest Point in the United States

600 feet

800 feet

1,000 feet

Shores of the Dead Sea (Israel)

1,200 feet

1,400 feet
1,292 feet (394 meters) below sea level

Lowest Point in the World

1,600 feet

1,800 feet

▶ **How much lower is the Dead Sea than Death Valley?**

Landforms

▶ **How much higher is Mt. Everest than Mt. McKinley?**

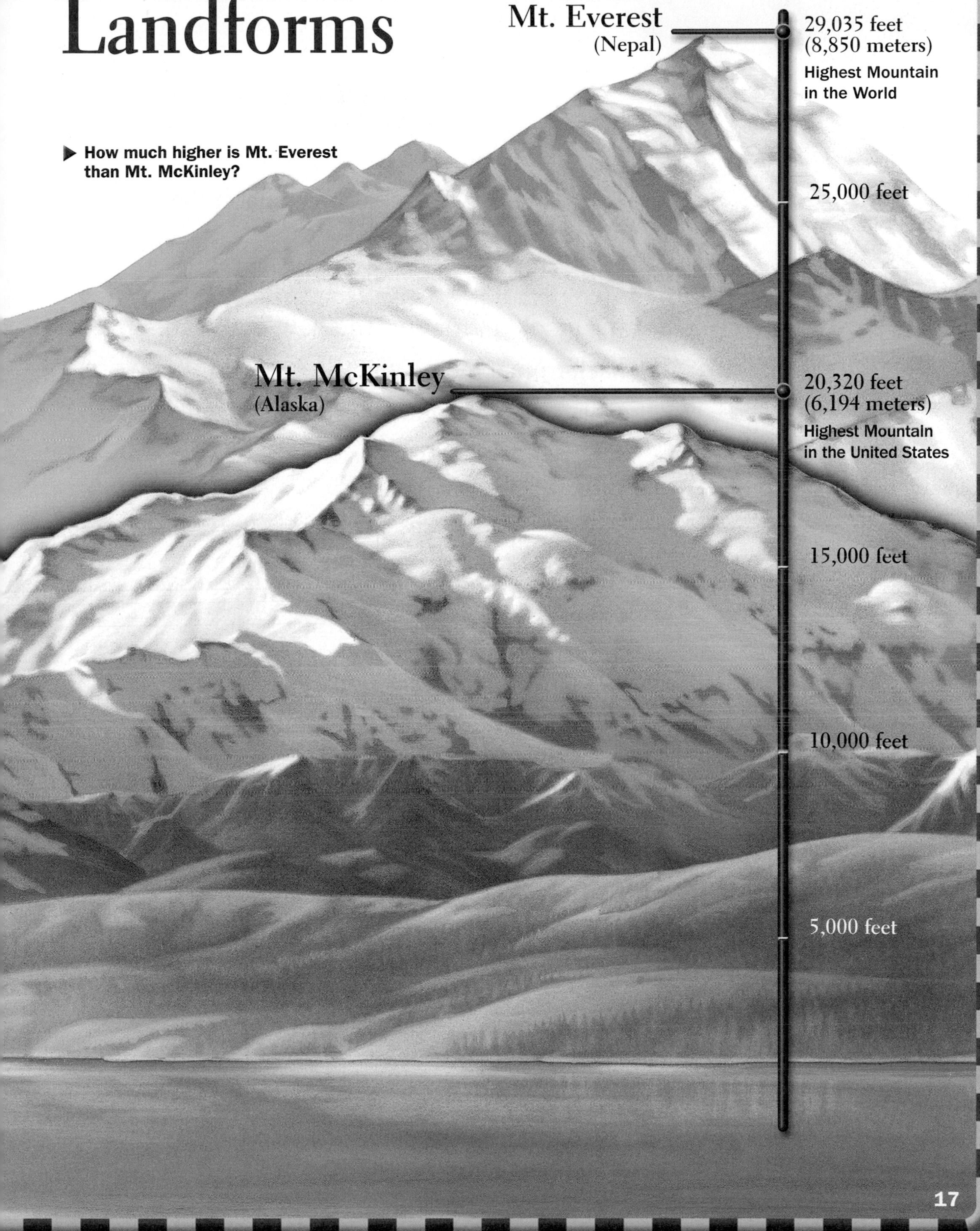

Mt. Everest
(Nepal)

29,035 feet
(8,850 meters)

Highest Mountain in the World

25,000 feet

Mt. McKinley
(Alaska)

20,320 feet
(6,194 meters)

Highest Mountain in the United States

15,000 feet

10,000 feet

5,000 feet

KANSAS

PREVIEW

Focus on the Main Idea
Many factors influence climate, which varies from region to region.

VOCABULARY
weather
climate
precipitation
temperature
humidity
equator
elevation
tropical climate
polar climate
subarctic climate
temperate climate

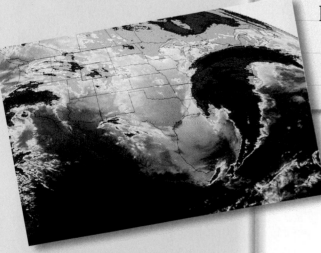

► Weather radar shows a cold front along the East Coast of the United States.

Climate

You Are There
It is the end of December. You and your family are relaxing in the main lounge of your motel in Honolulu, Hawaii. You have just come back from a hiking trip through the Manoa Valley on the island of Oahu. There you saw streams, flowering trees, and a 200-foot waterfall.

Your brother is watching a weather program on television. You see images of a snowstorm in Kansas. Minutes later, the image of an ice storm in New York State fills the screen. Trees are bent over under the weight of ice. But outside your motel in Honolulu, the weather is 75 degrees and sunny. You are amazed at the variety of climates across the United States!

Summarize As you read, look for things that affect climate in the United States.

Weather and Climate

In one way or another, we all pay attention to weather. You may just glance outside to see whether you will need an umbrella. Other people must pay more attention to weather when it directly affects their jobs or safety. For example, a pilot checks the weather to avoid flying into a dangerous storm.

Weather is the condition of the air at a certain time and place. Today's weather might be sunny and warm. Yesterday's weather might have been rainy and windy.

Climate is the weather of a place averaged over a long period of time. Climate includes the changes in weather that happen during seasons of the year. A farmer needs to know about the climate of an area in order to know what crops to plant and when to plant them.

Two major factors of weather and climate are precipitation and temperature. **Precipitation** is the amount of rain or snow that falls. **Temperature** is how warm or cold a place is.

Climate varies around the United States. In Florida, for example, temperatures are warm, and it rarely snows. And while Illinois can get very hot in summer, it can be very cold in winter and snow a great deal.

The map below shows how different the weather can be around the country. It shows average temperatures throughout the country in the month of January.

REVIEW Why is it important to know what the weather is going to be? **Draw Conclusions**

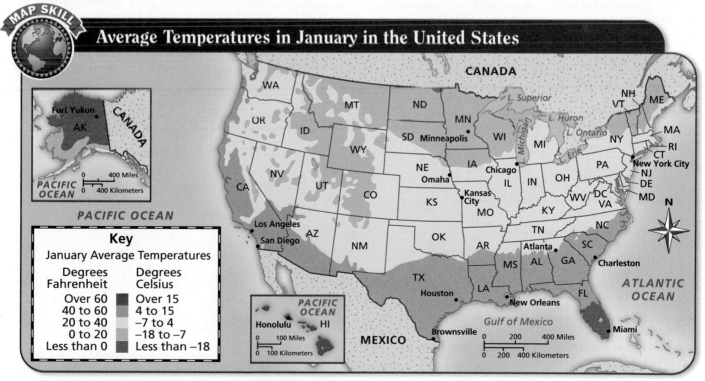

Average Temperatures in January in the United States

Key
January Average Temperatures

Degrees Fahrenheit	Degrees Celsius
Over 60	Over 15
40 to 60	4 to 15
20 to 40	−7 to 4
0 to 20	−18 to −7
Less than 0	Less than −18

▶ Temperatures vary greatly across the United States.

MAP SKILL Use a Map Key *What is the average range of temperatures in degrees Fahrenheit for Houston in January?*

Water in the Air

Water in the air is another major part of climate. About three-quarters of Earth is covered by water. Even though you cannot see it, the air around us contains water too. **Humidity** is the amount of moisture in the air.

How does water get from the ground into the air? Energy from the sun changes some water from oceans, lakes, rivers, and streams into a gas that rises into the air. This invisible gas is called water vapor. When air cools, the water vapor can form small drops. The drops gather together to form clouds. Within the clouds, the tiny drops join together and grow. The big drops fall to the ground as precipitation—rain or snow. The water in the air that can become rain in warm temperatures can become snow and ice in cold temperatures.

Rain falls into oceans, lakes, and onto the ground. Rain falling on land flows into rivers and streams and back to the seas and lakes. Then the cycle starts over again.

Different parts of the United States receive different amounts of precipitation. The map below shows the average amount of precipitation in the different parts of the United States.

___

REVIEW Describe how water gets into the air. ⟳ **Summarize**

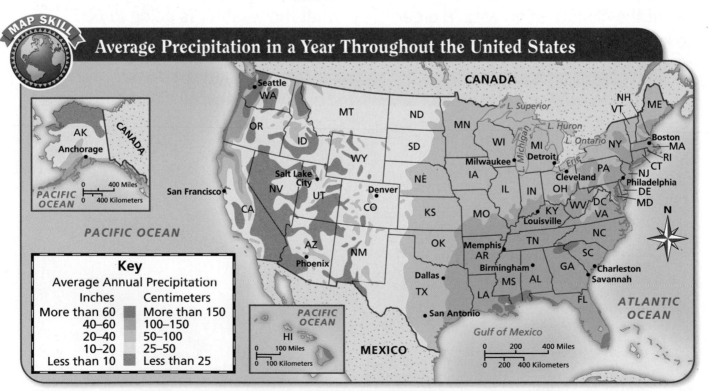

MAP SKILL

Average Precipitation in a Year Throughout the United States

Key
Average Annual Precipitation

Inches	Centimeters
More than 60	More than 150
40–60	100–150
20–40	50–100
10–20	25–50
Less than 10	Less than 25

▶ Annual precipitation amounts vary from less than 10 inches to more than 60 inches.

MAP SKILL Use a Map Key *What is the average precipitation in centimeters in a year for Memphis?*

What Causes Climate?

The climate of a place depends on its location. One factor is the distance a place is from the equator. The **equator** is an imaginary line that circles Earth halfway between the North and South Poles. The warmest climates are in places nearest to the equator. These areas are usually warm all year.

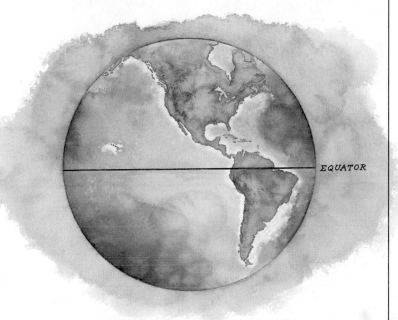

EQUATOR

A second factor that affects climate is how far a place is from a large body of water, such as an ocean. Places near an ocean usually have a milder climate than places far away from it. Land heats and cools faster than water. So in summer, water is cooler than land, and cool air from above the water cools the land nearby. In winter, the land is colder and the water is warmer, so the air from above the water warms the land. A place such as the state of Kansas, which is far from an ocean, is not affected by large bodies of water as much as a state on the Pacific coast.

The third factor that affects climate is elevation. **Elevation** tells how high a place is above sea level. Mountain climates are generally colder because the temperature is lower the higher you go. Very high mountains can have snow and ice throughout the year.

REVIEW How does a place's location affect its climate?
Main Idea and Details

The Rain Cycle

In cool air, water vapor changes into small drops of water in clouds.

Sun

Cloud

Energy from the sun changes water into water vapor, an invisible gas in the air.

Water drops fall to Earth as rain or snow.

Lake

Types of Climates

The United States has many different climates. An area with a **tropical climate** is usually very warm all year. Places with tropical climates are near the equator. The rays of the sun strike Earth most directly in this area. In the United States only the southern tip of Florida and Hawaii have a tropical climate. Some areas have a subtropical climate, which is not as warm as a tropical climate.

Areas around the North and South Poles have a **polar climate.** It is the coldest climate. A very small part of the United States, in Alaska, has a polar climate. Most parts of Alaska have a **subarctic climate** because they are closer to the North Pole. Warm periods in summer are short, and parts of the state are covered in snow for most of the year.

▶ **Palm trees grow in Hawaii's tropical climate.**

Climate Areas of the United States

MAP SKILL

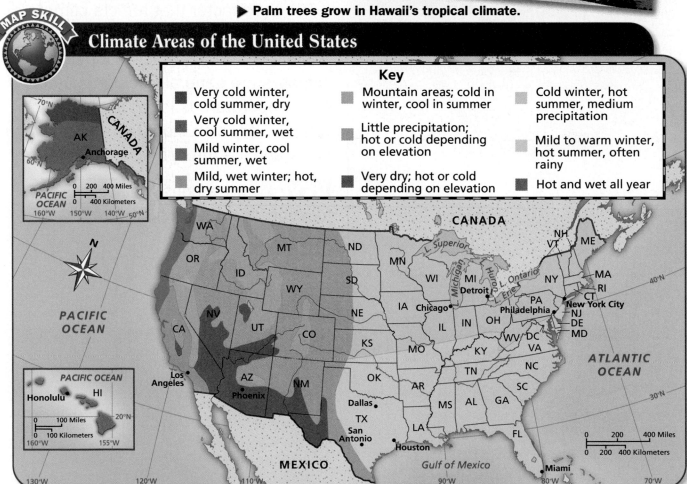

Key

- Very cold winter, cold summer, dry
- Very cold winter, cool summer, wet
- Mild winter, cool summer, wet
- Mild, wet winter; hot, dry summer
- Mountain areas; cold in winter, cool in summer
- Little precipitation; hot or cold depending on elevation
- Very dry; hot or cold depending on elevation
- Cold winter, hot summer, medium precipitation
- Mild to warm winter, hot summer, often rainy
- Hot and wet all year

▶ **The climates in the United States range from very cold winters with cool and dry summers to areas that are hot and wet all year.**

MAP SKILL Use a Climate Map *What state has the greatest variety of climates?*

Temperate climates are between the tropical and subarctic climates. Temperate climates are moderate in temperature, neither very hot nor very cold. The map shows some climate areas of the United States.

REVIEW Find your state's type of climate on the map. Now, find another state, far from yours. Make a list of the differences and similarities between the two climates.

Compare and Contrast

▶ Snow covers the ground for most of the year In Alaska.

Summarize the Lesson

- **Weather is the condition of the air at a certain time and place, and climate is the pattern of weather over a long period of time.**

- **Precipitation and temperature are factors of climate.**

- **Distance from the equator, distance from a large body of water, and elevation affect climate.**

- **The United States has many different climates.**

LESSON 2   REVIEW

Check Facts and Main Ideas

1. ⊙ **Summarize** On a separate sheet of paper, make a diagram like the one shown. Fill in some details of each type of climate.

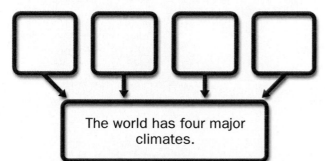

The world has four major climates.

2. Write a sentence describing the difference between **weather** and climate.

3. Describe the variations in **climate** in each region of the United States.

4. What are the three main factors that affect climate?

5. **Critical Thinking:** *Looking for Pictures* Choose two photos from this lesson and write a description about the weather of each place.

Link to ∞ Science

Learn About Plants Some plants grow well in some climates but cannot grow in others. Choose a climate shown on the map. Use reference materials to find out about the plants that grow well in the climate you chose.

Map and Globe Skills

Read Inset Maps

What? Maps show a large area on a small piece of paper. For example, you might find a map of the entire world printed on a sheet of paper no bigger than a page in this book. A map usually has a scale that shows how real distance compares with the distance shown on the map.

Sometimes a map needs to show places in different scales. For instance, to show all 50 states of the United States can be tricky. That is because two states, Alaska and Hawaii, will not fit easily on a map with the other 48 states. These two states can be shown in separate small maps. Each small map may have a separate scale. Such smaller maps that are related to the main map are called **inset maps.**

Why? Inset maps give information about places that are too large, too small, or too far away to be shown on the main map.

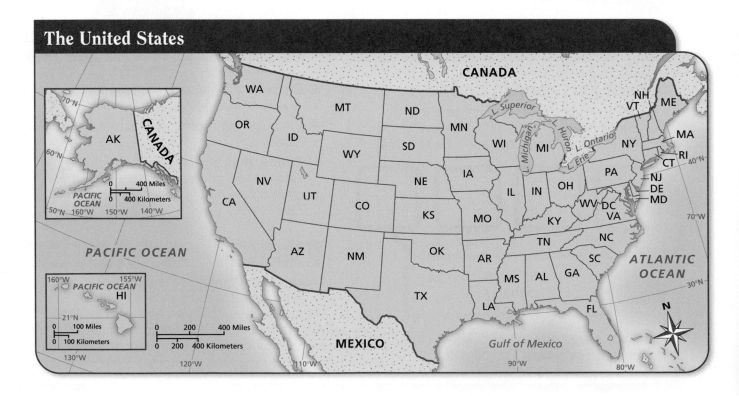

Some inset maps show how places relate to one another. This type of map might locate a country in a continent or a state within a region. Other inset maps give extra details. For example, a close-up map of a downtown section of a city can give details about the city that cannot be shown on the main map.

How? To read an inset map, first examine the main map. Notice its topic and its scale. Then study the inset map. Figure out how the inset map is related to the main map. Does it show a larger area? a smaller area? a distant area? What can you learn from the inset map that you could not find out from the main map?

Think and Apply

❶ What does the main map on page 24 show? What do the **inset maps** show?

❷ Why do you think the mapmaker decided to show the inset maps?

❸ What other inset maps might be useful for a person looking at the main map?

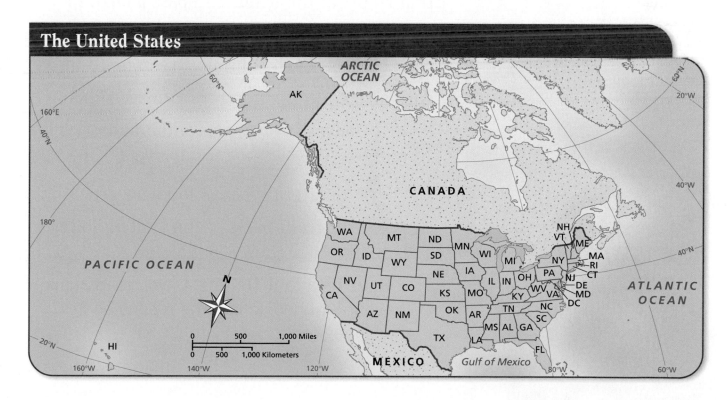

The United States

PREVIEW

Focus on the Main Idea
Each region has special resources.

VOCABULARY

natural resource
raw material
process
harvest
industry
manufacturing
product
capital resource
agriculture
conserve
renewable resource
recycle
nonrenewable resource
human resources
service

Regional Resources

You Are There

A huge herd of brown cattle thunders by you for what seems like a full five minutes. You and your family are driving by a cattle ranch just outside of Amarillo, Texas. You are on the first leg of a long car trip to Chicago, Illinois. This is the first long trip you have ever taken, and boy, are you excited! In central Oklahoma, you see huge fields of golden wheat that ripple in the wind. You pass a farm in Missouri where pigs run to the fence to watch your car pass by. In Illinois, green fields of corn stretch to the horizon. You see signs advertising apples and blueberries for sale. You are surprised to see that different types of food are grown in different parts of the United States.

Main Idea and Details As you read, think about how people use the resources in each region.

Natural Resources

You have read about the landforms and climates that make each of the five United States regions special. Each region also has materials known as natural resources. A **natural resource** is something in the environment that people can use. Forests, soil, water, and plants are examples of natural resources.

We can turn natural resources into raw materials. **Raw materials** are natural resources that have been changed or **processed** so that people can use them to make other products. For example, we can change an oak tree, which is a natural resource, into lumber, which is a raw material. Then the lumber can be used to build homes or furniture.

Some farmers in the Midwest and Southwest grow wheat. When the wheat is **harvested,** or cut for use, it is not ready to be eaten or sold to grocery stores. The wheat is a raw material that is processed into flour. The flour is then used to make such food items as bread, cake, and pancakes.

In the picture below look at all the various raw materials used to make a breakfast.

REVIEW Why are natural resources turned into raw materials?
Main Idea and Details

Using Resources

The resources in each region helped shape the businesses that grew there. The Northeast region was the nation's first center of industry. An **industry** is a form of business. For example, manufacturing is an industry. **Manufacturing** means making products to sell. **Products** are things that people make or grow.

When making products, people also need to use capital resources. **Capital resources** are things that people make in order to produce products. Tools, machines, and factory buildings are capital resources.

Manufacturing is important in the Northeast, but other industries are as well. Some parts of the Northeast are too rocky and hilly for large farms, so other industries have been built around the resources of the region. Fishing is an important industry along the coast. Coal is a natural resource also found in the Northeast, so industries that use coal developed there.

Soil is a valuable natural resource. In the Southeast, many people work in agriculture. **Agriculture** is using the soil to raise crops or animals. In the Southeast, farmers grow crops such as sugar cane, cotton and rice. These crops grow well in the warm climate. Cotton grown in the region is processed into cloth and then manufactured into clothing.

The fertile soil of the Midwest plains makes this region a great place to grow large crops of corn, soybeans, and wheat. Many people in the region raise cows and hogs. From the cows' milk, people make dairy products, such as cheese and butter. The Midwest also has large cities with manufacturing and other industries.

People moved to the West in search of silver, gold, and other valuable metals. Today, resources in the West include cattle that graze on the grassy plains; timber from the thick forests; fish from the ocean; and fruits, nuts, and vegetables from the fertile valleys.

The Southwest region has wide-open plains where cattle also graze. Cotton grows in its fields. Major natural resources of the Southwest are oil and natural gas. Many factories were built there to manufacture products from these resources.

REVIEW How might people use the following resources: trees, cotton, cattle, and fertile fields?
Draw Conclusions

Renewable and Nonrenewable Resources

"Close the refrigerator door!" "Turn off the lights when you leave!" Did you ever hear people say these things? They want to conserve resources. **Conserve** means to use resources carefully.

Some of the natural resources you've just read about are renewable and some are not. A **renewable resource** can be replaced. When we cut down trees to build houses or make furniture, we can plant more trees. Trees are renewable resources. But trees take a long time to grow, so we have to conserve them.

Soil and water are also renewable resources. We can use the same soil over and over to plant crops if we keep the soil nourished. Water is reused too. As you learned in the previous lesson, water rises into the air and then falls back down as rain. Just as we must conserve trees, we must be careful with soil and water. All of our

▶ **Oil is pumped from the ground.**

renewable resources can be damaged by pollution. Pollution can make water dirty, harm trees and other plants, and damage soil.

We can recycle resources as well as conserve them. **Recycle** means to use something again. People recycle materials such as paper, metal and plastic.

Nonrenewable resources cannot be replaced. There is a limited amount of each nonrenewable resource. When this type of resource runs out, there is no more.

Fuels such as coal, natural gas, and oil are nonrenewable resources. These fuels can be burned to make the energy we use to heat and light our homes, move our cars, and cook our food. Since these fuels are nonrenewable resources, it is important to conserve them by walking sometimes instead of driving, turning off lights we're not using, and closing the refrigerator door.

REVIEW Why should you try to conserve resources? **Draw Conclusions**

What About Your Region?

Use the information from this chapter and other sources, such as maps, encyclopedias, the Internet, people in your community, and books to fill out a form like the one below.

Then choose another region you would like to visit and explain why you would like to visit it and what you would do there.

REVIEW How can a form like the one below help you summarize facts about your region? ⟳ **Summarize**

FACT FILE

My Region

I live in the _____Northeast_____ region.

My town and state are _____Andover, New York_____.

Some other states in my region are _____Pennsylvania_____,
_____Maine_____, _____Massachusetts_____, _____New Jersey_____.
(List the state names.)

The landforms in my region include _____mountains_____,
_____lakes_____, and _____rivers_____.
(List types of landforms.)

I like the weather in my region is when it is _____cold and very snowy_____
_____in the winter._____
(List your favorite weather and when it happens.)

The natural resources in my region are _____soil, forests, and_____
_____water_____.
(List some resources.)

These natural resources are important because _____they provide_____
_____products we need to live_____.

Some things that make my region special are _____the different_____
_____types of weather and the beautiful places to visit._____

A Most Valuable Resource

You have read about natural and capital resources. Another very important resource is all around you, and is found in every region. **Human resources** are the people who make products or provide services. **Services** are jobs that people do for others.

People do service work everywhere. Teaching, repairing things, taking care of people, delivering products, and building houses are some kinds of service work.

REVIEW List some examples of service work. Main Idea and Details

Summarize the Lesson

- A natural resource is something from the environment that people can use.
- Each region has special resources.
- Renewable resources can be replaced and nonrenewable resources cannot.
- People use capital resources to make products and provide services.
- Human resources are people who make products or provide services.

LESSON 3   REVIEW

Check Facts and Main Ideas

1. **Main Idea and Details** On a separate sheet of paper, make a diagram like the one below. Fill in the main idea.

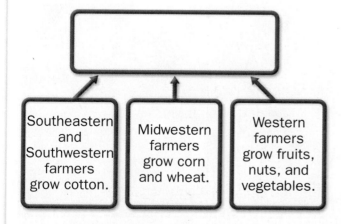

2. Why are people considered resources?
3. What is the difference between a **renewable** and a **nonrenewable resource?**
4. What resources are found in your region?
5. **Critical Thinking:** *Make Inferences* How do all the resources in a region help **industries** develop and grow?

Link to 〜 Writing

Write a Business Plan Suppose that you are going to start a small company that manufactures a simple product. What resources will you need? Write a plan that describes all the resources you will use and how you plan to make the product. Use the words **manufacture** and **product** in your business plan.

The United States and North America

The major landforms of the United States extend to its neighbors in North America. Mountains and plains reach north into Canada and south into Mexico. Huge chains of mountains run down the eastern and western sides of North America. The Appalachian Mountains are on the east, and the Rocky Mountains are on the west. Between the mountains, the land is mostly flat. The northern areas have large forests, while the central parts of the Great Plains are covered with flat, grassy lands. Each region within the United States has its own types of landforms and range of climates. Climate and resources affect all the living things within a region. People use the resources in many ways.

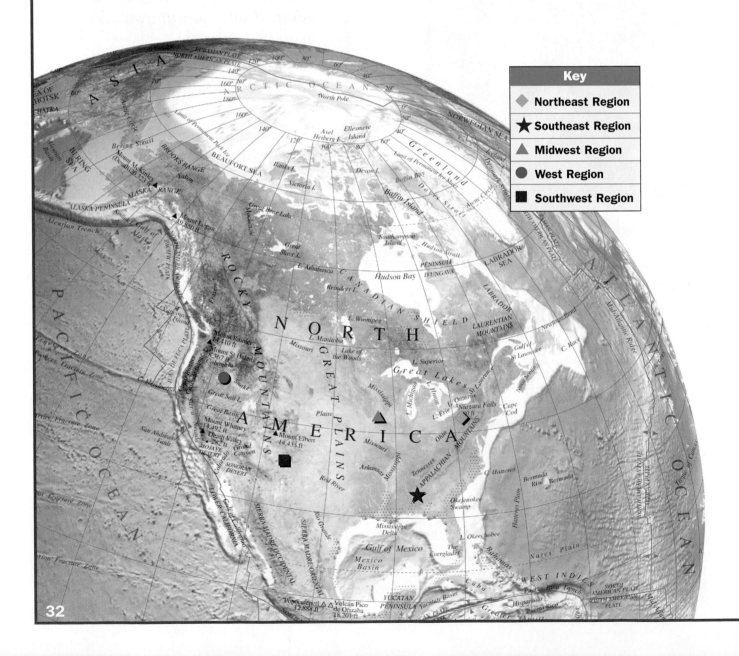

Key	
◆	Northeast Region
★	Southeast Region
▲	Midwest Region
●	West Region
■	Southwest Region

West

● **The Pacific Coast**
Waves crash along the rocky coast of Oregon.

West

● **Big Cities**
Its climate and resources have brought many people to Los Angeles. The parts of the city and surrounding areas are linked together by a system of roads.

Southwest

■ **Homes Made of Clay**
Many homes in Taos, New Mexico are built of sun-dried clay brick, called adobe. The Pueblo people lived in this region a thousand years ago. They used the resources of the area to build homes.

Southwest

■ **Carved by the Wind**
These strangely shaped rocks are in Monument Valley, Arizona. They have been carved by the wind.

Midwest

▲ **Faces on the Hills**
The heads of four great American presidents—George Washington, Thomas Jefferson, Theodore Roosevelt, and Abraham Lincoln—have been carved onto Mount Rushmore in South Dakota.

Midwest

▲ **Water Birds**
Many types of water birds, like this loon, spend the summer on the quiet lakes of Minnesota.

Midwest

▲ **Prairie Lands**
Flat land, fertile soil, and hot summers make the Midwest prairies ideal for farming.

Southeast

★ **Wetlands**
The beautiful Okefenokee Swamp is a large wetland in Georgia. Its warm climate makes it a comfortable home for many animals, including alligators and snakes.

Southeast

★ **Growing Fruit**
Florida and other parts of the Southeast have the right climate for growing citrus fruits. Farmers send their oranges, grapefruits, limes, and lemons all over the country.

Northeast

◆ **The Atlantic Coast**
Towns like this grew near the coast of the Atlantic Ocean. People who live here often use the resources of the sea.

Northeast

◆ **Traditional Farming**
Amish people live on this farm in Pennsylvania. They do not use any modern technology.

Southeast

★ **King Cotton**
The climate and soil of the Southeast are good for growing cotton. Large cotton farms can be seen in parts of the Southeast.

33

Chapter Summary

 Summarize

On a separate sheet of paper, make a diagram like the one shown. Fill in details about landforms in two more regions in the United States.

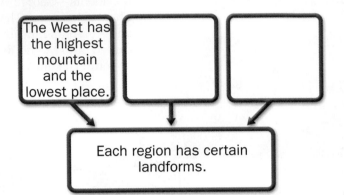

The West has the highest mountain and the lowest place. → □ □

→ Each region has certain landforms.

Vocabulary

Match each word with the correct definition or description.

1. **boundary** (p. 14)
2. **region** (p. 11)
3. **plateau** (p. 13)
4. **desert** (p. 13)
5. **canyon** (p. 13)
6. **plain** (p. 12)
7. **climate** (p. 19)
8. **precipitation** (p. 19)
9. **humidity** (p. 20)
10. **elevation** (p. 21)
11. **capital resources** (p. 28)
12. **renewable resource** (p. 29)

a. a large area of flat land, often with grass

b. the pattern of a place's weather over time

c. an area with similar characteristics

d. a resource that can be replaced

e. a line or natural feature that divides one area from another

f. the things people make in order to produce products

g. an area that gets very little rain

h. how high a place is above sea level

i. a deep valley with steep rocky hills

j. the amount of rain or snow that falls

k. the amount of moisture in the air

l. a large, flat, raised area of land

Facts and Main Ideas

1 What are the five regions of the United States?

2 What are three climate types?

3 Why do people try to conserve resources?

4 **Main Idea** What are some differences between the types of land in each region?

5 **Main Idea** How is climate affected by location?

6 **Main Idea** What are three main kinds of resources?

7 **Critical Thinking:** *Ask Questions* Write two questions about regions in the United States. Then write a short list of sources you might use to find answers.

Write About Geography

1 **Write a Region Riddle** Suppose that you are one of the United States regions. Without giving the name of the region, write a few hints. For example, if you were the West you could write, "I am the region with the tallest mountain." Exchange riddles with a classmate.

2 **Write an advertisement** for a particular place in the United States. Use illustrations and pictures from magazines to make your advertisement appealing.

3 **Write a travel article** explaining why someone should visit a region of your choice. Include locations you think are the most interesting.

Apply Skills

Use an Inset Map

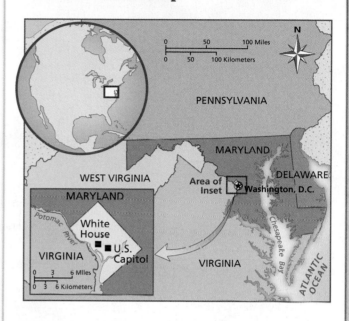

1 What is shown on the large map?

2 What is shown on the square inset map?

3 What is shown on the circular locator map?

Internet Activity

To get help with vocabulary and terms, select the dictionary or encyclopedia from *Social Studies Library* at **www.sfsocialstudies.com**.

CHAPTER 2

We All Live Together

Lesson 1

Americans All

Hundreds of years before the founding of our country, people from other lands made their way to North America.

1

Lesson 2

We the People

Americans have a strong voice in how the government of the nation is elected, organized, and run.

2

Lesson 3

The Strengths of Our Freedoms

Everyone who lives in the United States has certain basic rights that are protected by our Constitution.

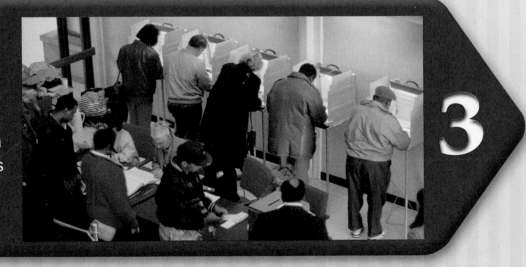

3

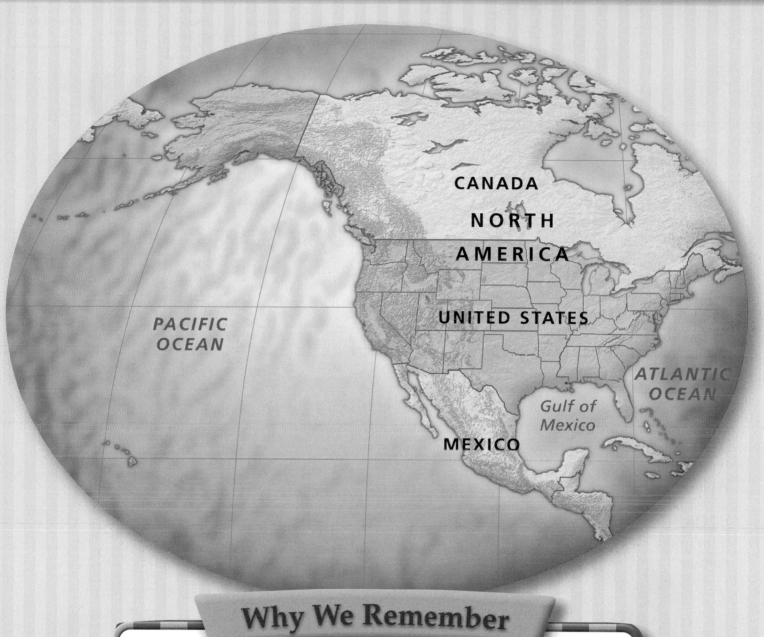

Why We Remember

From the 1500s to the 1800s, the number of people living in North America grew. Who was living on this land? Where did the new people come from? Why did they come? How did these people affect the United States? The United States is a nation of people from all over the world. Americans can be proud of working toward freedom for all cultures and peoples.

Mississippi River

1492
Columbus arrives in North America.

1803
The United States purchases the Louisiana Territory from France.

1819
The United States purchases Florida from Spain.

1845
Texas becomes a state.

1853
The area that is to become 48 of the 50 states is complete.

Americans All

PREVIEW

Focus on the Main Idea
The United States is a diverse nation made up of people from many different backgrounds and cultures.

PLACES
Bering Strait
Mississippi River
Louisiana Territory

PEOPLE
Christopher Columbus
Thomas Jefferson
Meriwether Lewis
William Clark

VOCABULARY
immigrant
culture

▶ **A brass box and compass from the 1400s**

Museum of the History of Science, Oxford

You Are There

It is October 1492. You are on the *Pinta*, one of the three ships in Christopher Columbus's exploration fleet. Columbus is on the *Santa María*. When you left Spain three months ago, you were excited about the adventure and the treasures you hoped to bring home from Asia. Now, everyone on the ships believes Columbus is lost. But then one of your shipmates runs up and tells you that Columbus has spotted tree branches with leaves and fruit floating by the ships. Columbus believes you must be close to land. He is offering a reward to the first person to spot land.

Suddenly, you hear the scream, "Land! Land!" Rodrigo de Triana has spotted land!

Main Idea and Details As you read, look for reasons why the United States came to include people of many different cultures.

The Earliest Americans

Although North America was a new world to Europeans, it was home to many people before **Christopher Columbus** arrived. When Columbus landed in America, he thought he had reached a group of islands between Asia and Australia. Those islands were known as the East Indies. Columbus therefore called the first North Americans he saw "Indians." Today, we refer to these people and their descendants as Native Americans or American Indians. How did Native Americans' ancestors come to this land?

Early Americans came to this part of the world from other places. Scientists differ about when they came and where they came from. Some scientists think that the first Americans came from Asia. They might have come when much of the Northern Hemisphere was covered with ice. Some scientists think they might have walked across the **Bering Strait** on land that then connected what we now know as Siberia and Alaska.

Other scientists think that the first Americans sailed from northern Asia. Others think that the first Americans sailed from South Pacific islands or Australia.

However they got here and whenever they came, people were living in North America over 11,000 years ago. Over time, they developed rich and varied cultures. Their cultures were shaped in part by the geography of the areas they settled. These early peoples became the hundreds of different Native American groups that occupied North America by the 1400s.

REVIEW What are some different ideas scientists have about where the first Americans came from?
Main Idea and Details

▶ Workers at a site in Colorado search for objects that are thousands of years old.

Explorers from Europe

Christopher Columbus and his fleet of ships arrived in 1492. His goal was to find a short route by sea to Asia. European countries, especially Spain, Portugal, France, and England, had been trading goods with China and India. Traders traveled there over land, but the routes were long and dangerous.

Columbus's voyages opened up a great age of exploration. European explorers came to the Americas in search of gold and other riches. These explorers also wanted to claim land for their rulers. The places they explored are shown on the map below.

In 1513 Spanish explorer Juan Ponce de León (Hwahn PAWN say de Lay AWN) landed in what is now Florida. He was hoping to find wealth and new lands. Ponce de León did not find the gold he was seeking. Another Spanish explorer, Hernando de Soto, also explored parts of what is now Florida. In 1539 his ships landed near what is now Tampa Bay. Francisco Vásquez de Coronado, a Spanish explorer who was seeking gold, traveled north from Mexico. In 1540 he explored parts of the area that is now New Mexico.

Explorers from France also came to North America for different reasons.

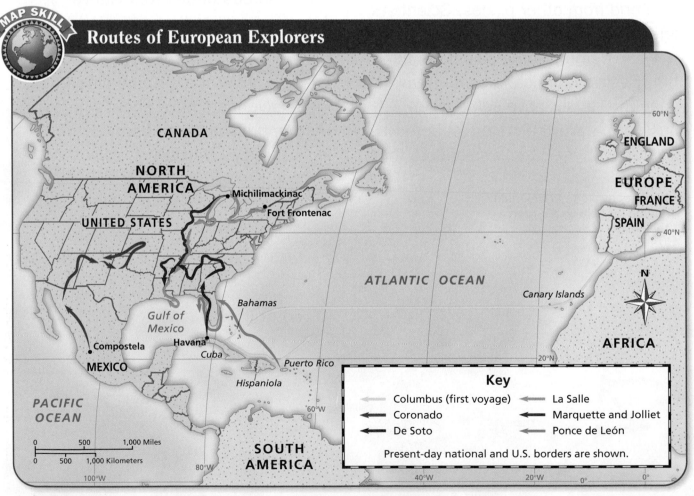

Routes of European Explorers

CANADA

NORTH AMERICA

Michilimackinac

Fort Frontenac

UNITED STATES

ENGLAND

EUROPE

FRANCE

SPAIN

60°N

40°N

ATLANTIC OCEAN

Canary Islands

AFRICA

Bahamas

Gulf of Mexico

Compostela Havana

Cuba

MEXICO

Puerto Rico

Hispaniola

PACIFIC OCEAN

20°N

N

Key
- Columbus (first voyage)
- Coronado
- De Soto
- La Salle
- Marquette and Jolliet
- Ponce de León

Present-day national and U.S. borders are shown.

0   500   1,000 Miles

0   500   1,000 Kilometers

SOUTH AMERICA

80°W

100°W   60°W   40°W   20°W   0°

▶ **European explorers traveled thousands of miles exploring North America.**

MAP SKILL Use Map Scale *About how many miles did Marquette and Jolliet travel?*

In 1534 Jacques Cartier (Zhahk Kar TEE ay) came in search of riches. Others, like Jacques Marquette (Zhahk Mar KET), wanted to bring Christianity to the Americas. In 1673 he and Louis Jolliet (JOH lee et) explored the Mississippi River. As they traveled, Marquette drew maps of the region. Another French explorer, Robert La Salle, traveled the **Mississippi River** to the Gulf of Mexico. He claimed land for France.

▶ **Jacques Marquette**

REVIEW Why did explorers come to the Americas? **Main Idea and Details**

The United States Grows

By the early 1700s, the Atlantic coast had many settlers. People traveled westward looking for good land. By 1783 the United States claimed land from the Atlantic coast to the Mississippi River.

Then, in 1803, the French sold land that was then called the **Louisiana Territory** to the United States. This included much of the land west of the Mississippi River to the Rocky Mountains.

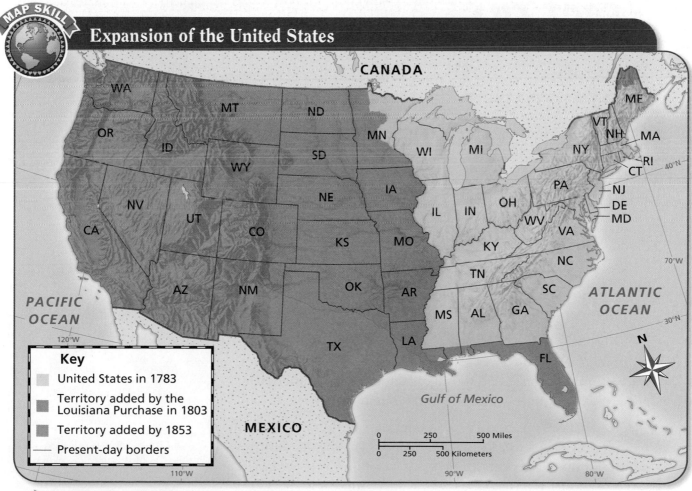

Expansion of the United States

Key
- United States in 1783
- Territory added by the Louisiana Purchase in 1803
- Territory added by 1853
- Present-day borders

CANADA

PACIFIC OCEAN

ATLANTIC OCEAN

Gulf of Mexico

MEXICO

0   250   500 Miles
0   250   500 Kilometers

▶ The growth of the United States occurred over many years.

MAP SKILL Observe Change Through a Map *How many years are represented by the changes shown on the map?*

President **Thomas Jefferson** sent **Meriwether Lewis** and **William Clark** on an expedition to discover what was on the land that had been purchased. In 1804 Lewis and Clark began their trip on the Missouri River at St. Louis. Eighteen months later, they reached the Pacific Ocean. They made maps and kept journals about what they saw.

Between 1803 and 1853, the United States continued to expand. Through treaties, purchases, and wars, new territory was added. In 1819 the United States purchased Florida from Spain. Texas was added to the United States in 1845. The next year, England ceded, or gave up, the Oregon Territory. As a result of the Mexican War in 1848, the United States purchased a huge area of land from Mexico. Then, in 1853, with the purchase of more land, the area that would become forty-eight of the fifty states in the United States was complete.

REVIEW List some of the ways the United States grew from the Atlantic Ocean to the Pacific Ocean.
➲ **Summarize**

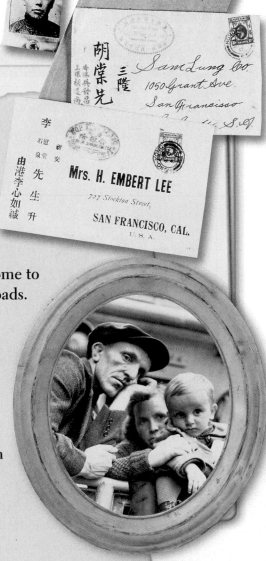

FACT FILE

Immigration Information

✔ Mid 1600s: Many people come to North America from England. About 50,000 people come during this time.

✔ Between 1730 and 1807: Over 40,000 Africans are brought to America against their will. In 1808 this practice is forbidden by law in the United States.

✔ Between 1860 and 1880: Nearly 200,000 Chinese workers come to the western United States. Many of them help to build railroads.

✔ Between 1880 and 1920: About 22 million immigrants from Europe come to the United States. Many pass through inspection stations at Ellis Island in New York City.

✔ Between 1910 and 1940: About 175,000 Chinese and other Asian immigrants come to Angel Island in San Francisco Bay and eventually enter the United States.

✔ Between 1960 and the 1990s: Thousands of immigrants from Southeast Asian, South American, and Caribbean countries settle in the United States.

Immigration

The English settlers who lived along the Atlantic coast in the 1600s were immigrants. An **immigrant** is a person who comes to live in a new land. Not all the people, however, who came to North America had a choice. Many Africans were forced to come.

Immigrants have continued to come to the United States throughout its history. Most people living in the United States are immigrants or descendants of immigrants. Each immigrant group has helped our country's culture grow.

REVIEW Why have immigrants continued to come to the United States? **Make Inferences**

▶ **Traditions and food are part of cultures across the United States.**

Cultural Riches

Culture is the way of life followed by a group of people. Food, clothing, music, art, religion, holidays, customs, stories, and games are all parts of a group's culture.

Language is another part of culture. Many words we use everyday show a variety of cultural influences. For example, the name *Kentucky* comes from the Iroquois Indian word *ken-tah-ten,* which means "land of tomorrow." The word *Michigan* received its name from the Chippewa Indian words for "great water." Lake Michigan is one of the largest fresh water lakes in the world. Florida received its name from the Spanish word *florida,* which means "flower."

Settlers named New York, New Jersey, and New Hampshire after places in England. Vermont got its name from the French words *vert mont*, which mean "green mountain."

REVIEW Why do you think the French named Vermont as they did? **Draw Conclusions**

Out of Many, One

Even our country's motto, *E pluribus unum*, is a phrase from another language. It is Latin and means "out of many, one." You can see this motto on our coins. Out of many states comes one nation. Out of many different backgrounds comes one people, united as a nation.

What binds us together as Americans? Some Americans say that we are held together by our common traditions, such as celebrating American independence on the Fourth of July or sharing Thanksgiving dinner with our families. Other people say that our government and our history unite us. Many believe that the foundation of our unity is respect for all people. Our nation's laws seek to respect people, despite differences in culture or beliefs. This respect is America's key to bringing many people together to form one nation.

REVIEW What is our nation's motto and what does it mean? **Main Idea and Details**

Summarize the Lesson

Pre-1492 Native American groups lived in North America for centuries.

1492 Columbus arrived in North America. Many more European explorers followed.

1803–1853 The United States grew with the addition of new lands.

Today People continue to come to America from all over the world.

LESSON 1   REVIEW

Check Facts and Main Ideas

1. Main Idea and Details On a separate sheet of paper, write a sentence that states the main idea for the details given.

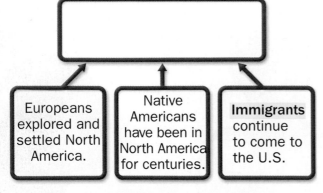

| Europeans explored and settled North America. | Native Americans have been in North America for centuries. | Immigrants continue to come to the U.S. |

2. Who was living in North America when Columbus arrived? What did you learn about these peoples? Use the word **culture** in your answer.

3. Why did European explorers and settlers come to North America?

4. How did the United States grow from the Atlantic Ocean to the Pacific Ocean?

5. Critical Thinking: *Make Decisions* Suppose you live in a different country. What might make you decide to move to the United States?

Link to ◁◦◦▷ Writing

Write About Your State Use encyclopedias and other books to find the answers to these questions. Write your answers and share them with the class.

Where did the name of your state come from?

Which Europeans first explored your state's region?

What words used today come from people who have lived in your region?

FIORELLO LA GUARDIA

1882–1947

Fiorello La Guardia (Fee uh REL oh Luh GWAHR dee uh) was the well-respected mayor of New York City from 1934 to 1945. His parents were Italian immigrants. Fiorello was born in New York City, but he spent much of his childhood in Arizona. His father was stationed with the army in Prescott, Arizona. There Fiorello met people from many different cultures. There were also children of all different backgrounds whose fathers were in the army. Sometimes children would make fun of Fiorello because his parents were immigrants.

BIOFACT

La Guardia read the Sunday comics over the radio to the people of New York City.

La Guardia became angry when he saw others being treated unfairly. For example, some companies sold the army rotten food to feed to soldiers. As a result of this, his father died from eating spoiled meat. These things made La Guardia want to fight for fairness, especially in government.

After his father died, La Guardia and his mother moved back to Europe. While in Europe, he learned seven different languages. When he returned to New York City, one of his first jobs was helping immigrants. La Guardia continued helping people, first as a congressman and later as mayor of the city.

Learn from Biographies

How do you think La Guardia's knowledge of languages helped him as mayor of New York City?

For more information, go online to *Meet the People* at **www.sfsocialstudies.com.**

MARYLAND
Washington, D.C.
VIRGINIA

We the People

PREVIEW

Focus on the Main Idea
Citizens of the United States elect representatives who make and enforce laws.

PLACES
Washington, D.C.

VOCABULARY
government
republic
represent
democracy
citizen
Constitution
federal
legislative branch
Capitol
executive branch
White House
judicial branch
Supreme Court
amendment
Bill of Rights

You Are There

People from all over town have gathered at your school tonight. They are here to talk about problems in the local park. They want to know why the mayor doesn't work harder to keep the local park clean and safe for everyone. You know that your mom has been thinking about this problem. You wait for her to speak up.

Once your mother starts talking, you notice that many people here seem to like her ideas. Later, a group of people stop to talk to your mom. She's as surprised as you are when you hear their request. They've just asked your mom to run for mayor.

 Summarize As you read, look for details to summarize how the government of the United States is structured.

A Government for the People

The **government** is made up of the rules, or laws, that we follow and the people who run our country. The government often does important jobs for us. For example, in many places the government makes sure that we have clean water to drink. The government builds and maintains our roads. It delivers our mail. It sets aside land for parks and playgrounds. The government tries to make sure that people have safe, pleasant places to live.

The United States is a republic. In a **republic,** the leaders are elected.

The leaders **represent**, or make decisions for, the people who elected them. Our type of republic is also called a representative democracy. In a **democracy,** every citizen has a right to take part in government. A **citizen** is an official member of a country. In the United States, the citizens elect the leaders who run the government. Our country follows a set of rules called laws. The elected leaders vote on the laws that all people must follow.

REVIEW Summarize the description of a republic.
Summarize

▶ **The United States Capitol in Washington, D.C.**

47

Government by the People

The founders of our country set up a very wise plan for governing our nation. This plan is a document called the **Constitution** of the United States of America.

The Constitution starts off with the words "We the People . . ." These three words show how important the idea of democracy is for the United States. The power of our government does not come from government leaders. It comes from citizens who elect those leaders.

There are three levels of government in the United States. The first level is the local government. The local government includes village, town, city, and county governments. The second level is state government—the government set up by the people of each state.

The third level of government is the national government—the government of our entire country. The national government meets in the capital city of the United States, **Washington, D.C.**

The Constitution explains how the national and state governments share power. A system of government in which the national and state governments share power is called a **federal** government. The Fact File on the next page tells more about the three levels of government and the leaders at each level.

REVIEW What are the three levels of government in the United States?
↪ **Summarize**

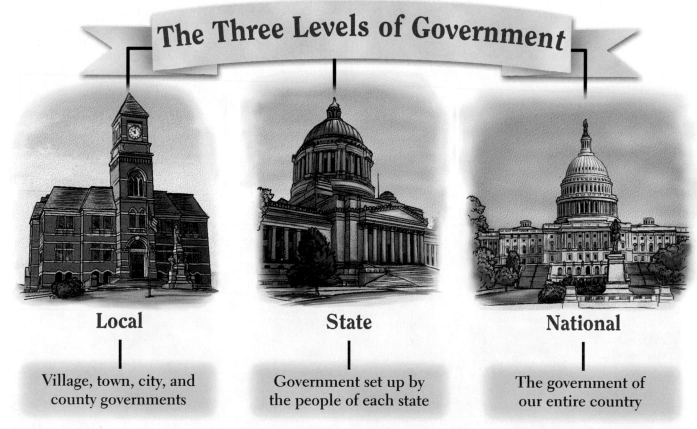

The Three Levels of Government

Local

Village, town, city, and county governments

State

Government set up by the people of each state

National

The government of our entire country

FACT FILE

Three Levels of Government

National

★ The President of the United States is the head of the national government.

★ The President gets authority to run the country from the United States Constitution.

★ Presidential duties include suggesting laws, making budgets, and choosing people to manage the services that the country needs.

★ The President is also the commander-in-chief of the armed forces.

★ Most of a President's decisions must be approved by Congress.

State

★ State governments are run by governors.

★ Governors get authority to run their state governments from state laws and the state constitutions.

★ Most of the laws that affect our daily lives, like driving laws, come from state governments.

Local

★ A city, town, or village is run by a top official. This official is often called a mayor, but may have a different title, such as village manager.

★ Mayors get their authority from the people and the state constitutions.

★ Some mayors have the responsibility to appoint people to manage city services.

★ City services may include providing police and fire protection, running the schools, and making sure that the water supply is clean and safe.

The Three Branches of Government

The Constitution describes the organization of the national government. The United States government has three branches. These branches are the legislative branch, the executive branch, and the judicial branch.

The **legislative branch** is the part of the government that makes our nation's laws. Congress is the legislative branch of the United States government. Congress has two parts. One part of Congress is the House of Representatives, which is also called the House. The Senate is the other part of the United States Congress.

The Congress meets in the building known as the United States **Capitol.**

The citizens of each state elect members to both the House of Representatives and the Senate. Each state has two senators. The senators are elected for six-year terms. The number of representatives for each state depends on the state's population. The larger the population, the more representatives a state has in the House of Representatives. For example, California has a large population, so it has fifty-two members in the House. Alaska has a small population. It has only one member in the House. Representatives are elected for two-year terms.

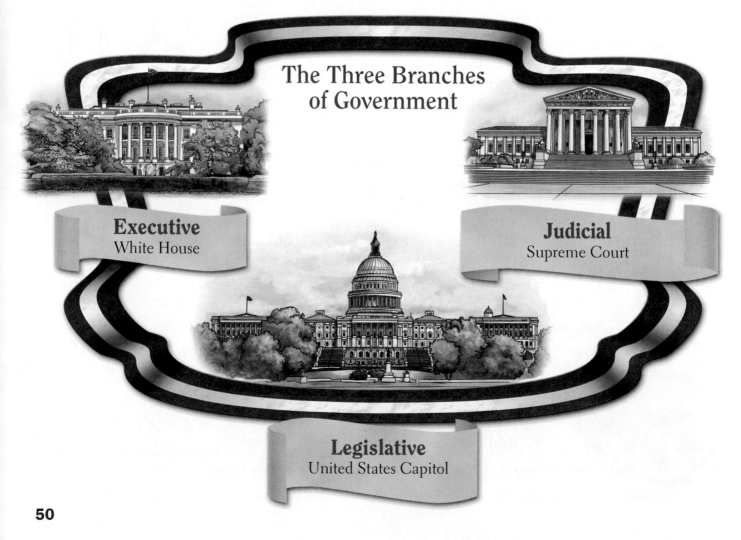

The Three Branches of Government

Executive
White House

Judicial
Supreme Court

Legislative
United States Capitol

Supreme Court Historical Society/Richard W. Strauss, Smithsonian Institute

▶ **The United States Supreme Court is made up of nine judges, appointed for life.**

The **executive branch** is in charge of enforcing our nation's laws. The President is the head of the executive branch. United States citizens vote to elect the President. The President serves a four-year term. A President can be reelected only once. The President lives and works in the **White House.**

The President has other duties besides enforcing the nation's laws. The President is in charge of our nation's armed forces. The President also suggests laws for Congress to pass.

The executive branch also includes the Vice-President. The Vice-President presides over, or heads, the Senate.

The **judicial branch** is in charge of interpreting our nation's laws. Judges in the federal courts decide whether the laws follow the Constitution. Our nation's highest court is called the **Supreme Court.** The nine judges who serve on the Supreme Court are called justices. Supreme Court justices and other federal court judges are appointed by the President and approved by the Senate. Once approved, all of these judges can keep their jobs for the rest of their lives. The United States Supreme Court meets in the Supreme Court building in Washington, D.C.

REVIEW Why do you think the President can be reelected only once? **Draw Conclusions**

The Flexibility of the Government

The United States government is flexible. That means that changes can occur. The government can be changed by laws and amendments. An **amendment** is a change to the Constitution. Amendments are passed by Congress and must then be approved by a majority of the states.

A number of amendments have been added to the Constitution since it was first written. The first ten amendments to the Constitution are known as the

▶ Congress in session

Bill of Rights. These amendments guarantee such freedoms as freedom of press, freedom of religion, and freedom of speech. Over time, our government has become a stronger, more representative democracy because of our amended Constitution.

REVIEW Why was it necessary to have an amendment that guaranteed freedom of speech? **Draw Conclusions**

Summarize the Lesson

- **The United States government has three levels: local, state, and national.**
- **The United States government has three branches: legislative, executive, and judicial.**
- **The United States government is structured according to the Constitution. It lists duties of the branches and describes how power should be shared between the national and state governments.**

LESSON 2 REVIEW

Check Facts and Main Ideas

1. **Summarize** On a separate sheet of paper, make a chart like the one below. Use it to summarize the government's other two branches.

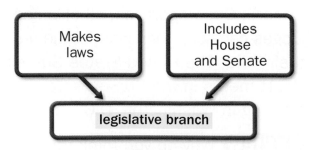

Makes laws

Includes House and Senate

legislative branch

2. What is the United States Constitution, and why is it important?

3. Describe each of the three levels of **government.**

4. How can the **Constitution** be changed?

5. **Critical Thinking:** *Draw Conclusions* The United States Constitution was written in 1787. Since then, there have been fewer than thirty **amendments** to the Constitution. What does this say about the original Constitution as a plan for government?

Link to —◯◯— **Art**

Make a Poster Make a poster inviting people in your community to a meeting of your local government. Include details about the meeting, including where and when the meeting will be held.

DANIEL INOUYE 1924–

In 1959 Hawaii became a state. Daniel Inouye (ih NOH way) was Hawaii's first representative in Congress. He was also the first Japanese American to be elected to either the House or the Senate.

Inouye's father had moved from Japan to Hawaii. Inouye's mother grew up in Hawaii. As an adult, she encouraged her family to meet and vote on family matters.

Daniel valued this experience. He also valued the different races and cultures of Hawaii and often spoke out against disrespect of cultural differences.

BIOFACT *Because of his bravery in war, Inouye won the Congressional Medal of Honor, the highest award given by the United States government.*

As a soldier in World War II, Inouye led troops in a battle to rescue his fellow American soldiers. During the battle, Inouye lost his right arm.

As both a representative and later as a senator from Hawaii, Inouye has continued to strengthen democracy by working for respect among all Americans.

"You can make a difference in your lives and in the lives of others if you simply care enough to try...."

Learn from Biographies

An experienced politician once told Inouye that it was important to follow the Golden Rule: Treat others the way you want to be treated. Why is this good advice?

For more information, go online to *Meet the People* at **www.sfsocialstudies.com**.

Map and Globe Skills

Read a Time-Zone Map

What? Before railroads crossed the country, each town and city set its own time. People noted when the sun was at its highest point in the sky. At that time, people would set their clocks to noon. However, the sun appears to travel across the sky from east to west. So noon would be a different time in a neighboring area.

Having slightly different times in different towns caused trouble for people making train schedules. The railroads decided to establish time zones. A **time zone** is a region where one standard time is used. In each time zone, clocks are all set to the same time. The United States adopted this plan in the 1880s. It is the basic plan we use for setting our clocks today.

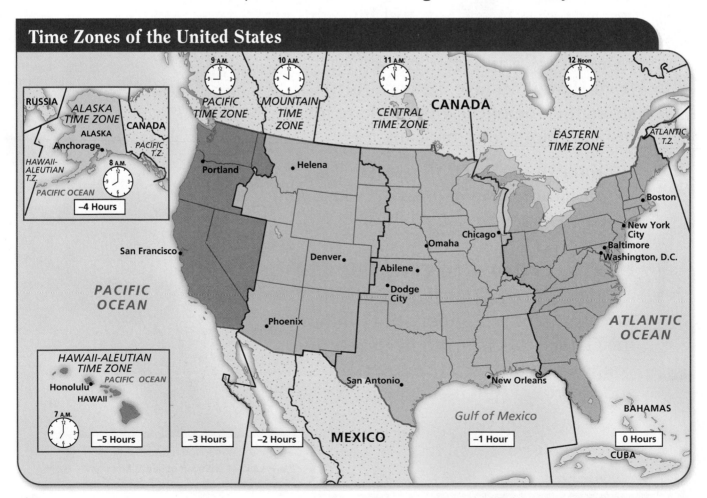

Time Zones of the United States

Why? You can best understand time zones by looking at a time-zone map. A **time-zone map** shows the boundaries of the time zones across a continent or for the entire Earth. Earth is divided into 24 time zones. Each time zone is an hour behind its neighbor to the east and an hour ahead of its neighbor to the west.

How? Look at the time-zone map. Note that the boundaries of each time zone are drawn with purple lines. Each time zone is shaded with a different color. Find the clocks on the map. There is one clock for each time zone. Notice that the clocks show that the time in each zone is different by one hour from the time in the zone next to it. The names of the time zones are

also given with each clock. What is the name of the time zone where you live?

Think and Apply

1. What time does this **time-zone map** show for the Pacific **time zone**? The Central time zone? The Eastern time zone?

2. When it is 10:00 A.M. in New York, what time is it in Portland?

3. If you lived in New York and you needed to call your friend in Portland at 8:00 P.M. Pacific time, what time would it be in New York when you called?

Hawaii

Texas

55

PREVIEW

Focus on the Main Idea
Citizens have rights as well as responsibilities.

VOCABULARY
passport
taxes
jury

The Strengths of Our Freedoms

You Are There

Today we cleaned up the school yard so that our class can have our fall track and field competition outside. Abby, our class representative on the student council, told us that everyone needed to pitch in and make the school yard neat and clean.

Abby pointed out that with rights come responsibilities. With the right to decide on activities comes the responsibility to get the school ready for the special event. Together we filled thirty garbage bags with litter. When we finished, the school yard was spotless. Tomorrow we will have a special recess because we did our job as responsible citizens.

 Summarize As you read, look for details to help you summarize the rights and responsibilities of all people living in the United States.

Our Constitutional Rights

As you have read, the Constitution guarantees United States citizens certain rights. A person who is born in the United States is a U.S. citizen. One can also become a citizen through a process established by the government.

Four years after the Constitution was ratified, or approved, the Bill of Rights extended citizens' rights by guaranteeing freedoms such as freedom of speech, freedom of press, and freedom of religion. As time has passed, it has become necessary to make more changes. These changes have extended our rights even more.

For example, the Thirteenth Amendment ended slavery. Slavery was legal when the Constitution was written. After the Civil War, it was not. On December 6, 1865, almost eight months after the war ended, the Thirteenth Amendment was ratified. It said, in part, "Neither slavery nor involuntary servitude...shall exist within the United States...." Servitude means that someone is forced to do work against his or her will.

On August 18, 1920, the Nineteenth Amendment was ratified. This amendment guaranteed women equal voting rights. For many years prior to this, many women and men had fought for this right. As with all of the amendments, once it was ratified, it became the law.

Another amendment that affected voting laws was the Twenty-Sixth Amendment. Ratified on July 1, 1971, this amendment gave citizens eighteen years of age and older the right to vote. Prior to this, a citizen had to be twenty-one to vote. Again, many people had fought for this amendment for a long time.

United States citizens have other rights as well. For example, a person can get a passport. A **passport** is a government document used in traveling to foreign countries. People who have United States passports can visit countries throughout the world. A United States passport shows people in other countries that the person is a United States citizen.

REVIEW List three special rights of United States citizens. ↺ **Summarize**

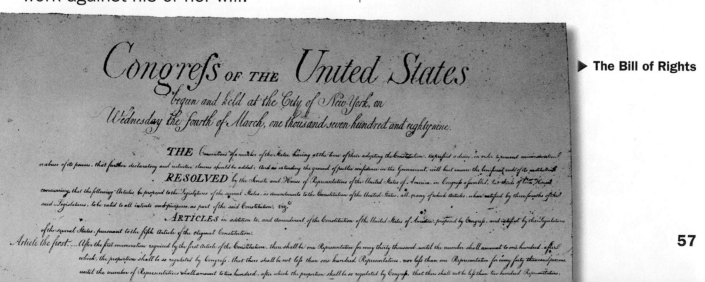

▶ The Bill of Rights

Responsibilities as Americans

All people living in the United States should respect the rights of others. They must respect all of the rights guaranteed by the Bill of Rights. This means that you should respect the rights of people who have ideas that are different from yours.

All people living in the United States are required to obey the laws of our country. Some laws require you to do particular things to fulfill your responsibilities as an American. For instance, people are required, by law, to pay the taxes they owe. **Taxes** are money the government collects to pay for its services, such as constructing and maintaining our roads, parks, and schools.

People pay taxes in several different ways. Taxes are taken out of paychecks. Taxes are added to the price of things you buy. Let's say you stop at a store to buy a soda that costs $1.00. You get to the cash register and find you have to actually pay $1.08. You may have just contributed toward new roads, fire and police protection, and maintaining your local park!

Another responsibility all adult citizens have is to serve on a jury when called upon. A **jury** is a panel of ordinary citizens who make decisions in a court of law. All Americans accused of a crime have a right to a jury trial. Serving on a jury is a way Americans help protect their right to a fair trial.

All Americans should work to make their communities and their country a good place to live. This is a responsibility for everyone, regardless of age. Make a list of ways you can help out. Which are the best choices for you?

All adult citizens have the responsibility to vote. By voting, people show how they want our government to be run.

▶ The court recorder works as the lawyer addresses the jury.

By voting, citizens make sure that the government represents the will of the people.

To make good decisions when they vote, people need to be educated. Adults need to stay informed of issues by reading newspapers, watching TV news broadcasts, and going to public meetings.

Children have responsibilities too. They are required by law to be educated. In school, they should learn about government and how it works. They should learn about our history. They should learn about decisions people have made that improve life for all Americans.

REVIEW How can you fulfill your responsibilities as a citizen?
⊙ Summarize

Summarize the Lesson

- **Everyone living in the United States has certain rights.**

- **People who are citizens of the United States have additional rights.**

- **Everyone who lives in the United States has certain responsibilities.**

▶ **Voting is an important responsibility.**

LESSON 3   REVIEW

Check Facts and Main Ideas

1. ⊙ Summarize On a separate sheet of paper, copy and fill in a chart like the one below to summarize responsibilities of all United States citizens.

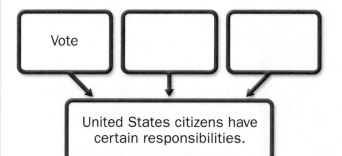

Vote

United States citizens have certain responsibilities.

2. What are two ways that a person can become a citizen of the United States?

3. List three types of government services that are paid for by **taxes.**

4. Why is voting an important responsibility?

5. Critical Thinking: *Evaluate Information* If a person wants to run for President, he or she must be born a United States citizen. Give a possible reason for this requirement, and tell whether or not you think the requirement is a fair one.

Link to ∞ Reading

Read About the Bill of Rights Find a copy of the Bill of Rights. Choose one of the ten amendments in the Bill of Rights. Work with a partner to read the amendment. Use a dictionary to look up words you do not understand. Then summarize the rights granted in that amendment.

Doing the Right Thing

Eight-year-old Seth and his brother Sam, five, were at the Sunland Park Mall in El Paso, Texas, on a Sunday in 1998. They entered a restroom where Sam found a bank deposit bag. When the brothers opened it, they saw the bag contained money. "It was exciting," Sam said. "There was a lot of money. We knew we couldn't keep it."

The boys decided to bring the bag to their father. Because the mall was about to close, the three took the money home with them. Police came to the family's El Paso home and counted out the money on the kitchen table. The total came to $23,399. The police also found a check among the money. The check gave the police a clue as to who the owner was.

As it turned out, the money belonged to a builder in the area. He met with the family to thank the boys for their honesty and to give them a cash reward.

BUILDING
CITIZENSHIP
Caring
Respect
Responsibility
Fairness
★ Honesty
Courage

▶ Seth and Sam
receive their awards
for honesty.

"He was extremely grateful to my children for returning the money," the boy's mother, Lynette, said. "He told us that losing the money would have been damaging to his business."

Police called the boys' heroes for returning the money. Seth responded, "We really didn't do anything special. My brother found the bag. When we opened it and saw all the money, we took it to my dad. We returned it to its rightful owner, which is what you're supposed to do."

"It felt good to return it because it wasn't our money."

Honesty in Action

Sometimes, doing the right thing can be hard. Write about someone who displayed honesty in a difficult situation. This person can be someone you know or a famous person from history.

Chapter Summary

 **Summarize**

On a separate sheet of paper, copy the chart. Use the details given to summarize information about the United States government.

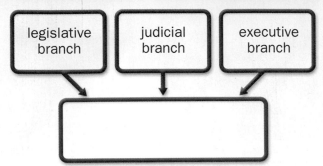

legislative branch	judicial branch	executive branch

Vocabulary

Match each vocabulary word with its definition.

1 culture (p. 43)

2 legislative branch (p. 50)

3 immigrants (p. 43)

4 government (p. 47)

5 Constitution (p. 48)

6 Bill of Rights (p. 52)

7 amendment (p. 52)

8 democracy (p. 47)

a. people who come and live in a new land

b. the laws of a country and the people who run it

c. our nation's plan for governing

d. the way of life followed by a group of people

e. a change to something, such as the Constitution

f. the part of government that makes laws

g. a republic

h. the first ten amendments to the Constitution

Vocabulary

Fill in the blank in each sentence with the correct word from this list.

judicial branch (p. 51)
passport (p. 57)
federal (p. 48)
jury (p. 58)
executive branch (p. 51)

1 The president is the head of the _____ of government.

2 The main responsibility of the _____ of government is to interpret laws.

3 A _____ is an official document used in traveling to other countries.

4 A _____ is a panel of citizens that makes decisions in a court of law.

5 The sharing of power between the state and national governments is called a _____ system.

Facts and Main Ideas

1. What are three parts of a culture?

2. Why is our government called a representative democracy?

3. List two rights guaranteed to citizens in the United States.

4. **Main Idea** Why do people sometimes say that the United States is and has always been a land of immigrants?

5. **Main Idea** What are the three branches of the United States government, and what is the main job of each?

6. **Main Idea** How are the rights that United States citizens have connected to the responsibilities that they have?

7. **Critical Thinking: *Solve Problems*** Two friends of yours get into an argument over differences of opinion about an issue at school. What could you say that would help convince your two friends to show respect for each other's opinion?

Write About It

1. **Write a menu** for a holiday that you celebrate or would like to celebrate. Give a description of each food and tell how the food is related to the holiday.

2. **Write a job description** of a government official who serves in the national government. Use the Internet or other sources to gather information.

3. **Write an action plan** for a project that would improve your school or your community. Write down the steps for carrying out your project. For each step, tell who would be in charge and who would work on it. Finally, write up a time line or a schedule for the project.

Apply Skills

Read a Time-Zone Map

Answer the questions about this map.

1. The President is giving a speech from the White House in Washington, D.C., at 7 P.M. You want to watch a live broadcast, and you live in Illinois. What time should you turn on your TV?

2. In what time zone will people be listening to the speech at 7 P.M.?

3. You want to talk about the broadcast with your uncle who lives in Wisconsin. What time would it be there if you called him at 8 P.M. in Illinois?

Internet Activity

To get help with vocabulary and terms, select the dictionary or encyclopedia from *Social Studies Library* at **www.sfsocialstudies.com**.

CHAPTER 3

Earning and Learning

Lesson 1

The Land of Plenty
What makes up our riches? The answer to this question has changed over the years.

1

Lesson 2

Trade Then and Now
People have used different methods of trading in different places and at different times.

2

Lesson 3

Transportation and Communication
The United States does business with countries all over the world.

3

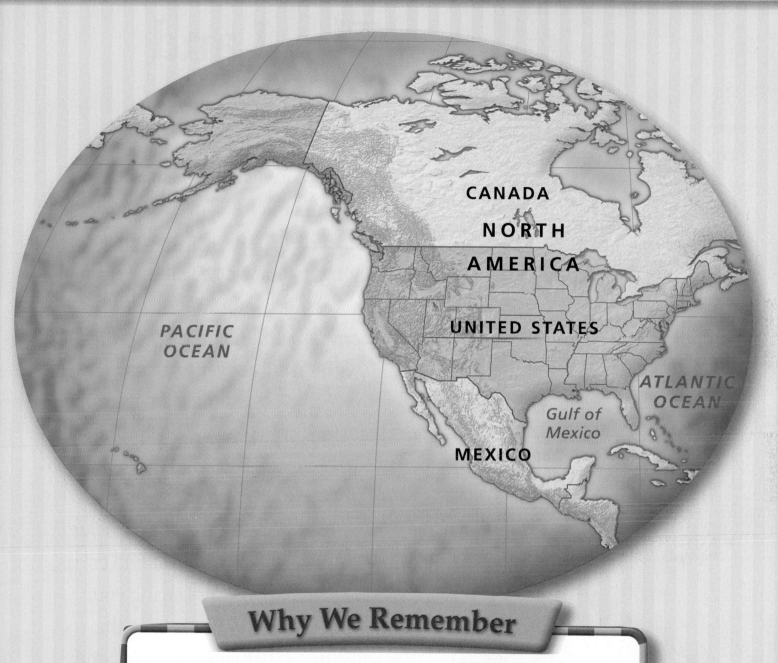

CANADA

NORTH

AMERICA

UNITED STATES

PACIFIC
OCEAN

ATLANTIC
OCEAN

Gulf of
Mexico

MEXICO

Why We Remember

How do people get what they want and need? Either they find or make things themselves, purchase what they want, or trade with others. Trade has been an important part of life for thousands of years. Native Americans had a vast trading network that spanned North America. Over time, trade has expanded even more.

Today, the United States does business with many, many different nations. Learning basic ideas about economics is important for understanding our nation and our world.

PREVIEW

Focus on the Main Idea
North America's rich resources have drawn many people to the continent and to specific regions of what today is our country.

VOCABULARY
technology
rural
urban

► **A covered wagon that once traveled the Oregon Trail**

The Land of Plenty

You Are There You are living in a small New England town in the 1850s. It's the night before your family is moving to a new place far away, "the land out west," as your father calls it.

Your father wants to find better land to farm—land with resources yet to be used. The place you are going will have many more trees so that you will have wood all winter to keep you warm and wood to build that new barn your father has wanted for so long. The new place will have rich soil that will provide wonderful, abundant fields of wheat and corn.

You are sad that you are leaving your friends, but you are excited about the new adventures that you and your family will have.

 Summarize After you read, summarize the reasons that people want to live in certain places.

A Land of Riches

When the first Americans came to North America, they arrived at a place full of natural resources. What they found convinced them to stay. They very likely came to this continent by accident, probably following a migrating herd of animals during a hunt. Once here, they found game animals, fish, fertile soil, and wild plants in abundance.

While some first Americans settled in one area and farmed, many continued to move and spread across North America. Different resources were available in different regions. Each group found ways to use their local resources. Sometimes the first Americans traded over very long distances for resources that were not available nearby.

In the early 1500s, Europeans also came to the Americas. Like the first Americans, they too were attracted to the continents by their rich resources.

In North America, the Europeans at first settled along the rivers near the coast. They traded with the Native Americans for resources found farther inland. But the Europeans began to move farther west and they, like the first Americans, settled in certain areas and farmed the rich land.

REVIEW What were some of the resources that convinced the first Americans to stay?
Main Idea and Details

Museum of Mankind, London

► These engraved knives were used for cutting blocks of snow by Native American groups living in cold regions.

► The first Americans hunted mammoths and other large mammals.

▶ **Wagon trains traveling west took many settlers to new homes.**

Moving Westward

By the 1700s European settlers realized that the greatest resource available in North America was the land. The settlers themselves were another great resource. They cleared trees and set up farms. They could use the crops they grew and the animals they raised to feed their families. They could sell or trade their extra farm products to others. There was an increase in demand for farm products due to the growing cities in North America and Europe. Producing crops and raising livestock soon came to be the nation's main economic activity.

Throughout the 1700s and the 1800s, people continued to come to North America to make a better life for themselves and their families. Cities along the Atlantic coast had become crowded. Settlers moved westward to find more land. They moved into places in the Midwest where they carved out farms on the plains. They moved into the Southwest where they raised sheep and cattle. Everywhere they moved, they cleared land for farms.

Another resource drew people westward. In 1848 a man in California found gold in a stream running through the land of his employer. Within months, tens of thousands of excited people were heading to the area to "strike it rich." Few people became wealthy in the rush to California for gold, but many stayed in the region. This caused a population boom along the West Coast.

REVIEW Why did agriculture become the main economic activity in America?
◑ **Summarize**

▶ Plentiful fields of wheat such as this are part of many Midwest farms.

▶ The discovery of gold in California caused many people to move west.

Lithograph by Currier & Ives

69

Growth of Industry

While settlers were moving steadily westward, industries were rapidly growing in other parts of the country. America was found to be rich in iron and coal, the raw materials necessary for industry.

By 1870 railroad workers had laid train tracks from coast to coast. Railroads linked resources of the West to markets in the East. The railroad was one example of a new technology. **Technology** is the development and use of scientific knowledge to solve practical problems.

Advances in other technologies occurred in the latter half of the century. For example, people came up with a new process of making steel that made it cheaper to produce. By the 1900s steel plants began turning out the steel frameworks that made skyscrapers, cars, and other new products possible.

New ways to produce electricity were also developed. Electricity powered lights and machines, such as the elevator. People learned how to drill deep underground for oil. This provided another source of power to run machines.

Coal, electricity, and oil were used to run engines and the new machines that were being invented. All these technologies led to the growth of other industries.

The rapid growth of industries changed the way people lived and worked in the United States.

"Detroit Industry," North Wall, 1932–1933, Diego M. Rivera, Gift of Edsel B. Ford, photograph—2001 The Detroit Institute of Arts

▶ **This famous painting is titled "Detroit Industry."**

Cities were centers for most of the new industries that arose in the late 1800s.

People came to the cities to find work. Many farmers left the land. They looked for better jobs in factories. In 1870 the United States was a **rural** nation. Most Americans lived in small towns or on farms. By 1920 the United States had become an **urban** nation with most of the people living in cities.

REVIEW How and why did the economy of the United States change in the late 1800s? 🔄 Summarize

Summarize the Lesson

- America's resources have attracted people from different countries and enabled many to build better lives.
- The growth of agriculture contributed to the movement of people from one region to another.
- Our economy has changed from an agricultural economy to an urban industrial economy in the centuries since the founding of our nation.

LESSON 1 ⟩ REVIEW

Check Facts and Main Ideas

1. 🔄 Summarize On a separate sheet of paper, write a sentence summary. Use the words **urban**, **rural**, and **technology** in your summary.

> People lived by hunting and gathering.

> Settlers moved to farms in the Midwest.

> Industries grew rapidly.

> [ ]

2. Why did the first Americans come to this continent?

3. What caused Americans to decide to move westward in the 1800s?

4. What happened in the late 1800s to change the way people lived in the United States?

5. **Critical Thinking: *Analyze Information*** Think of a product that is in your classroom. Make a list of the resources that were needed to make this product.

Link to 🔗 **Writing**

Write a Diary Entry Suppose you are with some of the first Americans traveling in search of food. You stop every night to rest, but each new day the journey begins again. Write about some of the adventures, dangers, and challenges you might face.

MISSOURI
St. Louis

Trade Then and Now

PREVIEW

Focus on the Main Idea
People trade for the goods and services that they need and want.

PLACE
St. Louis, Missouri

VOCABULARY
need
want
barter
producer
consumer
economy
free enterprise system
profit
supply
demand
opportunity cost

You Are There
You are a fur trapper in the 1600s. It's early fall, time to stock up before winter comes. You have collected several fur pelts, and you need to trade them for sacks of corn and wheat. You've traveled a long distance to reach the nearest trading post.

A farmer with sacks of grain catches your eye. He says he needs pelts to make clothing to keep his family warm in the winter. You have extra pelts to trade. He has extra sacks of grain to trade. You wonder how many pelts the farmer wants for his extra sacks of corn and wheat.

Summarize As you read, look for details to help you summarize how trade has changed over time.

72

Trading for Needs and Wants

Early in the history of the United States, people traded for the goods and services that they needed and wanted. A **need** is something that a person must have to live. People need food, clothing, and shelter. A **want** is something that a person would like to have, but can live without. People want things to make their lives easier and more comfortable.

People often bartered for what they needed and wanted. To **barter** is to trade one kind of goods or service for another. For example, people may have bartered fur pelts for food they needed. In the early 1800s, **St. Louis, Missouri,** grew because people came there to trade for fur.

Painting by Alfred Fredericks

In other situations, people skilled at building things may have bartered their services for another kind of service. For example, a person might help someone build a house. In exchange for that service, the building owner might help the other person harvest a crop.

In ancient times, people used shells, stones, and round metal disks as money. A person who was willing to sell something exchanged that good or service for a certain number of the shells, stones, or metal disks. In time, however, people relied less on bartering as a way of trading.

REVIEW Describe a time when you have bartered with a friend.
Apply Information

▶ **This famous painting shows a European explorer trading with Native Americans.**

73

Using Money

The use of money goes back thousands of years. About 2500 B.C., the early Egyptians used tiny bars of metal as money. Around 700 B.C., Greek cities produced flat pieces of metal with a picture or design on them. These are considered the first coins used as money. The Chinese, who had a shortage of metal, came up with the idea of paper money about 1,400 years ago.

Today, in the United States and in most countries around the world, people use paper bills, metal coins, and checks as money. Our money is divided into dollars and cents. People use this money to buy things that they need and want.

People who make goods or products to sell are called **producers.** A person who buys goods or services is a **consumer.** Producers in the United States can set the prices for the goods that they have made or for a service that they want to sell. This price covers their costs of production. Producers also think about what consumers are willing to pay in dollars and cents for the products or services.

REVIEW Tell the difference between a producer and a consumer.
Compare and Contrast

Literature and Social Studies

Josefina Saves the Day
by Valerie Tripp

Josefina Saves the Day is a story about a girl who lived in New Mexico in the 1820s. In this part of the story, Josefina's papá decides to trade his mules. He is excited because Señor Patrick has found people to buy the mules. Read to find out what he will get in return.

JOSEFINA SAVES THE DAY
A SUMMER STORY
~BOOK FIVE~

"I have good news. Señor Patrick has found traders who want to buy all of our mules."

"My friends will be glad to get the mules," said Patrick quickly. "Mules are sturdy. They do better than oxen on the wagon trails. Oxen are fussy eaters. They have delicate feet, and they get sunburned." Patrick pointed to his own red nose and joked, "Just like me!"

Everyone laughed, and Patrick went on. "I can get you silver for the mules," he said.

Silver! This was lucky indeed. Normally, Papá would have traded the mules for the goods from the americanos. Then he would trade the goods for sheep. Josefina knew Papá must be pleased. It would be much easier to buy the sheep they needed with silver.

74

FACT FILE

▶ A 1652 shilling

Money in the United States

The British colonists in America made their own coins and paper money. At times, they used beads and tobacco leaves as money.

▶ A 1794 silver dollar

The 1793 copper cent and the 1794 silver dollar were among the first coins made by the new United States government.

▶ A 1793 copper cent

▶ Tobacco leaves used as money

▶ An 1837 three-dollar bill made by a private bank in Ypsilanti, Michigan

After gold was discovered in California in 1848, miners used gold dust and nuggets as money in mining camps.

▶ A California gold nugget

Today, most United States coins have the image of a United States president on them. George Washington is on the quarter, Franklin D. Roosevelt is on the dime, Thomas Jefferson is on the nickel, and Abraham Lincoln is on the penny.

▶ Coins used today

75

Free Trade

In the United States our economy is based on the free enterprise system. An **economy** is the resources of a country, state, region, or community and how the resources are managed. A **free enterprise system** is one in which businesses have the right to produce any goods or provide any service that they want. The government does not tell these businesses what they can produce or sell. People or businesses decide what they want to make and sell.

Not every country in the world has a free enterprise system. Some governments limit what goods businesses can produce and what services businesses can provide. Some governments even choose which businesses can provide certain goods or services. In the United States, business people usually produce and sell goods or services in hopes of making a profit. A **profit** is the money a business person has left over after all the costs of the business are paid.

For example, if a business makes and sells T-shirts, it has to pay for the costs of the natural resources. It also pays for the capital resources—the machinery used to make the product. It has to pay the workers—the human resources—who make the shirts. When the business sells the shirts, it sets the price so that it can pay for all of its costs and still have money left over. The money left over is its profit.

Free Trade and Profit

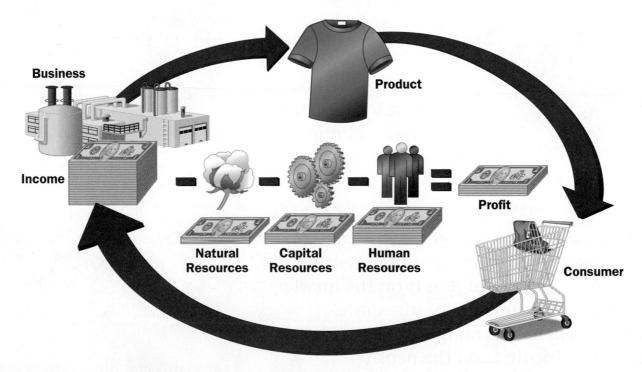

▶ Many factors affect profit.

DIAGRAM SKILL *What factors that affect profit are shown in this diagram?*

▶ Clearance signs are common sights when supply of a product is high.

product may go down. For example, if a business makes more robot dogs than people want to buy, the business may have to lower the price to try to get more people to buy the robots.

The quantity of an item that consumers are willing to buy at different prices is the **demand.** Sometimes demand increases because consumers want more of a product for various reasons. Then, the demand is great, and since the supply is low, the price for the product goes up. If people really want this product, they may be willing to pay a higher price to get it.

Business owners use their profits to improve their businesses and to buy the things that they need and want.

REVIEW How is an economy based on a free enterprise system different from one that is not?
Compare and Contrast

REVIEW How might an increase in supply benefit a customer?
Draw Conclusions

The Amount of a Product

In a free enterprise economy, businesses operate based on a system of supply and demand. The quantity of an item that sellers are willing to offer at different prices is called the **supply.** Usually, if a business has made too much of one particular product, there is a large supply. The price of the

Making Choices

You probably can't buy everything that you want. You have to make choices. Suppose you are at a fair. You have just enough money either to buy a ticket for a ride that you really want to take or to buy a stuffed toy at the dinosaur exhibit. You are just going to have to choose. If you choose to buy the toy, you can't take the ride. If you choose the ride, you can't buy the toy.

You decide that you are going to take the ride. You'll always be able to remember how much fun the ride was. The toy that you didn't buy is called your opportunity cost. An **opportunity cost** is what you give up when you choose one thing over another.

REVIEW Think of a choice that you had to make. What was your opportunity cost? Did you make a good choice or not? **Make Decisions**

▶ Home computers are becoming more and more common.

Facing the Future

We can all contribute to our nation's economy. If you buy something, you are a consumer. Every time you buy something, you make a contribution to the economy of the United States.

When you get older and begin working, you will also help the economy by producing goods or services. Preparing yourself for work is very important. You need to study and go to school to learn the skills that you will need as an adult in the workplace.

Our country is changing every day. New kinds of technology make the country a better place to live and work. Over the years, use of home computers has grown. Computers help us communicate quickly, do research, bank, and purchase products. The computer industry is creating new ways to work. What do you want to do when you grow up? What are some ways that you can prepare yourself for what you want to do?

REVIEW What are some ways that you can help the economy?
🕙 Summarize

Summarize the Lesson

- **Goods and services have been traded by barter and money.**
- **Our free enterprise system is based on supply and demand.**
- **You help the economy when you are a careful producer and consumer.**

LESSON 2 REVIEW

Check Facts and Main Ideas

1. 🕙 **Summarize** On a separate sheet of paper, fill in the summary statement for the details.

   ┌─────────────┐   ┌─────────────┐
   │ Businesses │   │ Businesses │
   │ choose what │   │operate on supply│
   │ to produce. │   │ and demand. │
   └─────────────┘   └─────────────┘

2. How does a business make a **profit?**
3. What is the difference between **supply** and **demand?**
4. How were goods and services traded by **barter?**
5. **Critical Thinking:** *Draw Conclusions* How have computers affected the economy of the United States?

Link to ⬥⬥ Reading

Read a Fable Read the story of "Jack and the Beanstalk." Tell the class what Jack got in return for his mother's cow. Decide if Jack's trade was a good one or a bad one. Explain why you think so.

CALIFORNIA MISSOURI

PREVIEW

Focus on the Main Idea
The regions of the United States and the nations of the world depend on each other.

VOCABULARY
transportation
interdependent
globalization
communication

▶ **Pony Express riders carried mail in sturdy leather pouches such as this one.**

St. Joseph Museum, Missouri

Transportation and Communication

You Are There It's 1860. William H. Russell's company has just hired you for the Pony Express. They need fast horse riders to get mail from Missouri to California. Mail takes from three weeks to six months to get across the country, either over land on trains and stagecoaches or by ship all the way around South America!

Your part of the route begins at Fort Kearny, Nebraska. You race toward the Rocky Mountains. When you arrive at the Platte station, your legs are wobbly and your horse is tired. First you hand the mail pouch to the next rider. Then you sit down to eat some beans and bacon before heading back. Even though the mail still has hundreds of miles to go, it will arrive in ten days. Now that's express!

 Summarize As you read, look for details to help you summarize how transportation and communication help the economy.

From Across the USA

The days of mail delivery by horseback are long gone in the United States. Today a letter sent from the state of Washington can arrive in Washington, D.C., overnight! How? Trucks, trains, ships, and airplanes provide transportation across the states. **Transportation** is the moving of goods, people, or animals from one place to another.

Why do we want to move goods across the states? Products grown in one state can be sent to people living in another state. For example, someone living in New York can buy Georgia peaches in their local grocery store. As you learned in Chapter 1, different regions have different climates. Because of differences in resources and climates, farmers grow different types of crops and produce different products in different regions.

No single region can produce everything that people in that region need and want. Each region depends on other regions for goods, services, and resources. When regions depend on one another in this way, they are economically **interdependent.**

Transportation helps the interdependent regions get almost anything they need and want. What would happen if we didn't have transportation? You could not get mail. If you lived in the Midwest, you would find mostly wheat and corn in the stores. You wouldn't find bananas or orange juice. If you lived in a community far from factories, you couldn't buy books, tennis shoes, or clothes.

REVIEW What does it mean for regions to be economically interdependent? **Main Idea and Details**

▶ A Pony Express rider (right) leaves St. Joseph, Montana on his way to California.

Around the World

The regions of the United States are economically interdependent. But trade and commerce stretch much farther than the borders of our country. Most of the countries of the world are tied together economically.

To understand how countries depend on each other, take a close look at a product you might find in your classroom or library: a computer. A computer works because it has a set of tiny electrical circuits called chips. The chips are made of silicon. The raw silicon might come from Germany. The design for the circuits might have been planned

▶ The manufacturing of computer parts requires very clean conditions. Dust and other dirt particles cannot get into the final product.

in Oregon, in the United States. The circuits might have been placed on the chips in Malaysia—a country in Asia.

The chips would have been sent to factories in different places where different computer parts are made. Some parts might have been made in Virginia. Other parts might have been made in England. The steel for the case around the computer might have been made in Poland. The computer might have been put together in Idaho. It might have been packaged in a big box made in Wisconsin and then sent to your school.

The making of your computer is an example of globalization. **Globalization** of businesses means that goods are produced using resources, raw materials, and services from several countries. Many businesses have factories in many places or use goods produced by other businesses. These companies also sell their products to businesses all around the world. With modern transportation, especially airplanes, companies can send goods halfway around the world in a day or two.

REVIEW Tell how the making of a computer is an example of globalization. **Main Idea and Details**

▶ A computer chip

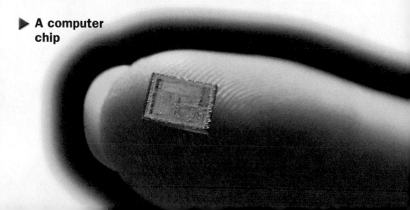

Map Adventure

Transportation has helped make globalization work. For example, a business can purchase raw materials or manufactured parts for a computer from several countries. The final product is then usually assembled in one place. Part of the trail of the making of a computer is shown below on the map. Study the trail and then answer the questions.

1. What parts came from Europe?
2. On the map below, what traveled the farthest to reach Idaho?
3. In which country will the computers be assembled?

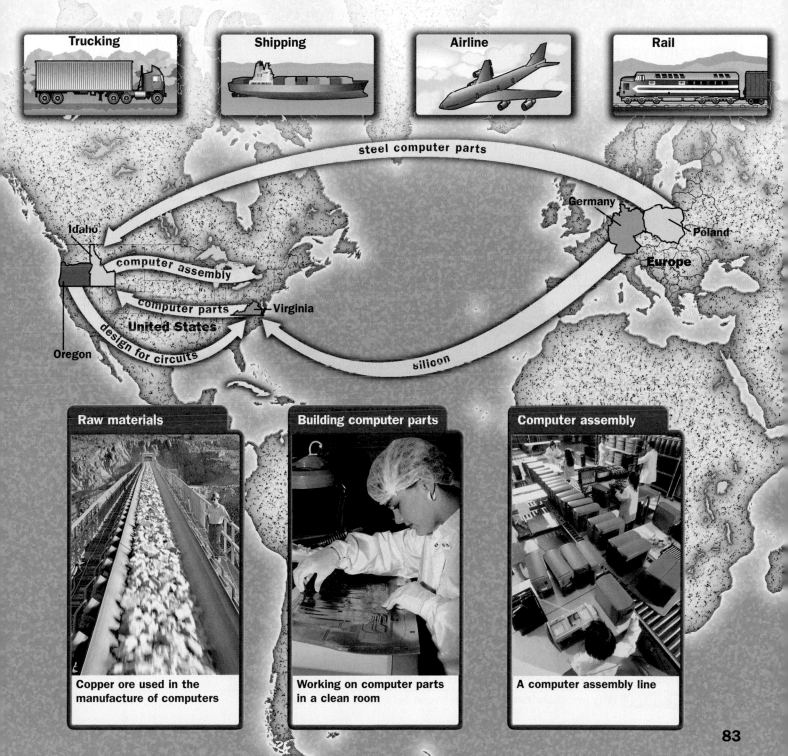

Trucking

Shipping

Airline

Rail

steel computer parts

Germany

Poland

Europe

Idaho

computer assembly

computer parts — Virginia

United States

design for circuits

Oregon

silicon

Raw materials

Copper ore used in the manufacture of computers

Building computer parts

Working on computer parts in a clean room

Computer assembly

A computer assembly line

Communication

Suppose that it's the late 1800s. You live on a dairy farm in Wisconsin. Your cows give you plenty of milk that you make into great ice cream. Everyone says you should sell your ice cream all over the country. Could you do that? Even though railroads are a part of everyday life, trains can't get goods to people's front doors. Even if they could, your ice cream would be melted and spoiled upon arrival.

Transportation in the 1800s was not fast. Airplanes had not been invented yet. Even if you decided to sell your ice cream to nearby places, the telephone and radio had only just been invented. To take orders, advertise, and get the goods to your customers, you need fast transportation and communication.

Communication is the way that people send and receive information. Fast communication helps local, national, and world trade. Suppliers communicate with stores to tell them about available goods. Consumers communicate with businesses to tell them what they want.

Fast communication and transportation are especially important for companies that sell goods that can spoil, such as fruit and milk. With today's fast communication and transportation, these companies can sell their goods in faraway places. The illustration below shows a possible path that goods can take to get to the consumer.

Communication and Transportation

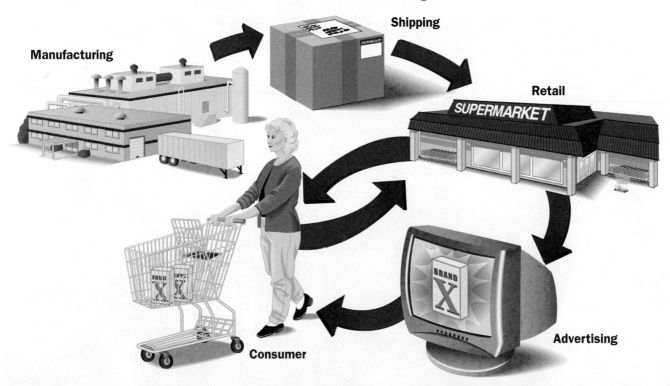

▶ Communication and transportation play a role in getting goods to the consumer.

DIAGRAM SKILL *Why are there two arrows between retail and consumer?*

Today, people can communicate instantly by telephone. With wireless telephones, people can make long distance calls from almost anywhere. They can make business decisions on the spot. People also communicate using their computers. With the Internet, people can send and receive messages and documents very quickly. Computers allow companies to do business easily over long distances.

REVIEW Why are fast transportation and communication important for world trade? ⊙ Summarize

Summarize the Lesson

- **Because no region can produce everything it needs, all the regions of the United States are economically interdependent.**

- **The globalization of businesses means that goods are produced using resources, raw materials, and services from several countries.**

- **Fast transportation and communication have made local and world trade easier.**

LESSON 3 REVIEW

Check Facts and Main Ideas

1. ⊙ Summarize On a separate sheet of paper, copy the diagram. Fill in the details that lead to the summary.

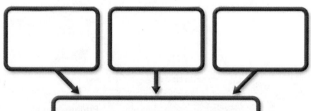

The U.S. economy depends on several important factors.

2. Give an example of a way that your region is economically **interdependent** with other regions in the United States.

3. What is an example of a way that your region helps the world economy?

4. How have **transportation** and **communication** been important in the growth of trade around the world?

5. Critical Thinking: *Identify Opinions* A newspaper ran a story about **globalization.** Part of the story said, "Globalization is not good for the economy of the United States. American companies have built factories in foreign countries." Which sentence is an opinion? Which is a fact?

Link to ⌘ Science

Learn About Transportation Go to the library to find a book about the history of transportation. Make a time line to show how transportation has changed from the founding of our country in 1776 to the present.

Map and Globe Skills

Use a Road Map and Scale

What? Road maps are maps that show roadways of a particular area, such as a city, a state, or an entire country. Maps that show a large area, like an entire country, include fewer types of roads because there is less room for detail. A road map of the United States, therefore, will show mostly major highways. On maps that show a small area, such as a city, more detail is included. City road maps include major highways, major paved streets, and certain side streets in local neighborhoods.

Why? People use road maps to plan routes from one place to another. Business travelers may want to figure out which route is fastest, while tourists might want to find a route that will take them through scenic areas.

Road Map of Ohio and Pennsylvania

Key
- Interstate highway (10)
- U.S. highway (90)
- ★ State capital
- • City

Others use road maps for local destinations, such as a trip to the museum or to a friend's house, or to find the best route to the airport.

How? First determine the area shown. Look for the map's title or label. This map's title indicates that this map shows Ohio and Pennsylvania. Then study the map key. Identify the symbols used to represent the different types of roads. According to the key for this map, double blue lines represent interstate highways. Find the road numbered "70" on the map. This road is shown as a double blue line, which means road "70" is an interstate highway.

After identifying the symbols in the key, you should identify the scale. The scale tells how many miles (or km) each inch (or cm) represents. For example, the scale for this map shows that one inch represents about 80 miles across land. If you

measured with a ruler along Route 33 on the map, you'd find that Columbus is about an inch from the city of Lima. This means that if you were to drive on Route 33 from Columbus to Lima, you would travel almost 80 miles. Understanding scale is an important part of using a road map. Without knowing the scale, it would be nearly impossible to use the map to figure out just how far one place is from another.

Think and Apply

Suppose that you want to visit Greenfield Village near Detroit, Michigan. You are in Cleveland, Ohio. Use the **road map** on page 86 to find the answers.

1 What major highways would you take to get from Cleveland to Detroit?

2 About how many miles is it from Cleveland to Toledo? from Toledo to Detroit?

3 How many miles would your cousin from Cincinnati have to travel to meet you in Detroit?

Chapter Summary

Summarize

Copy the diagram on a separate sheet of paper. Use the terms listed in the chart in a summary statement about the economy of the United States.

Free enterprise	Supply and demand	Prices

↓ ↓ ↓

Vocabulary

Fill in the blank in each sentence with the correct vocabulary word from the list below.

a. **producer** (p. 74)

b. **barter** (p. 73)

c. **opportunity cost** (p. 78)

d. **urban** (p. 71)

e. **rural** (p. 71)

f. **consumer** (p. 74)

g. **supply** (p. 77)

h. **free enterprise system** (p. 76)

i. **demand** (p. 77)

j. **interdependent** (p. 81)

k. **globalization** (p. 82)

l. **technology** (p. 70)

1 The countryside is considered a _____ area.

2 Putting scientific knowledge to practical use is called _____.

3 Businesses in a _____ have the right to produce any goods they want.

4 When you choose one thing over another, what you give up is the _____.

5 The process of making parts of a product in different places around the world is called _____.

6 A person who makes goods to sell is a _____.

7 Cities are _____ areas.

8 The amount of an item that sellers are willing to offer at different prices is the _____.

9 To trade one kind of goods or service for another is to _____.

10 A person who buys things is called a _____.

11 When regions depend on one another, they are economically _____.

12 The amount of an item that consumers are willing to buy at different prices is called the _____.

Facts and Main Ideas

1. List some resources that Native Americans or European settlers found in North America.

2. What is the difference between bartering and using money?

3. Why are transportation and communication very important in our modern economy?

4. **Main Idea** How did America's rich resources affect early settlement?

5. **Main Idea** How might a change in supply or a change in demand affect the price of objects?

6. **Main Idea** How are economic interdependence and globalization related to one another?

7. **Critical Thinking:** *Draw Conclusions* Having a healthy economy is important for our country. Why is this true?

Write About Economics

1. **Write an Ad** Suppose you are selling a product or service. Describe your product or service. Tell why the product or service is useful or important. List the price and explain why the price is a good one.

2. **Write a Newspaper Article** Write about certain goods that are in short supply. Many consumers wish to purchase these goods. Tell why the goods are in limited supply and why consumers want to buy them. Be sure to tell what will happen to the price for the goods.

3. **Write a Brochure** Tell why a particular type of business should move to your region. Think about the resources your region has and decide which type of new businesses would do well in your region. Discuss the communication and transportation networks in your region.

Apply Skills

Use a Road Map

Look at the map below. Then answer the questions.

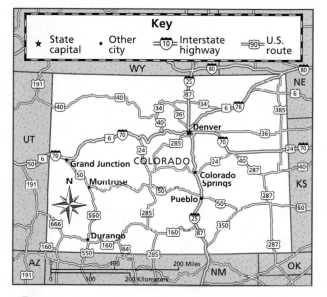

1. What information does this map give?

2. What is the scale of this map?

3. About how many miles is it from the New Mexico border to the Wyoming border traveling on Interstate 25?

Internet Activity

To get help with vocabulary and terms, select the dictionary or encyclopedia from *Social Studies Library* at **www.sfsocialstudies.com**.

End with a Song

America

The words to the song "America" were written in 1832 by Samuel F. Smith to celebrate George Washington's birthday. First sung July 4, 1832, it was unofficially regarded as our national anthem until the early part of the twentieth century.

America

Words by Samuel Francis Smith

Traditional Melody

1. My coun - try! 'tis of thee, Sweet land of
2. My na - tive coun - try, thee, Land of the

lib - er - ty, Of thee I sing; Land where my
no - ble free, Thy name I love; I love thy

fa - thers died, Land of the Pil - grims' pride,
rocks and rills, Thy woods and tem - pled hills;

From ev - 'ry __ moun - tain-side Let __ free - dom ring!
My heart __ with __ rap - ture thrills Like __ that a - bove.

Test Talk

Narrow the answer choices. Rule out answers you know are wrong.

Main Ideas and Vocabulary

TEST PREP

Read the passage below and use it to answer the questions that follow.

The United States is divided into regions. A <u>region</u> is an area defined by similar characteristics. The five regions of the United States are the Northeast, the Southeast, the Midwest, the Southwest, and the West.

Landforms help make the five regions different from one another. The Northeast has seacoasts and the Appalachian Mountains. The Appalachian Mountains also run through the Southeast. The Southeast has coastal areas and plains. The Midwest is mostly grassy plains. Like the Northeast, the Midwest also has land shaped by glaciers. The Southwest has canyons, high plateaus, and some deserts. The Rocky Mountains just touch the Southwest. The West also includes the Rocky Mountains and some deserts. But unlike the Southwest, the West has a

seacoast and a second range of mountains called the Cascade Mountains.

Climate differences also help make the regions distinct. The southern regions tend to be warmer than the northern regions. The regions that are lower in elevation tend to be warmer than the higher regions.

Each region has different <u>resources</u>. Resources are used to produce goods that people need or want. Some of the resources are related to the landforms and climates of a region.

The resources of each region contribute to the region's economy. Each region gets some things that it needs from other regions and sends things to other regions. For this reason, the regions are economically interdependent.

1 In the passage, the word <u>region</u> refers to
A an area with only one kind of landform
B an area with only one kind of culture
C an area of similar characteristics
D an area that is distinct from other areas on other continents

2 What are the regions listed in the passage?
A the plains and the plateaus
B the Appalachian Mountains, the Rocky Mountains, and the Cascade Mountains
C the Atlantic coast, the Pacific coast, and the coast of the Gulf of Mexico
D the Northeast, the Southeast, the Midwest, the Southwest, and the West

3 In the passage, the word <u>resources</u> means
A a mine
B a person
C the way a particular area, like a country, manages its goods and services
D something that can be used to produce goods that people want

4 What is the unstated main idea of the passage?
A People disagree on how the United States should be divided into regions.
B The five regions of the United States are distinct in their landforms, climate, resources, and economies.
C The equator determines climate.
D The five regions of the United States have similar characteristics.

Terms

Match each word with the correct description or definition.

1 **elevation** (p. 21)

2 **plateau** (p. 13)

3 **economy** (p. 76)

4 **legislative branch** (p. 50)

5 **landform** (p. 11)

a. a raised, flat area of land

b. how the resources of a place are managed

c. feature on Earth's surface

d. the branch of government that makes our nation's laws

e. how high above sea level a place is

Write About It

Design a Museum Exhibit As a class, design a museum exhibit about economics. Decide on a topic for your exhibit. You might consider designing an exhibit about methods of trading, about money, or about our nation's economy at any point in history. Decide what will be in your exhibit. Then divide into three groups. One group will describe the objects or displays in the exhibit. One group will write the labels to go with the objects or displays. One group will read the descriptions and the labels together and edit them. As you write and edit, make sure that the main idea you want to teach about economics is clear.

Apply Skills

Make a Map Game Ask an adult for old road maps or an old atlas. Pick one of the maps to use for a board game. Find or make playing pieces for your game. Decide where the starting and ending points will be. Make playing cards for the game. The cards could give directions for moving on the map. Decide on other rules for moving pieces along the map. Try out your game with a friend. After your trial game, revise the cards or the rules to improve the game.

Read on Your Own

Look for books like these in the library.

Discovery Channel School

UNIT 1 Project

Eye on Our Region

Take visitors on a video tour of your region. Show what's great about it.

1 Form a group and choose an interesting topic about your region.

2 Make a map of your region.

3 Make a list of facts about your topic. Draw pictures that illustrate your facts. Write a sentence or two to describe each picture.

4 Put your group's pictures together. Put them in the order in which you will show them. Use your map as an introduction. This is your video tour to share with the class.

Internet Activity

Learn more about geography. Go to **www.sfsocialstudies.com/activities** and select your grade and unit.

The Northeast

How has the Northeast welcomed
new people and new ideas?

"Gradually from week to week the character of each tree came out...reflected in the smooth mirror of the lake."

—Henry David Thoreau, *Walden*

Jasper Francis Cropsey's painting, *New England Landscape,* illustrates the lush countryside of the Northeast.

97

Welcome to the Northeast

Key
- New England states
- Middle Atlantic states
- ★ State capital
- ⊛ National capital
- — National border

CANADA

St. Lawrence River

MAINE

M O U N T A I N S

VERMONT

Augusta ★

Lake Champlain

Montpelier ★

WHITE MTS.

ADIRONDACK MTS.

NEW HAMPSHIRE

Lake Ontario

GREEN MTS.

Concord ★

NEW YORK

Connecticut River

Albany ★

Boston ★

Massachusetts Bay

MASSACHUSETTS

44°N

42°N

Lake Erie

CATSKILL MTS.

Cape Cod

66°W

Hartford ★

Providence ★

CONNECTICUT

N

PENNSYLVANIA

POCONO MTS.

Narragansett Bay

RHODE ISLAND

OH

ALLEGHENY MTS.

APPALACHIAN

Long Island

40°N

Allegheny River

Harrisburg ★

Trenton ★

ATLANTIC OCEAN

68°W

Ohio River

NEW JERSEY

Susquehanna River

WV

Potomac River

MARYLAND

Dover ★

0   100   200 Miles

0   100   200 Kilometers

Annapolis ★

Delaware Bay

Washington, D.C. ⊛

DELAWARE

38°N   70°W

VA

Chesapeake Bay

72°W

74°W

▶ **A northeastern lighthouse overlooks the Atlantic Ocean.**

► Thousands of lobsters are caught off the coast of Maine every year.

► The Statue of Liberty was a gift from the people of France to the United States in 1884.

► Boston is the largest city in New England.

► Designs like this one are painted on barns in Pennsylvania Dutch country.

► The Boardwalk in Atlantic City, New Jersey, is 60 feet wide and runs along the Atlantic Coast for $6\frac{1}{2}$ miles. It is lined with restaurants, hotels, shops, and theaters.

99

The Northeast

Sequence

Sequence means the order in which things happen.

- Clue words such as *first, then, next,* and *finally* can help you figure out the sequence of events.
- Dates and times of day are other clues to the sequence of events.
- Some events take place at the same time. Clue words such as *meanwhile* or *during* signal this.

Read this paragraph. **First, then,** and **finally** have been highlighted to show the sequence of events.

The brilliant colors of autumn leaves in the Northeast attract visitors from all over the country. When leaves change color they follow a pattern. **First,** leaves lose their green color. **Then,** yellow and orange pigments begin to show through, and red and purple pigments form from sugar that is trapped in the leaves. **Finally,** the leaves turn brown and fall from the tree.

Word Exercise

Precise Words Using precise words makes writing clearer and more interesting. Precise words, such as *shot* and *plunged*, paint a more vivid picture than the word *moved*. Use a word web to find more precise and exciting words for your ideas.

shot — plunged — moved — raced — scurried — dashed

An Exciting Sequence of Events Near the Falls

Niagara Falls is located at the border of New York and Canada. A boat at the bottom of the falls, called the *Maid of the Mist,* carries tourists near the waterfall. The very first *Maid of the Mist* sailed in 1846.

Farther down the river from the falls are dangerous rapids (part of a river's course where the water rushes quickly). An exciting event happened here in 1861 when the *Maid of the Mist*'s owner sold the steamboat. The boat had to be taken through the rapids to its new owner.

Joel Robinson, the *Maid of the Mist*'s captain, set out at 3:00 P.M. on June 6, 1861. First, the boat shot into the rapids. Then, huge waves crashed over the boat and tore off its smokestack.

Meanwhile, observers on the shore watched the boat being tossed about by waves. When the boat plunged into a whirlpool, Robinson grabbed the wheel and steered the boat out of the whirling water. The boat hurtled into the Devil's Hole Rapids.

Finally, the *Maid of the Mist* made it safely to Lake Ontario. The entire trip had taken only seventeen minutes.

Use the reading strategy of sequence to answer questions 1 and 2. Then answer the vocabulary question.

1. What sequence of events took place between the time Robinson began his journey and the time his boat arrived in Lake Ontario?

2. What happened at the same time that waves were crashing over the boat? How do you know?

3. Look for the word *tore* in the reading selection. What word could you use to replace it in the sentence?

CHAPTER 4

Land and Water in the Northeast

Lesson 1

Niagara Falls
Niagara Falls is a place of beauty and power.

1

Lesson 2

St. Albans, Vermont
The Northeast produces many products, such as maple syrup.

2

Lesson 3

Chesapeake Bay
Crabs and shellfish help support the economy of the Northeast region.

3

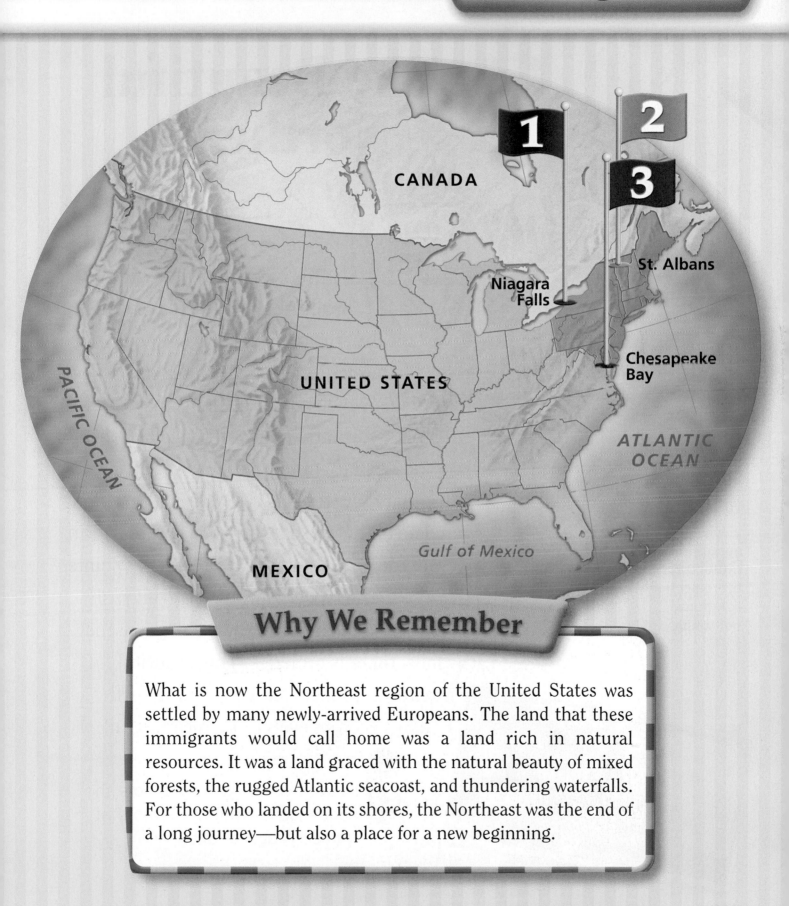

CANADA

Niagara Falls

St. Albans

Chesapeake Bay

UNITED STATES

PACIFIC OCEAN

ATLANTIC OCEAN

Gulf of Mexico

MEXICO

Why We Remember

What is now the Northeast region of the United States was settled by many newly-arrived Europeans. The land that these immigrants would call home was a land rich in natural resources. It was a land graced with the natural beauty of mixed forests, the rugged Atlantic seacoast, and thundering waterfalls. For those who landed on its shores, the Northeast was the end of a long journey—but also a place for a new beginning.

Niagara
Falls

The Beautiful Northeast

PREVIEW

Focus on the Main Idea
The Northeast region is one of incredible scenery and magnificent natural formations.

PLACES

Niagara Falls
Appalachian Mountain Range
Green Mountains
White Mountains
Catskill Mountains
Acadia National Park

VOCABULARY

glacier
gorge
hydropower
hydroelectricity
lighthouse
peninsula

 **You Are There**

You are so excited! Your class is taking a trip to Niagara Falls with thirty students visiting from Madrid, Spain. You will spend part of the day at the American Falls. Later you will all cross the border into Canada to see the Canadian, or the Horseshoe, Falls too. The students tell you that before they left Spain, everyone told them to be sure to see Niagara Falls, that they were indeed one of the natural wonders of the world. As the bus comes within view of the American Falls, your teacher points them out. The students from Spain all rush to one side of the bus, and as they see the falls, there is a silence. This beautiful natural wonder that you grew up with now becomes even more meaningful!

 Sequence As you read, note the sequence of natural events that formed Niagara Falls.

▶ Binoculars help visitors get a closer look at Niagara Falls.

Niagara Falls

On the border of the United States and Canada between Lake Erie and Lake Ontario, two of the five Great Lakes, is one of the natural wonders of North America—**Niagara Falls.**

Many thousands of years ago, glaciers covered what we now call the Northeast. A **glacier** is a huge sheet of ice that covers land. About 12,000 years ago, as the ice began to melt, it carved out the Great Lakes and the Niagara Gorge. A **gorge** is a deep, narrow valley, usually with a stream or river. At the Falls, the Niagara River plunges into this gorge, creating the site visited by millions of tourists throughout the year.

But the beauty of Niagara Falls is only part of its story. For hundreds of years, people have used hydropower to run mills and machines. **Hydropower** is power produced by capturing the energy of flowing water. Today, hydropower plants on the Niagara River take in water through power tunnels to produce hydroelectricity for millions of people. **Hydroelectricity** is electricity produced by water. Niagara is the largest producer of electricity in New York State, generating enough power to light 24 million 100-watt light bulbs at once!

REVIEW What sequence of events caused the formation of Niagara Falls?
◑ **Sequence**

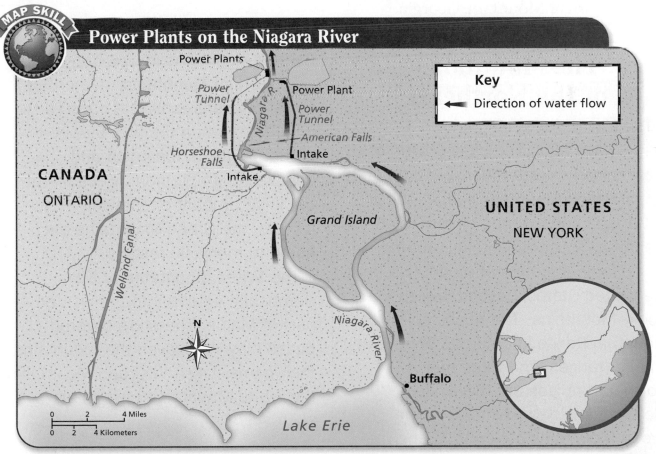

Power Plants on the Niagara River

Power Plants

Power Tunnel

Power Plant

Power Tunnel

American Falls

Niagara R.

Intake

Horseshoe Falls

Intake

Key
← Direction of water flow

CANADA
ONTARIO

Welland Canal

Grand Island

UNITED STATES
NEW YORK

N

Niagara River

Buffalo

0 2 4 Miles
0 2 4 Kilometers

Lake Erie

▶ Power plants on the Niagara River produce electricity for the United States and Canada.

MAP SKILL Understand Directions *What direction does the Niagara River flow?*

The Appalachian Trail

- The Appalachian Trail is the footpath that runs along the ridge of the Appalachian Mountain Range in the eastern United States.
- The trail is about 2,160 miles long, and it passes through fourteen states: Maine, New Hampshire, Vermont, Massachusetts, Connecticut, New York, New Jersey, Pennsylvania, Maryland, West Virginia, Virginia, Tennessee, North Carolina, and Georgia.
- The northernmost end of the trail is in Katahdin, Maine.
- The southernmost end of the trail is in Springer Mountain, Georgia.

- A man named Benton MacKaye had the idea for the Appalachian Trail. He thought hiking the trail would be a good getaway for city people.
- The Appalachian Trail is now part of the National Park System, but it is maintained by volunteers.

The Mountains of the Northeast

The Northeast is also known for its many mountains. The oldest chain of mountains in North America—the **Appalachian Mountain Range**—begins in Canada and extends all the way to Alabama. These mountains are one of the largest groups of mountains in the United States, second only to the Rocky Mountains. The Appalachian Mountain Range is made up of several smaller ranges. The three main Northeast ranges are the White Mountains in New Hampshire, the Green Mountains in Vermont, and the Catskill Mountains in New York.

The **Green Mountains,** named for the forest of evergreens that covered the mountains when the first European settlers arrived, run north and south through Vermont. Because of the large amount of snowfall they receive, the Green Mountains are home to many ski resorts.

The **White Mountains** of New Hampshire extend into the western part of Maine. The snow-covered peaks may have given the mountains their name. Like the Green Mountains, the White Mountains have many ski resorts.

The **Catskill Mountains** are about two hours north of New York City. These mountains, carved by glaciers thousands of years ago, make up one of the most beautiful areas in New York. The Catskills became famous in the 1800s as a setting for writers and painters. Today many vacationers there enjoy fishing, skiing, and other winter sports.

There are many other mountains in the Northeast, such as the Pocono Mountains in Pennsylvania and the Adirondack Mountains in New York. The Poconos are known for many spectacular waterfalls. These mountains are a popular spot for vacationers, especially in the fall when the autumn colors are at their peak.

▶ **A skier performs his jump in competition at Lake Placid.**

The Adirondack Mountains in New York have many beautiful lakes and resorts. One of the most famous lakes, Lake Placid, is at the edge of the village of Lake Placid. The Winter Olympics were held here in 1932 and 1980.

REVIEW What would be the sequence of mountain ranges you might cross if you traveled from Maine southwest to Pennsylvania?

🔄 **Sequence**

The Northeast Coastline

The Northeast region's coastline differs greatly from place to place. All but two of the Northeast states—Pennsylvania and Vermont—share their borders with the Atlantic Ocean. From the rocky coast of Maine to Chesapeake Bay, which is bordered by Maryland and Virginia, the Northeast Atlantic coastline is one of the most recognized in the world.

Maine is known for its beautiful shore on the Atlantic Ocean. The rocky coast is dotted with **lighthouses,** towers with bright lights that shine far out over the water to guide ships. Along the Maine coastline is **Acadia National Park,** the first U.S. National Park east of the Mississippi River. Huge rocks and cliffs make the Maine coastline a favorite of photographers and painters.

▶ **Bass Harbor Head lighthouse on Mount Desert Island, Maine**

Cape Cod is one of Massachusetts' most interesting features. Cape Cod is a **peninsula,** a piece of land almost surrounded by water, or extending far out into the water. The Cape, as it is commonly known, is home to tourists during the warm summer months. Its location and climate have made it one of the most well-known fishing areas in the world.

Thousands of vacationers visit New Jersey's shore every year. Many come to enjoy the warm sandy beaches on the Atlantic coast. All along the beaches in the summer, vacationers play volleyball, swim in the warm waters of the Atlantic, or just gather to relax in the sun.

From famous Atlantic City to beautiful Cape May, the New Jersey coastline is known as "the shore."

REVIEW If you took a boat ride from Maine to Maryland, what sequence of coastline sights might you see? ⊙ **Sequence**

Summarize the Lesson

- The Niagara Falls area provides not only a natural wonder but hydroelectricity for millions.
- The Appalachian Mountain Range, the oldest in North America, runs from Canada to Alabama and includes many smaller ranges in the Northeast.
- The coastline of the Northeast ranges from rocky cliffs to sandy beaches.

▶ Colorful, old houses such as this are common sights in Cape May, New Jersey.

LESSON 1   REVIEW

Check Facts and Main Idea

1. ⊙ Sequence On a separate sheet of paper, copy the diagram below. Fill in sights you would like to see if you traveled south from the northern part of the Northeast region to its southern part.

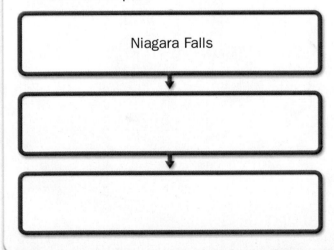

Niagara Falls

2. Niagara Falls is located between what two Great Lakes?

3. What are the three main Northeast mountain ranges in the Appalachian Mountains?

4. What two Northeast states do not share borders with the Atlantic Ocean?

5. **Critical Thinking:** *Solve Problems* The demand for electricity is always high. What could you and others do to reduce this demand? Use the word **hydropower** in your answer.

Link to ⬤⬤ Writing

Write a Poem Make a list of words that might describe the beauty and power of Niagara Falls. Use these words to write a poem about this natural wonder. Use the words **glacier** and **gorge** in your poem.

Read a Cross-Section Diagram

What? A cross-section diagram is a drawing that shows you what you would see if you could cut through something and look inside. It may show how something works.

Why? Sometimes it's hard to imagine what something looks like or how it works simply by reading about it. You have to see it.
Look at the cross-section diagram of a dam and a hydroelectric power plant. The plant is similar to power plants on the Niagara River. The diagram shows parts that are inside the plant. With your finger, trace the path of water through the plant.

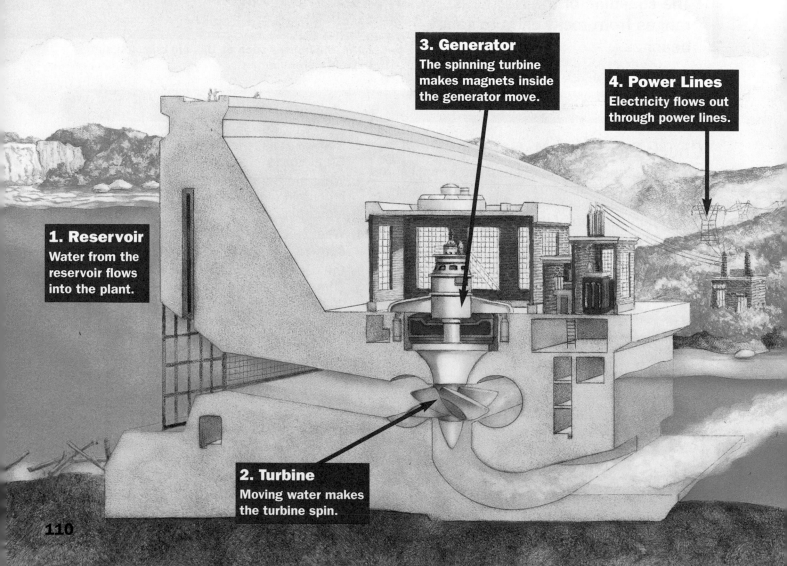

3. Generator
The spinning turbine makes magnets inside the generator move.

4. Power Lines
Electricity flows out through power lines.

1. Reservoir
Water from the reservoir flows into the plant.

2. Turbine
Moving water makes the turbine spin.

Moving water makes the power plant work. Find the reservoir (REZ er vwar) behind the power plant. A **reservoir** is a place that holds water. When water is released from the reservoir, it flows past a turbine (TER bin). The moving water makes the turbine spin. The turbine is connected to the generator. In the generator, magnets move past coils of copper wire. This action produces electricity.

How? Study a cross-section diagram in steps. First, gather information from the labels you see on the diagram. Second, study each labeled part. Try to figure out how each part of the plant works. Third, look at the numbers that show the way water is converted into electricity. Note that the water pushes the turbine to move the generator.

Think of the terms that are used in this diagram. These terms can help you understand and remember how a hydroelectric power plant makes electricity.

Think and Apply

Use the **cross-section diagram** to answer the questions.

1 What is a **reservoir?**

2 What happens when water is released from a reservoir?

3 How does a power plant use renewable resources?

• St. Albans

South
Carver

Resources of the Northeast

PREVIEW

Focus on the Main Idea
The Northeast produces products for the world to enjoy.

PLACES
Lake Seneca
South Carver, Massachusetts
St. Albans, Vermont

VOCABULARY
vineyard
bog
sap
mineral
quarry

You Are There

As your dad drives into the parking lot, you spot the beginning of the rows and rows of grapevines. You are so excited! Each year, you and your brothers have a contest to see who can pick the most grapes. Last year when you were here, your older brother won—he picked five more baskets than you did. This year, you're ready to win! It is so much fun to walk up and down all of the rows of the beautiful purple berries. The best part, though, is thinking of the grape jelly that your mom will make from all of the baskets and baskets of grapes. It's really hard work, but you'll have grape jelly all winter long!

Sequence As you read, pay attention to the many steps it takes to grow and produce some products.

Grapes and Cranberries

Grapes are just one of the many products of the Northeast. Grown in **vineyards,** places where grapevines are planted, thousands of tons of the large purple berries are produced every year.

The vineyards are usually found in hilly areas where the climate is right for the grape's long growing season, which is often as long as 205 days.

Some of the largest vineyards in the Northeast are in New York, near Lake Erie, one of the Great Lakes, and in the Finger Lakes region, an area with several long, finger-shaped lakes. **Lake Seneca,** the largest of the Finger Lakes, is over 600 feet deep and never freezes. The warm air that surrounds the lake helps create just the right conditions for a plentiful grape production.

Another berry grown in the Northeast is the cranberry. Of the 1,000 cranberry farms in the United States, 500 of them are in Massachusetts. Most cranberries are grown in bogs. A **bog** is an area of soft, wet, spongy ground. To prepare a cranberry bog, swampy land must be leveled and cleared. Then it is covered with sand for good drainage. Finally, small, new cranberry plants are pressed into the sand.

As the plants grow, they form a covering over the bottom of the bog. In winter the bogs are covered with water that freezes and protects the plants. When spring arrives, the bogs are drained. They are once again covered with water to protect the plants against insects and disease.

As fall approaches, water becomes very important to the harvest. Since cranberries have small air pockets in the center, they rise when they are flooded. Raking the bog knocks the berries from their vines. They are then collected. Each year, the harvest is celebrated at the Annual Massachusetts Cranberry Harvest Festival in **South Carver, Massachusetts,** home to a cranberry museum!

REVIEW What are steps used to prepare a cranberry bog? **Sequence**

▶ **Raking a cranberry bog**

Other Resources

Another famous Northeast product known around the world is maple syrup. Maple syrup is a sweet liquid made from the sap of sugar maple trees. **Sap** is the liquid that circulates through a plant carrying water and food. Since a great many sugar maple trees grow in Vermont, more maple syrup is produced there than in any other state in the United States.

In order for the sap to flow, the weather in early spring must grow warmer and warmer until temperatures rise above freezing. To get the sap, one or more holes are drilled into the tree. A spout, either metal or plastic, is then placed in the hole. The sap runs through the spout and into a bucket, which is then emptied into a large barrel and taken to a place called a sugar house. Some producers use what is known as a pipeline system where the sap flows through tubes.

At the sugar house, workers boil the sap. As the sap boils, water evaporates until pure maple syrup remains. This process takes many hours. About forty gallons of sap are needed to produce one gallon of syrup!

▶ **Beginning to collect sap**

To celebrate Vermont's maple harvest, every year people from the area and around the world attend the Vermont Maple Festival in **St. Albans, Vermont.** Here visitors enjoy a parade, carnival rides, crafts, pancake breakfasts, and food shows, including maple candy-making demonstrations.

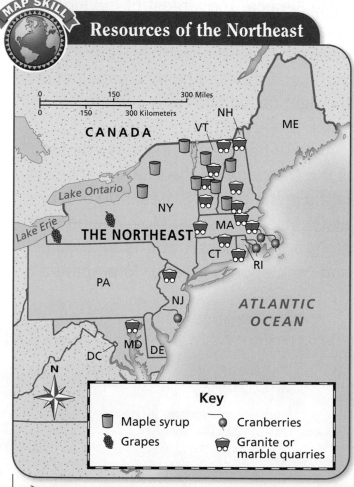

Resources of the Northeast

▶ **Vermont, New Hampshire, and Massachusetts have many quarries.**

MAP SKILL Use a Resource Map *According to the map, what states grow cranberries?*

114

▶ A northeastern granite quarry

such as granite and marble, are combinations of minerals. New Hampshire, known as the Granite State, has many **quarries**, places where stone is dug, cut, or blasted out for use in building. The products from the quarries are often used in building construction. For example, marble from Vermont is in the Supreme Court Building in Washington, D.C.

REVIEW What has to happen for sap to start flowing in maple trees?
Cause and Effect

Minerals are also an important resource of the Northeast. A **mineral** is a material that was never alive and is found in the earth. Most rocks,

Summarize the Lesson

- Grapes and cranberries are two important products grown in the Northeast.
- Vermont is a leading producer of maple syrup.
- Minerals are an important resource of the Northeast.

LESSON 2   REVIEW

Check Facts and Main Idea

1. ⟳ Sequence On a separate sheet of paper, copy the chart below. Fill in the missing information to show the sequence of steps needed to produce maple syrup.

```
┌─────────────────────────────────┐
│      The days grow warmer.      │
└─────────────────────────────────┘
                 ↓
┌─────────────────────────────────┐
│                                 │
└─────────────────────────────────┘
                 ↓
┌─────────────────────────────────┐
│   Sap is collected in buckets.  │
└─────────────────────────────────┘
                 ↓
┌─────────────────────────────────┐
│                                 │
└─────────────────────────────────┘
```

2. Why are **vineyards** able to grow in certain areas of the Northeast?
3. What is the name of the largest lake of the Finger Lakes?
4. Why is water important in the production of cranberries? Use the word **bog** in your answer.
5. Critical Thinking: *Make Inferences* Why are annual festivals in the Northeast so popular?

Link to ⊶⊷ Science

Give a Report Do research in the library or on the Internet to find out more about how sap nourishes trees and other plants. Gather your notes and present your report to the class.

Chesapeake Bay

PREVIEW

Focus on the Main Idea
Chesapeake Bay and other bays in the Northeast provide seafood for millions.

PLACES
Chesapeake Bay
Delaware Bay
Massachusetts Bay

VOCABULARY
bay
inlet
watermen
crab pot

The Plentiful Sea

You Are There
The wind is blowing in your face as you smell the fresh salt air. Uncle Rob and Aunt Ellen have decided to take you fishing with them on Chesapeake Bay. They are watermen, the third generation in their family to follow this profession.

All day long you help them hook and pull their crab pots. The blue crabs you catch are amazing! You pass a sailboat and wave at the watermen on board. They are harvesting oysters with large nets. There are so many oysters in their catch!

As the sun starts to go down, you head toward the docks. It's been a long day. Uncle Rob pats you on the head. Aunt Ellen smiles. You have done well. They are very proud.

Sequence As you read, look for the sequence of events in the day of a waterman.

Great Shellfish Bay

Chesapeake Bay got its name from the Native American word *Chesepiook* (cheez PEE ook), which means "Great Shellfish Bay." A **bay** is a part of a sea or lake that cuts into a coastline. Chesapeake Bay also has inlets that go into the shore. An **inlet** is a narrow opening in a coastline. An inlet is usually smaller than a bay.

Maryland surrounds part of Chesapeake Bay. Maryland is one of the Middle Atlantic states. Others are New York, New Jersey, Pennsylvania, and Delaware.

Chesapeake Bay is rich in crabs, oysters, clams, and other shellfish. About two hundred different kinds of fish live in the bay as well. Because of this abundance, many families in the Chesapeake Bay area earn their livings harvesting the sea.

The people who fish the bay are called **watermen.** These men and women gather different kinds of seafood in different seasons.

Watermen who catch crabs are called "crabbers." Crabbers fish for crabs in the summer using crab pots. As you can see from the above photo, a **crab pot** isn't really a pot at all—it is a large wire cage with several sections. Crabs can swim into the pot, but they cannot swim out of it.

To harvest crabs, a crabber pulls the crab pot into the fishing boat, empties the pot, and sorts the catch by size and type. Then the crabber takes the catch to market.

REVIEW How is a bay like an inlet? How are they different?
Compare and Contrast

Challenges to Chesapeake Bay

Pollution of the land around Chesapeake Bay threatens the bay's fish and shellfish. Some factories around the bay dump waste onto the land, polluting the soil. When it rains or snows, the polluted soil washes into rivers that drain into the bay.

Pollution harms the natural habitat, making it difficult for fish and shellfish to reproduce. The result is a decrease in their numbers. However, pollution is not the only reason that fish and shellfish populations have become smaller.

Overfishing also challenges the balance of life in the bay. Overfishing means taking oysters, crabs, and fish from the bay faster than natural processes can replace them.

People are trying to stop pollution and overfishing. One organization, the Chesapeake Bay Foundation, is working to educate people about the environment. Its slogan is "Save the Bay!"

REVIEW List factors that harm the fish population of Chesapeake Bay.
Main Idea and Details

Then and Now

Nantucket

Between 1800 and 1840, Nantucket was known as the "Whaling Capital of the World." Whaling ships sailed from the island of Nantucket, off the coast of Massachusetts, to hunt whales. Today, there is no longer a whaling industry on Nantucket. But the Nantucket Historical Association's Whaling Museum contains many artifacts from this famous period in history. About 80,000 people visit the Whaling Museum each year.

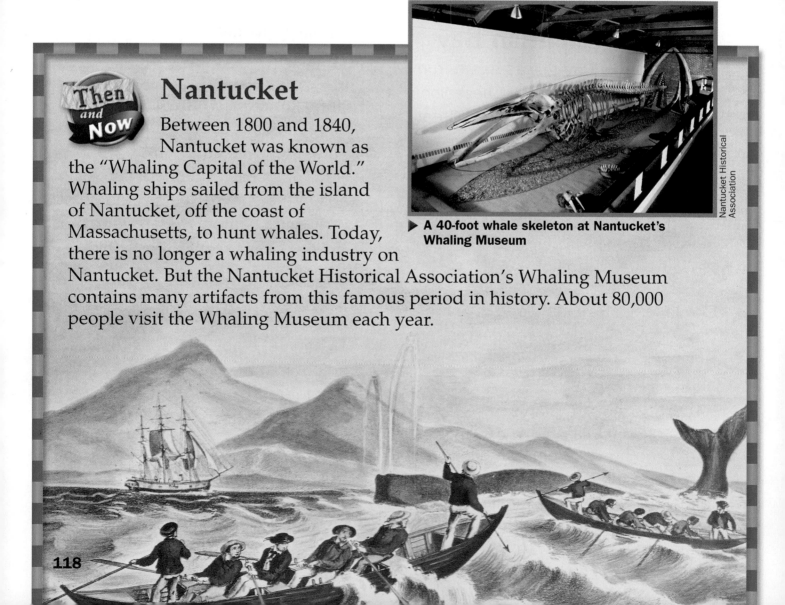

▶ **A 40-foot whale skeleton at Nantucket's Whaling Museum**

Nantucket Historical Association

118

Other Northeast Bays

Chesapeake Bay is only one of many bays of the Northeast known for plentiful products from the sea. For example, north of Chesapeake Bay is Delaware Bay. It forms part of the border between New Jersey and Delaware. Oyster fishing is popular in this bay.

Farther north is Massachusetts Bay. It is near the city of Boston. Many other cities and towns around Massachusetts Bay serve as tourist, fishing, and boating centers.

REVIEW Name other bays along the Northeast Atlantic coast, starting from the north. ⊙ Sequence

▶ A fisherman off the coast of Massachusetts hauls in his catch of shrimp.

Summarize the Lesson

- Chesapeake Bay is one major bay of the Atlantic Ocean and a rich source of fish and shellfish.
- Pollution and overfishing challenge Chesapeake Bay.
- Several other bays are along the coast of the Northeast.

LESSON 3   REVIEW

Check Facts and Main Ideas

1. ⊙ Sequence On a separate sheet of paper, explain how pollution from a factory gets into Chesapeake Bay. Be sure to list the steps in the correct sequence.

Factories produce waste.

↓

↓

↓

↓

Pollution reaches the Bay.

2. What are the people who fish Chesapeake Bay called?
3. Why is Chesapeake Bay important to the Northeast region?
4. What is the purpose of the Chesapeake Bay Foundation?
5. **Critical Thinking:** *Draw Conclusions* What are some kinds of businesses that would grow near bays?

Link to ⚭ Reading

Research Nantucket Go to the library or online and find information about the whaling industry on Nantucket in the early 1800s. Share what you learn with the class.

Chesapeake Bay and Shark Bay, Australia

Bay Life

Fishing is a way of life for the watermen of Chesapeake Bay, but it is also a way of life for people in other parts of the world. In western Australia, for example, many people fish Shark Bay. They catch several different kinds of fish, including pink snapper and whiting. As you can see from the map of page 121, Shark Bay is an inlet of the Indian Ocean. Look closely at the map. Does the shape of Shark Bay remind you of a shark? Many early settlers in Australia thought so. However, the bay was named after the many sharks in its waters.

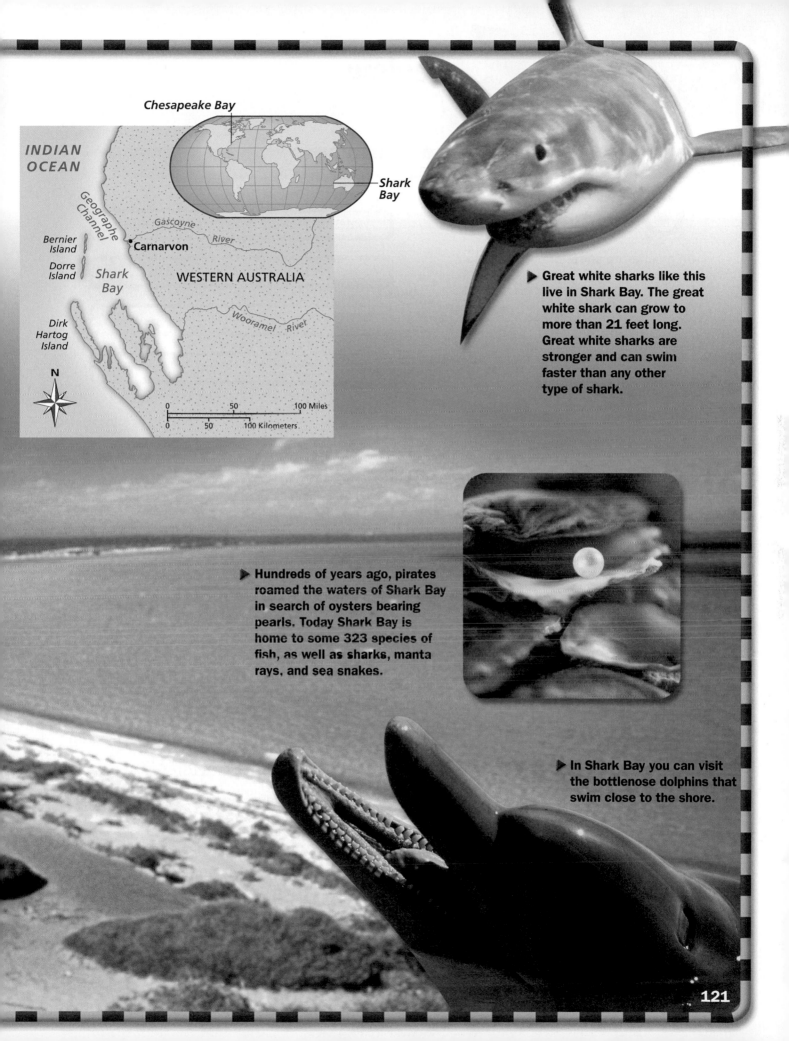

INDIAN OCEAN

Chesapeake Bay

Shark Bay

Geographe Channel

Bernier Island

Dorre Island

Shark Bay

Dirk Hartog Island

Carnarvon

Gascoyne River

WESTERN AUSTRALIA

Wooramel River

N

0   50   100 Miles

0   50   100 Kilometers

▶ Great white sharks like this live in Shark Bay. The great white shark can grow to more than 21 feet long. Great white sharks are stronger and can swim faster than any other type of shark.

▶ Hundreds of years ago, pirates roamed the waters of Shark Bay in search of oysters bearing pearls. Today Shark Bay is home to some 323 species of fish, as well as sharks, manta rays, and sea snakes.

▶ In Shark Bay you can visit the bottlenose dolphins that swim close to the shore.

121

Chapter Summary

Sequence

On a separate sheet of paper, make a diagram like the one shown. Fill in the steps it takes to catch crabs and get them to market.

Waterman lowers crab pots into the bay.

↓

↓

↓

▶ **A blue crab from Maryland**

Vocabulary

1 **glacier** (p. 105)

2 **gorge** (p. 105)

3 **hydroelectricity** (p. 105)

4 **peninsula** (p. 108)

5 **bog** (p. 113)

6 **sap** (p. 114)

a. piece of land almost surrounded by water

b. a deep, narrow valley

c. soft, wet, spongy ground

d. a sheet of ice that covers land

e. liquid in a plant that carries water and food

f. electricity produced by water

Places

Write a sentence or two describing an important fact about each of the following places.

1 **Niagara Falls** (p. 105)

2 **Appalachian Mountain Range** (p. 106)

3 **Lake Seneca** (p. 113)

4 **St. Albans, Vermont** (p. 114)

5 **Chesapeake Bay** (p. 117)

Facts and Main Ideas

Write your answers on a separate sheet of paper.

1 Why is Niagara Falls important for reasons other than its beauty?

2 How does the coastline of the Northeast change from Maine to New Jersey?

3 What does a waterman do?

4 **Main Idea** Describe three important geographic features of the Northeast.

5 **Main Idea** What are some foods that are grown or produced in the Northeast region?

6 **Main Idea** How do many people who live near Chesapeake Bay earn a living?

7 **Critical Thinking:** *Evaluate* Why is there a need for groups such as the Chesapeake Bay Foundation?

Write About the Region

1 **Write a journal entry** as a tourist visiting Niagara Falls for the first time. What are some of the things you notice about the waterfalls?

2 **Write an advertisement** for grape jelly made from grapes grown in the Finger Lakes region of New York. Create a brand name for your jelly. Use words in your ad that will convince the reader to buy your jelly.

3 **Write a letter to the editor** of a Chesapeake Bay area newspaper. State the problems that affect the bay. Explain the causes of the problems. Then suggest possible solutions.

Apply Skills

Read a Cross-Section Diagram

Look at the cross-section diagram of a grape. Then answer the questions.

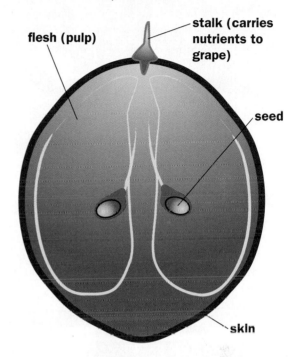

flesh (pulp)

stalk (carries nutrients to grape)

seed

skin

1 What is another word for the flesh of a grape?

2 What carries the nutrients to the grape?

3 Name the parts of a grape from the outside to the inside.

Internet Activity

To get help with vocabulary and places, select dictionary or encyclopedia from *Social Studies Library* at **www.sfsocialstudies.com**.

Lesson 1

Charlestown, Rhode Island
The Narragansett meet European settlers.

1

Lesson 2

Ellis Island, New York
Many Europeans come to the United States to look for opportunities.

2

Lesson 3

Seneca Falls, New York
Women join together to win the right to vote.

3

Lesson 4

Pittsburgh, Pennsylvania
Pittsburgh becomes a center of industry in the Northeast region.

4

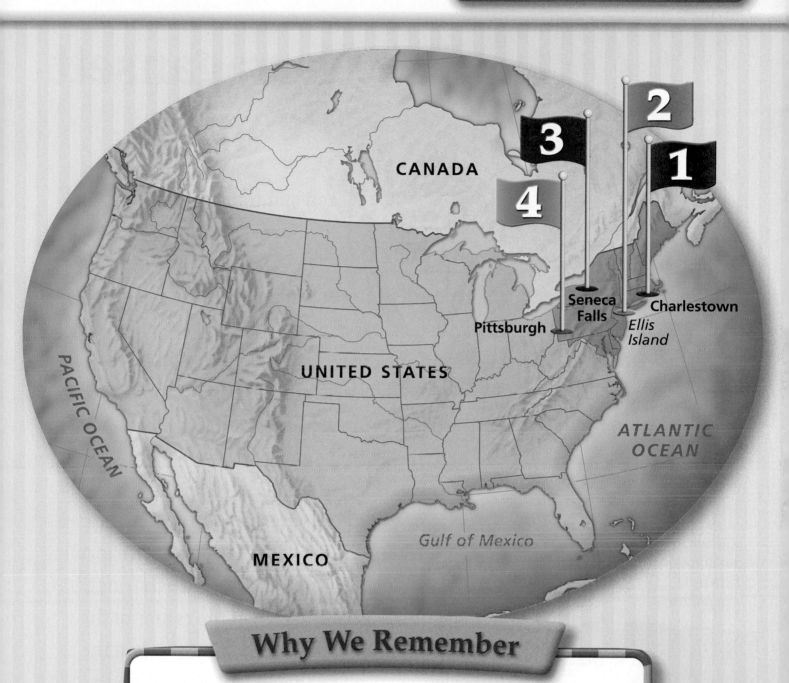

CANADA

3

2

1

4

Seneca
Falls

Pittsburgh

Charlestown

Ellis
Island

UNITED STATES

PACIFIC OCEAN

ATLANTIC
OCEAN

Gulf of Mexico

MEXICO

Why We Remember

The people who came to the Northeast region came with new ideas. They learned to use the land and to thrive on what it gave them. Strong-willed people, they fought for their rights until they won them. The Northeast represents strength and new beginnings, from cities developing their industries to people rediscovering their heritage.

Narragansett Bay

Charlestown

PREVIEW

Focus on the Main Idea
The Narragansett lived in the Northeast region before European settlers came to North America.

PLACE
Charlestown, Rhode Island

PEOPLE
Roger Williams
Canonicus

VOCABULARY
cooperation
wigwam
sachem
reservation
powwow
confederacy

The Narragansett People

You Are There

You and your friend are visiting the Narragansett Indian Reservation during the group's Annual Meeting. You are standing in a field with a crowd of people, waiting for a dance to begin. You see a group of Narragansett men dressed in fringed leather pants and beaded necklaces. You ask a woman next to you how long the Narragansett have lived here. She tells you that Narragansett Indians have lived in this area for hundreds of years.

You turn toward the clearing as the dance begins. Three dancers dressed in fringed leather pants dance in the center of the clearing. You are glad that you had the chance to come to the reservation to see this joyful dance.

Sequence As you read, keep track of the order in which things happen.

▶ **Narragansett chief**

The Narragansett Way of Life

For hundreds of years, the Narragansett (nair uh GAN sit) Indians lived in what is now the state of Rhode Island. They lived on the west side of Narragansett Bay. They hunted, fished, and grew corn and vegetables for food.

▶ A Narragansett wigwam made from tree bark and animal hides

The Narragansett lived in a society that was based on **cooperation,** or working together to get things done. When a family needed a field cleared for planting vegetables, all of their neighbors and friends helped. Several families also shared a home. The Narragansett home was a **wigwam,** a cozy hut made of wooden poles covered with bark.

The Narragansett lands were divided up into a number of territories. Each territory had its own chief, or sachem. **Sachem** means "ruler."

The first Europeans to set foot on the Narragansett lands were Dutch, French, and English fishermen and fur traders. The traders brought goods such as iron axes and hoes and brass kettles. They traded these goods with the Narragansett in exchange for their animal furs. The Narragansett had used tools made of stone and shell. They were happy to use the stronger tools made of metal. The traders also brought glass beads and other attractive items.

REVIEW Describe how the Narragansett organized their government. **Main Idea and Details**

Changes in the Narragansett Way of Life

In 1636 an English settler named Roger Williams visited the Grand Sachem, Canonicus. Williams came to buy land from the Narragansett for a colony that was later called Rhode Island.

Williams was friendly with the Narragansett. He learned their language and earned their trust. He helped keep peace between the Native Americans and the colonists.

At first, the two groups got along well. Gradually, though, the Narragansett and the Europeans began to mistrust each other. Some Europeans took part of the Narragansett's land. The Narragansett and other Native Americans tried to keep their land and their independence by resisting expansion of the Europeans.

In 1675 Native Americans in Massachusetts attacked the English settlers. Because the Narragansett were angry about losing their land, they sided with the other Native American groups. Many Narragansett were killed in battles that followed. The Narragansett scattered. Many moved to Canada or joined other Native American groups. Some Narragansett remained on their lands, even after the State of Rhode Island sold part of their land in 1880.

In 1978 Rhode Island returned about 1,800 acres of land to the Narragansett reservation. A reservation is an area of land set aside for Native Americans. Some Narragansett live on the reservation today. Other Narragansett live throughout the Northeast.

Every August, the Narragansett hold their Annual Meeting Powwow and Green Corn Festival on their reservation in Charlestown, Rhode Island. A powwow is a festival of Native Americans. The Narragansett's powwow is a time for dancing, singing, and renewing old friendships. During this meeting, they also hold elections and settle disputes.

REVIEW How did the Europeans change the way the Narragansett lived? **Main Idea and Details**

▶ A Narragansett dancer at the annual powwow in Charlestown, Rhode Island

▶ **Iroquois boys in their traditional dress gather on the Onondaga Reservation in New York State.**

Other Native Americans of the Northeast

The Iroquois Confederacy was the strongest Native American organization. A **confederacy** is a union of groups, countries, or states. Five Native American groups—the Seneca, Mohawk, Oneida, Onondaga, and Cayuga—had formed the Iroquois Confederacy by 1722. The groups selected fifty representatives who made up a Great Council. The representatives made decisions that affected the whole Confederacy. The Tuscarora later joined the Confederacy.

The Iroquois Confederacy still exists today. Great Council representatives meet on the Onondaga Reservation in New York State.

REVIEW How is the Iroquois Confederacy like the government of the United States? Draw Conclusions

Summarize the Lesson

- **Before Europeans arrived, the Narragansett lived in present-day Rhode Island.**
- **The Europeans changed the way the Narragansett lived.**
- **Five Native American groups formed the Iroquois Confederacy.**

LESSON 1   REVIEW

Check Facts and Main Ideas

1. **Sequence** On a separate sheet of paper, make a diagram like the one shown. Then fill in events that affected the Narragansett in the order they occurred.

> The Narragansett lived in what is now the state of Rhode Island.

↓

> [ ]

↓

> [ ]

↓

> Every August, the Narragansett gather in Charlestown, Rhode Island, for a festive, two-day meeting.

2. What is a **sachem?**
3. What did the Europeans receive from the Native Americans in exchange for the goods they traded?
4. Describe the Iroquois **Confederacy.**
5. **Critical Thinking: Draw Conclusions** Why did five tribes decide to form the Iroquois Confederacy?

Link to ◯─◯ Art

Draw a Poster Based on what you've read in this lesson, draw a poster showing the items that the Narragansett and Europeans traded.

1770   1810   1850   1890

1776
The Declaration of Independence is signed.

1787
The U.S. Constitution is written.

1820
The first of several waves of immigration to the United States begins.

1892
Ellis Island immigration station opens.

The Land of New Beginnings

PREVIEW

Focus on the Main Idea
The Northeast saw the beginnings of the American Revolution, the writing of our nation's Constitution, and the start of many new lives as immigrants arrived in the United States.

PLACES
Plymouth, Massachusetts
Lexington, Massachusetts
Philadelphia, Pennsylvania
New York City, New York
Ellis Island

PEOPLE
John Adams
Benjamin Franklin
Alexander Graham Bell
Albert Einstein
Andrew Carnegie
Madeleine Albright

VOCABULARY
colony
revolution

EVENTS
American Revolution

You Are There

It is a hot day in Philadelphia, and yet the windows and the shutters are closed. The meeting hall is very stuffy. Tempers are rising. The delegates are trying to write a constitution, or a plan of government. There are so many issues yet to be decided.

For example, should little Rhode Island have as many representatives in the government as big New York? There are fewer southern states than northern states. What about their say in the government? It is hard work, but eventually the delegates reach their decisions. The result is the United States Constitution. It begins "We, the People . . ."

Sequence As you read, note the order of events that led from the arrival of early colonists to the immigrants who come to the United States today.

A New Nation

The Constitution set up the government of our new nation. The Northeast played an important role in the beginning of this nation. One of the first English colonies in North America began at **Plymouth, Massachusetts,** in 1620. A **colony** is a settlement of people who come from one country to live in another. By the early 1700s there were thirteen American colonies. Nine of them were in the Northeast.

All of the colonies protested when they felt that England was passing unjust laws and collecting taxes unfairly. Some of the strongest protests came from the colony of Massachusetts. The first shots of the **American Revolution** were fired at **Lexington, Massachusetts,** a town near Boston. A **revolution** is a fight to overthrow the government. Shortly after that, colonial leaders met in **Philadelphia, Pennsylvania,** to write and sign the Declaration of Independence. This document was dated July 4, 1776, and it marked the beginning of the United States of America. **John Adams,** from Massachusetts, provided strong leadership in the writing of the document. Later as our nation's second president, his leadership skills were once again important.

After the United States won independence from England, it became necessary to form a government. In 1787 delegates met in Philadelphia to write the Constitution. **Benjamin Franklin** from Pennsylvania played an important role. He helped settle disputes between the states. At eighty-one, he had become a famous publisher, inventor, and statesman.

Before Washington, D.C., was built, our first two capitals were in the Northeast. **New York City, New York,** was our capital from 1789 to 1790. This is where George Washington took the oath of office and became our first president. In 1790 Philadelphia became our second capital city. The capital moved to Washington, D.C., in 1800.

REVIEW What were some events that led to the development of the new nation? ⟳ Sequence

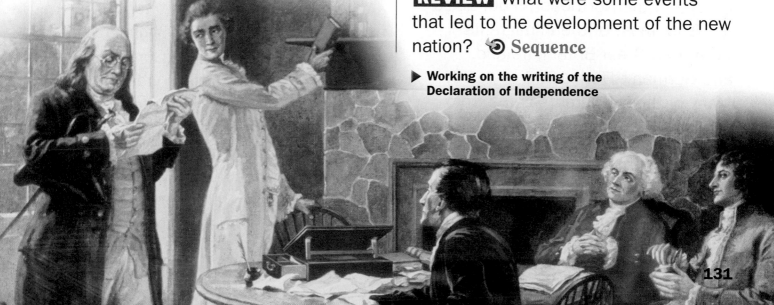

▶ Working on the writing of the Declaration of Independence

A Land of Promise

Even before the American Revolution, the American colonies attracted many people from other nations. After the United States became a nation, many more immigrants came to start a new life in the new nation.

Why did they come? Some were looking for jobs. The growing cities and industries of the Northeast needed plenty of workers. Others wanted to own their own land. Still others hoped to escape war or other hardships in their countries of origin. All of them hoped to find a better life in the United States.

Immigrants came to the United States from all around the world. Since the early 1800s, there have been several waves of immigration from Europe to the Northeast. From 1820 to 1860, most of the immigrants were from Great Britain, Ireland, and Germany. From 1860 to 1890, many of the immigrants came from Scandinavia, a region in northwestern Europe. Many Scandinavians moved westward and started family farms in the Midwest. From 1890 to 1910, many of the immigrants came from southern and eastern Europe.

The Bettmann Archive

▶ **The Ellis Island Registration Hall in 1915**

Most European immigrants came to the United States through the port of New York. In 1892 the United States government opened a huge immigration station on **Ellis Island** in New York harbor. Inspectors there checked the immigrants' papers. They also checked to make sure the immigrants were in good health. By the time the immigration station was closed in 1954, more than 12 million immigrants had passed through the inspection station at Ellis Island. Then they began a new life in the United States.

Immigrants to the United States have contributed much to our nation. **Alexander Graham Bell,** the inventor of the telephone, was a Scottish immigrant. So was **Andrew Carnegie,** who introduced an important steel-making process to the United States. **Albert Einstein,** one of the world's most important scientists, immigrated to the United States from Germany. **Madeleine Albright,** the United States' first female Secretary of State, was an immigrant from eastern Europe.

Today immigrants continue to come to the United States from all parts of the world. Most immigrants are seeking a better way of life, just as the waves of

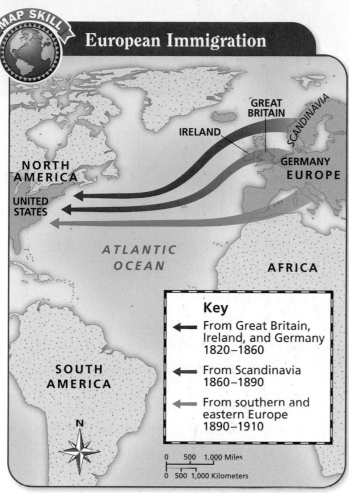

European Immigration

Key

← From Great Britain, Ireland, and Germany 1820–1860

← From Scandinavia 1860–1890

← From southern and eastern Europe 1890–1910

0   500   1,000 Miles

0   500 1,000 Kilometers

▶ Many immigrants came to the United States from Europe.

MAP SKILL Trace Movement on a Map *How many years are represented by the three waves of immigration shown on the map?*

immigrants who came before them. In time many immigrants become citizens of the United States. They contribute to their communities in the Northeast and throughout our nation.

REVIEW Why would the United States set up an immigration station such as the one at Ellis Island? **Draw Conclusions**

Summarize the Lesson

1620 A colony was founded at Plymouth, Massachusetts.

1776 The Declaration of Independence was signed.

1787 The U.S. Constitution was written.

1820 The first of several waves of immigration to the United States began.

1892 Ellis Island immigration station was opened.

LESSON 2 REVIEW

Check Facts and Main Ideas

1. **Sequence** On a separate sheet of paper, fill in the sequence of events that led to the founding of the United States of America.

> Colonies are founded in North America.
>
> ↓
>
> [ ]
>
> ↓
>
> [ ]
>
> ↓
>
> [ ]
>
> ↓
>
> U.S. Constitution is written.

2. Where were the first shots of the American **Revolution** fired?

3. What two Northeastern cities were capitals of the United States before Washington, D.C.?

4. What are some reasons immigrants came to the United States?

5. **Critical Thinking:** *Make Inferences* Why do you think so many European immigrants first arrived in the Northeast region?

Link to ∞ Writing

Write a Letter Suppose that you are on a ship sailing from a nation in Europe to the United States in 1895. Write a letter to your friends back in your old home explaining what you are thinking and how you are feeling.

Use a Vertical Time Line

What? A **vertical time line** shows important events that happened over a period of time. The events are listed along a vertical line, or line that runs up and down.

Why? Sometimes it's difficult to keep track of events that you read about or to understand how the events may be related. A vertical time line lists important events and helps you see their relationship to each other.

How? Page 135 shows an example of a vertical time line. To use the time line, begin at the top and read down. As you read, try to understand how each event relates to the events around it. Also think about what was happening elsewhere in the world at the same time.

Think and Apply

To make sure you understand how to read a **vertical time line,** answer these questions.

1 The most inventions occurred between what years?

2 How many years passed between the invention of the automobile and the invention of the airplane?

3 After the invention of the locomotive, how many years passed without a major invention?

Famous Inventions Time Line

1775

1793 Cotton Gin
The cotton gin makes it profitable for farmers in the South to grow cotton.

1800

1819 Steamship
The first steamship crosses the Atlantic Ocean in 3 weeks, up to 2 months faster than a ship with sails.

1825

1830

1830 American Locomotive
Peter Cooper constructs a small, steam-powered locomotive nicknamed the *Tom Thumb*.

1850

1876 Telephone
Alexander Graham Bell invents the telephone.

1877 Phonograph
Thomas Alva Edison invents the phonograph.

1875

1879 Electric Light Bulb
The electric light bulb is the first electric lighting that can be used in homes.

1880

1885 Automobile
The earliest cars can go only 8 miles per hour.

1885

1895 Radio
Italy's Guglielmo Marconi invents the radio.

1900

1903 Airplane
Orville and Wilbur Wright build *Flyer*, the world's first successful airplane.

1830	1855	1880	1905	1930

1833
American Anti-Slavery Society is formed.

1848
First women's rights convention in the United States is held.

1865
Thirteenth Amendment abolishes slavery in the United States.

1920
Nineteenth Amendment grants women the right to vote.

PREVIEW

Focus on the Main Idea
The Northeast was the birthplace of the abolitionist movement and the women's rights movement.

PLACES
Philadelphia, Pennsylvania
Seneca Falls, New York

PEOPLE
William Lloyd Garrison
Frederick Douglass
Sojourner Truth
Elizabeth Cady Stanton
Lucretia Mott
Susan B. Anthony

VOCABULARY
abolitionist
slave
convention

TERMS
Thirteenth
   Amendment
Nineteenth
   Amendment

► Frederick
   Douglass

The Granger Collection

Taking a Stand

You Are There The room is hushed. A tall, muscular man takes his place, front and center. His name is Frederick Douglass. As he begins to speak, you realize that his voice is as powerful as his body.

He tells the crowd that he was born into slavery in Maryland. He says that the wife of one of his owners taught him to read. He explains how he read about slavery and learned about freedom. He also speaks about beatings and punishment. He describes his escape to New York, disguised as a free sailor. He warns that even now, slave hunters could track him down and return him to his master.

Everyone in the crowd is moved by his story. They promise to take a stand against slavery.

Compare and Contrast As you read, think about the similarities and differences between the abolitionist movement and the women's rights movement.

The Abolitionists

During the 1800s, many reforms, or changes, took place in American society. Many of these reform movements began in the Northeast. One of the most important was the abolitionist movement. An **abolitionist** was a reformer who believed that slavery should be erased, or abolished, from the land.

Since the early days of the colonies, Africans had been captured and brought to the Americas to work as slaves on farms and in homes. A **slave** is a person who is owned as property by another person. A slave often has no rights and must do whatever his or her master wishes.

Some people spoke out against slavery. Even some people in the South, where slavery was widespread, were against it. The movement grew in the Northeast, however. Abolitionists organized groups and published newspapers against slavery. African Americans and whites joined together to seek an end to slavery.

In **Philadelphia** in 1833, abolitionists met to form the American Anti-Slavery Society. One strong abolitionist, **William Lloyd Garrison,** published a newspaper called *The Liberator.* The word *liberator* means "one who brings freedom." Speakers such as **Frederick Douglass** and

The Bettmann Archive

▶ **Sojourner Truth**

Sojourner Truth addressed abolitionist meetings and told about their lives as slaves. They convinced many people to fight against slavery. They also worked for freedom for all people.

Disagreements about slavery and other issues grew between Northern and Southern states. These tensions led to the Civil War. In 1865, after this war, the **Thirteenth Amendment** to the Constitution made slavery illegal in the United States.

REVIEW Why were Frederick Douglass and Sojourner Truth able to convince many people to join the abolitionist cause? **Draw Conclusions**

Votes for Women

Before the 1900s, women in the United States did not have the same rights as men. For example, women did not have the right to vote. In the 1800s reformers began to fight for women's rights.

Elizabeth Cady Stanton and **Lucretia Mott** organized the first women's rights convention in the United States. A **convention** is a meeting held for a special purpose. The convention took place in 1848, in **Seneca Falls, New York.** **Susan B. Anthony** was one of the leaders of the women's rights movement.

► Susan B. Anthony

The struggle was long and hard. In 1920, seventy-two years after the Seneca Falls convention, the **Nineteenth Amendment** to the Constitution gave women the right to vote.

REVIEW Where was the first women's rights convention in the United States held? **Main Idea and Details**

Summarize the Lesson

— **1833** American Anti-Slavery Society was formed.

— **1848** First women's rights convention in the United States was held.

— **1865** Thirteenth Amendment abolished slavery in the United States.

— **1920** Nineteenth Amendment granted women the right to vote.

LESSON 3   REVIEW

Check Facts and Main Ideas

1. **Compare and Contrast** On a separate sheet of paper, list the similarities and differences between the abolitionist movement and the women's rights movement.

Similarities	Differences
Both were reform movements.	

2. Why were the antislavery reformers called **abolitionists?**

3. Name two important women's rights reformers and state one fact about each.

4. Why did women fight for the right to vote?

5. **Critical Thinking:** *Make Inferences* Why might Frederick Douglass and Sojourner Truth work for both the abolitionist movement and the women's rights movement?

Link to ⚭ **Geography**

Research a City Find Seneca Falls, New York, on a map. Use an encyclopedia or other resource to find out more about the history and geography of Seneca Falls. Present your findings in a report.

ELIZABETH CADY STANTON
1815–1902

Elizabeth Cady was born in Johnstown, New York. When Elizabeth was eleven years old, Eleazar, her only living brother, died. Elizabeth's father was very sad and said to her, "Oh, my daughter, I wish you were a boy!" From then on, Elizabeth tried to act as if she were her father's son. To her, acting like a man meant studying, learning as much as possible, and having courage.

Elizabeth read many books, including her father's law books. However, Elizabeth did not go to college. Most colleges did not accept women then. She attended Troy Female Seminary in Troy, New York. At this school women received the same type of education that men received in college.

BIOFACT

Elizabeth tried wearing bloomers instead of long skirts.

Elizabeth fought for the rights of all people. When she was twenty-four years old, she married Henry B. Stanton. Her husband also worked for equal rights for all.

Learn from Biographies

How did Elizabeth Cady Stanton's childhood experiences help her prepare for her work as a leader of the women's rights movement?

For more information, go online to *Meet the People* at **www.sfsocialstudies.com**.

Winning the Right to Vote

Women did not have the right to vote in the United States until 1920. For many years, people worked long and hard for women's suffrage—the right for women to vote. Here are some of the ways they tried to persuade others to join their fight.

Pro-suffrage buttons

The Pro Faction and the Anti–Suffragists

Women needed men to support suffage as well; without men's votes, the Nineteenth Amendment never would have passed in Congress. A nationwide political campaign produced buttons and other materials that supported the suffragists' cause. Anti-suffrage groups did the same.

Anti-suffrage buttons

How Long Must Women Wait?

In January 1917, the National Woman's Party began protesting in front of the White House. This angered Mrs. Wilson, the first lady, who nevertheless invited them to come in from the cold. They refused. The group was later arrested for protesting at the White House.

Suffrage sash over armor

A Suffragist's Cape

A suffragist wore this cape and sash in the early 1900s. Women suffragists wore this uniform to show their unity and gain publicity for their cause.

Marching On to Victory

Support for women's suffrage took many forms. This sheet music honored the suffragists of the world. The cover shows a suffrage herald who raises her trumpet to announce a new day.

A March on Washington

Suffrage supporters held a parade in Washington, D.C., on March 3, 1913. The parade drew five to eight thousand marchers. This is the official program from that march.

Cities Grow and Change

PREVIEW

Focus on the Main Idea
Northeastern cities and their industries have grown and changed.

PLACES
New York City, New York
Boston, Massachusetts
Philadelphia, Pennsylvania
Pittsburgh, Pennsylvania

VOCABULARY
commerce
import
export
diverse

You Are There
You're excited. You're looking down from the observation deck of the Empire State Building. All of New York City is spread out before you. You spot Broadway, where you and your family saw a musical last night. In the distance you see New Jersey. Your sister finds the Brooklyn Bridge and you spot the Statue of Liberty out in the harbor.

There are more tall buildings than you've ever seen. Among the buildings, you see a big patch of green. It's Central Park—your next stop. There your family plans to see the zoo. And if there's time, you'll cross the street to see the dinosaurs at the American Museum of Natural History. There are so many different things to do in New York!

Cause and Effect As you read, note why the cities of the Northeast grew to be so important to commerce and industry.

Cities of the Northeast

The large cities of the Northeast are centers of culture, transportation, and commerce. **Commerce** is the buying and selling of goods, especially in large amounts between different places. The three largest cities— **New York City, New York; Boston, Massachusetts;** and **Philadelphia, Pennsylvania**— began as ports where ocean-going ships docked. Trade with Europe was very important to the early colonies, so cities grew up around natural harbors. Providence, Rhode Island, and Baltimore, Maryland, are also important port cities.

Merchants set up shop in port cities to sell imported goods. An **import** is an item that is brought from abroad to be offered for sale. Also, industries grew in port cities to make goods to export. An **export** is an item sent from one country to be sold in another country. Stores and industries provided jobs and attracted people to the great port cities of the Northeast.

As the colonies spread westward, new cities grew beside rivers and canals. **Pittsburgh, Pennsylvania,** was founded at the point where three major rivers meet. Boats used these rivers to bring natural resources and raw materials to the industries that grew

▶ **Workers unload merchandise from ships in New York City in the 1880s.**

in Pittsburgh. After the Erie Canal was built, Buffalo, New York, became an important port on Lake Erie. The Erie Canal linked Lake Erie to the Hudson River and New York City. Because of good transportation and plentiful natural resources, many of the cities of the Northeast became centers of industry.

Shipping and transportation are still important to the cities of the Northeast. The region's cities have also become centers of banking, health care, and high-tech industries.

REVIEW Why did cities grow around natural harbors? **Cause and Effect**

Map Adventure

Northeastern Landmarks

A. You have ridden the swan boats in the Boston Commons. Now you want to visit the Liberty Bell in Philadelphia. In what direction would you travel?

B. If you walked on the Boardwalk in Atlantic City, New Jersey, what ocean would you see?

C. If you wanted to see two famous landmarks in one day, which might be the easiest to see in that time period? Why?

D. On what body of water is Baltimore?

City Landmarks

If you visit Philadelphia, you can see the Liberty Bell and walk through Independence Hall. The Declaration of Independence and the Constitution were both signed in this historic building.

Boston's Freedom Trail winds past the city's historic sites. It begins near the Public Gardens, with its lagoon and famous swan boats. It ends in the nearby city of Charlestown, near the top of Bunker Hill. It passes by Paul Revere's house and a number of other important historic places.

New York City is famous for its skyscrapers and its theater. The Empire State Building, built in 1931, is still one of the world's tallest buildings. The bright lights of Broadway attract theatergoers from all over the globe. Out in New York's harbor, the Statue of Liberty still welcomes newcomers to the United States.

REVIEW Name one landmark that tourists can visit in each of the cities named above. **Main Idea and Details**

Centers of Industry

The cities of the Northeast are centers of industry. The types of industries have changed over the years, however.

For example, Pittsburgh was once so famous for its steel mills that it was called the "Steel City." Coal and limestone, two important ingredients for making steel, were plentiful around Pittsburgh. Iron ore was mined in the Midwest and transported to the city. In the 1870s, Andrew Carnegie brought a new steel-making process to Pittsburgh from England. Soon the city was supplying the world with steel for railroads, bridges, and, eventually, skyscrapers.

The steel industry brought money and jobs to Pittsburgh, but it also polluted the air. In fact, sometimes the air was so thick with smoke that the streetlights came on during the day. In the mid-1900s, the citizens of Pittsburgh passed laws to clean up the city. At the same time, the demand for steel was decreasing. The economy of Pittsburgh began to change.

Today, Pittsburgh boasts a **diverse,** or varied, group of industries. High-tech businesses such as computer software companies and factories that make robots have headquarters there. The city is also a center of health-care and environmental research.

The story of Pittsburgh's changing economy is similar to that of other cities of the region. Northeastern cities are still centers of industry.

REVIEW What sequence of events led Pittsburgh to develop a diverse economy? ⊙ **Sequence**

▶ **Present-day Pittsburgh**

▶ Crowded city streets have become a common sight.

Hubs of Commerce

Northeastern cities are hubs of commerce. Each day, millions of people go to these cities to work, to shop, and to enjoy themselves. Whether they are doing business on New York's Wall Street or assembling robots in Pittsburgh, citizens of the Northeast's cities help build the economy of the region. In turn, a healthy economy makes the cities of the Northeast good places to live and good places to visit.

REVIEW Why do cities attract a large number of workers? **Draw Conclusions**

Summarize the Lesson

- **Because trade was important, businesses and cities grew near places where transportation by water was easy.**
- **Northeastern cities have many important places to visit.**
- **Industries in Northeastern cities, such as Pittsburgh, have changed over the years.**
- **Northeastern cities are centers of commerce and good places to live or visit.**

LESSON 4 REVIEW

Check Fact and Main Idea

1. **Cause and Effect** On a separate sheet of paper, copy the diagram below and fill in the cause.

Cause	Effect
	Businesses and cities grew where transportation was easy.

2. How did trade and the need for good transportation affect where Northeastern cities grew? Use the words **import** and **export** in your answer.

3. Explain the importance of Philadelphia's Independence Hall, Boston's Freedom Trail, and New York City's Empire State Building.

4. What was once Pittsburgh's major industry? What are some of its important industries today?

5. **Critical Thinking:** *Cause and Effect* Describe how a city's people and its economy affect each other. Use the words **commerce** and **diverse** in your answer.

Link to ᴑᴑ Reading

Read About a City Choose one of the cities mentioned in this lesson. Then find and read a book about the city. Share what you learned about the city with classmates.

ANDREW CARNEGIE
1835–1919

Andrew Carnegie was born in Scotland. When he was twelve years old, his family moved to the United States and settled in Pittsburgh. Carnegie started working in a cotton factory and went to school at night.

Years later, after he started working for the Pennsylvania Railroad, Carnegie spent time in England. While there, he learned that the British made bridges from steel. He brought his knowledge of the British steel-making process to the United States and built steel and iron factories around Pittsburgh. He also formed the Carnegie Steel Company.

BIOFACT

Carnegie started out as a bobbin boy. He fed yarn into factory looms from bobbins like the ones here.

When Carnegie sold his company to the United States Steel Corporation, he became the richest person in the world. He then gave much of his time and money toward helping people.

Carnegie gave money to schools and to other institutions. He also paid for the building of libraries. His words are carved over the doors of the Carnegie Library in Pittsburgh: "Free to the People."

Learn from Biographies

Why do you think Andrew Carnegie built libraries?

For more information, go online to *Meet the People* at **www.sfsocialstudies.com.**

► **Ethan took photographs of the ruins of the World Trade Center, as well as people placing candles at memorials. He also photographed fellow students who came together to paint two giant murals honoring the victims and heroes of September 11, 2001.**

Capturing History

The World Trade Center attacks on September 11, 2001, shocked and saddened the entire country. On that day, police and firefighters rushed to the burning World Trade Center towers to help people escape. Hundreds of other people volunteered their help at the scene of the disaster.

Police officers and firefighters came from all over New York City to the site of the Trade Towers. They were responding to their duty to help others during an emergency. On that day, they did their jobs under very difficult and dangerous conditions.

Volunteers took on responsibility for handing out food and water to the rescue workers. Other people photographed or reported on the collapse of the towers. One photographer, named Ethan, was a senior at nearby Stuyvesant High School. Stuyvesant is located just four blocks north of the World Trade Center.

Ethan is a staff photographer for *The Spectator*, the Stuyvesant High School newspaper. While the towers were burning, Ethan left the school building to make a phone

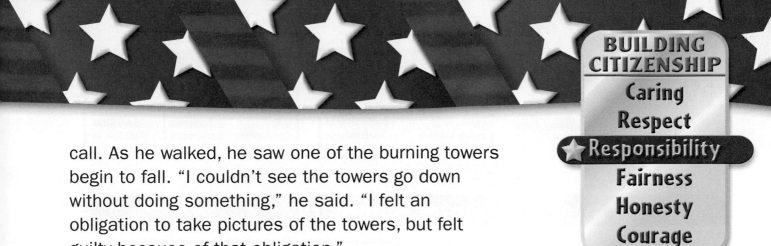

BUILDING CITIZENSHIP

Caring

Respect

★ Responsibility

Fairness

Honesty

Courage

call. As he walked, he saw one of the burning towers begin to fall. "I couldn't see the towers go down without doing something," he said. "I felt an obligation to take pictures of the towers, but felt guilty because of that obligation."

Later, Ethan talked with a family friend who is a professional photographer. Ethan told him that he felt guilty for taking pictures of a disaster in which so many people lost their lives. Ethan wrote about this conversation in a special edition of *The Spectator.* "I told him I was ashamed to be taking pictures, but he said that it was our responsibility. He told me that through our photographs, even more than our writing, the world would remember what happened on September 11, 2001."

Ethan could have chosen to stay home and avoid the destruction and sorrow that filled New York after the attacks. But he decided to go back with his camera to help record history.

Responsibility in Action

The people who took action on September 11, 2001, showed responsibility during a major emergency. However, it is also important to act responsibly in situations that don't involve emergencies. We all have things we should do every day. Just as the heroes of September 11 followed through on their responsibilities, it is important for us to follow through on the responsibilities we have to others. What are your responsibilities?

CHAPTER 5
REVIEW

1620

1775   1800   1825

1620
Plymouth
colony founded

1776
Declaration of
Independence
signed

1787
U.S.
Constitution
written

1820
European
immigration
continues

1833
American
Anti-Slavery
Society formed

Chapter Summary

 Sequence

On a separate piece of paper, show the
sequence of events that changed the
population of the Northeast region.

The Narragansett and other Native American
peoples lived in the Northeast.

↓

↓

↓

Vocabulary

Match each word with the correct definition or
description.

1 **sachem** (p. 127)

2 **confederacy**
(p. 129)

3 **revolution**
(p. 131)

4 **import** (p. 143)

5 **export** (p. 143)

6 **diverse** (p. 145)

a. a ruler

b. fight to overthrow
   a government

c. item brought from
   abroad to be sold

d. a union of groups,
   countries, or
   states

e. varied

f. item sent from
   one country to be
   sold in another

People

Write a sentence or two explaining why each
of the following people was important.

1 **Roger Williams** (p. 128)

2 **John Adams** (p. 131)

3 **Benjamin Franklin** (p. 131)

4 **William Lloyd Garrison** (p. 137)

5 **Susan B. Anthony** (p. 138)

1850   1875   1900   1925

1848
First women's rights convention held in U.S.

1865
Thirteenth Amendment abolished slavery.

1892
Ellis Island immigration station opened.

1920
Nineteenth Amendment granted women the right to vote.

Facts and Main Ideas

1 In the 1600s the Narragansett people lived on land that is now what state?

2 In what year was the U.S. Constitution written?

3 **Main Idea** What caused changes in the lives of the Narragansett and other Native American peoples in the Northeast?

4 **Main Idea** What was the purpose of the American Revolution?

5 **Main Idea** Why are the Thirteenth and the Nineteenth Amendments important?

6 **Main Idea** What do the Northeast cities of New York, Boston, and Philadelphia have in common?

7 **Critical Thinking:** *Make Inferences* Why do you think that some cities that are not on water have grown in recent years?

Write About History

1 **Write a journal entry** telling which city in the Northeast you would like to visit.

2 **Write a letter** to a friend's older relative. Explain that you have been reading about when people immigrated to the United States. Ask about his or her ancestors.

3 **Write quiz questions** about the people, places, and events in this chapter. Exchange questions with a partner to review the chapter.

Apply Skills

Vertical Time Line

Look at the vertical time line below. Then answer the questions.

1815 Elizabeth Cady was born. (When she married, her name changed to Elizabeth Cady Stanton.)

1848 The Seneca Falls Convention was held.

1850 The first national convention of the women's movement was held.

1870 The 15th Amendment was passed, giving African American men the right to vote.

1878 The 19th Amendment was introduced to Congress.

1920 The 19th Amendment was ratified, giving women the right to vote.

1 In what year were African American men given the right to vote?

2 How many years passed between the Seneca Falls Convention and the passing of the 19th Amendment?

3 Using the dates on the time line, do you think that it is likely that Elizabeth Cady Stanton ever voted in an election?

Internet Activity

To get help with vocabulary and people, select the dictionary or encyclopedia from *Social Studies Library* at
www.sfsocialstudies.com.

NIAGARA

Carl Sandburg

Close your eyes and see if you can imagine Niagara Falls.
Listen to the sound of the water as it rushes over the rocks.

The tumblers of the rapids go white, go green,
go changing over the gray, the brown, the rocks.
The fight of the water, the stones,
the fight makes a foam laughter
before the last look over the long slide
down the spread of a sheen in the straight fall.
    Then the growl, the chutter,
    down under the boom and the muffle,
    the hoo hoi deep,
    the hoo hoi down,
        this is Niagara.

Main Ideas and Vocabulary

TEST PREP

Read the passage below and use it to answer the questions that follow.

The Northeast region is beautiful. There are mountain ranges and miles of coastline. One of the most beautiful and famous landforms in the country is in this region—Niagara Falls. These waterfalls provide <u>hydropower</u>, or power produced by capturing the energy of running water.

When the English arrived in this region, the Narragansett and other Native Americans lived there. One of the English settlers, Roger Williams, was friendly with the Narragansett. In 1636 Williams went to the Grand Sachem, Canonicus, the ruler of the Narragansett, to buy land. The land became the colony of Rhode Island. Today the Narragansett have a reservation in Rhode Island.

People and places of the Northeast region played an important part in the founding of our country. The Declaration of Independence was signed in Philadelphia, Pennsylvania. John Adams, from Massachusetts, played an important role. The Constitution was also written there. Benjamin Franklin from Pennsylvania was an important

representative. Also, the first two capitals of the new nation were in the Northeast—New York City and Philadelphia.

As the nation grew, many people immigrated to the United States to find a better life. Ellis Island in New York was the gateway for many of these immigrants. Some came for jobs. Others wanted to own their own land. Still others came to escape war or hard times.

The Northeast was also home to two important reform movements. One was the abolitionist movement. Abolitionists believed that slavery was wrong and should be ended. In 1865 the Thirteenth Amendment ended slavery. Another reform movement worked to give women the right to vote. In 1920 the Nineteenth Amendment gave women that right.

Port cities of the Northeast have grown into centers of commerce and industry. Rural areas produce products like cranberries, grapes, and maple syrup. Tourism is also a big business. People visit for the beauty of the Northeast as well as for its history.

1 In the passage, the word <u>hydropower</u> means
  A wetland
  B power produced by the energy of water
  C power produced by the energy of wind
  D an airplane that can float on water

2 According to the passage, one of the early capitals of the nation was in
  A Rhode Island
  B Massachusetts
  C Pennsylvania
  D Washington, D.C.

3 According to the passage, why did many immigrants come to the Northeast?
  A They were looking for adventure.
  B Everyone they knew was immigrating.
  C They wanted to come to a land where everyone was happy.
  D They were seeking a better life.

4 According to the passage, slavery was ended by
  A the Thirteenth Amendment
  B the Nineteenth Amendment
  C the Declaration of Independence
  D the U.S. Constitution

Vocabulary and People

Choose six of the vocabulary words and people. Then write a story that uses all six.

1 slave (p. 137)

2 cooperation (p. 127)

3 powwow (p. 128)

4 convention (p. 138)

5 abolitionist (p. 137)

6 reservation (p. 128)

7 Frederick Douglass (p. 137)

8 Canonicus (p. 128)

9 William Lloyd Garrison (p. 137)

10 Elizabeth Cady Stanton (p. 138)

11 Sojourner Truth (p. 137)

Apply Skills

Create a Poster Make a poster with a vertical time line. List several important events that you read about in this unit.

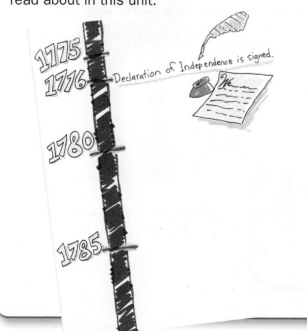

Write and Share

Write and Publish a Newspaper Many newsworthy events have taken place in the Northeast region over the history of the nation. Choose an event or a person and write a newspaper article telling about the occasion. Remember to include the important parts of a news story—who, what, where, when, why, and how. Write a catchy headline. Work with classmates to combine your news articles into a newspaper. Share the historical "news" with other classrooms in your school.

Read on Your Own

Look for books like these in the library.

Discovery Channel School

UNIT 2 Project

On the Spot

Life was often challenging for America's early settlers, as well as for Native American groups who had lived in the Northeast for hundreds of years. Make a documentary about their experiences.

1 Form a group and choose Native Americans or early European settlers who settled in the Northeast.

2 Write sentences about their experiences and observations. Include a variety of topics.

3 Make a diorama or model to show the environment and settlements. Include where they lived, other buildings, and the physical setting.

4 Present your documentary. Show the diorama or model to the class.

Internet Activity

Explore the Northeast on the Internet. Go to **www.sfsocialstudies.com/activities** and select your grade and unit.

The Southeast

How have resources and events affected the Southeast?

"Beautiful is the land, with its prairies and forests of fruit-trees; Under the feet a garden of flowers . . ."

—Henry Wadsworth Longfellow, describing the banks of a Southeastern bayou in his poem *Evangeline*.

Jacquelyn Modesitt Schindehette's 1999 painting *Pines on the Bayou* was inspired by the scenery of St. Vincent Island in Florida.

Welcome to the Southeast

Key

★ State capital

PA

OH

IL

IN

NJ

MD

DE

WEST
VIRGINIA

VIRGINIA

Charleston

Richmond ★

Chesapeake Bay

MO

Ohio River

Frankfort ★

KENTUCKY

36°N

KS

Outer
Banks

Raleigh ★

NORTH
CAROLINA

OK

Nashville ★

TENNESSEE

Tennessee River

APPALACHIAN

MOUNTAINS

BLUE RIDGE MOUNTAINS

ARKANSAS

Arkansas River

Little
Rock ★

Columbia ★

SOUTH
CAROLINA

32°N

Atlanta ★

Mississippi River

MISSISSIPPI

ALABAMA

GEORGIA

ATLANTIC
OCEAN

LOUISIANA

Alabama River

Jackson ★

Montgomery ★

Red River

TX

Okeefenokee
Swamp

Baton ★
Rouge

Tallahassee ★

Mississippi
Delta

28°N

76°W

FLORIDA

Gulf of Mexico

Lake
Okeechobee

N

0   100   200 Miles

0   100   200 Kilometers

92°W

The
Everglades

80°W

88°W

Florida Keys

24°N

84°W

▶ The magnolia is a type of flowering tree that grows wild in the Southeast.

▶ Georgia farmers grow thirty-eight percent of the nation's peanuts.

▶ Manatees live along the coast of Florida. They are also called "sea cows." Adult manatees are about 10 feet long and weigh 800 to 1,200 pounds.

▶ Many people visit Charleston, South Carolina to see the city's historic buildings.

▶ Space Shuttle missions lift off from the John F. Kennedy Space Center in Florida.

Reading Social Studies

The Southeast

Main Idea and Details

Learning to find the main idea and details will help you understand what you read.

- A main idea is the most important thought in the paragraph or passage.
- The supporting details give more information about the main idea.

Read this paragraph. The **main idea** and **supporting details** have been highlighted.

The Mississippi River is one of the longest and deepest rivers in the world. In some places, it is more than 400 feet deep, which is equal to the height of a building that is 40 stories high. It starts at Lake Itasca in Minnesota and goes south to the Gulf of Mexico, a distance of 2,350 miles.

Word Exercise

Context Clues Sometimes you can use clues from the text and what you already know to figure out the meaning of an unfamiliar word. Look at the sentence below and try to determine the meaning of the word *deposits*.

They made *deposits* at the bank and watched their accounts grow.

Context Clues		What I already know		What I think *deposits* means
•The deposits took place at the bank. •Their accounts grew.	+	Banks hold money for people.	=	Money that people put into the bank

The Big River

The Mississippi River affects the land and people of the Southeast. It is the largest river in the United States. It is wide—a mile and a half across in some places. It curves back and forth on its long journey like a big ribbon.

As the Mississippi approaches the Gulf of Mexico, its waters fan out into smaller, marshy rivers. These marshy rivers are called bayous (BEYE yooz). As the Mississippi flows south, it carries dirt, sand, and mud. These materials are deposited at the mouth of the river, the place where the river flows into the Gulf of Mexico. Over thousands of years, land has been built up by these deposits. This rich, flat land is called a delta. The delta of the Mississippi River juts out into the Gulf of Mexico. It covers thousands of square miles.

The Mississippi River is also a water highway. Native Americans used it as a main trade route. Today, the river is still a major route for ships and barges loaded with many different goods. One of the nation's busiest ports is located on the Mississippi. It is called the Port of South Louisiana. New Orleans and Baton Rouge, Louisiana, and Memphis, Tennessee, are some other Mississippi River ports.

Apply it!

Use the reading strategy of main idea and details to answer questions 1 and 2. Then answer the vocabulary question.

1 Which sentence is the main idea of the whole passage?

2 What details tell how the Mississippi delta was formed?

3 Find the word *deposits* in the reading selection. From the other words in that paragraph, what does *deposits* mean? Use a dictionary to check your definition.

CHAPTER 6

The Land of the Southeast

Lesson 1

Myrtle Beach, South Carolina
Plains line the coasts, while the Appalachian Mountains rise inland.

1

Lesson 2

Key West, Florida
Mild climates bring many visitors to the Southeast.

2

Lesson 3

Everglades National Park
Plants of the Southeast provide homes for animals and food for people.

3

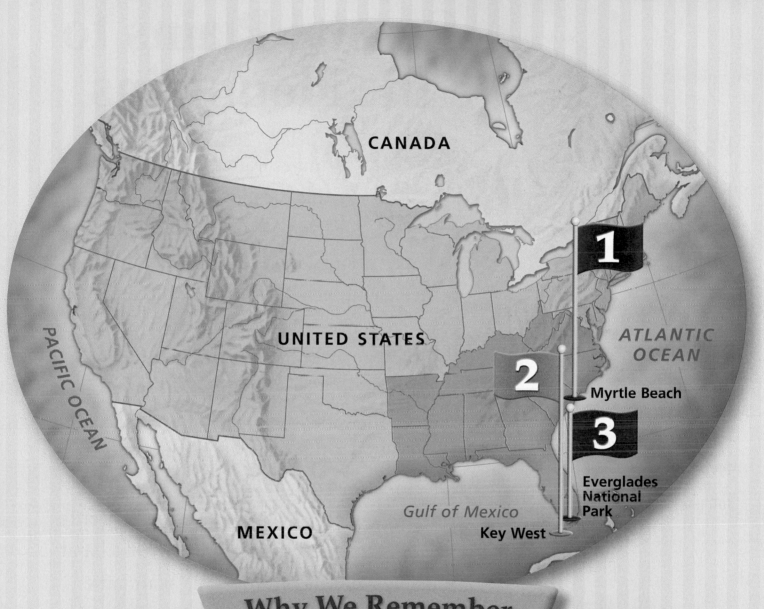

CANADA

UNITED STATES

PACIFIC OCEAN

ATLANTIC OCEAN

Myrtle Beach

Everglades National Park

Gulf of Mexico

MEXICO

Key West

1

2

3

Why We Remember

Sights and sounds frame the Southeast. Listen to the sounds that surround that mighty river, the Mississippi, and the rhythm of waves crashing onto miles of beaches. Think about the stillness of forests in the Appalachian Mountains. These contrasts make up the Southeast. People settled this land to farm, to fish, and to trade. People come to enjoy warm weather when the rest of the nation is cold. They also come to work in the growing cities of the region.

Myrtle Beach

Coastal Plains to the Mountains

PREVIEW

Focus on the Main Idea
The main areas of the Southeast region include the coastal plains, the Piedmont, and Appalachia.

PLACES
Myrtle Beach, South Carolina
Outer Coastal Plain
Inner Coastal Plain
Piedmont
Appalachia

VOCABULARY
barrier islands
wetlands
fall line

You Are There
You've waited a long time for this vacation trip. The drive from Atlanta to Myrtle Beach took many hours, but you didn't mind. You're excited about seeing the Atlantic Ocean. You've never seen an ocean before!

After you put your suitcases in your hotel room, your family heads off for the beach. Your mother puts sun block lotion all over your back, and then you run to the shore. Waves roll toward you as you put your toes into the cold ocean water. As you bend over to pick up some pretty seashells, you feel a hand grabbing yours. "Come on, Pal," your father says. "Just hold my hand. I'll show you how to dive into these waves!"

Main Idea and Details As you read, notice how the Southeast region changes as you travel from the seacoast to the mountains.

Along the Coasts

Most of the states of the Southeast lie along the Atlantic coast, the coast of the Gulf of Mexico, or both. Beaches, such as **Myrtle Beach** in South Carolina, line some of the shore.

Off the shore are groups of long, low islands. Thousands of years ago, when glaciers began to melt, the rising waters of the ocean deposited sediment, material such as sand and mud left by a glacier, into shallow areas off the coast. These islands, known as **barrier islands,** were formed over thousands of years as more and more sediment was deposited by ocean waves, currents, and mainland rivers.

Inland from the shore is an area known as the **Outer Coastal Plain.** This area is very flat and has very low elevation.

The Outer Coastal Plain has different kinds of wetlands. **Wetlands** are lands that are at times covered with water. Swamps, bogs, and marshes are kinds of wetlands. A huge swamp, the Dismal Swamp, is between Virginia and North Carolina.

Farther inland is the **Inner Coastal Plain.** The elevation here is slightly higher than in the Outer Coastal Plain.

REVIEW How does the land change as you move inland from the coast?
 Main Idea and Details

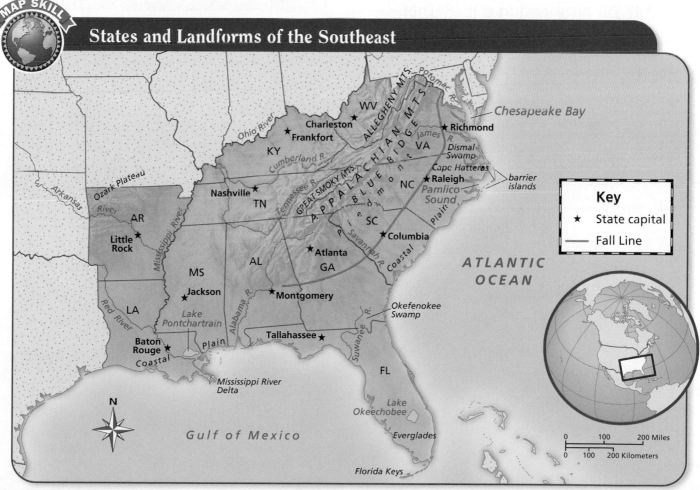

States and Landforms of the Southeast

Chesapeake Bay

Key
★ State capital
— Fall Line

ATLANTIC OCEAN

Gulf of Mexico

▶ The Southeast has plains, mountain ranges, rivers, and lakes.

MAP SKILL Understanding Continents and Oceans *In what body of water are the barrier islands?*

167

Toward the Mountains

An area of rolling hills and beautiful valleys lies inland from the coastal plains. This area is known as the **Piedmont.** The word *piedmont* means "foot of the mountain." Its elevation is higher than that of the coastal plains.

The soil of the Piedmont is different from the sandy soil of the coastal plains. Piedmont soil is dark brown or reddish and feels like clay. It is very rich soil and can be good farmland.

Many rivers flow through the Piedmont toward the Atlantic Ocean. The rivers tumble through waterfalls from the higher Piedmont to the lower coastal plains. On a map the waterfalls seem to be arranged in a line. This line is called the **fall line.** The fall line

▶ **The Callasaja Falls tumble down the fall line between the Piedmont and the coastal plains of North Carolina.**

▶ **The hilly landscape of the Piedmont**

168

marks the boundary between the Piedmont and the coastal plains.

Rising above the Piedmont is part of the Appalachian Mountain Range. The Appalachians in this area are rugged and steep, with narrow valleys. Farms in this area tend to be small.

The Blue Ridge Mountains are a chain that forms part of the eastern edge of the Appalachians. Mount Mitchell in North Carolina is in this chain. It is the highest peak east of the Mississippi River. The Great Smoky Mountains form part of the western edge of the Appalachians.

One area in and around the Appalachian Mountains is known as **Appalachia.** This area is known for its rich natural resources, such as coal, and its dense forests. Most of Appalachia lies in the Southeast region. Virginia, West Virginia, Kentucky, North Carolina, South Carolina, Tennessee, Georgia, and Alabama all include parts of Appalachia.

REVIEW What areas lie inland from the coastal plains?
◉ **Main Idea and Details**

Summarize the Lesson

- **Beaches and wetlands line the shores of the Southeast region.**
- **The elevation of the land increases as you go farther inland from the coast.**
- **The fall line is the border between the coastal plains and the Piedmont.**
- **The Appalachian Mountains extend through the Southeast region.**

LESSON 1 REVIEW

Check Facts and Main Ideas

1. ◉ **Main Idea and Details** On a separate sheet of paper, make a diagram like the one shown. Fill in the details that support the main idea.

> In the Southeast, the elevation becomes greater as you travel inland.

2. What parts of the Southeast might be popular as vacation spots?
3. How were the **barrier islands** formed?
4. Describe the Appalachian Mountains.
5. **Critical Thinking:** *Draw Conclusions* Why might it be difficult to have a large farm in the Appalachian Mountains?

Link to ━━ **Science**

Prepare a Report Learn more about the **fall line.** Do research in the library or on the Internet. Present your report to the class.

Read Elevation Maps

What? Maps help you locate different places and find out about a region. Different kinds of maps can show you different kinds of things. An **elevation map** shows you how high the land is. Elevation is height above **sea level**. A place that is at sea level is at the same height as the surface of the ocean's water.

This elevation map uses color to show elevation. The map below uses color to show the average height of the land across the Southeast. It also gives the elevations of some mountains.

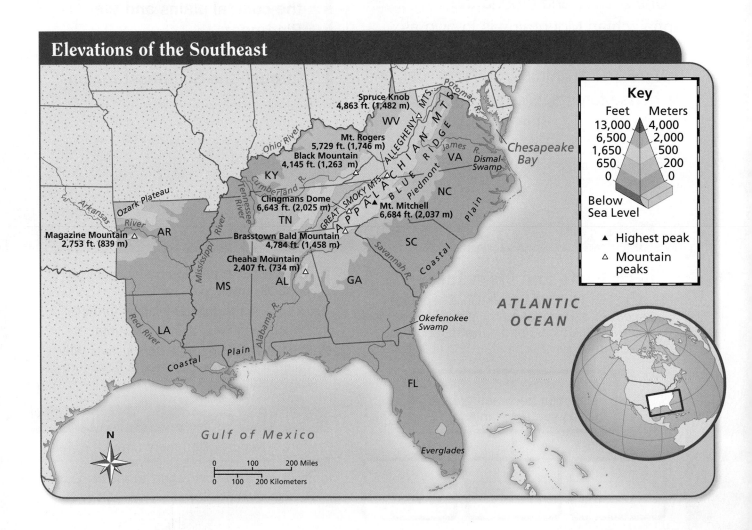

Elevations of the Southeast

Spruce Knob
4,863 ft. (1,482 m)

WV

Mt. Rogers
5,729 ft. (1,746 m)

Black Mountain
4,145 ft. (1,263 m)

Ohio River

ALLEGHENY MTS.

Potomac R.

A P P A L A C H I A N   M T S.

B L U E   R I D G E

James R.

Chesapeake Bay

VA

Dismal Swamp

KY

Cumberland R.

Tennessee River

Clingmans Dome
6,643 ft. (2,025 m)

GREAT SMOKY MTS.

Piedmont

NC

Plain

Ozark Plateau

Arkansas River

TN

Mt. Mitchell
6,684 ft. (2,037 m)

Magazine Mountain
2,753 ft. (839 m)

AR

Brasstown Bald Mountain
4,784 ft. (1,458 m)

Savannah R.

SC

Coastal

Cheaha Mountain
2,407 ft. (734 m)

Mississippi River

MS

AL

GA

ATLANTIC OCEAN

Red River

LA

Alabama R.

Okefenokee Swamp

Coastal   Plain

FL

N

Gulf of Mexico

Everglades

Key

Feet	Meters
13,000	4,000
6,500	2,000
1,650	500
650	200
0	0

Below Sea Level

▲ Highest peak
△ Mountain peaks

0   100   200 Miles

0   100   200 Kilometers

Why? Elevation maps can help you locate important landmarks. They can show you the location of important features in a region and help you better understand what that region is like.

How? To read an elevation map, first look at the map key. Notice that there are numbers next to each color on the map key. The numbers show the range of elevation that each color represents. Notice that on the elevation map on page 170, dark green represents the lowest elevations. The range for dark green is between 0 and 650 feet above sea level.

▶ **The view from Magazine Mountain, the highest point in the Boston Mountains of Arkansas.**

Think and Apply

① What is the elevation range of the coastal plain that borders the Atlantic Ocean? that borders the Gulf of Mexico?

② Based on the **elevation map,** what is the name of the highest elevation range? Explain how you know.

③ What is the difference in elevation in feet between Mt. Mitchell and Magazine Mountain?

Key West

PREVIEW

Focus on the Main Idea
The mild climates of the coastal areas of the Southeast bring many tourists, but the area has some natural hazards.

PLACES
Key West, Florida
Florida Keys

VOCABULARY
key
hurricane
hurricane season

Sunlight and Storms

You Are There The little boat is bobbing up and down and from side to side. It's hard to hold onto the fishing pole because your safety vest is so big. It's December, but you feel warm. The sun is bright and the winds are gentle.

Just yesterday, you were wearing boots, mittens, and a heavy jacket. It was snowing in Boston, and the winds almost blew you down. You helped your father shovel snow.

Now, your father is helping you hold your fishing pole. You feel very lucky to be in Key West, Florida. December here is not at all like it is in Boston. You can see why so many people like to come here, especially in the winter. Now, if only you could catch a really big fish!

Main Idea and Details As you read, find the details about the different climates of the Southeast.

Enjoying the Climate

Key West, an island off the southern coast of Florida, is one of a chain of islands called the **Florida Keys.** A **key** is a low island.

Mild, sunny weather attracts many tourists to Florida in winter. The northern part of the state gets cool in winter—in the 50 degree range. The southern part usually stays warm—in the 70 degree range. In the summer, though, all of Florida is hot and humid. Cool ocean or gulf breezes make the coastal beaches good places to visit in the summer!

Louisiana, Mississippi, and Alabama also have hot, humid climates in the summer. Louisiana is also one of the rainiest states. The average yearly rainfall there is 57 inches.

States in the coastal plains— Georgia, South Carolina, North Carolina, and Virginia—have warm climates most of the year. When you get into the Appalachian Mountains, however, the temperature drops. Snow falls in the mountains in winter.

REVIEW How does the climate of the Southeast change as you move north?
Main Idea and Details

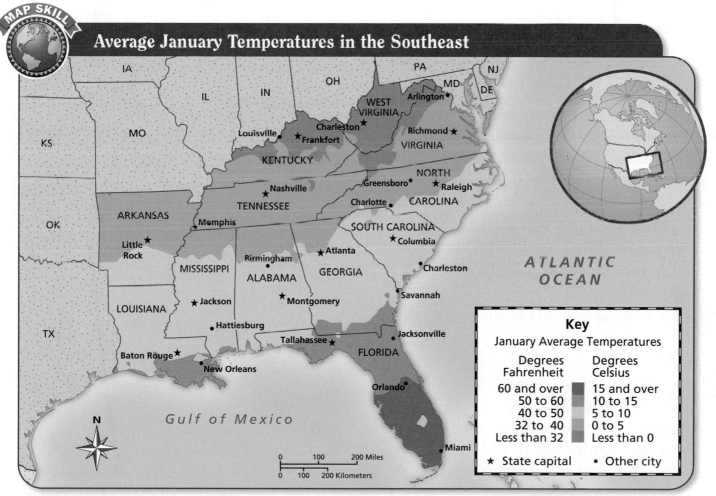

MAP SKILL

Average January Temperatures in the Southeast

Key
January Average Temperatures

Degrees Fahrenheit	Degrees Celsius
60 and over	15 and over
50 to 60	10 to 15
40 to 50	5 to 10
32 to 40	0 to 5
Less than 32	Less than 0

★ State capital   • Other city

► In January, the Southeast is usually warmer than many other parts of the United States.

MAP SKILL Use Intermediate Directions *In what direction would you travel from Savannah, Georgia to Atlanta, Georgia?*

Watch Out!

People in the Southeast enjoy mild weather much of the time, but sometimes the weather can be dangerous. Hurricanes sometimes occur along the Atlantic and Gulf coasts. A **hurricane** is a violent storm that forms over the ocean. Its strong winds move in a circular path. Along with the winds are very heavy rains. A hurricane smashing into the coast can be very destructive.

Hurricane winds can be strong enough to send large objects flying. They can uproot trees and damage buildings. The huge waves pound the shore and often cause flooding.

Hurricanes mainly occur from June until the end of November. This time of year is known as **hurricane season.** Weather forecasters have the equipment and technology to help them figure out the path that a hurricane will most likely take. This information helps people prepare for hurricanes and move to safety. People usually move inland, away from the coast.

The rocky shorelines are another hazard of the coastal areas. Long ago, as in the Northeast, people built lighthouses to

Map Adventure

Visiting Lighthouses

Take a trip along the outer coast of North Carolina to visit some famous lighthouses. Use the map to plan your trip.

1. Your first stop is the Bodie Island Lighthouse. What road will take you to the Cape Hatteras Lighthouse?

2. What body of water is to the east of the Cape Hatteras Lighthouse?

3. What types of transportation take you to the Ocracoke Lighthouse from the Cape Hatteras Lighthouse? In what direction would you be traveling?

4. What body of water is to the north of the Ocracoke Lighthouse?

Bodie Island Lighthouse

12

Atlantic Ocean

Pamlico Sound

Roads

Ferry route

12

Ocracoke Lighthouse

Cape Hatteras Lighthouse

Atlantic Ocean

help sailors avoid the rocky coastlines. The lighthouses warned the sailors of dangerous rocks and currents along the Southeast coast. The strong lights were very bright, and many could be seen as far as twenty miles out to sea. Lighthouses were built in different shapes and colors. In the daytime, sailors could tell where they were because they could recognize the lighthouses. At night, each lighthouse had a light using a special pattern. This helped sailors know which lighthouse they were near.

Sailors now use other tools and technology to help them find their way. Many lighthouses are no longer working, but people still enjoy visiting these colorful buildings.

REVIEW What are some natural hazards of living near the coast in the Southeast? ⊙ Main Idea and Details

Summarize the Lesson

- **The mild climates of the Southeast attract many tourists.**

- **Hurricanes are dangerous storms that can strike coastal areas.**

- **Lighthouses were built to warn sailors about rocky shores and also to help sailors determine their location.**

▶ **The Bodie Island Lighthouse is near the coast of North Carolina.**

LESSON 2 REVIEW

Check Facts and Main Ideas

1. ⊙ **Main Idea and Details** On a separate sheet of paper, draw a diagram like the one shown. Fill in some details that support the main idea.

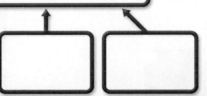

Many tourists visit the Southeast, especially from November to June.

Temperatures are warm in the winter.

2. When do **hurricanes** usually occur?
3. Why are hurricanes dangerous?
4. Why were lighthouses built?
5. **Critical Thinking:** *Make Inferences* Why is living near the Southeast coast both good and bad?

Link to ⚭ Science

Learn about Hurricanes Use reference materials to learn what causes hurricanes. Find out why they are more likely to occur at certain times of the year. Prepare a brief report and present it to the class.

Hurricanes

The sea covers about two-thirds of our planet. Strong winds constantly disturb the surface of the oceans, producing waves that break as they reach the shore. During severe storms, particularly hurricanes, winds push seawater high onto the shore. Areas close to the shore can become flooded. At high tides, the risk of serious flooding during storms increases. People living on the coast are not the only ones who are at risk. Ships can sink in stormy weather, leaving passengers and crew members stranded in dangerous waters.

In Deep Water

High seas are stormy seas with dangerous waves that can sink a ship or leave it stranded. Air-sea rescue helicopters rush to the aid of survivors. The helicopters hover above the sea while a rescuer is lowered on a winch to lift the survivors clear of the water.

A rescuer is lowered to the sea by a search and rescue helicopter.

Tearing Along

Crashing waves damage the coastlines. The waves dissolve pieces of rock and break off parts of cliffs. As the sea becomes stormier and its level becomes higher, the erosion becomes greater.

Collapsed coastal road was caused by wave erosion.

Stormy Sea

When Hurricane Hugo hit the West Indies and southeastern United States in 1989, it produced a sudden surge 6 feet (2 m) high in open water. This wall of water rose to 18 feet (6 m) in some places. The sudden and dramatic rise in sea level when a hurricane reaches land is caused by low air pressure at the storm's center.

Wall of Water
An ocean wave begins as wind blows across the sea's surface, making the water swing up and down, and back and forth. When the wave nears the shore, where the sea becomes shallower, the movement is broken, and the water topples over, forming a breaker. Huge breakers, such as this one, are sometimes called "dumpers." They send water crashing in all directions if they hit the shore.

This huge wave is on the verge of breaking.

Wildlife and Resources

PREVIEW

Focus on the Main Idea
The Southeast is rich in different resources. These resources are used in different industries throughout the region.

PLACES
Everglades National Park

VOCABULARY
endangered species
extinct
pulp
fossil fuel

You Are There

You and your family are riding in a boat through the Everglades. Your boat glides underneath cypress trees and past high grasses. Suddenly, something moves in the water. Seconds later, you hear an enormous splash! You look out over the water. You see only a pair of eyes looking back at you from the surface. The eyes come nearer and nearer as the creature swims closer to your boat. You see its long, low head first, and then you stare in fascination as you recognize it as an alligator. Your mom tells you that alligators have lived in the Everglades for hundreds of years!

 Main Idea and Details As you read, look for details that describe the resources of the Southeast.

Fins, Feathers, and Fur

If you visit a swamp in the Southeast, you may see alligators. In Florida many alligators live in swamps, canals, and lakes. But alligators were not always so common in Florida and other parts of the Southeast. In the 1960s many alligators were hunted for food or for their hides. By 1967 the alligator became an endangered species. An **endangered species** is a kind of animal or plant that is thought to be in danger of becoming **extinct,** or no longer existing.

After 1967 it was against the law to hunt alligators. The numbers of alligators slowly grew. By 1987 alligators had made a comeback. The United States Fish and Wildlife Service took the alligator off the list of endangered species.

Many other animals, including herons, turtles, and fish, can be found in the wetlands of the Southeast. The **Everglades National Park,** a huge area of wetlands in southern Florida, is home to about 600 different kinds of birds and other animals. About a dozen kinds of animals that live in the Everglades, including the Florida panther and the manatee, are endangered.

The Coastal Plain and Piedmont are also home to a wide variety of animals, such as deer and birds. In the Appalachian Mountains, black bears, deer, and other animals live in the forests.

REVIEW How have certain laws affected the number of alligators? **Cause and Effect**

Literature and Social Studies

The Yearling

Marjorie Kinnan Rawlings wrote this famous novel about farm life in central Florida in the late 1800s. In the passage below, a 12-year-old boy named Jody finds a young deer, a one-year-old fawn, known as a yearling, in the forest.

Under a scrub palmetto he was able to make out a track, pointed and dainty as the mark of a ground-dove. He crawled past the palmetto.

Movement directly in front of him startled him so that he tumbled backward. The fawn lifted its face to his. It turned its head with a wide, wondering motion and shook [scared] him through with the stare of its liquid eyes. It was quivering [shaking]. It made no effort to rise or run. Jody could not trust himself to move.

He whispered, "It's me."

The fawn lifted its nose, scenting [smelling] him. He reached out one hand and laid it on the soft neck.

THE YEARLING
by MARJORIE KINNAN RAWLINGS
Illustrated by N.C. WYETH

▶ Orange grove near Orlando, Florida

Harvesting a Bumper Crop

In addition to forests and swamps, the coastal plains of the Southeast contain wide stretches of good farmland. Land for farming is a valuable resource. Farming has been an important industry ever since the first settlers came to the Southeast. Today, the major crops of the region include cotton, corn, peanuts, rice, oranges, and soybeans. Soybeans are used to make vegetable oil and food for livestock. They also can be made into many other healthful foods.

The coastal plains have warm temperatures and plenty of rain, which makes this area excellent for farming. Most parts of the Southeast coastal plains have a long growing season, the time of year when it is warm enough for crops to grow. A long growing season makes it possible to grow crops like cotton, peanuts, and sugar cane. These crops cannot grow well in colder regions.

Citrus fruits, such as oranges, lemons, limes, and grapefruits, grow well in Florida because of the long growing season. Throughout the state nearly 107 million trees produce citrus fruits. Many of them are shipped to colder regions of the United States.

Directly to the north of Florida, Georgia produces more peanuts than any other state. Farms sometimes produce more than 1.5 billion pounds of peanuts a year.

Rice is also a major product of the Southeast. In fact, the Southeast produces more rice than any other part of the United States. Arkansas and Louisiana are two major producers of rice. One-third of the rice harvested in the United States is grown in Arkansas.

The agriculture industry is very important in the Southeast. Agriculture was the basis of the Southeast region's economy until the mid-1900s. However, since then manufacturing and other industries have also become important in the region.

REVIEW Why is the Southeast a good region for agriculture?
🔁 **Main Idea and Details**

Agriculture in the Southeast

Key to Symbols

- oranges
- peanuts
- peaches
- soybeans
- corn
- tobacco
- sugarcane
- rice
- cotton

Miles 100 200 300 400

0 100 300 500 700
Kilometers

▶ The Southeast is an important agricultural region.

Diagram Skill *What two crops are grown both in states bordering the Mississippi River and states bordering the Atlantic Ocean?*

Valuable Trees

Trees are another important resource of the Southeast. Some farmers in the Southeast grow and harvest trees, just like other crops.

Trees are also harvested from the pine forests of the coastal plains and parts of Appalachia. The trees are used to make boards for the lumber industry. They are also used for other wood products, such as furniture. Some trees are made into **pulp,** a combination of ground-up wood chips, water, and chemicals. Pulp is used in the production of paper. The book you are reading right now is made from pulp!

Trees are also important to the environment. They help cool the earth, provide homes for animals, and give off oxygen we need to breathe. So that we always have enough trees, companies replant new trees where others have been harvested. This is known as reforestation. It guarantees that we will always have this very important renewable resource.

REVIEW Why are trees valuable?
⟳ **Main Idea and Details**

▶ **Trees can be used to make furniture and many other products.**

182

Coal Mining in the Southeast

Trees are a resource that grow high into the air. Deep underground, there is another resource that is important in the Southeast. This nonrenewable resource is a black fossil fuel called coal. A **fossil fuel** is a fuel that is formed in the earth from the remains of plants or animals. Coal forms over millions of years. Coal is found in some parts of Appalachia, including parts of Kentucky and West Virginia. Many electric power plants burn coal to run their generators. Chemicals made from coal are used to produce nylon, paints, plastics, aspirin, and many other products.

REVIEW What is coal used for?
◉ **Main Idea and Details**

▶ **A piece of coal**

Summarize the Lesson

- **The Southeast is home to many different types of animals.**
- **Some crops grow in the warm climate of the Southeast that cannot grow in colder regions of the United States.**
- **In some areas of the Southeast, trees are grown as crops.**
- **Coal mining is important to the Appalachian economy.**

LESSON 3 REVIEW

Check Facts and Main Ideas

1. ◉ **Main Idea and Details** On a separate sheet of paper, make a diagram like the one shown. Fill in the diagram with two more details that support the main idea.

The resources of the Southeast are used in many ways.

Trees are used to make lumber, paper, and furniture.

2. Name a renewable and a nonrenewable resource found in the Southeast.

3. Why is coal an important resource? Use the term **fossil fuel** in your answer.

4. What have you eaten in the past week that might have been grown in the Southeast?

5. **Critical Thinking: Draw Conclusions** Why is it important to protect **endangered species**?

Link to ⚭ Music

Find a Song Many folk songs have been written about coal mining. Find one or think of one you know. Write down the words. If your song mentions a specific place, find that place on a map. Share your song and its meaning with your classmates.

Chapter Summary

 Main Idea and Details

On a separate sheet of paper, make a diagram like the one shown. Fill in details that support the main idea.

The Southeast has many different types of land.

Vocabulary

For each vocabulary word, write a sentence that defines or shows what the word means. Show how the word relates to the Southeast region.

1. **wetlands** (p. 167)

2. **fall line** (p. 168)

3. **key** (p. 173)

4. **hurricane** (p. 174)

5. **extinct** (p. 179)

6. **pulp** (p. 182)

7. **fossil fuel** (p. 183)

Places

Complete the sentences by filling in the correct place from the list below.

Piedmont (p. 168)
Appalachia (p. 169)
Everglades National Park (p. 179)

1. _____ is a huge area of wetlands in southern Florida.

2. The _____ is an area of rolling hills and valleys inland from the coastal plain.

3. One area around the Appalachian Mountains is called _____.

Facts and Main Ideas

1 What areas of the Southeast contain large stretches of good farmland?

2 What is a hurricane and where do hurricanes form?

3 Which area of the Southeast has a warmer climate, the mountains or the coastal plains?

4 **Main Idea** What are some differences between the Inner Coastal Plain, Outer Coastal Plain, Piedmont, and mountains of the Southeast?

5 **Main Idea** Which states in the Southeast have warm climates most of the year?

6 **Main Idea** What are some important resources of the Southeast coastal plain? of Appalachia?

7 **Critical Thinking:** *Evaluate* If you moved to the Southeast, which area or state would you choose to live in? Why?

Internet Activity

To get help with vocabulary and places, select the dictionary or encyclopedia from *Social Studies Library* at **www.sfsocialstudies.com.**

Write About Geography

1 **Write a poem** that tells about one of the geographic features of the Southeast.

2 **Write a television newscast** about a hurricane that is offshore from the Southeast region. Describe the hurricane, including its wind speed and where it is heading. Tell people in that area what they should do to stay safe during the hurricane.

3 **Write a Letter** If you took a trip to the Everglades in Florida, you would see many different kinds of plants and animals. Write a letter to a friend describing several different plants and animals that you see.

Apply Skills

Using Elevation Maps
Study the map below. Then answer the questions.

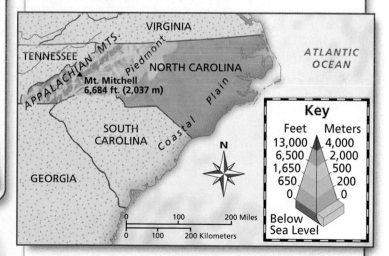

1 What does this map show?

2 Which part of North Carolina has the highest elevation?

3 What is the elevation range in feet in the Piedmont region?

Lesson 1

Qualla Boundary, North Carolina
The Cherokee way of life changes after Europeans arrive.

1

Lesson 2

St. Augustine, Florida
The Spanish build the first permanent European settlement.

2

Lesson 3

Charleston, South Carolina
Events starting at Fort Sumter change the whole Southeast.

3

Lesson 4

Atlanta, Georgia
Cities in the Southeast grow quickly.

4

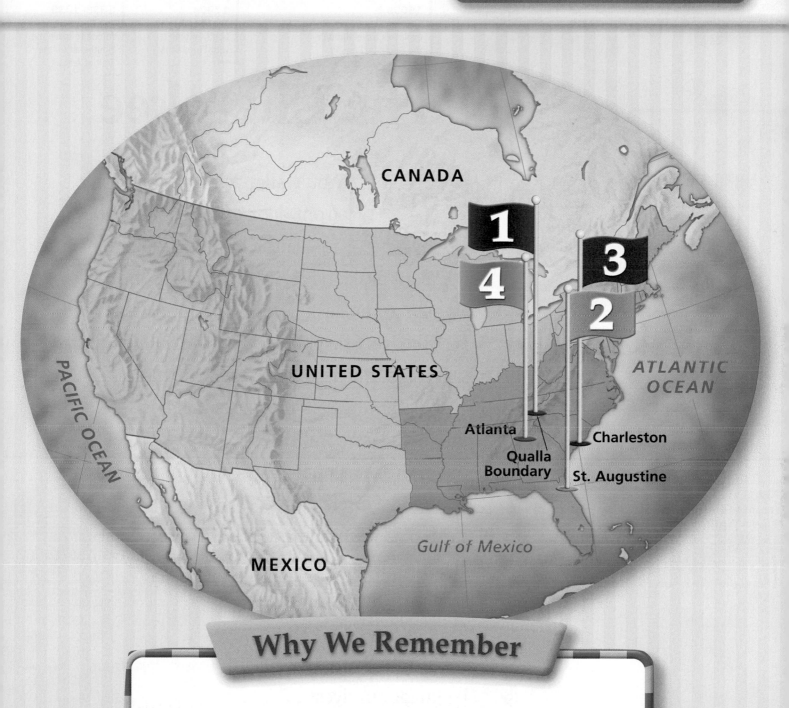

CANADA

1

4

3

2

UNITED STATES

ATLANTIC
OCEAN

PACIFIC OCEAN

Atlanta

Charleston

Qualla
Boundary

St. Augustine

Gulf of Mexico

MEXICO

Why We Remember

Before 1865, many enslaved people worked on farms and plantations in the Southeast. Many people, especially those living in the Northern states, thought that slavery was wrong. Other issues divided the North and the South, and war resulted. After the Civil War, the Southeastern states needed to rebuild. Today, Southeastern cities continue to grow.

Qualla Boundary

1500 — **1700** — **1900**

1500s
First European explorers travel through the Southeast region.

1700s
The Cherokee begin trading with Europeans.

1838–1839
The Cherokee are forced to leave the Southeast on the Trail of Tears.

The Cherokee

PREVIEW

Focus on the Main Idea
The Cherokee have contributed greatly to the history of the Southeast.

PLACES
Qualla Boundary, North Carolina

PEOPLE
George Washington
Sequoyah

VOCABULARY
consensus
Trail of Tears

You Are There

You walk up the path to the front door of the school. Once inside the building, you go to the front desk and check in. You ask the woman at the desk if your first-grade teacher is still here. She points down the hallway and says, "Yes. She is at the end of the hall."

Quietly you walk down the hall and look into the classroom. On the wall is a poster of the Cherokee alphabet. The children are all sitting in a circle on the carpet. As you walk into the classroom, they start singing a song—a welcome song in Cherokee. How wonderful that your ancient language survives!

North Wind Picture Archives

Cherokee Alphabet.

▶ Cherokee alphabet

 Main Idea and Details

Target Skill As you read, notice events and changes that affected the Cherokee and how the Cherokee responded to them.

Early Cherokee Culture

Hundreds of years ago, the Cherokee made their homes in the mountains of southern Appalachia. They lived in villages. They farmed in family units on land in their villages. They grew corn, squash, beans, and other crops. They hunted in the forests. Cherokee hunters traveled for hundreds of miles through shared territory that no single group claimed but many used. They trapped rabbits and shot deer with bow and arrow. They also hunted wild turkeys and bears and fished in the region's many streams, rivers, and lakes. They gathered wild fruits and nuts. The land provided many resources

▶ The Cherokee made spoons like these to use in cooking.

that they used.

In the summer, the Cherokee lived in rectangular houses. In the winter, they lived in smaller, warmer round huts. Their huts had thick walls made of clay and poles. The center of the

▶ Cherokee dance mask

Cherokee village was a large meeting house. There, the villagers gathered to celebrate religious holidays and to make important decisions. All adults in the village could express their thoughts about issues. The Cherokee debated issues until all could come to agreement. This method of decision-making is called **consensus.**

REVIEW How did the Cherokee make their living? What were their villages like? ↻ **Main Idea and Details**

▶ In this model of a Cherokee village, the large building is the meeting house.

Changes in Cherokee Culture

Life for the Cherokee began to change when Europeans first came to the region. In the early 1500s, Spanish explorers traveled through the Southeast. Some explorers had diseases that were new to North America. Many Cherokee and other Native Americans became ill with the new diseases.

The first Europeans to settle on Cherokee land were traders. They brought goods such as knives, hoes, guns, cloth, and beads to trade for the Native Americans' deerskins and furs. By the mid-1700s, this trade was very important.

Around the same time, conflicts grew between the settlers and the Native Americans. The Cherokee were forced to give up land and to move westward, away from the settlers.

In the late 1700s, the newly formed United States government tried to help end these conflicts. President George Washington encouraged the Cherokee to stop hunting and to focus more on farming instead. The government gave the Cherokee horses, plows, and other farm tools. They hoped that the Cherokee would change to fit in with the surrounding culture.

Many Cherokee took up Washington's offer. They built large farms. They went to school to learn English. They also learned how to read and write in their

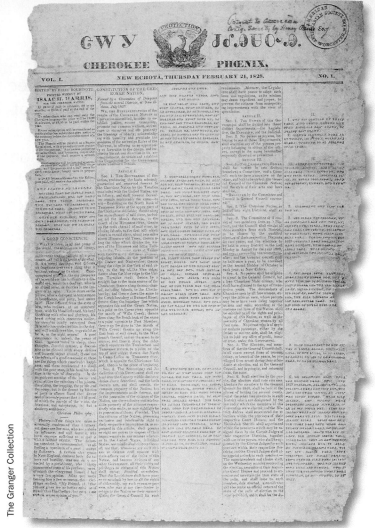

The Granger Collection

▶ The *Cherokee Phoenix* newspaper was written in both Cherokee and English. This copy is from February 21, 1828.

own language. A Cherokee man named Sequoyah made up an alphabet for the Cherokee language. He was one of the few people to ever develop an alphabet on his own. With the new alphabet, many Cherokee learned how to read and write in their own language.

Although many Cherokee took up new ideas and changed their ways of life, it did not end conflicts with the settlers and government.

REVIEW What changes occurred in Cherokee culture after the Europeans came? ⟳ **Main Idea and Details**

The Cherokee Leave Their Lands

After the American Revolution, settlers continued to try to gain control of Cherokee land. In the early 1800s, the Cherokee decided that forming a new government would help them hold onto their land. They wrote a constitution in 1827. It stated that the land belonged to the Cherokee nation.

The Cherokee constitution was similar to the United States Constitution in many ways. The Cherokee constitution stated that a head chief would be elected once every four years. The constitution also established a senate and a house of representatives.

After gold was discovered on Cherokee land in 1828, settlers were even more determined to force the Cherokee off their lands. In the 1830s, the United States government ordered the Native American groups of the region, including the Cherokee, to give up their land. The Native American groups would occupy new territory west of the Mississippi River. American soldiers forced the Cherokee families to move west to what is now Oklahoma. Forced to walk hundreds of miles without enough food or warm clothing, thousands of Cherokee died. Their journey came to be called the **Trail of Tears.**

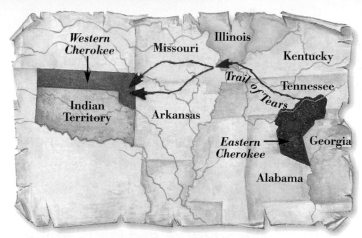

▶ **The Trail of Tears led from Tennessee to what is now Oklahoma.**

The Cherokee who traveled to Oklahoma became known as the Western Cherokee. However, some Cherokee stayed in the Southeast. Several hundred Cherokee bought land together in a mountainous part of North Carolina. A few simply hid in the mountains when soldiers came to round them up. All of these people came to be known as the Eastern Cherokee. Together, the Western and Eastern Cherokee are now the largest Native American group in the United States.

Today, the Eastern Cherokee number more than 11,000. Many live on **Qualla Boundary,** a Cherokee reservation in western North Carolina.

REVIEW How was the Cherokee constitution similar to the U.S. Constitution? **Compare and Contrast**

▶ *The Trail of Tears,* a painting by Robert Lindneux, shows the Cherokee on their long journey west.

191

The North Carolina Cherokee

The Cherokee who remained in the Southeast found new ways to support themselves and keep their culture alive. Today, many Cherokee artists belong to an organization called Qualla. They make artworks and crafts that are sold in stores across the country. The Cherokee also run a number of businesses, including a lumber business and shops for tourists.

Some Cherokee leaders fear that their language is dying out. Many Cherokee in their fifties and younger can speak only a few phrases. To

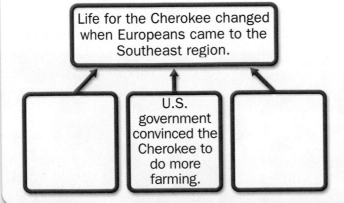

▶ **Mask made by a Qualla artist**

keep the language alive, Cherokee speakers have begun to lead special classes in Cherokee school.

Recently, elementary school teachers began teaching the Cherokee language to their students for at least twenty minutes a day. Now, many people are learning the Cherokee language.

REVIEW How do the Eastern Cherokee keep their culture strong?
⤷ **Main Idea and Details**

Summarize the Lesson

- **Before 1500s** Cherokee followed their traditional lifestyle.
- **1500s** Europeans came to the Southeast.
- **1830s** Cherokee were forced to move off their land and go west.
- **Today** Many Eastern Cherokee live in the Southeast.

LESSON 1 REVIEW

Check Facts and Main Ideas

1. ⤷ **Main Idea and Details** On a separate sheet of paper, make a diagram like the one shown. Fill in the diagram with two more details that support the main idea.

> Life for the Cherokee changed when Europeans came to the Southeast region.

> U.S. government convinced the Cherokee to do more farming.

2. What was the Cherokee culture like before Europeans came to the region? Use the word **consensus** in your answer.

3. How has work changed for the Cherokee people?

4. Why was the Cherokee journey to Oklahoma called the **Trail of Tears?**

5. **Critical Thinking: Draw Conclusions** How might developing a written language change a culture?

Link to ⟞⟠⟝ Writing

Write a Poem What if you had lived in a Cherokee village hundreds of years ago? Write a poem about life in the village.

SEQUOYAH
1763?–1843

Some Cherokee thought that white people had magic powers—reading and writing. Sequoyah disagreed. Sequoyah could not read. But he did not think that the marks on paper were special charms. He thought they stood for words. Sequoyah was determined to find a way to write the Cherokee language. He hoped that reading and writing would help Native Americans develop a stronger government and gain more respect.

BIOFACT

Giant redwood trees of the Pacific coast were named "Sequoia" in honor of Sequoyah.

Sequoyah began working on his writing system for the Cherokee language in 1809. At first, he made up a symbol for each word. Sequoyah decided that working with sounds would be easier than using a separate symbol for every word.

He based his alphabet not on single sounds but on syllables. Sequoyah made up a symbol for each of the 85 syllables in the Cherokee language. This system is called a *syllabary* after the syllables that the letters represent. Cherokee leaders officially adopted the writing system in 1821. This written language made it possible for the Cherokee to start their own newspaper, *The Cherokee Phoenix.* Sequoyah's syllabary is still used today.

Learn from Biographies

How could Sequoyah's writing system help the Cherokee keep their traditions and culture?

For more information, go online to *Meet the People* at **www.sfsocialstudies.com.**

1565   1765

1565
Spanish build St. Augustine, Florida.

1587
British start a colony on Roanoke Island, Virginia.

1607
British start a colony at Jamestown, Virginia.

1776
American colonies declare independence from Britain.

Early History of the Southeast

PREVIEW

Focus on the Main Idea
Exploration, settlements, agriculture, and slavery all shaped the early growth of the Southeast region.

PLACES

St. Augustine, Florida
Roanoke Island
Jamestown, Virginia
Monticello

PEOPLE

Juan Ponce de León
Hernando de Soto
Robert La Salle
Thomas Jefferson
James Madison
Andrew Jackson

VOCABULARY

pioneer
backwoodsman
plantation

▶ Juan Ponce de León led an expedition to a land he named Florida.

You Are There The year is 1513. You are sitting with a group of Spanish soldiers around a crackling campfire in Puerto Rico. One soldier is telling stories he heard from the native people of Puerto Rico. "Across the sea, there is an island called Bimini, where the fountain of youth flows. Anyone who drinks from this fountain will stay young forever," he says.

The other soldiers are clearly interested in the tale. The leader of the group rises to his feet and says, "I propose an expedition to search for Bimini. Who is with me?" Several soldiers rise to their feet, and you step forward, shouting "Aye!" with the soldiers. You feel ready to face the dangers of exploring a land you know nothing about.

Main Idea and Details As you read, notice how European settlements in the Southeast region developed over time.

194

The Explorers

The Spanish governor of Puerto Rico, **Juan Ponce de León,** believed the Native Americans' stories about the fountain of youth. He set sail to find the island of Bimini in 1513. Ponce de León sailed to the eastern shore of present-day Florida. He mistakenly believed it to be the island of Bimini. He named the land "Florida" because he first saw the land on Easter Sunday, which in Spanish is *Pascua Florida*, or "flowery Easter." He claimed the land for Spain. He was the first European to explore Florida, but he never found the fountain of youth.

Another Spanish explorer, **Hernando de Soto,** landed in Florida in 1539. He was searching for gold. He explored a large area of what was to become the Southeastern United States, including present-day Georgia, the Carolinas, Tennessee, and Alabama. He was the first European to see the Mississippi River, but he never found any gold.

The first European to sail down the Mississippi River and reach the Gulf of Mexico was French explorer **Robert La Salle.** In 1682 La Salle headed an expedition that sailed through the Great Lakes and down the Mississippi. When he reached the end of the Mississippi, La Salle

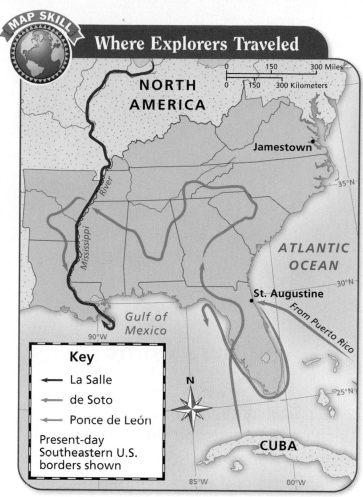

NORTH AMERICA

Jamestown

35°N

Mississippi River

ATLANTIC OCEAN

30°N

St. Augustine

From Puerto Rico

Gulf of Mexico

90°W

N

25°N

Key

← La Salle
← de Soto
← Ponce de León
Present-day Southeastern U.S. borders shown

CUBA

85°W   80°W

▶ Explorers from Spain and France traveled through the Southeast.

MAP SKILL Movement *Which explorer went north and west and crossed the Mississippi River?*

▶ **Robert La Salle**

claimed the Mississippi River valley (the land surrounding all the rivers that flow into the Mississippi) for his king, Louis XIV of France. In honor of the king, La Salle named the region Louisiana.

REVIEW Who were the major explorers of the Southeast?

◑ **Main Idea and Details**

Settlers Come to the Southeast

The Spanish founded a city that became **St. Augustine** on the east coast of Florida in 1565. This city became the first permanent European settlement in any area that is now part of the United States. The Spanish built a fort there called the Castillo de San Marcos. They built the fort to protect themselves against attacks. Today, this enormous stone fort is the largest remaining Spanish structure in the United States.

A famous colony in the Southeast is called the "Lost Colony." In 1587 a group of about 100 settlers sailed from England to establish a colony in North America. They arrived on **Roanoke Island** in what is now North Carolina. Their leader, John White, left the colony to go to England for more supplies. When White returned to Roanoke in 1590, the colony had disappeared. The only clue left was the word "CROATOAN" carved on a fence post. No one has ever found out what happened to the lost colony.

The first successful British colony in North America was **Jamestown, Virginia.** In 1607 a group of 105 settlers landed on an area of marshy land on the James River in Virginia. The land turned out to be a breeding ground for diseases. Many settlers became ill and died. The nearby Powhatan Indians offered the colonists food and helped them survive.

The success of Jamestown led to the founding of more colonies up and down the Atlantic coast. The Southeast became home to the oldest English settlements in North America.

REVIEW Name the early colonies of the Southeast and the countries that founded them. ⟳ **Main Idea and Details**

Building the Nation

Many early leaders of the United States were born in the Southeast. George Washington, who was born in Virginia in 1732, led the Colonial forces against the British army in the Revolutionary War. Some important battles of the Revolutionary War were fought in the Southeast.

George Washington became the first President of the United States in 1789. Washington is known for his honesty, bravery, dedication, and service to his country. As the "Father of His Country," he set an example for other presidents to follow.

Another leader of the Revolutionary War was **Thomas Jefferson,** the author of the Declaration of Independence. In this document, the American colonies declared themselves free and independent from Great Britain in 1776.

Jefferson was born in Virginia in 1743, and became President of the United States in 1801. As president, he doubled the size of the United States when he purchased the Louisiana Territory from France. He designed his home, **Monticello,** which is in Virginia.

Another famous Virginian, **James Madison,** is often called the "Father of the Constitution." Madison was one of the leaders of the Constitutional Convention of 1787. Here, political leaders met to write the Constitution of the United States. In 1809 Madison became the fourth President of the United States.

Andrew Jackson, who became president in 1829, was the first president to be born in poverty. Jackson was born in South Carolina in 1767. Jackson received wide support from ordinary working people who believed that he understood their needs.

REVIEW What major contributions did four early presidents from the Southeast make to the nation?
🔁 **Main Idea and Details**

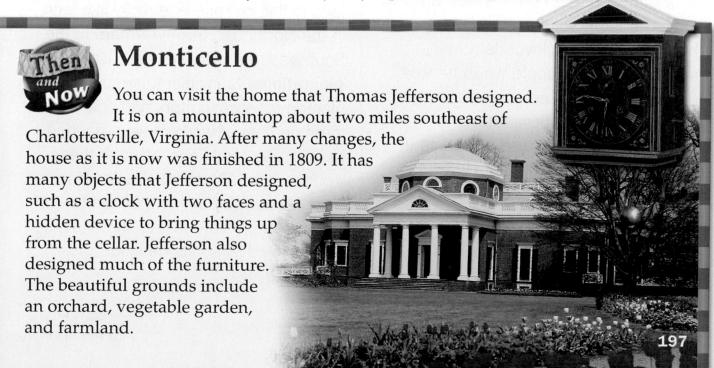

Monticello

Then and Now

You can visit the home that Thomas Jefferson designed. It is on a mountaintop about two miles southeast of Charlottesville, Virginia. After many changes, the house as it is now was finished in 1809. It has many objects that Jefferson designed, such as a clock with two faces and a hidden device to bring things up from the cellar. Jefferson also designed much of the furniture. The beautiful grounds include an orchard, vegetable garden, and farmland.

197

Pioneers and Backwoodsmen

American settlers moving west created their own folklore and legends. Pioneers and backwoodsmen became popular figures in stories and songs of the day. A **pioneer** was a person who settled in a part of the country and prepared it for others. A **backwoodsman** was a person who lived in forests far away from towns.

Daniel Boone was a pioneer. He explored Kentucky and developed the Wilderness Road, a route followed by many pioneers traveling west. Daniel Boone was born in Pennsylvania in 1734. As a teenager, he moved to North Carolina with his family.

David, also known as "Davy," Crockett, was born in the backwoods of Tennessee in 1786. He was a skilled hunter, soldier, scout, and humorist. This backwoodsman surprised many people when he was elected a Tennessee congressman in 1827. He was a successful and popular leader. After leaving office in 1835, he moved to Texas. He was killed in 1836 while fighting at the Alamo, a battle fought in Texas.

The Burstein Collection

▶ **David "Davy" Crockett**

REVIEW What contributions did Daniel Boone and David Crockett make to the region? **Main Idea and Details**

Farmers and Plantations

Settlers who came to farm the Southeast's coastal plains were able to build large farms. This is because the land is flat, not hilly and rocky like land in the Northeast. Some farmers in the Southeast built large farms called **plantations.** Many plantation owners planted tobacco, cotton, and rice. A great number of workers were needed to work on plantations. Most of these workers were African slaves. Slaves are held against their will and forced to work without pay. A slave is usually considered to be owned by someone else.

By 1776 slaves made up close to half the population in some states. Many Southerners owned slaves who worked in the cotton fields. Farmers who had the largest plantations and the most slaves planted the largest crops. These farmers grew rich growing cotton and became very powerful.

REVIEW How does the farmland in the Southeast compare with farmland in the Northeast? Compare and Contrast

Summarize the Lesson

1500s to 1600s Explorers from Spain and France traveled through the Southeast.

1607 British colony was started at Jamestown, Virginia.

1700s Plantations grew.

1776 American colonies declared independence from Great Britain.

▶ **Boone Hall Plantation near Charleston, South Carolina**

LESSON 2 REVIEW

Check Facts and Main Ideas

1. **Main Idea and Details** On a separate sheet of paper, make a diagram like the one shown. Fill in the diagram with two more details that support the main idea.

Early leaders from the Southeast have made major contributions to the nation.

President Jefferson bought territory from France.

2. What areas did Juan Ponce de León, Hernando de Soto, and Robert La Salle explore?

3. When was the first permanent European settlement founded in North America, and what was its name?

4. Why were some farmers able to build huge farms called **plantations** in the Southeast?

5. **Critical Thinking:** *Point of View* Of all the qualities listed for George Washington, which one do you think is most important for a president to have? Why?

Link to ∞ Reading

Read About Plantations Find a book in the library that describes life on a plantation. Report to your class about what you read.

Speaking Out

Have you ever stood up for a belief you thought was right, even though other people said you were wrong? In the 1830s, sisters Sarah and Angelina Grimké had the courage to speak out against slavery. Even though their words made it dangerous for them, the sisters continued speaking and writing against slavery.

Before 1850, some people who lived in the Southeast believed that slavery should be ended, or abolished. People who wanted to abolish slavery were called Abolitionists. **Sarah and Angelina Grimké** (GRIM-kee) were Abolitionists who grew up in Charleston, South Carolina. Sarah visited Philadelphia, Pennsylvania, where she met people who were opposed to slavery. After several visits, Sarah decided to leave her home permanently in 1821. Her sister followed her in 1829. Angelina wrote a letter supporting abolition that was printed in an Abolitionist newspaper. From then on, the sisters were deeply involved in the antislavery movement.

In 1836 Angelina wrote an antislavery booklet that was sent to women across the South.

▶ **Angelina Grimké**

BUILDING
CITIZENSHIP
Caring
Respect
Responsibility
Fairness
Honesty
★ Courage

In the booklet, she urged Southern women to speak out against slavery. Sarah wrote a similar booklet to religious leaders in the Southeast, urging them to support the Abolitionists. Many people in South Carolina were angry at the sisters for writing the booklets.

The Grimké sisters were among the first women to give speeches in public in the United States. Many people paid attention to the sisters' words, in part because the sisters were wealthy Southerners speaking out against slavery. Sarah, Angelina, and Angelina's husband, Theodore Dwight Weld, wrote a booklet, *Slavery as It Is: Testimony of a Thousand Witnesses*, in 1839. Harriet Beecher Stowe, a writer and Abolitionist, was said to have based parts of her novel, *Uncle Tom's Cabin*, on this booklet. Abolitionists like Weld, Stowe, and the Grimké sisters gradually convinced many people that slavery was wrong. The Grimké sisters lived to see their dreams made reality when slavery ended in 1865.

▶ Sarah Grimké

Courage in Action

Research other people who have stood up for what they believed, even when they were criticized for their beliefs. You may choose important figures in history or people from the present day who are not well-known. What beliefs did they stand up for? How did they respond to people who attacked their beliefs?

201

1860   1880

1861
The Civil
War begins.

1865
The Civil
War ends.

1877
Reconstruction
ends.

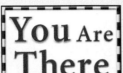

Charleston

The Nation Divided

PREVIEW

Focus on the Main Idea
The Civil War had a major impact on the history of the Southeast.

PLACES
Charleston, South Carolina

PEOPLE
Abraham Lincoln
Dr. Martin Luther King, Jr.

VOCABULARY
Civil War
Union
Confederacy
secede
Reconstruction
civil rights
segregate

You Are There

Dear Mary,
    We've known for a long time that a war could break out. But I didn't think that it would happen here in Charleston. As you may have heard, there was shooting at Fort Sumter in our harbor. We heard that a Union ship was bringing food and supplies to the Union soldiers there. Our Southern soldiers attacked the fort before the supply ship arrived.

    We could see the whole battle from the city. People clapped whenever a shell blew up near the fort. We were happy when the soldiers at the fort surrendered. No one was killed. I hope nothing worse happens.

        Your loving cousin,
        Lucy

Main Idea and Details As you read, note why the Civil War was important in the history of the Southeast region.

▶ A bugle used by soldiers in the Civil War.

The Civil War

Many people of **Charleston, South Carolina,** were excited by the battle at Fort Sumter. They were ready for war.

The **Civil War** began in 1861 and lasted for four years. It is called a civil war because it was a war between two groups in one country. On one side were the Northern states, called the **Union.** They continued to call themselves the United States of America.

On the other side were the Southern states, called the Confederate States of America, or the **Confederacy.** A confederacy is a group of countries or states. Because the war set Northern states against Southern states, some people call the Civil War the "War Between the States."

North Wind Picture Archive

Slavery was one important issue of the Civil War. Northerners and Southerners argued over whether slavery should be allowed in the new states added to the nation. Northerners did not want slavery to expand. Southerners thought they had a right to bring slaves as their property.

How people felt about their state and their country was another important issue. Many Southerners thought that each state

▶ **Abraham Lincoln**

should have more control over what its citizens could do. Many Northerners thought that the national government should have more power.

Abraham Lincoln, who was running for president in 1860, agreed with these Northerners. When he won, seven Southern states **seceded,** or pulled out, of the United States. They thought that Lincoln would work against the Southern states and might even pass laws to abolish slavery. In time, four more states seceded. These eleven states formed their own country, called the Confederate States of America.

REVIEW Summarize some reasons the Civil War began. **Summarize**

▶ **People of Charleston watched the battle at Fort Sumter in 1861.**

▶ **This field and bridge in Virginia were left in ruins after the Civil War.**

The Civil War's Effects on the Southeast

The Civil War was a time of great suffering. Confederate soldiers who fought in the war often had little food. Many people died from wounds or diseases that spread through army camps.

After four years of fighting, the South surrendered. Many soldiers returned home to find only ruins. During the war, cities had been burned down and factories had been destroyed. Farms had been burned and trampled.

The war did not just change the South physically. It also changed Southern society. One in four Confederate soldiers died in the war. Many families lost sons or fathers or both. Life was sad and difficult for many people.

The greatest change in the South came with the end of slavery. After the end of the Civil War, in 1865, the United States government passed the Thirteenth Amendment to the United States Constitution. This amendment made slavery illegal in the United States. Former slaves became new American citizens.

REVIEW Why was the Civil War a time of great suffering for people in the Southeast? **Summarize**

Rebuilding the Region

Slowly, the South began to recover from the war. **Reconstruction** is the period of time after the Civil War when the South's buildings and its economy were rebuilt. Reconstruction lasted from 1865 to 1877. Farmers again plowed their overgrown fields and planted crops. Factory owners rebuilt their factories. Rail lines were repaired. The government established the Freedmen's Bureau in 1865. For a time it provided food, clothing, and medical care to former slaves. The Bureau also built more than 1,000 schools for African Americans.

During Reconstruction, Southern states were readmitted to the United States government. To rejoin the United States, each Southern state had to promise African Americans their **civil rights.** Civil rights include the right to vote and to have the protection of the law.

Many former slaves remained on the farms of landowners. Because many had few skills for other jobs and no land of their own to farm, most former slaves lived in poverty. Many landowners tried to keep African Americans in a condition very close to slavery. After 1877 many Southeastern states enforced "Jim Crow" laws. These laws separated black people from white people on buses, in schools, and in other public places. This separation is known as **segregation.**

REVIEW How did the Southeast change during Reconstruction?
◉ **Main Idea and Details**

▶ The Freedmen's Bureau set up schools like this one for newly-freed African Americans. This school was in Richmond, Virginia.

The Granger Collection

The Civil Rights Movement

In the 1950s and 1960s, many people began to work for civil rights. An important leader of the civil rights movement was **Dr. Martin Luther King, Jr.** He was born in Atlanta, Georgia. He spoke out against segregation and other kinds of unfair treatment.

Dr. King urged people to protest unfair treatment without violence. He believed that nonviolent protest was a powerful way to win the fight for civil rights. Dr. King said,

". . . nonviolent resistance is the most potent [strongest] weapon available to oppressed [treated unjustly] people in their struggle for freedom."

Many people agreed with Dr. King. A new law was written and Congress passed the Civil Rights Act of 1964. According to this law, segregation in schools and other public places was no longer allowed.

REVIEW How did Dr. King and his followers protest segregation?
Main Idea and Details

Summarize the Lesson

- **1861** The Civil War began.
- **1865** The Civil War ended.
- **1865–1877** The South began to rebuild during Reconstruction.
- **1964** Congress passed the Civil Rights Act of 1964.

▶ **Dr. Martin Luther King, Jr.**

LESSON 3 REVIEW

Check Facts and Main Ideas

1. **Main Idea and Details** On a separate sheet of paper, fill in the diagram with details that support the main idea.

> The Civil War had a major impact on the land and people of the Southeast.

2. What were two conflicts between North and South that led to the **Civil War**?

3. Compare the Northern and the Southern pre-Civil War view of state governments and their importance.

4. How did the Freedmen's Bureau help former slaves during **Reconstruction?**

5. **Critical Thinking:** *Draw Conclusions* Why was the Civil Rights Act of 1964 important for everyone in the United States?

Link to ⊶ **Writing**

Write a Book Report Look in the library for a book about Dr. Martin Luther King, Jr. After you read the book, write a short book report. Use the words **civil rights** and **segregation** in your answer. Share your report with the class.

ROSA PARKS 1913–

Rosa Parks grew up in a small town in Alabama. During that time in the South, many whites treated blacks unfairly. Rosa Parks' family taught her to be proud of herself and her culture. Rosa Parks said about her mother:

". . . she believed in freedom and equality for people, and did not have the notion that we were supposed to live as we did."

Montgomery, Alabama has named a street in honor of Rosa Parks.

ROSA L PARKS AV 800

When Rosa Parks became an adult, she lived in Montgomery, Alabama. There she worked to get fair treatment for African Americans. She joined the National Association for the Advancement of Colored People (NAACP). The NAACP is an organization that works for the fair treatment of African Americans and other minority groups. Rosa Parks became secretary of the NAACP.

During the 1950s, many African Americans in the South did not like the way they were treated on city buses. When Rosa Parks was arrested in 1955 for refusing to give up her seat to a white man, a bus boycott began. A **boycott** is the policy of refusing to buy something as a form of protest. After the boycott succeeded, Rosa Parks became famous for her action.

Learn from Biographies

What did Rosa Parks learn during her childhood that might have inspired her to fight segregation?

For more information, go online to *Meet the People* at **www.sfsocialstudies.com**.

Identify Fact and Opinion

What? A fact is a statement that can be checked. It can be proved to be true. An **opinion** tells about personal feelings. It cannot be proved to be true or false.

Why? Facts and opinions help you understand the world. However, you need to be able to tell the difference between facts and opinions.

Writers often combine facts and opinions. They may use facts to support their opinions. They may also use opinions to make a story lively or to persuade others.

Suppose you found a diary with the following page written by a young man who lived in Georgia during the 1860s. In 1864 his family was forced to leave their farm when the Union army advanced through Georgia. They stayed with relatives until the Civil War was over. When the family returned, the young man wrote about what they found.

Our farm stood directly in the way of the Union troops advancing from Atlanta to Savannah in 1864. When we heard about the army's approach, my family left the farm to stay with our relatives in Columbus, 120 miles away. My mother, sister, and I made the journey back to our farm in May of 1865. When we arrived, it was wonderful to see that our house was still standing. Where a field of corn had stretched to the horizon, there was a sea of burned stalks. The field of vegetables that I had planted was trampled with what looked like hundreds of footprints. In my opinion, our land was ruined.

My mother was silent until now. "We'll plant again," she said, looking around. "We'll put in another crop of corn and maybe some peach trees." I felt better as I thought about the new crops we could plant. "Peaches are the best fruit in the world," I said.

How? To tell the difference between a fact and an opinion, follow these steps.

- First, read the diary entry on page 208.

- Then, ask yourself, "What statements can be proved to be true?" These statements are facts. You can use reference sources such as encyclopedias, almanacs, and maps to check facts. The first sentence of the entry is a fact. Historical records would show that the farm stood between Atlanta and Savannah.

- Ask yourself, "What statements cannot be proved to be true or false?" These statements are opinions. Sometimes statements of opinion begin with clues such as *I believe* or *In my opinion*. Opinions are also signaled by words such as *wonderful, horrible, best,* and *worst*.

1 What is an example of another **fact** from the passage on page 208? What is one way to prove that this fact is true?

2 What is an example of an **opinion** from the passage? What words signal the opinion?

3 How does reading for facts and opinions help you to understand the passage?

•Dahlonega
•Atlanta

The Glittering Cities

PREVIEW

Focus on the Main Idea
Cities in the Southeast are growing and changing.

PLACES
Dahlonega, Georgia
Atlanta, Georgia

VOCABULARY
gold rush
public transportation system

You Are There

It's so bright! Even though the sun is not shining directly on it, the golden dome looks as if it's all lit up. You're looking out the window at the Georgia State Capitol as the train pulls into the station. You're riding a MARTA train through Atlanta. You've just been to Centennial Olympic Park in downtown Atlanta. You're glad that the train runs above the ground here so that you can see the beautiful dome. Later, you'll get back on the train to go to the Dr. Martin Luther King, Jr., National Historic Site.

It's your first visit to Atlanta. There's so much to do and see!

Main Idea and Details As you read, look for details that describe Atlanta.

▶ Georgia State Capitol, Atlanta, Georgia

The Golden Dome

In 1828 gold was found in **Dahlonega,** a town in a mountain area in northern Georgia. The first **gold rush** in the United States started soon afterward. People rushed to Dahlonega to look for gold. The town quickly filled with people mining and panning for gold. If you go to Dahlonega, you can visit the Dahlonega Courthouse. The Courthouse was made with bricks that contain gold.

The dome of the state capitol in **Atlanta** gleams with gold from Georgia that the people of Dahlonega gave to the state. The Georgia State Capitol was modeled after the United States Capitol in Washington D.C. The Georgia Capitol has a Georgia Hall of Fame, with pictures of governors and other famous Georgians. The building also contains the State Museum of Science and Industry.

Before the Civil War, Atlanta was an important city in the Southeast. During the war, the city was destroyed. After the war, Atlanta was rebuilt, and soon became an important city again. It became the capital of Georgia in 1868, after the Civil War. The new capitol building was dedicated on July 4, 1889.

REVIEW What is the source of the gold that covers the dome of the Georgia State Capitol?

↻ **Main Idea and Details**

▶ **A street in Atlanta after the Civil War**

Getting Around

Atlanta started as a railroad center in 1837. It was the western end of a new railroad line. As the railroad grew, Atlanta also grew and prospered. Trains carried goods, especially cotton, to the cities in the North. Atlanta is a center of transportation today. It is still a railroad center, and many major highways pass through it. Atlanta's airport is one of the busiest in the United States.

Like many other large cities, Atlanta has a public transportation system to take people to work or to other places. A **public transportation system** is made up of of trains and buses that carry many people through a city. Public transportation helps cut down on automobile traffic. Atlanta's public transportation system is called MARTA, which stands for Metropolitan Atlanta Rapid Transit Authority.

REVIEW How do public transportation systems save fuel? **Draw Conclusions**

▶ **MARTA trains carry people around Atlanta.**

The Growing Cities

Cities in the Southeast are growing. Many people are moving to the South from colder climates in the North. Atlanta is growing quickly. Shiny new buildings are going up all over town. New industries are moving into Atlanta. People are moving here for the jobs that the industries provide. Because Atlanta is the state capital, many people who work for the state government live in Atlanta.

Communications is a major industry in Atlanta. Television stations broadcast all over the world from Atlanta. Financial centers, such as banks and insurance companies, have their headquarters in the city too.

Other Southeastern cities are also among the fastest growing in the United States. Among these cities are Myrtle Beach, South Carolina, and the cities of Naples and Orlando in Florida. The warm climate and the availability of jobs in these cities encourage people to move there.

Charleston, South Carolina, is another growing city. This city has many beautiful old buildings. Near its harbor is the South Carolina Aquarium. There you can see plants and animals from all areas of the state.

▶ The Rocky Reef exhibit at the South Carolina Aquarium in Charleston, South Carolina

Photograph by Eric Horan

Another fast-growing area is called the Triangle Region of North Carolina. This area includes the cities of Raleigh, Durham, and Chapel Hill. This area is a center for research in medicine, computers, and many other industries. It is also important as a center for business and education.

Many cities in the Southeast lead the country in population growth. The region is well-known not only for its warm climate and beautiful beaches, but also for its growing economy and industries.

REVIEW What are some reasons why people are moving into cities in the Southeast? ⟳ **Main Idea and Details**

Summarize the Lesson

- **The Georgia State Capitol has a dome covered with gold that came from mines In Georgia.**

- **Atlanta started as a railroad center, and now has a public transportation system to move people throughout the city.**

- **Atlanta and many other cities in the Southeast are growing.**

LESSON 4 REVIEW

Check Facts and Main Ideas

1. ⟳ **Main Idea and Details** On a separate sheet of paper, make a diagram like the one shown. Fill in the main idea and some facts to support it.

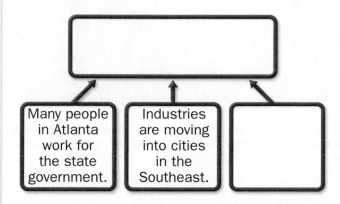

Many people in Atlanta work for the state government.

Industries are moving into cities in the Southeast.

2. Where was the first **gold rush** in the United States?

3. How has transportation affected Atlanta?

4. In what way is Atlanta a center of industry?

5. **Critical Thinking:** *Fact and Opinion* A friend says, "The Southeast is the best part of the country to live in." Is this a fact or an opinion? How can you tell?

Link to ⟷ Writing

Write a Comparison In what ways are Atlanta and the other cities in the lesson like your home town? In what ways are they different? Make a chart that shows the ways that your hometown compares with one of them.

Spoleto Festival —of— Two Worlds

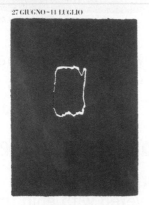

27 GIUGNO–11 LUGLIO

SPOLETO FESTIVAL 1968

▶ **A poster from the festival in Italy**

Every summer, a music festival is celebrated in two countries. Charleston, South Carolina, in the United States and Spoleto in Italy, come alive with dance, music, theater, opera, and visual art. The Spoleto Festival of Two Worlds is a festival founded by Italian-born composer Gian Carlo Menotti. People from all around the world come to both Spoleto and Charleston to enjoy the festival events.

▶ **If you visit Charleston in late May and early June, you might see puppet shows, circuses, jazz bands, or chamber music concerts.**

▶ **A dancer at the Spoleto Festival in Charleston**

Charleston

Spoleto

▶ A cathedral stands in the middle of Spoleto, Italy. The cathedral's colorful windows and mosaics are a beautiful background for the festival.

1550   1600   1650

1565
Spanish built
St. Augustine.

1607
British started
Jamestown colony.

Chapter Summary

Main Idea and Details

On a separate sheet of paper, make a diagram like the one shown. Fill in details that support the main idea.

▶ A Cherokee water drum

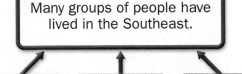

Many groups of people have lived in the Southeast.

Vocabulary

Match each word with the correct definition or description.

1. **plantation** (p. 198)

2. **consensus** (p. 189)

3. **secede** (p. 203)

4. **civil rights** (p. 205)

5. **segregate** (p. 205)

a. a method of decision-making in which all people agree

b. pull out of

c. to separate people by race

d. a very large farm

e. the right to vote and to have protection of the law

People and Places

Tell how each of the following was important in the Southeast region.

1. **George Washington** (p. 190)

2. **Sequoyah** (p. 190)

3. **Qualla Boundary** (p. 191)

4. **Roanoke Island** (p. 196)

5. **Jamestown, Virginia** (p. 196)

6. **Charleston, South Carolina** (p. 203)

7. **Dr. Martin Luther King, Jr.** (p. 206)

8. **Dahlonega, Georgia** (p. 211)

1700   1750   1800   1850   1900

1700s
Cherokee traded with Europeans.

1776
American colonies declared independence.

1838
Cherokee were forced to move.

1861–1865
Civil War

Facts and Main Ideas

1 **Time Line** How many years passed between the American colonies declaring independence and the start of the Civil War?

2 **Main Idea** What issues did Northerners and Southerners disagree about that caused them to go to war?

3 **Main Idea** Compare the Cherokee lifestyle before and after the Europeans came.

4 **Main Idea** How did Jamestown's success affect the settlement of North America?

5 **Main Idea** Name several growing cities of the Southeast and explain what is attracting people to these cities.

6 **Critical Thinking:** *Evaluate* What was the most important event in the history of the Southeast region? Give two or more reasons.

Apply Skills

Identify Facts and Opinions

Read the advertisement. Then answer the questions.

Come to Jamestown!

Jamestown is the first successful English colony in North America! You will enjoy the beautiful Virginia landscape. The food in Jamestown is the best in North America.

1 **List a sentence** that contains a fact.

2 **List two sentences** that contain opinions.

3 What words are clues that these two sentences are opinions?

Write About History

1 **Write a Story** Suppose that you are a colonist living in Jamestown. Write a short story about your life in the colony. Describe the colony and what kind of work you do.

2 **Write a travel brochure** about Atlanta. Use the information in Lesson 4 to help you write your description.

3 **Make a time line** about the Civil War and Reconstruction or about the exploration and settlement of the Southeast. Show six or more key events. Illustrate your time line.

1860   Abraham Lincoln is elected President of the United States.

1861   The Civil War begins with the Battle at Fort Sumter.

Internet Activity

To get help with vocabulary, people, and places, select the dictionary or encyclopedia from *Social Studies Library* at **www.sfsocialstudies.com.**

End with a Song

Shenandoah
American River Shanty

The Shenandoah River flows through parts of Virginia. It is surrounded by the beautiful Shenandoah Valley, which lies between the Blue Ridge and Allegheny Mountains. People who worked on ships sang a type of song called a shanty. This shanty tells about the longing people have for their faraway home.

Shenandoah

Capstan Sea Shanty

Call—Shantyman

1. Oh, Shen - an - doah, I long to hear you, ___
2. Oh, Shen - an - doah, I'm bound to leave you, ___
3. 'Tis sev'n long years since last I saw you, ___
4. When first I took a ram - bling no - tion ___

Response—Crew

And ___ see ___ you roll - in' riv - er, ___
A - way ___ you roll - in' riv - er, ___
And ___ heard ___ you roll - in' riv - er, ___
To ___ leave ___ you roll - in' riv - er, ___

Call—Shantyman

Oh, Shen - an - doah, I long to hear you, ___
Oh, Shen - an - doah, I'll not de - ceive you, ___
'Tis sev'n long years since last I saw you, ___
To sail a - cross the brin - y o - cean, ___

Response—Crew

A - way, ___ I'm bound a - way, 'Cross the wide ___ Mis-sou - ri.

UNIT 3 Project

This Just In

Report breaking news in your state's history.

1 **Choose** an important event in your state's history.

2 **Choose** roles to play for a press conference about the event: government officials or experts, news reporters, eyewitnesses, and other participants.

3 **Research** the event, focusing on one or two important details of the event. Work together to write questions and answers about the event.

4 **Create** a poster that a TV news station might use to announce breaking news about an event.

5 **Hold** your press conference as a class activity.

Internet Activity

Learn more about the United States. Go to **www.sfsocialstudies.com/activities** and select your grade and unit.

The Midwest

Why does our country need a wheat-growing region?

"O beautiful for spacious skies, for amber waves of grain . . ."

—from "America, the Beautiful," written by Katharine Lee Bates in 1893

Grant Wood painted *Stone City* in 1930. It shows the rich farmland and green landscape of the Midwest.

Welcome to the Midwest

Key

Great Lakes states

Plains states

★ State capital

National border

N

CANADA

Lake of the Woods

0   125   250 Miles

0   125   250 Kilometers

Red Lake

Lake Superior

MT

NORTH DAKOTA
★ Bismarck

MINNESOTA

MICHIGAN

Lake Huron

SOUTH DAKOTA
★ Pierre

St. Paul ★

WISCONSIN

Lake Michigan

Lake Ontario

BLACK HILLS

BADLANDS

WY

Missouri

★ Madison

★ Lansing

Lake St. Clair

Lake Erie

NY

NEBRASKA

River

IOWA
★ Des Moines

PA

Platte   River

ILLINOIS

River

OHIO

Columbus ★

Lincoln ★

★ Indianapolis

CO

Illinois

Springfield ★

INDIANA

Ohio

WV

Topeka ★

KANSAS

River

Jefferson City ★

NM

MISSOURI

KY

OK

AR

Mississippi

TN

TX

AL

MS

▶ Thousands of people enjoy sailing on the Great lakes every year.

▶ Nearly half of the corn grown in the United States is grown in Iowa, Illinois, Indiana, and Ohio.

▶ Sculptor Gutzon Borglum spent more than 14 years carving the faces of four United States Presidents on Mt. Rushmore in South Dakota.

▶ The 630-foot Gateway Arch in St. Louis, Missouri, is the nation's tallest monument. It is a monument to the spirit of western pioneers.

▶ The moose is Minnesota's largest animal. Moose can grow to be 6 1/2 feet high at the shoulder.

▶ An old schoolhouse sits on the prairie in the Midwest.

The Midwest

Target Skill

Cause and Effect

Finding causes and effects can help you understand what you read.

A cause is why something happens. → An effect is what happens.

- Sometimes writers use clue words such as *so, since,* or *because* to signal cause and effect.
- An effect can have more than one cause.
- One cause can have many effects, as in the paragraph below.

Read the following paragraph. **Causes** and **effects** have been highlighted.

A tornado is a type of violent storm that sometimes happens in the Midwest. Tornadoes are sometimes called "twisters" because their winds spin around in a whirling funnel-shaped cloud. Tornadoes are dangerous because they can cause serious damage. Effects of tornadoes include destroyed buildings, uprooted trees, and objects as large as trucks being thrown in the air.

Word Exercise

Comparatives The passage describes the Midwestern plains as flat. The word *flat* is an adjective that means "smooth and even." Doubling the *t* and add *-er* forms the word *flatter*, which means "more smooth and even." Adding the *-est* ending forms *flattest*, which means "the most smooth and even."

Word	More	Most
flat	flatter	flattest

Causes and Effects of the Rainfall Patterns in the Midwest

The Midwest region stretches from the state of Ohio at the east to the states of the Dakotas, Nebraska, and Kansas at the west. The patterns of rainfall vary across the Midwest. The western part of the region is much drier than the central and eastern parts are.

What causes this difference? The dry weather of the western Midwest is caused by the presence of mountain ranges to the west of the region. Because weather in the United States generally moves from west to east, much of the moisture in the air from the Pacific Ocean falls as rain on the western slopes of the Sierra Nevada and the Rocky Mountains. By the time the air gets to the eastern slopes, it is very dry. That is why the flat, Midwestern plains on the eastern side of the Rocky Mountains get so little rain.

The dry climate of the western plains affects the types of crops grown there. Farmers plant wheat and other products that do not need much water.

The central and eastern plains of the Midwest receive more rain. This is because moist air from the Gulf of Mexico flows northward. This moist air brings rain to the central and eastern parts of the Midwest.

Apply it!

Use the reading strategy of cause and effect to answer questions 1 and 2. Then answer the vocabulary question.

1. What causes the western part of the Midwest to be dry?

2. What effect does the lack of rainfall have on the farmers of the western plains?

3. In the reading selection, find the word *dry* and the comparative form *drier*. What word means "most dry"?

CHAPTER 8

Water and Land of the Midwest

Lesson 1

Lake Huron
The Great Lakes and other waterways connect the Midwest to the world.

1

Lesson 2

Badlands National Park
The Badlands look back in history—to the days of the dinosaurs!

2

Lesson 3

Hoopeston, Illinois
The Midwest is one of the best agricultural regions in the world.

3

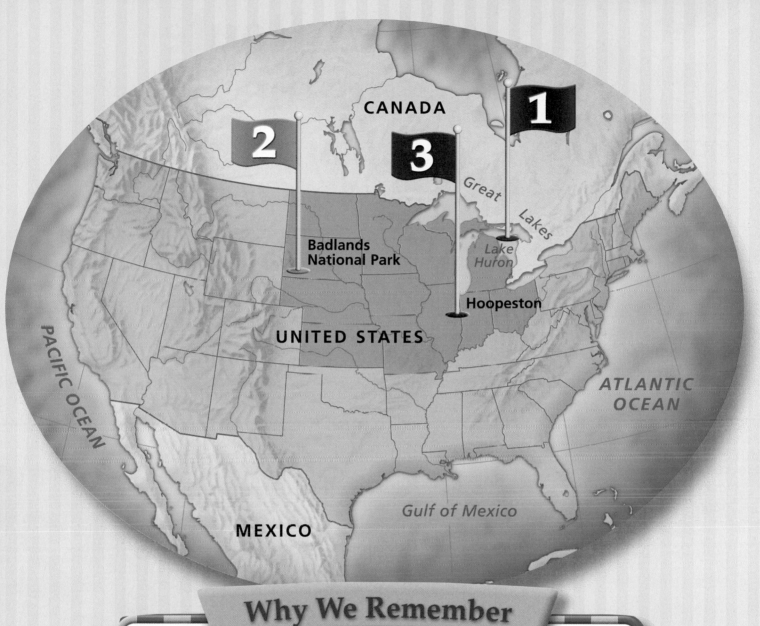

CANADA

2

3

1

Great Lakes

Badlands National Park

Lake Huron

Hoopeston

UNITED STATES

PACIFIC OCEAN

ATLANTIC OCEAN

Gulf of Mexico

MEXICO

Why We Remember

Fields of wheat blowing in the wind, tall cornstalks in neat rows, a scarecrow, cows in a pasture, beaches with beautiful lakes—you'll see all these in the Midwest. You might also see the Arch in St. Louis, Missouri; the Sears Tower in Chicago, Illinois; the sand dune beaches in Indiana; and the cheese made in Wisconsin. Read why many people call the Midwest "America's Heartland."

Great Lakes

Lake Huron

PREVIEW

Focus on the Main Idea
The Great Lakes link the Midwest region to the Gulf of Mexico and to the Atlantic Ocean.

PLACES

The Great Lakes
Illinois Waterway
Mississippi River
St. Lawrence Seaway

VOCABULARY

waterway
canal
lock
barge

A Route to the Sea

You Are There You are riding on a boat in the Chicago River. You are going to go through the locks into Lake Michigan. Your teacher explains that locks are gated parts of a canal or river. She says that the gates could be closed at each end separately to raise or lower the water level. You stop. You see the gate close behind you. The boat is trapped in this little area. As you look over the side of the boat, you see the water rising. The water rises until the boat is at Lake Michigan level. The gate opens and the boat moves forward. As you look behind, you see the Chicago River lock closing. You are on Lake Michigan now!

Cause and Effect As you read, look for the effects the glaciers had on the formation of the Great Lakes.

Visit the Great Lakes!

Lake Superior
Lake Huron
Lake Ontario
Lake Michigan
Lake Erie

The History of the Great Lakes

The states of the Midwest that are near the Great Lakes are called the Great Lakes states. The **Great Lakes** are Lake Ontario, Lake Erie, Lake Huron, Lake Michigan, and Lake Superior. The Lakes are connected to each other. The Great Lakes are the largest group of freshwater lakes in the world. They contain about one-fifth of the world's freshwater—water that is not salty. They are so large that they appear to be seas. In most places, you cannot see the opposite shore.

The Great Lakes were formed many thousands of years ago during the last Ice Age. At that time, much of North America was covered by thick sheets of ice called glaciers. Movement of the glaciers caused deep pits to form in the Earth. As the Ice Age ended, the glaciers melted. The melting water of the glaciers filled the pits, forming the Great Lakes.

REVIEW What happened at the end of the last Ice Age that caused the Great Lakes to form?

⊙ Cause and Effect

▶ Lake Michigan is a huge, deep lake. It was formed when glaciers melted and moved.

Connecting the Midwest to the World

The Great Lakes are part of a system that links the Midwest with the rest of the world. The system forms a **waterway,** which consists of rivers, lakes, and canals through which many ships travel. A **canal** is one kind of waterway that has been dug across land for ships to go through. The **Illinois Waterway** connects Lake Michigan to the **Mississippi River.** This waterway consists of several rivers and canals. The Mississippi River flows into the Gulf of Mexico.

Another waterway, the **St. Lawrence Seaway,** links the Great Lakes with the St. Lawrence River. The St. Lawrence River flows into the Atlantic Ocean.

Some parts of waterways are at higher or lower levels than other parts. Locks were built so that ships could be raised or lowered to a different level. A **lock** is a gated part of a canal or river. Between the gates, water can be let in or out to raise or lower the water level.

The Chicago River originally flowed into Lake Michigan. Engineers dug a canal to connect the Chicago River to the Illinois River, which flows into the Mississippi. The canal and locks forced

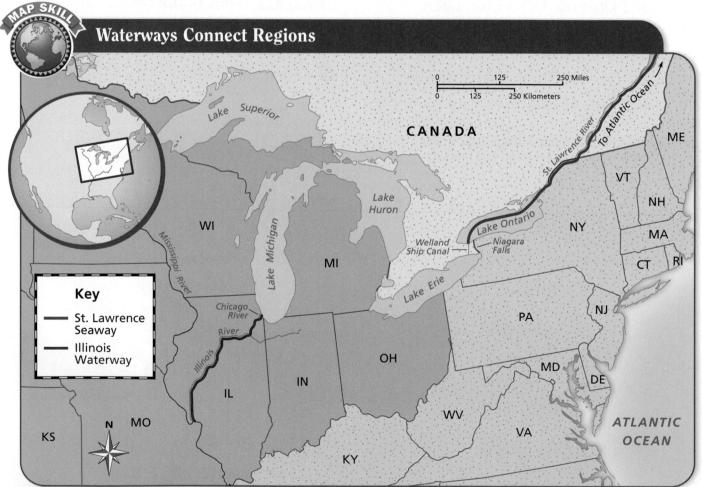

Waterways Connect Regions

Key
— St. Lawrence Seaway
— Illinois Waterway

▶ The Great Lakes, rivers, and canals combine to form a large network of water routes.

MAP SKILL Using Routes *What route would goods take if they are shipped by water from Chicago to New York state?*

234

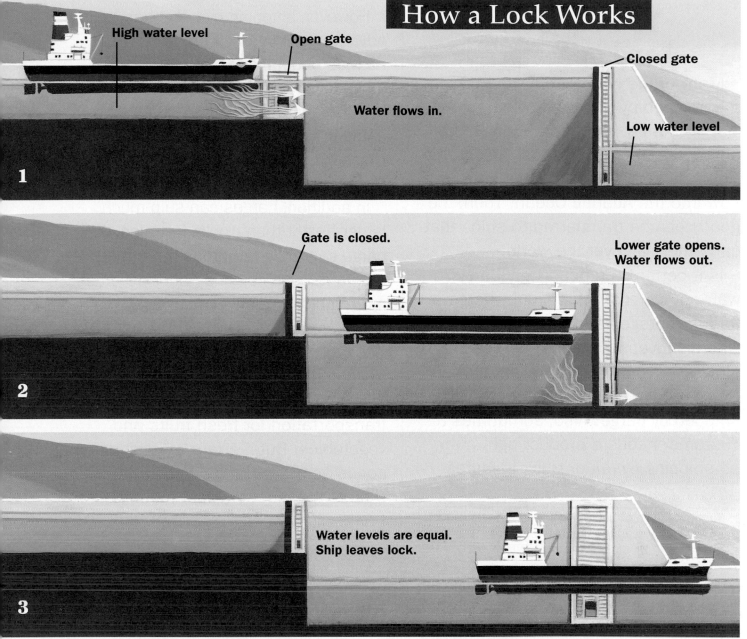

How a Lock Works

1 High water level | Open gate | Closed gate

Water flows in.

Low water level

2 Gate is closed. | Lower gate opens. Water flows out.

3 Water levels are equal. Ship leaves lock.

▶ A lock system helps ships pass through rivers or canals that are at different levels.

the Chicago River to flow backwards so that it would link Lake Michigan to the Mississippi. Engineers solved the problem of how to let boats travel from Lake Michigan to the Mississippi River.

The builders of the St. Lawrence Seaway, however, faced a different problem. Boats could not use the Niagara River to get from Lake Erie to Lake Ontario. Boats could not travel through Niagara Falls. So engineers designed the Welland Ship Canal between the two lakes. The St. Lawrence Seaway has a number of other canals and locks as well. These canals and locks make the seaway a smooth passageway to the ocean.

REVIEW What effect did changing the flow of the Chicago River have on transporting goods from Lake Michigan?
↻ **Cause and Effect**

To Ship Over Land or Water?

Many of the goods from the Midwest are shipped by boat and by barge. A **barge** is a flat-bottomed boat. Barges and boats transport goods through the Great Lakes and on rivers that eventually flow into the Atlantic Ocean. Then, the goods can be transferred to ships that carry them all over the world.

Is it better to transport goods by water or by land? Shipping by barge has advantages and disadvantages. One disadvantage is that barges are slow, averaging only six miles per hour. Since food can spoil, it is not usually shipped by barge. Also, sometimes a customer needs a product right away, so shipping by rail or truck is faster.

▶ **Tugboats push or pull barges. Sometimes, several barges are connected together.**

However, shipping by water has a big advantage. Barges can move large or heavy products long distances at a much lower cost than trucks or trains can. Barges use less fuel to ship the same amount of product than trucks or trains do. Barges also do not require as much maintenance as trucks or trains.

In addition, barges can ship much larger freight than trucks or trains. A barge can move 15 times more material than a railroad car, and about 60 times more material than a truck. Coal and metals are often shipped on barges.

However, barges cannot provide door-to-door shipping the way trucks can. Trucks are the main method of transportation for fresh fruits and vegetables. But if a farmer is shipping goods across great distances, then a train is the most efficient means of transportation.

► **Freight train**

Trains can carry much heavier loads than trucks can, and at faster speeds. Freight trains can travel at 75 miles per hour, while trucks travel at up to 65 miles per hour, depending on the speed limits of different highways. Barges travel much more slowly than trucks or trains.

Several cities in the Midwest are major transportation centers. Trains and trucks transport more freight through Chicago, Illinois, than through any other city in the nation. Ships and barges dock in St. Louis, Missouri, one of the busiest port cities on the Mississippi River.

As you can see, shipping by water has advantages and disadvantages. It is up to the person in charge of shipping a product to decide if shipping by water is the best method of sending the product.

REVIEW What are some of the positive effects of shipping by water?
Cause and Effect

Summarize the Lesson

- **The Great Lakes formed thousands of years ago from glaciers carving channels in the land and then filling them with melted ice.**
- **The Great Lakes are linked to the Mississippi River through the Illinois Waterway and to the Atlantic Ocean through the St. Lawrence Seaway.**
- **The waterways of the Midwest provide an inexpensive way for people to ship products worldwide.**

LESSON 1   REVIEW

Check Facts and Main Ideas

1. **Cause and Effect** On a separate sheet of paper, make a diagram like the one shown. Complete it by listing the missing causes and effect.

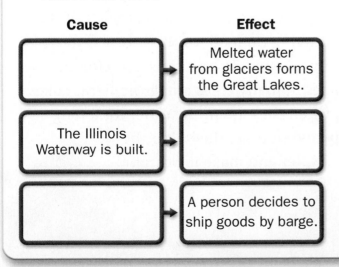

Cause	Effect
	Melted water from glaciers forms the Great Lakes.
The Illinois Waterway is built.	
	A person decides to ship goods by barge.

2. How did glaciers help form the geography of the Midwest?

3. What are **locks** and why are they important?

4. What helps link the Great Lakes and the Atlantic Ocean? Use the words **canal** and **waterway** in your answer.

5. **Critical Thinking:** *Evaluate* Suppose you need to send fresh fruit from a farm in the Midwest to a city in the Northeast. What shipping method would you use? Explain.

Link to ∞ **Science**

Learn About Glaciers With a partner, research other places in the world where glaciers can still be found. Compare what you learn with what your classmates find.

ZEBRA MUSSEL INVASION

International trade on the waterways of the Midwest is great for the region's economy. However, it can bring with it a problem that is difficult to solve!

In 1988, a new type of shellfish was discovered in the waters of Lake Erie. This creature is called the zebra mussel, because it has a dark and light striped shell.

Where on Earth did they come from? Zebra mussels are native to Europe and Asia. They arrived in the United States undetected, probably in 1986. Zebra mussels traveled across the Atlantic Ocean in European ships.

Adult zebra mussels attach to hard surfaces, including boat hulls, water pipes, and the rocky bottom of lakes and rivers. They grow rapidly in thick colonies. There can be 500,000 zebra mussels in an area smaller than your teacher's desk.

▶ **Zebra mussels clog the inside of water pipes.**

These small creatures can cause big problems. They can eat most of the small plants floating in the water, leaving no food for the fish. They can cause the deaths of many larger clams. The mussels also clog the water intake pipes in many cities along the Great Lakes. Yet, when they are in the water for a long period of time, they filter the water and make it clearer.

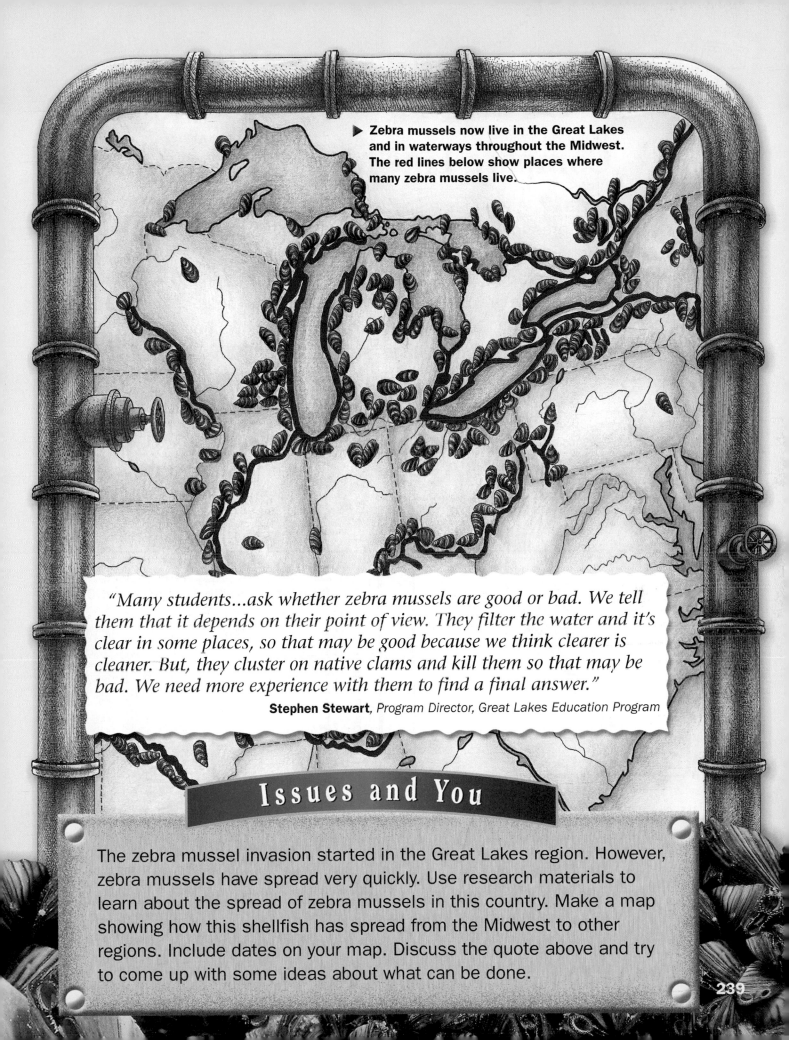

▶ Zebra mussels now live in the Great Lakes and in waterways throughout the Midwest. The red lines below show places where many zebra mussels live.

"Many students...ask whether zebra mussels are good or bad. We tell them that it depends on their point of view. They filter the water and it's clear in some places, so that may be good because we think clearer is cleaner. But, they cluster on native clams and kill them so that may be bad. We need more experience with them to find a final answer."

Stephen Stewart, *Program Director, Great Lakes Education Program*

Issues and You

The zebra mussel invasion started in the Great Lakes region. However, zebra mussels have spread very quickly. Use research materials to learn about the spread of zebra mussels in this country. Make a map showing how this shellfish has spread from the Midwest to other regions. Include dates on your map. Discuss the quote above and try to come up with some ideas about what can be done.

Chart and Graph Skills

Compare Line and Bar Graphs

What? A graph is a special kind of picture. It shows and compares information. Two common kinds of graphs are line graphs and bar graphs.

A **line graph** can show how something has changed over time. A line on the graph goes up or down to show these changes. For example, the line on the line graph below shows how the population of Illinois changed from 1850 to 2000.

A **bar graph** can also show how something changes over time. The bar graph below shows the same information as the line graph.

Line Graph

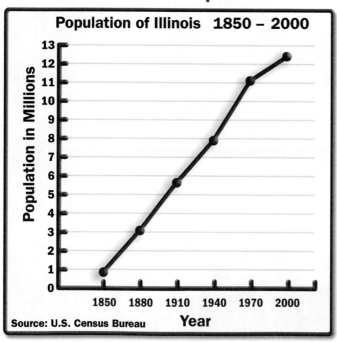

Bar Graph

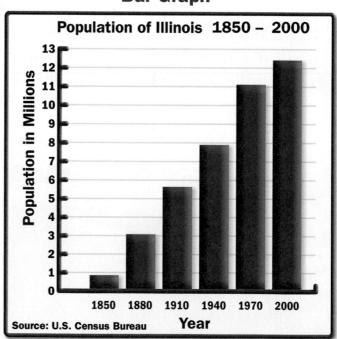

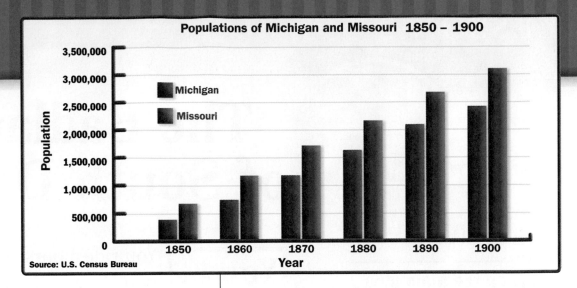

Populations of Michigan and Missouri 1850 – 1900

Population

- Michigan
- Missouri

Source: U.S. Census Bureau

Year

A bar graph can also be used to compare amounts. This bar graph compares the populations of Michigan and Missouri from 1850 to 1900.

Why? Line graphs and bar graphs show facts in a clear, simple picture. They help you find information quickly and easily. They also help you compare information. Choose the type of graph for the information you want to show.

How? Always read the title of a graph and the labels on the graph. This information tells you what the graph is showing.

Look at the line graph on page 240. The dates at the bottom tell you when the population was measured. The numbers at the left show the number of people living in Illinois. Each dot stands for the total number of people living in Illinois in a given year. Did the population of Illinois grow slowly or quickly from 1880 to 1940?

Look at the bar graph on page 240. It shows another way of presenting the same information that is in the line graph. How is this bar graph different from the line graph? Now look at the bar graph above. How is it different from the bar graph on page 240?

Think and Apply

1 Would you choose a **bar graph** or a **line graph** to show changes in your height each year since your birth? Why?

2 Suppose you wanted to compare the number of workers in two Illinois industries. What kind of graph would best show that information?

3 Look at the graphs on page 240. In which 30-year period did the population of Illinois change the fastest? How did you find the answer?

Badlands National Park

The Badlands of South Dakota

PREVIEW

Focus on the Main Idea
Erosion has shaped the South Dakota Badlands.

PLACES
Badlands National Park

PEOPLE
Sue Hendrickson

VOCABULARY
badlands
erosion
prairie

► Sue Hendrickson and the *Tyrannosaurus* skull

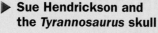

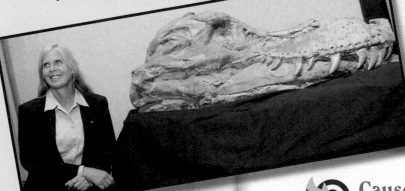

You Are There
You ride a horse down a trail that winds between sand-colored hills. You and your family are riding with a group through the rock formations of the South Dakota Badlands. You were excited when you learned you were coming here because you wanted to look for fossils along the rocky trails.

Your guide says, "Many dinosaur fossils have been found in these hills. A scientist named Sue Hendrickson discovered one of the most complete *Tyrannosaurus rex* fossils ever found. The fossil was named 'Sue' in her honor." Perhaps you are about to make an incredible discovery of your own!

Cause and Effect As you read, look for the ways that the South Dakota Badlands have changed over time and some of the causes of these changes.

Changes in the Badlands

The Great Lakes states are one part of the Midwest. Another part is known as the Great Plains. The badlands are in the Great Plains.

Sue Hendrickson found her famous fossil in the badlands of South Dakota. **Badlands** are regions of dry hills and sharp cliffs formed of crumbling rock. The badlands of western South Dakota are among the most beautiful landscapes in the United States.

Let's travel back in time to when *Tyrannosaurus rex* roamed this region, very long ago. There were no badlands then. Instead, broad rivers flowed through a lush, green plain. Many plants and animals lived on the plain. The climate was warmer and more humid than it is today.

Over millions of years, the climate became cooler and less humid. The Rocky Mountains and the Black Hills rose to the west. These mountains affected the region's climate. They blocked some of the rain that once fell on the region. Over the next millions of years, the land began to change. Rivers, wind, and rain carved the landscape we see today.

REVIEW How did the climate of this region change? ➲ **Cause and Effect**

▶ The *Tyrannosaurus rex* named "Sue" is on display at the Field Museum in Chicago.

HERE AND THERE

United States and Thailand

BIG FARMS
& Little Farms

Farms in the Midwest region of the United States and farms in Thailand, in Southeast Asia, raise important food crops. However, while corn is often grown on Midwestern farms, rice is the most important crop on Thai farms. Corn is grown in soil that is moist, but not wet. Rice is planted in flooded fields called rice paddies.

UNITED STATES
Midwest Region

THAILAND

■ Most Thai farms are 1–5 acres.

A Midwest farm might be more than 500 acres.

▶ In the Midwest, professional farmers use big machines called combines to harvest corn.

250

▶ Some baskets are used in Thailand for measuring or carrying rice. The larger basket is a *tanan*, used for measuring rice. The smaller basket is a *katip*, or lunch box, used for carrying sticky rice.

▶ In Thailand, entire families work together on farms. Rice is usually planted, cared for, and harvested by hand. Rice seedlings are planted one at a time. Harvesting is done with a sickle or knife.

251

Chapter Summary

 Cause and Effect

On a separate sheet of paper, fill in the effects related to the causes.

▶ **The Badlands**

Cause	Effect
The temperature of the Earth rises at the end of the Ice Age.	
Sand is flung by the wind against cliff faces.	
Soybean plants add necessary materials to the soil.	

Vocabulary

For each vocabulary word, write a sentence that defines or shows what the word means.

1. **barge** (p. 236)
2. **canal** (p. 234)
3. **lock** (p. 234)
4. **waterway** (p. 234)
5. **badlands** (p. 243)
6. **erosion** (p. 244)
7. **prairie** (p. 245)
8. **crop rotation** (p. 248)
9. **irrigation** (p. 248)

Places

Describe each place, tell where it is located, and why it is important in the Midwest region.

1. **The Great Lakes** (p. 233)
2. **Mississippi River** (p. 234)
3. **Illinois Waterway** (p. 234)
4. **St. Lawrence Seaway** (p. 234)
5. **Badlands National Park** (p. 244)
6. **The Central Plains** (p. 247)

Facts and Main Ideas

Write your answers on a separate sheet of paper.

1. How did the Great Lakes form?

2. How did erosion shape the South Dakota Badlands?

3. What factors make the central Midwest a rich agricultural region?

4. **Main Idea** Describe the waterway that connects the Midwest with the Atlantic Ocean.

5. **Main Idea** What part of the Midwest has rich fossil beds?

6. **Main Idea** Name two Midwest states and crops they produce other than corn and soybeans.

7. **Critical Thinking:** *Make Generalizations* The central Midwest has many large cities. Based on what you have learned about the Midwest, give a reason why cities have flourished in this part of the region.

Apply Skills

Using Graphs

Study the bar graph below. Then answer the questions.

1. What does this bar graph show?

2. Of the three Midwestern states shown—Illinois, Indiana, and Kansas—which one had the largest population in the year 2000? in the year 1990?

3. About how many people lived in Illinois in the year 2000?

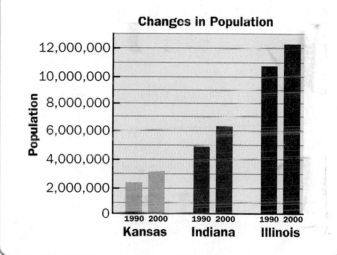

Changes in Population

Write About Economics

1. **Write a story** using what you have learned about different types of transportation for getting goods to market. Tell why you chose this route.

2. **Write a radio advertisement** encouraging tourism in the Midwest.

3. **Write a journal** describing how you plan to transport a Midwestern farmer's soybeans to market.

Sending Beans to Market

Julie wonders, "How should I send my soybeans to Chicago? By truck or by train?"

Internet Activity

To get help with vocabulary and terms, select the dictionary or encyclopedia from *Social Studies Library* at **www.sfsocialstudies.com.**

People of the Midwest

Lesson 1

Duluth, Minnesota
The Ojibwa settle near the Great Lakes.

1

Lesson 2

Sault Sainte Marie, Michigan
The French trade with Native Americans.

2

Lesson 3

Wapello County, Iowa
Settlers rush to claim land.

3

Lesson 4

St. Louis, Missouri
The Gateway Arch celebrates the western growth of the United States.

4

CANADA

1

2

4

Duluth

Sault Sainte Marie

3

Wapello County

St. Louis

UNITED STATES

ATLANTIC OCEAN

PACIFIC OCEAN

Gulf of Mexico

MEXICO

Why We Remember

Native Americans who lived in the northern Midwest moved around their villages to plant crops along riverbanks, fish in peaceful lakes, and hunt in the deep woods. They often traveled by canoes made from the bark of birch trees. Today, the Midwest is the transportation hub of the nation, linking all the regions by train, by plane, and by superhighways.

Duluth
Milwaukee
Mt. Pleasant

The Ojibwa

PREVIEW

Focus on the Main Idea
The Ojibwa have maintained important cultural traditions and have contributed to the culture of the Midwest.

PLACES
Duluth, Minnesota
Milwaukee, Wisconsin
Mt. Pleasant, Michigan

VOCABULARY
fur trade

▶ Ojibwa Talking Stick

You Are There

Today your friend Ron, an Ojibwa, has brought his talking stick to class. You and your classmates are sitting in a circle while Ron speaks. He says that the Ojibwa use the talking stick to make sure that each person in a group has a chance to express his or her thoughts. Whoever holds the stick has the right to talk. Everyone else has to show respect and remain silent. When the speaker is finished talking, he or she passes the stick on.

The students in your class decide to use the talking stick to talk about what they wish were different in the world. You enjoy listening to your classmates and thinking about what they are saying. You decide to ask Ron more about Ojibwa culture after class.

Cause and Effect As you read, think about the effects the Europeans had on the changing ways of the Ojibwa.

Early Ojibwa Culture

The Ojibwa (oh JIB way) lived along the coast of the Atlantic Ocean. Centuries ago, they decided to move westward. They traveled along the St. Lawrence River and other rivers and lakes in what is now Canada. By 1641 they had reached the northern Great Lakes region. They settled in the present-day cities of **Duluth, Minnesota; Milwaukee, Wisconsin;** and **Mt. Pleasant, Michigan.**

The new Ojibwa homeland was covered with thick forests. The hunting was excellent. Fish from the region's many lakes and rivers were another plentiful source of food. The Ojibwa also gathered wild rice and berries from the forests, marshes, and waterways. In most of the region, they grew only a small amount of vegetables. The forests were too thick, the summers were too short, and the soil was not rich enough for much farming.

The Ojibwa had to travel widely to hunt, fish, and gather food. They traveled through the northern Great Lakes region in canoes made from the bark of birch trees. These lightweight, durable boats would later become a main method of transportation for European traders.

REVIEW Why did the Ojibwa rely on fish, game, and wild rice instead of farming as their main sources of food?
Main Idea and Details

▶ **This historic photo shows an Ojibwa couple carrying a birchbark canoe ashore in Minnesota.**

Native Americans of the Midwest Today

In the mid-1600s, Europeans first came to the northern Great Lakes region where the Ojibwa lived. The Europeans traded cloth, guns, and knives for skins from beavers trapped by the Ojibwa. This **fur trade** changed Ojibwa culture. The Ojibwa started to spend more time trapping and trading than they had done before. They no longer produced everything they wanted and needed.

Today, many Ojibwa still live in the northern Great Lakes region. Some live on reservations. These reservations resulted from treaties, or agreements that the Ojibwa made with the United States government. Some Ojibwa still hunt and fish and make traditional crafts. Many have also left the reservation and have gone to live and work in cities. Centers like the American Indian Center in Chicago, Illinois, offer technology training for Native Americans. The centers also teach the skills of different trades.

The Sioux (SOO) Indians also live on the Great Plains. The Sioux belong to several different groups: Lakota, Nakota, and Dakota. Today, many Sioux live on reservations in several Midwestern states. They live in South Dakota, North Dakota, Minnesota, and Nebraska.

Some Sioux live in cities, such as Minneapolis and St. Paul in Minnesota. Many Sioux who live in cities keep their ties to their culture by visiting the reservations for special occasions, such as traditional ceremonies. Many urban Sioux also take part in Native American cultural activities at urban social centers.

▶ **This Ojibwa boy is wearing a traditional costume.**

Other Native Americans who live in the Midwest include the Ottawa and the Potawatomi. Originally, these groups are thought to have come with the Ojibwa from the Atlantic coast to the Great Lakes region. The Ottawa and the Potawatomi supported themselves like the Ojibwa by hunting, fishing, and gathering wild rice. They

▶ **Ojibwa harvesting wild rice**

also grew corn on their farmland. Today, some Ottawa and Potawatomi still live in the Midwest. Some Ottawa live in Michigan. Some Potawatomi live in Kansas, Michigan, and Wisconsin.

REVIEW Name one way that the Sioux and Ojibwa have continued to follow their traditions. **Main Idea and Details**

Summarize the Lesson

- **The Ojibwa live in the northern Great Lakes region.**
- **Hundreds of years ago, the Ojibwa adapted to life in the region by hunting, fishing, and gathering wild rice and other plants.**
- **Many Ojibwa and other Native American tribes still live in the Midwest.**

LESSON 1 REVIEW

Check Facts and Main Ideas

1. **Cause and Effect** On a separate sheet of paper, list the effect that goes with the appropriate cause and the cause that goes with the appropriate effect.

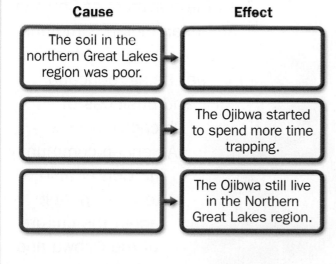

Cause	Effect
The soil in the northern Great Lakes region was poor.	
	The Ojibwa started to spend more time trapping.
	The Ojibwa still live in the Northern Great Lakes region.

2. Describe the places where the Ojibwa traveled before the Europeans came to the Great Lakes region.

3. What is one way that Ojibwa use of the land changed after Europeans came to the region? Use the term **fur trade** in your answer.

4. How do some Native Americans help other Native Americans today?

5. **Critical Thinking:** *Point of View* What special relationship do the Ojibwa have with the United States government?

Link to ⟨⟩ Mathematics

Make a Bar Graph Find out the population of the Ojibwa in the four different midwestern states where most Ojibwa live: Michigan, Wisconsin, Minnesota, and North Dakota. Make a bar graph that shows the Ojibwa population of these states.

Keeping a Culture Strong

How do you make a community stronger? One way is by celebrating holidays and other events together. Joseph Podlasek, an Ojibwa, works hard to keep his community and its culture strong.

Joseph Podlasek's mother, a member of the Ojibwa from the Lac Courte Oreilles (La COO TOO Ray) Reservation in Wisconsin, had always taught him to respect his Native American roots. In 1989, when Joseph was looking for a new career, he turned to the American Indian Center for help. The organization allowed him to use his construction skills in exchange for taking courses in a computer technology program. Joseph then began a life-long journey teaching people to respect his culture.

Joseph Podlasek is now the Executive Director of the American Indian Center. The American Indian Center has become a symbol of Chicago's American Indian community. The center promotes the well-being, education, and business of Chicago's Native American community. The Center also teaches people about the culture of the Ojibwa and other Native Americans.

BUILDING CITIZENSHIP

Caring

Respect

Responsibility

Fairness

Honesty

Courage

The American Indian Center has a program for students in Illinois. The program includes storytelling, drumming, and other traditions. But most important of all, students learn about the talking stick. People pass the talking stick around a circle. A person who receives the stick may speak. Everyone else is silent, showing respect to the speaker. Many students who visit the American Indian Center make a talking stick to take home.

Joseph Podlasek enjoys working at the center because of what it has taught him.

"It is about going full circle and giving back to the community. I was taught that if and when possible, you should provide back to the community that has helped you grow."

Respect in Action

Show how people in the community can teach and demonstrate respect for their cultures.

Research and Writing Skills

Use a Search Engine on the Internet

What? You can find out more about a topic by doing **research.** One place to find lots of research information is on the Internet. The **Internet** is a huge network of computers. It contains many World Wide Web (Web) sites. One of the quickest ways to find information on the Internet is to use a search engine. A **search engine** is a special Web site that locates other Web sites that can provide information on the topic you are researching.

Why? A search engine can provide links to Web sites from all over the world. The search engine usually gives you the title of the Web site and a little information about it. From the search engine, you can choose a link to find out more about the topic you are researching.

Q: How do I begin my search?

A: Start with a search engine. Then type in a keyword or keywords for the information you want.

Search Engine

search keyword
Ojibwa

.gov

.org

.edu

How? To use a search engine, follow these steps.

- First, select a search engine. A teacher or librarian can help you choose a search engine that will best help you conduct your search.
- Next, type in a keyword or two. A keyword is a word or phrase related to your topic, such as "Ojibwa." Then click on "Search." You may have to experiment with different words and phrases. If you need help, click on "Help" or "Search Tips."
- If your search brings no results, try another keyword, or ask for help from someone with Internet experience.
- Check the facts you find on the Internet with another source such as an encyclopedia.

Think and Apply

1. What is one way that the **Internet** can be a useful **research** tool?

2. What words or phrases would you type in a **search engine** to begin a search of Native Americans in the Midwest?

3. How would you choose which sites to visit from the list that appears on a search engine?

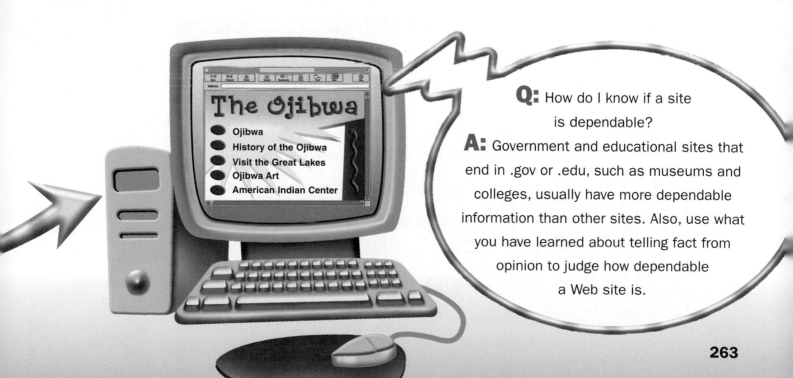

The Ojibwa

- Ojibwa
- History of the Ojibwa
- Visit the Great Lakes
- Ojibwa Art
- American Indian Center

Q: How do I know if a site is dependable?

A: Government and educational sites that end in .gov or .edu, such as museums and colleges, usually have more dependable information than other sites. Also, use what you have learned about telling fact from opinion to judge how dependable a Web site is.

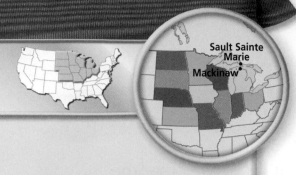

Sault Sainte Marie
Mackinaw

1650   1700   1750

Middle 1600s
French fur traders come to the Midwest.

1673
Marquette and Jolliet explore midwestern waterways.

1680s
The French build forts as trading posts.

1700s
Settlements grow around the French forts.

PREVIEW

Focus on the Main Idea
European settlement in the Great Lakes region and the Mississippi valley began with the fur trade. Many of the region's cities and towns began as fur trading centers.

PEOPLE
Jacques Marquette
Louis Jolliet
Jean Baptiste Point du Sable

PLACES
Mackinaw, Michigan
Sault Sainte Marie, Michigan

VOCABULARY
mission
trading post

The Fur Trade

You Are There
You are a trapper. Today you leave on your journey down river. Two young Ojibwa men will be your guides. You are taking beaver and fox furs to trade. The Ojibwa have provided you with sturdy birchbark canoes. They have given you corn and smoked meat to eat on your journey. You have traded metal tools for their goods. As you travel down the rivers you will watch the beauty of the spring flowers blooming and the trees budding. It will be a long journey but you are excited because you know you will see many new things along the way.

▶ Top hat made from beaver fur

Cause and Effect As you read, look for ways that the fur trade affected the settlement of the Midwest.

The Fur Trade in the Midwest

The French were the first Europeans to come to the Midwest. They came in the mid-1600s in search of furs. The French and the Native Americans trapped and skinned beaver, mink, and otter. The animal furs were very valuable. Europeans used the furs to make coats and hats.

In 1673 a French priest and explorer, **Jacques Marquette,** and a French Canadian, **Louis Jolliet**, explored areas of the Midwest. They traveled in birchbark canoes from Michilimackinac **(Mackinaw)** in present-day Michigan, across Lake Michigan, and down river to the Mississippi River. On their return journey, they followed the Illinois River to a place near present-day Chicago. They stopped at a mission on Green Bay in present-day Wisconsin. A **mission** is a settlement set up by a religious group to teach their religion and to help the people of an area. Marquette stayed at the mission. Jolliet continued on to **Sault Sainte Marie, Michigan.** Trace Marquette and Jolliet's journey on the map.

REVIEW Why did the French trap animals for their furs?
Main Idea and Details

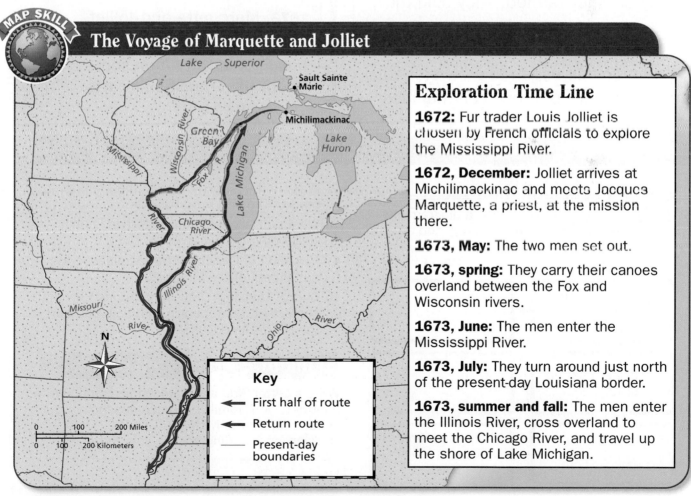

MAP SKILL

The Voyage of Marquette and Jolliet

Lake Superior

Sault Sainte Marie

Michilimackinac

Green Bay

Lake Huron

Wisconsin River

Mississippi River

Fox R.

Lake Michigan

Chicago River

Illinois River

Missouri River

Ohio River

N

0   100   200 Miles
0   100   200 Kilometers

Key
← First half of route
← Return route
— Present-day boundaries

Exploration Time Line

1672: Fur trader Louis Jolliet is chosen by French officials to explore the Mississippi River.

1672, December: Jolliet arrives at Michilimackinac and meets Jacques Marquette, a priest, at the mission there.

1673, May: The two men set out.

1673, spring: They carry their canoes overland between the Fox and Wisconsin rivers.

1673, June: The men enter the Mississippi River.

1673, July: They turn around just north of the present-day Louisiana border.

1673, summer and fall: The men enter the Illinois River, cross overland to meet the Chicago River, and travel up the shore of Lake Michigan.

▶ Marquette and Jolliet explored areas around rivers of the Midwest.

MAP SKILL Intermediate Direction *In what direction did the explorers travel along the Fox River?*

Trade Grows at French Forts

Where Marquette and Jolliet traveled, French fur traders soon followed. They built many forts in the Midwest, setting them up as trading posts. A **trading post** is a sort of store at which goods are bought and sold. The traders exchanged tools for fur from the Native Americans.

▶ **Cannon at a French trading post**

The Ottawa, Ojibwa, and Huron tribes brought furs to trade at the forts. Some Native Americans settled at the forts as well. In places where the soil was good, they farmed. They sold their extra crops to the traders at the nearby forts. They also made canoes.

Communities began to grow around the forts. Many of these communities eventually grew into major cities. Sault Sainte Marie and Chicago are two Midwestern cities that began as forts or trading posts. On the next page you can read how **Jean Baptiste Point Du Sable's** trading post became the city of Chicago.

REVIEW Describe some changes that took place as French fur traders came to the Midwest. **Sequence**

Summarize the Lesson

- **middle 1600s** Fur traders from France came to the Midwest.
- **1673** Marquette and Jolliet explored waterways.
- **Today** Cities stand on some sites where the French built forts.

LESSON 2 REVIEW

Check Facts and Main Ideas

1. 🔄 Cause and Effect Make a diagram like the one shown. Fill in the cause and effects.

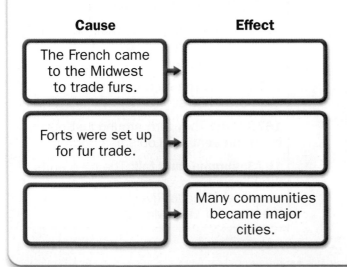

Cause	Effect
The French came to the Midwest to trade furs.	
Forts were set up for fur trade.	
	Many communities became major cities.

2. Why did the French come to the Midwest in the 1600s?

3. What did Jacques Marquette and Louis Jolliet do?

4. How did the French fur trade influence the settlement of the Midwest?

5. **Critical Thinking:** *Draw Conclusions* How did contact with Europeans both help and hurt the Native Americans?

Link to ⬮⬮ Writing

Write a Letter You are a French fur trader. Write a letter to your family in France describing your life at a fort in the Midwest. Use the terms **mission** and **trading post** in your letter.

JEAN BAPTISTE POINT DU SABLE

1745?–1818

Jean Baptiste Point Du Sable (Zhahn Bah TEEST Pwahnt DOO SAH Bluh) has been called "the father of Chicago." Born in Haiti, Du Sable was a black pioneer. In 1784 he brought his family to the shores of Lake Michigan, in a region the Algonquin Indians called "Chicago."

Du Sable's trading post grew to be the largest in the Midwest. It had a mill, a bakehouse, a dairy, a smokehouse, a workshop, a poultry house, a horse stable, and a barn. He sold items to all the trappers, traders, and loggers that passed through it. Soon Chicago became known as the best trading post for people living in Wisconsin and Michigan. Du Sable sent wheat, baked goods, meats, and furs to trading posts in Detroit and Canada. Soon Chicago became part of the trading route.

BIOFACT

The location of Jean Du Sable's trading post is now a busy intersection in Chicago.

Learn from Biographies

Chicago is located on Lake Michigan by the Chicago River. Why do you think Du Sable chose to build his trading post there?

For more information, go online to *Meet the People* at **www.sfsocialstudies.com**.

Trading for Goods

European countries explored North America looking for wealth. Many searched for gold. Although the French and English did not find gold, they found something almost as valuable: beaver fur.

British flag

French flag

Spanish flag

Chief Ho Nee Yeath Taw No Row

By 1750, the English had steady trade with some Native American nations. But the Iroquois, who traded with the French, handled most of the beaver fur. This helped the French control most of the fur trade. The conflict for control of the trade eventually helped lead to war between the French and English.

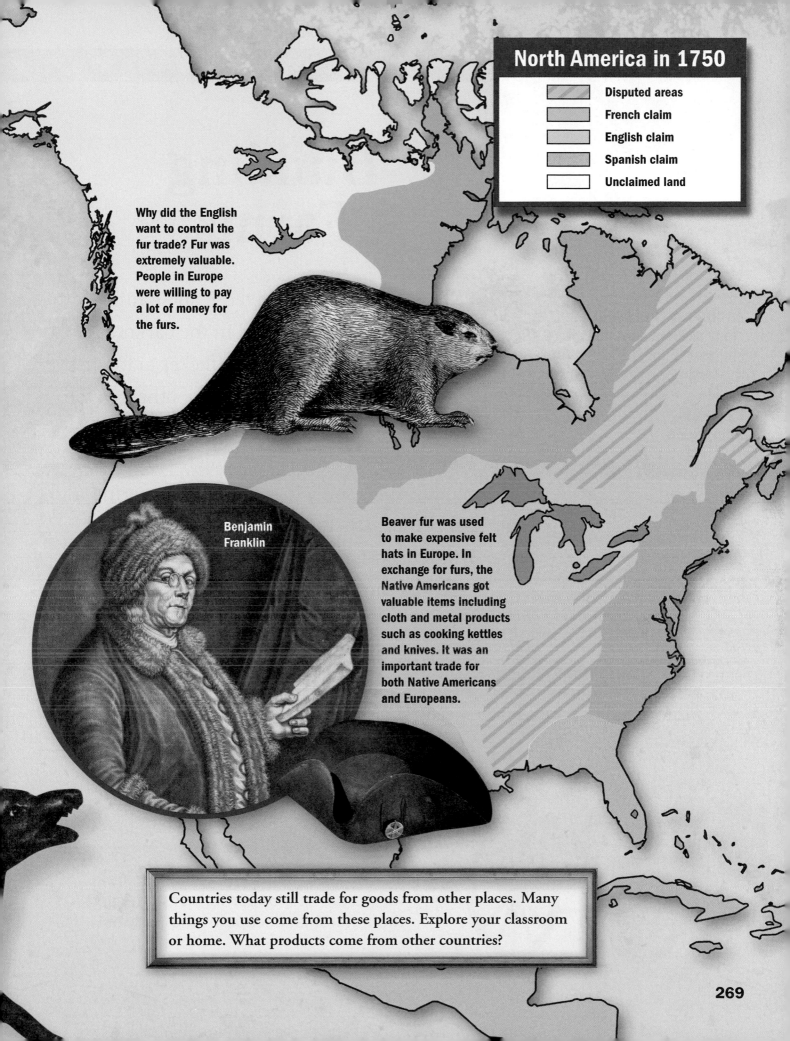

North America in 1750

Disputed areas
French claim
English claim
Spanish claim
Unclaimed land

Why did the English want to control the fur trade? Fur was extremely valuable. People in Europe were willing to pay a lot of money for the furs.

Benjamin Franklin

Beaver fur was used to make expensive felt hats in Europe. In exchange for furs, the Native Americans got valuable items including cloth and metal products such as cooking kettles and knives. It was an important trade for both Native Americans and Europeans.

Countries today still trade for goods from other places. Many things you use come from these places. Explore your classroom or home. What products come from other countries?

Wapello County

Building Farms

PREVIEW

Focus on the Main Idea
Many settlers came to the Midwest in the 1800s to farm the land.

PEOPLE
John Deere

VOCABULARY
sod
drought
Dust Bowl

PLACE
Wapello County, Iowa

▶ Covered wagon

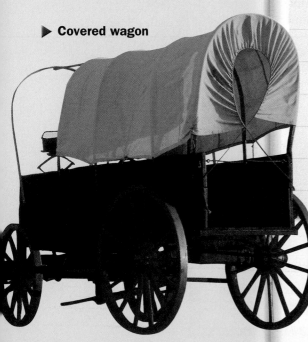

You Are There

You stand tense and waiting with your family. In the darkness of the night, the flicker of torches lights up the faces of hundreds of others in the crowd around you. A man near you cracks a joke, and people break into quiet laughter. A mother sings softly to soothe a whimpering baby. Your father pulls out his pocket watch. It will be just a few minutes now.

When the cannon fires, you and everyone around you will run forward to stake claims on the land. The date is May 1, 1843. The place is Wapello County, Iowa. You are part of a land rush. People enter an area at the same time to claim land for homes, farms, and businesses. Your family is among the first white settlers in this part of the state.

Cause and Effect As you read, look for ways that pioneer farmers changed the natural landscape of the Midwest.

Before the Settlers

The settlers of **Wapello County** were not rushing forward onto empty land. For many centuries, Native Americans had lived in this part of Iowa.

Some Native American groups of the Midwest had farmed. Others had hunted bison, or buffalo, that roamed the prairies. Still others had combined farming and bison hunting. Each group had claimed a particular area as its homeland. Throughout the 1600s and 1700s, the Europeans who had settled on the East Coast had been moving westward.

By the early 1800s, centuries of suffering had weakened many Native American groups. Then settlers started coming by the thousands to the Midwest. The United States forced Native Americans to sell their land to the government and move to reservations farther west. Once the Native Americans left, pioneers rushed in to claim the land.

REVIEW What were some factors that led some Native American groups in the Midwest to lose their land? **Main Idea and Details**

▶ **This painting shows settlers racing for their piece of land during a land rush.**

Starting a Farm, Building a Home

Almost all of the settlers who came to the Midwest in the early 1800s built farms. First, a settler claimed land by hammering a wooden stake into each of the four corners of the area. Then, the family built their home.

Midwestern farmhouses in the 1800s were small and simple. Most had a single room about the size of a modern living room. Most were log cabins, made of trees the farmers cut on their own land. However, some parts of the Midwest had very few trees. These regions were prairies. A prairie is a grassland that stretches for miles and miles. Many pioneers who settled on the prairie built homes out of **sod.** Sod is made of the grass, roots, and dirt that forms the ground's top layer. Settlers cut the prairie sod into thick bricks, stacking them to form walls. They rolled out sod strips to cover the roof.

Sod houses were warm in the winter and cool in the summer. But sod houses were small and hard to keep clean. Most families moved into wooden houses as soon as they could.

REVIEW Contrast the two main types of homes that Midwestern pioneers built. **Compare and Contrast**

▶ Some families lived in houses made of sod, such as the one pictured below.

Farming in the Midwest

In some parts of the Midwest, farming the land was easy. In many river valleys, Native Americans had already cleared the land for farm fields. The settlers who took over only had to

▶ Farmers in the Midwest in the 1800s used horse-drawn plows like this one.

On the Banks of Plum Creek

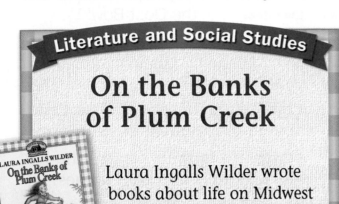

Laura Ingalls Wilder wrote books about life on Midwest farms in the 1800s. Many stories came from her family's experiences. This is a part of one book.

Laura went . . . into the dugout. It was one room, all white. The earth walls had been smoothed and whitewashed. The earth floor was smooth and hard.

When Ma and Mary stood in the doorway the light went dim. There was a small greased-paper window beside the door. But the wall was so thick that the light from the window stayed near the window.

That front wall was built of sod. Mr. Hanson had dug out his house, and then he had cut long strips of prairie sod and laid them on top of one another, to make the front wall. It was a good, thick wall with not one crack in it. No cold could get through that wall.

plant their own corn. In most places, farmers had to clear the land before they could plant. It took a lot of hard work to chop down trees and dig up the stumps to make a field.

In still other places, Midwestern farmers had to plow up the tough prairie sod. In the early 1800s this was not easy. The plows of the time had great difficulty breaking through the tangled prairie grass roots. In the 1850s farmers could get a new steel plow made by **John Deere.** Then, farming on the prairies became easier.

Many farmers raised cattle, pigs, and chickens. They made money by selling the animals or the milk or eggs the animals produced. In the early 1800s, farmers close to the Mississippi and other big rivers and lakes could ship farm products to the cities of the Northeast and the Southeast. In the mid-1800s, railroads were built across the Midwest. The region quickly became a center of farming and shipping, supplying the nation with food.

REVIEW What challenges did Midwestern settlers face and how could they overcome these challenges?
Main Idea and Details

Using Farm Land

Farmers who came to the Midwest in the 1800s did not realize that the way they farmed could harm the land. During times of little rain, or **drought,** the soil turned to dust and blew away in huge dust storms.

Years of drought struck the Midwest in the 1930s. Farmers suffered greatly. The area became known as the **Dust Bowl.** Soil from the Dust Bowl darkened the skies for weeks and even blew as far as the East Coast.

Today, farmers plow and plant in curves to help stop soil from washing or blowing away. They plant different crops to help keep the soil fertile. In

▶ **A family escaping from the Dust Bowl, 1936**

some areas, they have let the prairie grasses grow back.

REVIEW What did farmers do that contributed to the cause of the Dust Bowl?
🔄 **Cause and Effect**

Summarize the Lesson

• In the 1800s thousands of settlers came to the Midwest to start farms.

• Midwestern farmers cleared the land, plowed it, and built homes.

• Improved farm equipment allowed Midwestern farmers to become important food producers.

• Midwestern farmers learned better ways to farm the land.

LESSON 3 REVIEW

Check Facts and Main Ideas

1. 🔄 **Cause and Effect** Make a diagram like the one shown below. Complete it by listing the missing cause and effects.

Cause	Effect
Many settlers moved west, looking for opportunities. →	
The pioneer family would build a house and begin farming. →	
→	The **Dust Bowl** developed.

2. What affected Native Americans in the Midwest from the 1600s to the early 1800s?

3. What kind of houses did the pioneers build and why?

4. What effect did advances in technology in the mid-1800s have on the economy of the Midwest?

5. **Critical Thinking: *Draw Conclusions*** In the early and mid-1800s, money was scarce in the Midwest. What could a family with little money do to buy what they needed?

Link to 🔗 Art

Make a Mural With a partner, design a mural that shows the history of the Midwest from the 1600s to the 1800s.

JOHN DEERE
1804–1886

John Deere was a blacksmith who moved to Illinois from Vermont. A blacksmith is a craftsperson who makes and repairs metal items such as horseshoes and tools for working in the fields. The farmers in Illinois were always bringing in their iron plows for sharpening. Farmers complained that the thick clay soil stuck to the blade and made it dull. They couldn't plow more than a few furrows before they had to stop and clean the blade.

BIOFACT

To use John Deere's plow, the farmer walked behind it, holding the reins of the horse.

That gave Deere an idea. Deere used a broken steel saw to make the blade for his new plow. It worked much better than the old iron plow blades. John Deere was soon in the plow-making business. He called his steel plow the "Self-Polisher" because it stayed clean as it plowed the soil.

John Deere was an entrepreneur. An entrepreneur is someone who organizes and manages a new business. Today the company that John Deere founded is one of the largest manufacturers of farm equipment in the world.

Learn from Biographies

How did Deere use problem-solving skills to improve the plow?

For more information, go online to *Meet the People* at **www.sfsocialstudies.com.**

St. Louis • Cahokia

1804
Lewis and Clark
Expedition begins.

1869
Transcontinental
Railroad is
completed.

1950s
Interstate highway
system is built.

PREVIEW

Focus on the Main Idea
The Midwest has been a trade
and transportation hub, from
long ago to the present.

PLACES
St. Louis, Missouri
Cahokia, Illinois

PEOPLE
Meriwether Lewis
William Clark

VOCABULARY
mound
steamboat
hub
transcontinental railroad
Interstate highway system

Hub of the Nation

You Are There The tram ride is an exciting one, taking you up a steep, curved path to the top of the Arch. With each upward yank of cables, the round car twists and turns as it climbs the arch. When you get out of the tram, the view amazes you. You can see so many things! Barges that look like toys travel down the silver strip of the Mississippi River. You feel the slight sway of the Arch in the wind. Outside the other window you see the stadium. The guide announces that the tram is about to leave. You and two others pile into the egg-shaped car. As it cranks and juts forward, you smile at the thought that you were at the top of the Gateway Arch in St. Louis!

Cause and Effect As you read, look for events that caused the Midwest to become an important center for trade and transportation.

Cahokia

You can visit Monks Mound near Cahokia, Illinois. When Cahokia was at its peak, around A.D. 1100, about 20,000 people might have lived there. Archaeologists continue to dig up more of the mounds to learn about life in this ancient city.

Cahokia: Early Trade Center of the Midwest

If you are in the St. Louis area, you can spot them. The mounds were built by Native Americans who lived in the area more than 1,000 years ago. A mound is a pile of earth or stones. Some mounds were burial sites for important people. Other mounds were platforms where important members of the community built their homes. Still other mounds probably were places where ceremonies were held.

The biggest of these mounds is in Cahokia Mounds State Park in Illinois. Called Monks Mound, it is the largest structure built by any group of Native Americans north of Mexico. Monks Mound towered over a huge plaza.

Thousands of people gathered at the Cahokia plaza for festivals and perhaps for markets.

Cahokia was once a key trading center in the Midwest. It was close to the junction of three rivers—the Illinois, the Missouri, and the Mississippi. Traders from the Great Lakes area and from the western plains shipped copper, lead, and bison bones on these rivers to Cahokia. Southern traders in the Mississippi valley shipped shells, jewelry, and pottery to Cahokia. With its widespread trade, Cahokia was a meeting place of many cultures.

REVIEW What caused Cahokia to be a key trade center?
↻ **Cause and Effect**

A Gateway to the West

Native Americans were not the only people who used the area near present-day St. Louis as a center for trade. The French set up a fur-trade center there in the 1700s.

In the early 1800s, the United States bought the area from the French. Thomas Jefferson, who was the United States President at the time, wanted to expand trade. He also wanted to learn about the land and peoples of the West. He wanted to see if St. Louis could connect the Midwest not only with the Northeast and the Southeast, but with the West as well. He sent two explorers, **Meriwether Lewis** and **William Clark,** on an expedition to travel up the Missouri River to its source. Jefferson hoped that once they reached the source of this eastward-flowing river, Lewis and Clark would find a nearby river flowing westward all the way to the Pacific Ocean. With a water route to the Pacific Ocean, the United States could expand the fur trade. He asked Lewis and Clark to keep a record of their trip.

Lewis and Clark set out on their expedition from the area near St. Louis in 1804. On their way up the Missouri River, they met many different Native American groups. They tried to get each group to promise to trade with pioneers. They asked for advice on routes to the Pacific. Lewis and Clark had many adventures, as shown on the map on the facing page. However, they learned that there was no direct water route connecting the Midwest with the Pacific Ocean.

REVIEW What were two main goals of the Lewis and Clark expedition?
Main Idea and Details

▶ A page from Lewis's journal with his drawing of a sage grouse

▶ **William Clark**

▶ **Meriwether Lewis**

Map Adventure

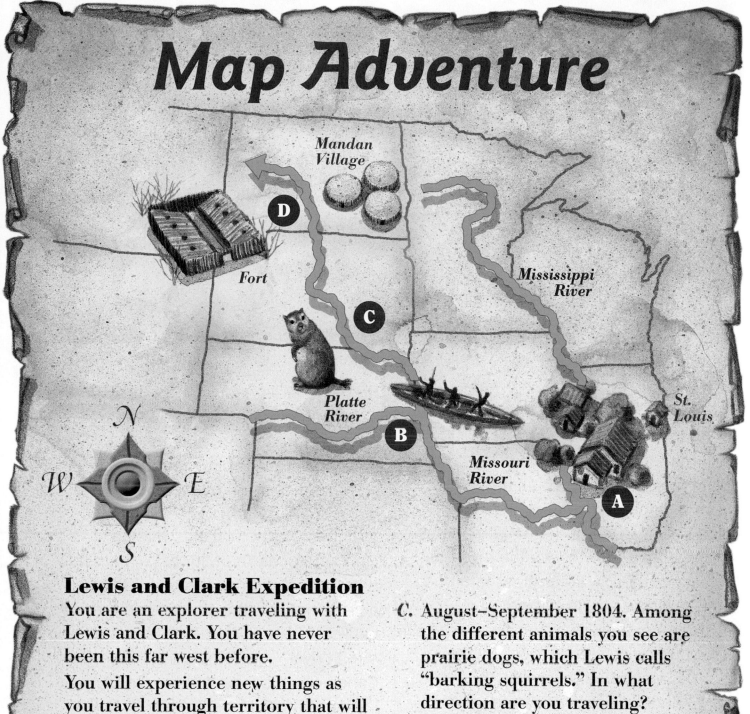

Lewis and Clark Expedition

You are an explorer traveling with Lewis and Clark. You have never been this far west before.

You will experience new things as you travel through territory that will some day form part of the Midwest. The following questions match locations on the map.

A. May 1804. You leave your camp near St. Louis to begin your up-river journey. What two rivers meet near the site of your camp?

B. July 1804. Your party reaches the Platte River. In what direction is St. Louis?

C. August–September 1804. Among the different animals you see are prairie dogs, which Lewis calls "barking squirrels." In what direction are you traveling?

D. October–November 1804. You encounter a grizzly bear. Two weeks later you feel the weather turning cold. Winter is coming. You help the party set up a fort by a Mandan Indian village. You will stay here until spring of 1805. In what direction will you go to return to St. Louis?

▶ A steamboat race on the Mississippi River in the early 1800s

Steamboats Chug Upstream

Within fifteen years of the Lewis and Clark expedition, St. Louis had grown from a small trading post into a bustling city. One of the main reasons for this rapid growth was the invention of steamboats. A **steamboat** is a boat powered by a steam engine.

Steamboats were bigger and faster than human-powered boats. By the 1820s, steamboats carrying tons of cargo and hundreds of passengers chugged up rivers at speeds as fast as 10 miles per hour. In the 1820s, that was very fast. Such steamboats turned the great rivers of the Midwest into major highways.

In the first three decades of the 1800s, the fur trade held the biggest share of St. Louis's shipping business. However, the steady stream of settlers coming into the region or heading westward from there also made business grow quickly. Farmers shipped their grain by steamboat to sell in markets in St. Louis.

By the 1830s St. Louis ran into competition as the Midwest's main hub of transportation and trade. A **hub** is a center of activity. Chicago, on the banks of Lake Michigan, became a strong rival. The completion of the Erie Canal, which connected the Great Lakes with the Hudson River in New York, drew business to Chicago. In time, the building of railroad lines across the United States would further increase competition between St. Louis and Chicago.

REVIEW How did the invention of steamboats affect the city of St. Louis? ↻ **Cause and Effect**

Railroads Crisscross the Nation

By the mid-1800s the steamboat was no longer the most modern form of transportation. Railroads had several advantages over water transportation. Rail lines could be built almost anywhere. Weather also did not affect train travel as much as it did travel on steamboats. Ice generally would not keep the trains from running. But ice-clogged rivers stopped steamboat traffic for months during Midwestern winters.

In the 1860s the United States government decided to help build a transcontinental railroad. Such a rail line would cross the entire country. While the Civil War was raging, Congress planned a northern route for the railroad. Since Chicago was farther north, it became a more important rail center than St. Louis. In 1869 the transcontinental railroad was completed.

Railroads remained important for travel and trade for almost a century. But by the middle 1900s, cars and trucks had taken over as the main form of transportation in the United States.

REVIEW How did the Civil War affect transportation decisions made at that time? ⟳ **Cause and Effect**

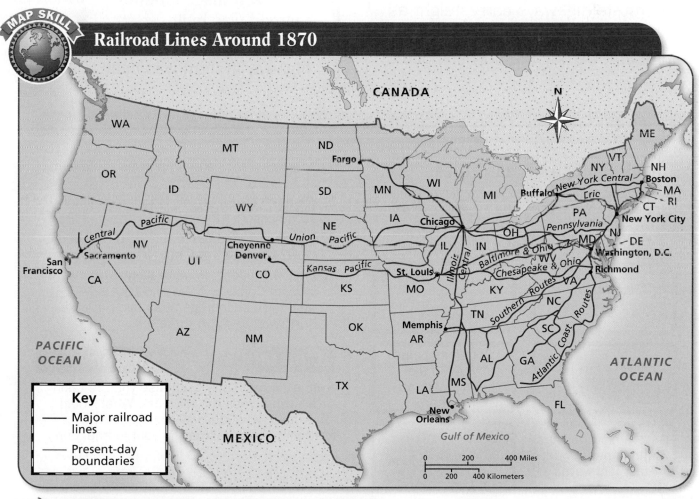

MAP SKILL

Railroad Lines Around 1870

Key
— Major railroad lines
— Present-day boundaries

▶ In 1869 the transcontinental railroad was completed.

MAP SKILL Use a Transportation Map *What rail lines would you have taken to go from Chicago to Sacramento?*

Superhighways Span the States

In the early 1900s automobiles began to catch on in the United States. People liked being able to travel when they wanted to instead of following a railroad schedule. However, there were few good roads.

The government started building better roads for automobiles in the early 1900s. By the 1950s the government decided that the nation needed a set of wide, fast, interconnecting highways to link all the states. They built the **Interstate highway system**, commonly called superhighways.

Interstate highways carry freight as well as car passengers. Most of the things that we buy are now shipped by truck over the interstate highways. Because of the Midwest's central location, its highways are important for trade.

REVIEW What effect did the building of interstate highways have on shipping? ⟳ **Cause and Effect**

Summarize the Lesson

- **More than 1,000 years ago** Native Americans built mounds at Cahokia.
- **1804** Lewis and Clark set out to find a water route to the Pacific Ocean.
- **1820s** Steamboats carried trade on rivers in the Midwest.
- **1869** A transcontinental railroad was built.
- **1950s** The Interstate highway system was built.

LESSON 4 ‹ REVIEW

Check Facts and Main Ideas

1. ⟳ **Cause and Effect** Make a diagram like the one shown. Complete it by filling in the cause and effects.

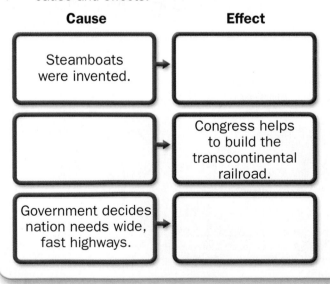

Cause	Effect
Steamboats were invented.	
	Congress helps to build the transcontinental railroad.
Government decides nation needs wide, fast highways.	

2. Why was Cahokia an important trade center around 1100?

3. What did the Lewis and Clark expedition accomplish?

4. How did **steamboat** traffic help St. Louis to grow? Use the word **hub** in your answer.

5. **Critical Thinking:** *Point of View* If you were living in Chicago in the mid-1800s, why would you encourage a relative from the Northeast to move there?

Link to ⟳ Writing

Write a Journal Entry Suppose you are taking a train trip across the Midwest. What would you write in your journal? Use the term **transcontinental railroad** in your journal entry.

MARK TWAIN

1835–1910

Mark Twain's real name was Samuel Langhorne Clemens. Mark Twain was one of America's most popular writers. He grew up in the small, riverfront town of Hannibal, Missouri. According to Twain, life in Hannibal centered on the steamboats that visited daily. Twain's love of the great river began when he took a trip downstream, intending to go to South America.

Halley's Comet appeared in 1835, the year that Mark Twain was born. The next time it appeared was 1910, the year that Twain died.

Twain started his career in writing when he worked as a printer's assistant. His first story was about life on the Mississippi.

However, Twain longed to work on the steamboats. In 1859 he became a steamboat pilot and worked on the river for another two years. Twain's years on the Mississippi gave him many stories to tell. It also gave him his pen name. On the riverboats the crew measured the depth of the water using a rope with flags. When someone shouted, "Mark one," the rope went down to its first mark. At this measurement, the water was six feet deep. At "mark twain" the rope was at its second mark. "Mark Twain," or twelve feet, meant the water was deep enough for riverboats to travel safely. Samuel Clemens took this riverboat cry as his name. It represented his love for the Mississippi and the riverboats.

Learn from Biographies

In what ways did working on a steamboat help Twain in the career he later chose as a writer?

For more information go online to *Meet the People* at **www.sfsocialstudies.com**.

CHAPTER **9**

REVIEW

1800   1810   1820

1804
Lewis and Clark
expedition began.

1820s
Steamboats
travel on rivers.

Chapter Summary

 Cause and Effect

Make a diagram like the one shown at the right. Complete the empty boxes.

▶ **Ojibwa hunting tools**

Cause	Effect
In the Ojibwa homeland, forests were too thick for farming.	
	Farmers used available materials such as sod to build homes.
Interstate highways are built.	

Vocabulary

Match each word with the correct definition or description.

1 **mission** (p. 265)

2 **sod** (p. 270)

3 **drought** (p. 272)

4 **transcontinental railroad** (p. 281)

5 **interstate highway system** (p. 282)

a. little precipitation over a long period

b. rail lines that cross the country

c. roads that link all states

d. a settlement set up by a religious group

e. earth materials used for building

People

Describe each person, and tell why each has been important in the Midwest region.

1 **Jacques Marquette** (p. 265)

2 **Jean Baptiste Point Du Sable** (p. 266)

3 **John Deere** (p. 273)

4 **Meriwether Lewis** (p. 278)

5 **Mark Twain** (p. 283)

1830	1840	1850	1860	1870

1843
Wapello County
land rush

1869
Transcontinental
railroad was completed.

Facts and Main Ideas

Write your answers on a separate sheet of paper.

1 How did the Ojibwa of the 1600s adapt to living in the northern Great Lakes region?

2 **Main Idea** Why was the fur trade very important to the Midwest?

3 **Main Idea** What was the result of special treaties the Ojibwa had with the United States government?

4 **Main Idea** Why were Cahokia and St. Louis good places for trade?

5 What advances in technology and transportation in the mid-1800s helped Midwestern farmers be successful?

6 **Time Line** About how many years were there between the Lewis and Clark expedition and the Wapello County land rush in Iowa?

7 **Critical Thinking:** *Make Generalizations* How can the Midwest be called the "Hub of the Country"?

Write About History

1 **Write an advertisement** for your favorite form of transportation. Include pictures and a slogan or a plan for a videotape.

2 **Write a diary entry** telling what it was like for someone your age to live in the Midwest some time long ago. You might be a member of a Native American family or a member of a pioneer family.

3 **Write a story** from the point of view of a railroad worker living in what is today South Dakota, near the Missouri River. Describe the changes you hope to see in the area after the tracks are laid.

Apply Skills

Using a Search Engine

Look at the following list to be used to search the Web for information:

- Samuel L. Clemens
- Hannibal, Missouri
- Steamboats
- Famous American writers

1 What is this research probably about?

2 What other words and phrases might you add to the list? Why?

3 Would you be more likely to find the information you want at a .gov, .com, or .edu site? Why?

Create your own list of search terms for another topic in the chapter.

Search Engine

search keyword
Mark Twain

Internet Activity

To get help with vocabulary, people, and terms, select the dictionary or encyclopedia from *Social Studies Library* at **www.sfsocialstudies.com.**

End with a Song

I've Been Working on the Railroad

People came from many countries to build the railroads that cross the United States. In the 1800s men worked to the rhythm of this song as they laid the first railroad tracks.

Work Song from the United States

A *With a swing*

I've been work-ing on the rail - road, All the live-long day;

I've been work-ing on the rail - road, Just to pass the time a - way.

Don't you hear the whis-tle blow - ing? Rise up so ear-ly in the morn.

Don't you hear the cap-tain shout - ing: "Di - nah, blow your horn!"

B G
Di - nah, won't you blow,
C
Di - nah won't you blow,

D₇
Di - nah, won't you blow your
1. G
horn? _____
2. G
horn?

C G
Some - one's in the kitch - en with Di - nah,

G
Some-one's in the kitch - en, I
D₇
know. _____

G
Some-one's in the kitch-en with Di - nah,
C
D₇
Strum-min' on the old ban - jo.
G

G
Fee, fie, fid-dle-ee i o,
3
fee, fie, fid-dle-ee i o, _____
3
D₇

slight ritard
G
Fee, fie, fid-dle-ee i o,
3
a tempo
C
D₇
Strum-min' on the old ban - jo.
G

287

Review

Test Talk

Look for details to support your answer.

Main Ideas and Vocabulary

TEST PREP

Read the passage below and use it to answer the questions that follow.

The Midwest region is at the center of the United States. Its waterways connect the Midwest to the rest of the United States and to the world.

In the 1700s the French came to the Midwest region. The French also used the waterways for trade. They built fur-trading posts on the rivers. These trading posts grew into large cities.

In the early and mid-1800s, many people traveled on waterways as they settled in the Midwest. However, in the 1900s, automobiles began to catch on in America. People liked being able to travel when they wanted to instead of following a railroad schedule. Soon the Interstate highway system was developed.

The Midwest has served as a center, or hub, of transportation. In the early 1800s steamboats brought traffic to the region's many rivers and lakes. In the mid-1800s railroads became the most popular form of transportation. Trains from the Northeast and Southeast regions connected to trains going westward. Today the vast superhighways carry traffic across the country.

1 According to the passage, which became large cities?
  A Native American hunting grounds
  B French fur-trading posts
  C farms beside the Great Lakes
  D railroad repair yards

2 In the passage the phrase Interstate highway system means
  A a large road
  B transportation
  C a set of roads that connect states
  D traffic jams

3 The passage as a whole illustrates
  A how the Midwest became a transportation hub
  B how the Midwest became popular
  C why people chose to move to the Midwest
  D why wheels also have hubs

4 In the passage the word superhighways means
  A the waterways of the Midwest
  B the Midwest's central locations
  C unpaved roads
  D large roads that carry goods and people across the country

People and Places

Match each person or term with its description.

1 **Illinois Waterway** (p. 234)

2 **Cahokia** (p. 277)

3 **Louis Jolliet** (p. 265)

4 **Jean Baptiste Point Du Sable** (p. 267)

5 **William Clark** (p. 278)

a. canoed down the Mississippi River to claim land for France

b. traveled the Missouri River

c. connects Lake Michigan to Mississippi River

d. built a trading post in area that became Chicago

e. ancient city that was a center of trade

Apply Skills

Make a Bar Graph There is an Arts Camp located in Michigan. Students from all over the United States attend this camp. With the following data, create a bar graph showing how many students come from each state:

The number of students ranges from 0–400.

73 from Florida
225 from Illinois
50 from Indiana
350 from Michigan
60 from New York
140 from Ohio

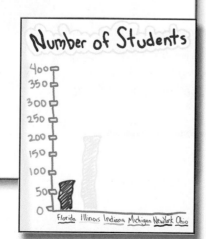

Write and Share

Write a Poem As a class write a poem about how the Midwest has changed from the 1600s to the present. Divide up the centuries and form small groups to write a stanza about each time division. Decide whether or not you want your poem to rhyme. After all the groups have finished writing their stanzas, get together with the other groups and read your stanzas in time order.

Read on Your Own

Look for books like these in the library:

UNIT 4 Project

Point of View

People often have different ideas about one topic. Take sides and discuss different points of view.

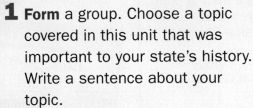

1 **Form** a group. Choose a topic covered in this unit that was important to your state's history. Write a sentence about your topic.

2 **Find** two sides of the topic. Write sentences with facts that support each side.

3 **Decide** who will argue each side.

4 **Debate** your topic for the class.

Internet Activity

Explore the Midwest on the Internet. Go to **www.sfsocialstudies.com/activities** and select your grade and unit.

The Southwest

Why might people want to live in or visit the Southwest?

"... **keep it for your children, your children's children, and for all who come after you ...**"

—President Theodore Roosevelt, May 6, 1903, on his first visit to the Grand Canyon.

Edward H. Potthast's 1910 painting, *The Grand Canyon*, pictures the vast area of the canyon.

Welcome to the Southwest

Key
★ State capital
— National border

WY

NE

UT

CO

KS

MO

Lake Powell

ROCKY MOUNTAINS

Lake Mead

NV

GRAND CANYON

Santa Fe ★

OKLAHOMA

Arkansas River

AR

CA

ARIZONA

Colorado River

NEW MEXICO

Oklahoma City ★

Lake Texoma

Red River

★ Phoenix

Gila River

SONORAN DESERT

Pecos River

TEXAS

Brazos River

Colorado River

LA

Rio Grande

Austin ★

MEXICO

N

Gulf of California

Gulf of Mexico

0	125	250 Miles
0	125	250 Kilometers

▶ Yellow blossoms of the prickly pear cactus can be seen throughout the Southwest.

▶ This bowl was made by the Anasazi, a group of Native Americans who lived in Arizona and New Mexico long ago.

▶ The roadrunner, the state bird of New Mexico, prefers running to flying. It can run as fast as 17 miles per hour.

▶ Astronauts are trained at Johnson Space Center in Houston, Texas, for the work they will do in space.

▶ A boy rides a sheep during an Oklahoma rodeo event.

▶ The Lighthouse is one of the rock formations in Palo Duro Canyon in Texas.

The Southwest

Draw Conclusions

Authors do not always tell you everything. Instead, they may give you a few details about what happens and expect you to draw conclusions.

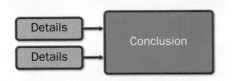

- A conclusion is a decision you reach after you think about details that you have read.

- You can use the details and what you already know about a subject to draw conclusions about it.

Read the paragraph at the right. The **conclusion** was reached from the **details** in the paragraph.

The Grand Canyon is one of the nation's most popular national parks. In the year 2000, almost 5 million people visited the park. Most of them drove there in their cars, but the park does not have many roads or parking spaces. This combination caused traffic jams. Park managers concluded that they must find a better way for tourists to travel in the park.

Word Exercise

Inferring Meaning Sometimes the same word can be used as two different parts of speech. Knowing the meaning of the word when it is used as one part of speech can help you understand the meaning of the word when it is used as another part of speech. For example, the verb *preserve* means to keep something safe. Sometimes, people create a place where animals and plants can be kept safe. The name of this place is a noun, and if you remembered what it means to **preserve** something, you would know exactly what this place was for as soon as you heard its name. It's called a **preserve**.

Draw Conclusions About the Grand Canyon

After Major John Wesley Powell explored the Grand Canyon and wrote reports about his trip, many people became interested in this natural wonder. Miners came to search for minerals. Tourists came to see the wonders Powell had written about. Some miners found that there was more wealth in guiding tourists than in digging for minerals.

In 1882, the United States government began a movement to protect the canyon. A bill was introduced in Congress to make the Grand Canyon a national park. It took more than thirty years for the Grand Canyon to win this honor. In the meantime, the area became the Grand Canyon Forest Preserve. Mining and cutting trees for lumber were still allowed.

In 1903, President Theodore Roosevelt visited the Grand Canyon. He was impressed by its beauty. He said, "Leave it as it is. . . . keep it for your children, your children's children, and for all who come after you as one of the great sights which every American . . . should see." In 1908, the Grand Canyon became a national monument. Then, in 1919, part of the Grand Canyon became a national park.

Apply it!

Use the reading strategy of drawing conclusions to answer questions 1 and 2. Then answer the vocabulary question.

1 Why did the government make the Grand Canyon a national park?

2 Do you think that the Grand Canyon should have been made a national park? Why or why not?

3 What does the name "Grand Canyon Forest Preserve" mean? How can you tell?

CHAPTER 10

Land and Resources of the Southwest

1

2

3

CANADA

1

2

Grand
Canyon
National
Park

UNITED STATES

3

PACIFIC OCEAN

Saguaro
National
Park

ATLANTIC
OCEAN

Beaumont

Gulf of Mexico

MEXICO

Why We Remember

When you think of the Southwest, what images come to mind? The Painted Desert? The Grand Canyon? Majestic mountains? Sunny, warm climate? If you thought of any of these, you would be right! The Southwest has a varied climate, unusual plants, and amazing landforms, including one of the seven natural wonders of the world—the Grand Canyon. It also has state-of-the-art technology and much more. Turn the page and find out just what the Southwest has to offer.

Grand Canyon National Park

ARIZONA

A Land of Canyons

PREVIEW

Focus on the Main Idea
The Grand Canyon dazzles visitors with its size and beauty.

PLACES
Grand Canyon National Park

PEOPLE
García López de Cárdenas
Francisco Vásquez de Coronado
John Wesley Powell
Theodore Roosevelt

VOCABULARY
adobe
pueblo

You Are There

Finally, you are going hiking in the Grand Canyon. You can feel the excitement as your guide signals the beginning of your adventure down Bright Angel Trail. As you look down you think, "I'd better watch my step, or I might find myself down there faster than I planned." On the rim, two mule deer pass by. Out from behind a fallen boulder some rock squirrels chase one another. Overhead a beautiful butterfly flits through the air. Below you in the canyon, some jet black ravens roll and tumble like acrobats. What an adventure this is going to be!

▶ **Binoculars**

Draw Conclusions As you read, draw conclusions about why the Grand Canyon attracts so many tourists.

The Role of Erosion

Scientists still don't know exactly how the Grand Canyon was formed. What they do know is that erosion played a part in it. This gradual process of wearing away soil and rock can be caused by gravel and sand, by water from rushing rivers, by rainwater, by melting and moving glaciers, and even by the wind.

Many scientists think that the rushing water of the Colorado River helped dissolve and wear away the rock of the Grand Canyon. The sand, gravel, and boulders carried by the river most likely helped cut the canyon as well. Rainwater also causes erosion by dissolving certain kinds of rock, such as limestone, causing it to wear away.

Wind may also play a part in the canyon's continued erosion. Sand is often picked up by wind and blown against the canyon's walls. If you have felt sand, you know how sharp its edges can be. Blowing sand can wear away the surface of the rock.

Because erosion takes place all the time, the Grand Canyon may never stop changing. However, these changes happen very slowly—over thousands of years. Hikers and visitors may never see any changes at all.

REVIEW How might the canyon continue to change because of erosion? ↻ **Draw Conclusions**

▶ Rafting through the Grand Canyon on the Colorado River is an exciting experience. The river's swift waters helped carve the canyon.

People and the Canyon

For centuries, people have hunted, farmed, and lived around the Grand Canyon. Scientists have found artifacts in the canyon that are more than 3,000 years old.

Hundreds of years ago, people we call the Anasazi (ah nuh SAH zee) lived in the Southwest and as far north as Colorado. Some lived near the Grand Canyon. *Anasazi* means "ancient ones" in the Navajo language.

The Anasazi were skilled basket makers and potters. They also built networks of roads. Anasazi farmers built irrigation systems to bring water to their crops.

Some Anasazi homes were one- or two-story houses of **adobe,** or mud brick. The Anasazi also built large, apartment-like homes on cliffs. These cliff dwellings had many rooms and housed many families.

Native Americans still live in the canyon area today. Some, such as the Pueblo peoples, may be the descendants of the Anasazi. **Pueblo** means "village" in Spanish. Some Pueblo still live in villages of adobe homes similar to those of the Anasazi.

The Havasupai (hah vah SOO peye) live in Havasu Canyon, a part of the Grand Canyon. *Havasupai* means "people of the blue-green water." There are no roads to their reservation, only hiking and mule

▶ **Anasazi buildings within Grand Canyon**

trails. Even so, tourists hike or ride in to see the beautiful waterfalls and blue-green pools along Havasu Creek.

Spanish explorer Captain **García López de Cárdenas** (CAR deh nas) and a small band of soldiers were the first Europeans to see the Grand Canyon. Their leader, **Francisco Vásquez de Coronado,** explored the Southwest in search of gold. He had heard rumors of a great river that flowed through a golden canyon. Coronado sent Cárdenas and the soldiers to see if the rumors were true. In 1540, they found the river and the canyon, but no gold.

There was not much interest in the Grand Canyon until 1869, when Major **John Wesley Powell** explored it. He made a dangerous trip by boat down the Colorado River and through the canyon. His report led others to want to see this natural wonder. Powell was the first to call it the "Grand Canyon."

In the 1880s, miners came to the canyon in search of zinc, copper, lead, and other minerals, but the steep canyon walls made mining difficult. At the same time, tourists came to see the Grand Canyon. Some miners began taking tourists into the canyon. They charged for the tour.

In 1903, President **Theodore Roosevelt** visited the Grand Canyon. He wanted to preserve its beauty for years to come. In 1919, part of the Grand Canyon became a national park.

REVIEW Why did Spanish explorers come to the Grand Canyon?
Draw Conclusions

FACT FILE

Grand Canyon Facts

- The Grand Canyon is about 277 miles long and about 6,000 feet deep at its deepest point. That is the height of four Sears Towers.

- At its widest point, the Grand Canyon is more than 18 miles wide.

- At the South Rim the average temperature in July is 69°F. In the same month, the average temperature on the canyon floor is 92°F.

▶ Guided mule rides below the rim are popular with tourists to Grand Canyon National Park.

Visiting the Grand Canyon

If you visit Grand Canyon National Park, you can walk along the rim of the canyon to see the breathtaking view. You can hike into the canyon on one of the trails. Park rangers can tell you about the wildlife and earth science of the canyon. You can also explore the site of a Native American village.

REVIEW Why do people want to visit the Grand Canyon? ⟳ Draw Conclusions

Summarize the Lesson

- The Grand Canyon is a magnificent landform.
- Erosion carved out and is still carving the features of the canyon.
- Native Americans, Spanish explorers, miners, and tourists have played a part in the history of the Grand Canyon.

LESSON 1 REVIEW

Check Facts and Main Ideas

1. ⟳ Draw Conclusions On a separate sheet of paper, write a conclusion about people living in the Grand Canyon from the details given.

Details

Scientists have found artifacts in the canyon that are over 3,000 years old.

The Anasazi lived in and near the Grand Canyon hundreds of years ago.

Native Americans live in the canyon area today.

Conclusion

2. What is the Grand Canyon and why do so many people travel to the Grand Canyon each year?

3. How might the Grand Canyon have been formed?

4. How does erosion affect the Grand Canyon today?

5. Critical Thinking: *Predict* How might the Grand Canyon be different today if the Grand Canyon National Park had not been formed?

Link to ∞ Science

Do Research About Erosion Erosion can help create beautiful landforms, such as the Grand Canyon. It can also wear away topsoil needed for growing crops. Find out about other landforms that may have been shaped by erosion. Share your findings with classmates.

John Wesley Powell   *1834–1902*

The year was 1869. Major John Wesley Powell gathered nine brave men and four sturdy boats to take a trip through nearly a thousand miles of canyons.

Powell had lost part of his right arm in the Civil War, but that didn't stop him. This journey had been a lifelong dream of this college professor and geologist. On May 24, 1869, Powell and his crew set off on the Green River in Wyoming.

Nearly two months into the trip, the crew reached the place where the Green River meets the Colorado River in Utah. The Colorado River is rough with many dangerous rapids as it passes through the Grand Canyon.

By August 29, 1869, Powell and his crew had braved the danger and traveled through the Grand Canyon! Powell made the first scientific exploration of the Grand Canyon. His account of the canyon sparked interest in this awe-inspiring landform. In a report about his trip he wrote,

BIOFACT

A chair was tied to Powell's boat so that he could see ahead and signal the other boats.

> *"The Grand Canyon is a land of song. . . . This is the music of waters."*

Learn from Biographies

Powell was a scientist who kept a detailed journal of his trip. How do you think this journal influenced people?

For more information, go online to *Meet the People* **www.sfsocialstudies.com.**

Thinking Skills

Make Generalizations

What? A generalization is a statement that applies to many examples. It explains how many facts have one idea in common. Sometimes, clue words such as *all, most, some, none,* and *many* signal the use of a generalization.

In Lesson 1, you learned these facts:

Peoples of the Grand Canyon	What they did there
Anasazi	Lived and farmed
Spanish Explorers	Looked for gold
John Wesley Powell	Explored

From these statements of fact, you can form this generalization:

Many different people have lived in or explored the Grand Canyon.

▶ **Anasazi cliff dwellings**

Why? Generalizations help you see the big picture. They make it easier for you to remember many facts. They help you understand new information.

How? To make a generalization, you need to identify the topic and gather facts about it. Then you figure out what these facts have in common. Finally, you make one statement that is true for all the information.

This passage is about tourists and the Grand Canyon:

There are six lodges and three campgrounds on the South Rim of the Grand Canyon. Two main roads lead into the South Rim, which is open year-round. Only one road leads to the tourist area on the North Rim, which has only one lodge and one campground. Because of snow, the North Rim is closed from late autumn until mid-spring. Most tourists to the Grand Canyon visit the South Rim.

The last sentence of the paragraph is a generalization. Based on the information, it is a valid generalization—one that is supported by facts.

Think and Apply

Based on the paragraph about the Grand Canyon at left, which of the following statements are valid **generalizations** and which are not valid? Why?

❶ The South Rim of the Grand Canyon is more beautiful than the North Rim.

❷ There is more traffic at the South Rim.

❸ Park rangers would rather work at the North Rim.

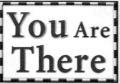

ARIZONA

Saguaro
National Park

Climates in the Southwest

Focus on the Main Idea
The Southwest climate can vary greatly. It is dry in some places and moist in others.

PLACES
Sonoran Desert
Saguaro National Park

VOCABULARY
arid
savanna

► The tiny elf owl may nest in a hole in the trunk of a saguaro cactus.

You Are There You are walking outside on a hot summer day. You are wearing a hat, but you can still feel the sun beating down on your head. You think, "Whew, it's really hot! But I'm not sweating." Even the air around you feels dry. You take out your water bottle and take a long drink. That cool water tastes good!

You look around and see plants growing here. You wonder, "Where did that squirrel come from?" You notice birds flitting from one cactus to another. You think, "How can living things survive in such a hot, dry climate? Where do they get the water they need to live?"

Draw Conclusions As you read, draw some conclusions about living in a climate that is hot and dry.

A Region of Varied Climates

The Southwest region has a variety of climates with wide differences in temperature and precipitation. Some parts of the Southwest are deserts. Remember, a desert is an area that gets less than ten inches of rain each year. The rains may come in heavy downpours, but they don't last long.

Some parts of the Southwest have an **arid** climate. They are dry, but are not deserts. For example, parts of Arizona, Oklahoma, New Mexico, and Texas receive more than ten inches of rain each year, but they are still very dry. These areas might go for a long time without rain.

Because Texas is so large, the state has several types of climate. The eastern part of Texas has a hot, humid climate. Western Texas is also hot, but it is usually dry.

Oklahoma sometimes has humid and windy weather. When cold and warm air masses meet over the state, Oklahoma can experience thunderstorms, blizzards, or tornadoes.

REVIEW How would you describe the climate of the Southwest?
Main Idea and Details

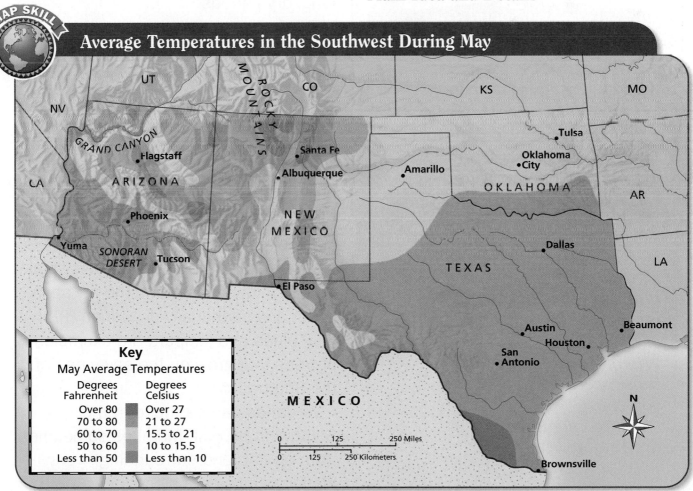

MAP SKILL

Average Temperatures in the Southwest During May

Key
May Average Temperatures

Degrees Fahrenheit	Degrees Celsius
Over 80	Over 27
70 to 80	21 to 27
60 to 70	15.5 to 21
50 to 60	10 to 15.5
Less than 50	Less than 10

► **Temperatures in the Southwest vary greatly during the month of May.**

MAP SKILL Use a Climate Map *What Southwestern state has the highest average temperatures in May? Which states in the Southwest have the lowest average temperature in May?*

Plants of the Southwest

The saguaro (sa WAR oh) is a kind of cactus that grows naturally in the **Sonoran Desert,** which stretches through Arizona, parts of Mexico, and southern California. This cactus is the symbol of the Southwest. Its white, night-blooming blossom is Arizona's state flower. You can see many of these spectacular plants in **Saguaro National Park** near Tucson, Arizona.

The saguaro is well suited for living in the desert. To grow big and strong, the saguaro spreads its long, shallow roots to drink in the rainwater. Its

▶ **Saguaro in the Sonoran Desert**

ribbed trunk and branches expand to store water. The saguaro can store enough water to stay alive through long, dry periods.

The saguaro's relationship with desert animals is good for all. The saguaro provides shelter for gila woodpeckers, elf owls, bluebirds, warblers, cactus wrens, wood rats, and lizards. Many animals return the favor by eating insects that could cause disease and destroy the saguaro.

Other types of plants grow in a climate region of the Southwest called a savanna. A **savanna** is a grassy plain on which few trees grow. The savanna is hot and seasonally dry. Piñon (PIN yon) pines and junipers are examples of trees that grow on the savannas of the Southwest.

Wetlands can be found in the Southwest as well. Marshes sometimes form on flat land surrounding rivers. Wetlands provide a place for water birds such as ducks and cranes.

Literature and Social Studies

The Desert Is Theirs

Byrd Baylor collected folktales from the Southwest. Here is part of a poem based on a tale told by the Papago people who live in the Sonoran Desert.

*Even then
Coyote
was around
giving advice
and scattering seeds
on the sides
of hills.
Where he dropped
those seeds,
you see
saguaro cactus
growing now.*

▶ A Southwestern Savanna

▶ Wetlands in Bosque del Apache National Wildlife Refuge in New Mexico

Marsh plants include reeds, grasses, and wild grains.

REVIEW Name three types of plants that grow in the Southwest.
Main Idea and Details

Summarize the Lesson

- **Much of the Southwest has an arid climate, but not all of the region is desert.**

- **The saguaro is a cactus that is well suited to growing in the Sonoran Desert of the Southwest.**

LESSON 2   REVIEW

Check Facts and Main Ideas

1. ⊙ Draw Conclusions Make a diagram like the one shown. Draw a conclusion about the saguaro from the facts given in the diagram.

Details

Its roots spread wide to drink in rainwater.

Its trunk and branches expand to store water.

Animals help the saguaro by eating harmful insects.

Conclusion

2. How does the climate of the Southwest vary?

3. In what area of the Southwest do the saguaro grow?

4. Describe a **savanna.**

5. Critical Thinking: *Make Generalizations* What do plants and animals of the Southwest have in common?

Link to ⌯⌯ Writing

Describe the Climate Write a postcard to a friend describing the climate of the Southwest. On the front of the postcard, draw a picture to show what the Southwest is like. Use the word **arid** in your postcard message.

Sonoran Desert

Nyiri Desert

▶ The saguaro cactus begins to bloom when it is 50 to 75 years old.

Giant Plants

The saguaro cactus is a large plant that grows in the Sonoran Desert in the Southwest. Giant plants grow in many other places in the world. The giant baobab tree grows in the Nyiri Desert and on the savannas of Africa. The baobab has a very wide trunk. Both the saguaro and the baobab tree can grow as tall as 60 feet. Many different animals make their homes in both the saguaro and the baobab.

▶ Most saguaros grow their first branches after they are 80 years old.

Big Hug for a Big Tree It would take about 15 students touching hands to go all around the trunk of an average baobab.

▶ People and animals, including bats, use the hollowed-out trunk of the baobab for shelter.

▶ The trunk of the baobab tree can be 30 feet wide.

Comparison Height Graph

Height in Feet

60
50
40
30
20
10
0

saguaro cactus   baobab tree   4th grade student   4 story townhouse

Los Alamos
Albuquerque
Beaumont
Houston

Oil and Technology

Preview

Focus on the Main Idea
The Southwest is a region of discovery and research.

PLACES
Beaumont, Texas
Albuquerque, New Mexico
Los Alamos, New Mexico
Houston, Texas

PEOPLE
Pattillo Higgins
Anthony Lucas

VOCABULARY
gusher
refinery

You Are There It's 10:30 in the morning on January 10, 1901. You're watching a crew drilling on Spindletop Hill near Beaumont, Texas. All of a sudden the earth begins to rumble. All at once, mud begins gushing from the ground! Drilling string and pieces of equipment fly high into the air. Then comes the oil! Everyone runs for cover. Safe at last, but covered with oil, the drillers rejoice. "We have struck 'black gold'!"

▶ Gusher at Spindletop

Draw Conclusions As you read, draw conclusions about how oil and technology play an important role in the economy of the Southwest.

Using Oil

The gusher at Spindletop had an effect on Texas history. A **gusher** is an oil well that produces a large amount of oil. After the gusher at Spindletop many people came to Texas in search of oil and natural gas. By 1902, more than 500 Texas companies were doing business in **Beaumont** and other Texas towns.

Pattillo Higgins, a businessman and scientist, thought that there might be oil beneath Spindletop. He saw signs that there might be natural gas in the area. He thought if there was underground gas, there might also be oil. Higgins hired **Anthony Lucas,** a mining engineer, to drill at Spindletop.

Lucas's crew drilled the gusher.

Oil comes out of the ground in the form of a thick, black liquid called crude oil. This liquid must be separated, or refined, into different groups of chemicals. The factory that does this separation is called a **refinery.** From the refinery the chemicals go to other factories to be made into many different products.

Oil is a natural resource, and it is nonrenewable. A nonrenewable resource is one that cannot be replaced by nature.

REVIEW Using details from this page, draw a conclusion about the importance of oil. **Draw Conclusions**

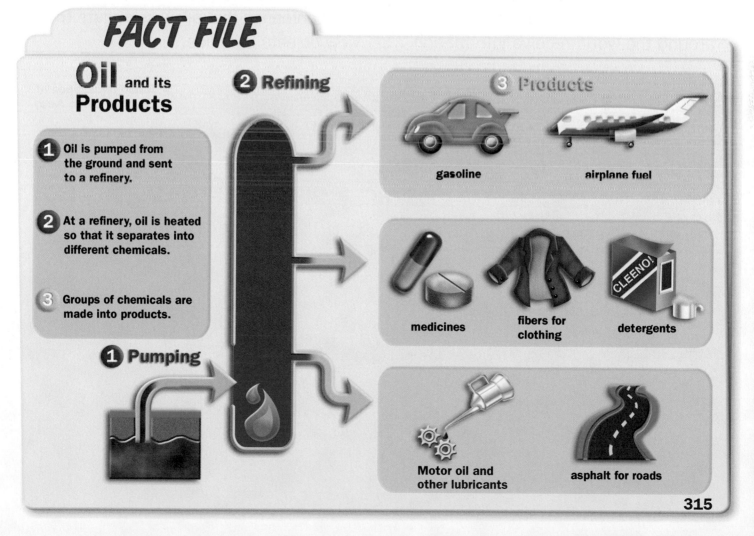

FACT FILE

Oil and its Products

1 Oil is pumped from the ground and sent to a refinery.

2 At a refinery, oil is heated so that it separates into different chemicals.

3 Groups of chemicals are made into products.

1 Pumping

2 Refining

3 Products

gasoline   airplane fuel

medicines   fibers for clothing   detergents

Motor oil and other lubricants   asphalt for roads

Technology in the Southwest

The oil industry is important to the economy of the Southwest. Technology is another important part of the Southwestern economy.

Arizona factories manufacture electronic equipment, aircraft, space vehicles, and missiles. You can see some of these products at the Pima Air and Space Museum near Tucson.

Companies in New Mexico make computer chips and computers. Researchers study telecommunications, medicine, and genetics. At the Sandia National Laboratories in **Albuquerque,** workers develop military resources. Scientists in **Los Alamos** study nuclear energy. Astronomers from around the world receive information

▶ Pima Air and Space Museum

about space from one of the world's largest radio observatories, the Very Large Array in the desert of central New Mexico. The observatory has 27 radio antennas that allow scientists to view objects in space.

▶ Radio telescopes at the Very Large Array

Texas industries make computers, radios, calculators, and electronic equipment. Texas is also home to the Johnson Space Center in **Houston.** Scientists and engineers at the Johnson Space Center manage space flights and conduct research.

Oklahoma companies assist the electronic, aviation, and space industries. Many NASA astronauts train at Vance Air Force Base in Oklahoma.

REVIEW How does technology in the Southwest affect people all over the world? Draw Conclusions

Summarize the Lesson

- **Oil is a nonrenewable natural resource found in the Southwest.**
- **Technology is important to the economy of the Southwest.**

▶ **This jet, the SR-71 Blackbird, is one of the fastest planes in the world.**

LESSON 3 REVIEW

Check Facts and Main Ideas

1. Draw Conclusions On a separate sheet of paper, complete the chart about the importance of oil to the development of the Southwest.

Details

Oil brought many businesses to Beaumont, Texas.

Conclusion

Oil has been important to the development of the Southwest.

2. Why is oil called a nonrenewable natural resource?

3. Name one technology industry for each state in the Southwest.

4. How has technology in the Southwest helped the rest of the United States?

5. Critical Thinking: *Evaluate* How have the lives of the people of the Southwest been affected by the discovery of oil? Use the words **gusher** and **refinery** in your answer.

Link to ⚭ Science

Conserve Resources Research different types of nonrenewable resources and ways to conserve their use. Make a poster showing ways to conserve a nonrenewable resource.

Flying to Help

When her dream of flying in space didn't come true, Jerrie Cobb decided to use her skills to help others in need. Because Jerrie Cobb cared, many people in the Amazon rain forest lead healthier lives.

Geraldyn (Jerrie) Cobb was born in 1931 in Norman, Oklahoma. When she was only twelve years old, her father taught her to fly a plane. After Project Mercury, a major space project, was announced in 1958 by NASA, Jerrie was chosen to take physical tests to compare women's and men's abilities to become astronauts. In 1960, Jerrie easily passed the 75 tests and was named one of the participants in the women's astronaut training program.

A change in the rules, however, kept Jerrie Cobb from her dream of going into space. NASA made a rule that astronauts must be military jet pilots and at that time only men could be military jet pilots. So the 13 women chosen for *Mercury 13* lost their chance to go into space.

Jerrie was discouraged, but she decided to use her skill as a pilot to help others. She knew that the people of the Amazon rain forest needed medicine, clothes, food, and doctors. For more than 35 years, Jerrie has flown doctors and supplies into this South American rain forest.

BUILDING
CITIZENSHIP
★ Caring
Respect
Responsibility
Fairness
Honesty
Courage

▶ Cobb's plane takes her to parts of the Amazon rain forest that cannot be reached on foot or by car.

Her flights have helped more than 6 million people living in parts of Brazil, Colombia, Bolivia, Peru, Venezuela, and Ecuador. Because of her caring efforts, Jerrie Cobb was nominated for a Nobel Peace Prize.

Jerrie Cobb organized this project on her own. Her work in the Amazon has given her a new dream. She hopes to go on a mission to study the Amazon from space one day.

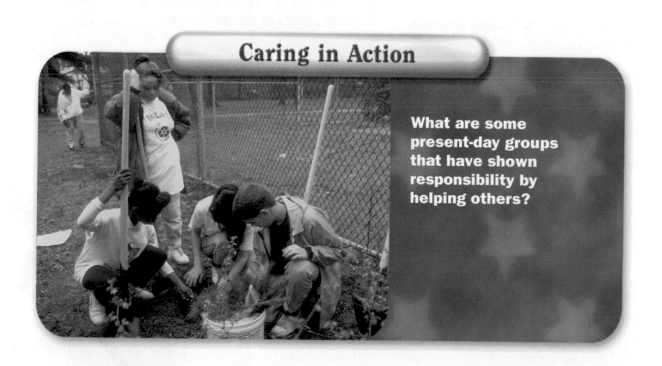

Caring in Action

What are some present-day groups that have shown responsibility by helping others?

319

Chapter Summary

Draw Conclusions

On a separate sheet of paper, fill in three details that would lead you to draw this conclusion about the Southwest.

Details

Conclusion

The Southwest has many natural resources.

Vocabulary

Match each word with the correct definition or description.

1 adobe (p. 302)

2 pueblo (p. 302)

3 arid (p. 309)

4 savanna (p. 310)

5 refinery (p. 315)

a. grassy area with little rainfall

b. mud brick

c. village

d. a factory where crude oil is separated

e. dry

People and Places

Write a sentence explaining why each of the following people or places is important to the Southwest. You may use two or more people or places in one sentence.

1 García López de Cárdenas (p. 302)

2 John Wesley Powell (p. 302)

3 Theodore Roosevelt (p. 303)

4 Sonoran Desert (p. 310)

5 Beaumont, Texas (p. 315)

6 Pattillo Higgins (p. 315)

Facts and Main Ideas

1 Why was Major John Wesley Powell important to the history of the Grand Canyon?

2 How does the arid climate of the Southwest affect the kinds of plants that grow there?

3 How was oil found at Spindletop?

4 **Main Idea** How has erosion affected the Grand Canyon?

5 **Main Idea** Describe three types of climate you might find in the Southwest.

6 **Main Idea** Name four technology industries found in the Southwest.

7 **Critical Thinking:** *Cause and Effect* How did the discovery of oil affect the development of the Southwest?

Apply Skills

Make Generalizations

Read the paragraph below. Which numbered statement is a generalization?

The saguaro cactus is well suited to grow in the desert. The saguaro has long, shallow roots that take in water quickly when it rains. Saguaros have ribbed trunks and branches that expand as water is taken in. The cactus can store huge amounts of water that keep the plant alive during dry periods.

1 The saguaro cactus is well suited to grow in the desert.

2 The cactus can store huge amounts of water.

3 Saguaros have ribbed trunks and branches.

Write About Geography

1 **Write a diary entry** about a day at the Grand Canyon.

2 **Write a report** describing ways to conserve oil and reasons for doing so.

3 **Write a newspaper article** describing the plants and animals of the Southwest.

Internet Activity

To get help with vocabulary, people, and places, select dictionary or encyclopedia from *Social Studies Library* at **www.sfsocialstudies.com**.

CHAPTER 11

The People of the Southwest

Lesson 1

Window Rock, Arizona
The Navajo have lived in the Southwest for hundreds of years.

1

Lesson 2

Santa Fe, New Mexico
The Spanish established cities and missions in the Southwest.

2

Lesson 3

King Ranch, Texas
Cattle ranches became legendary in the Southwest.

3

Lesson 4

Tucson, Arizona
Cities in the desert are growing quickly.

4

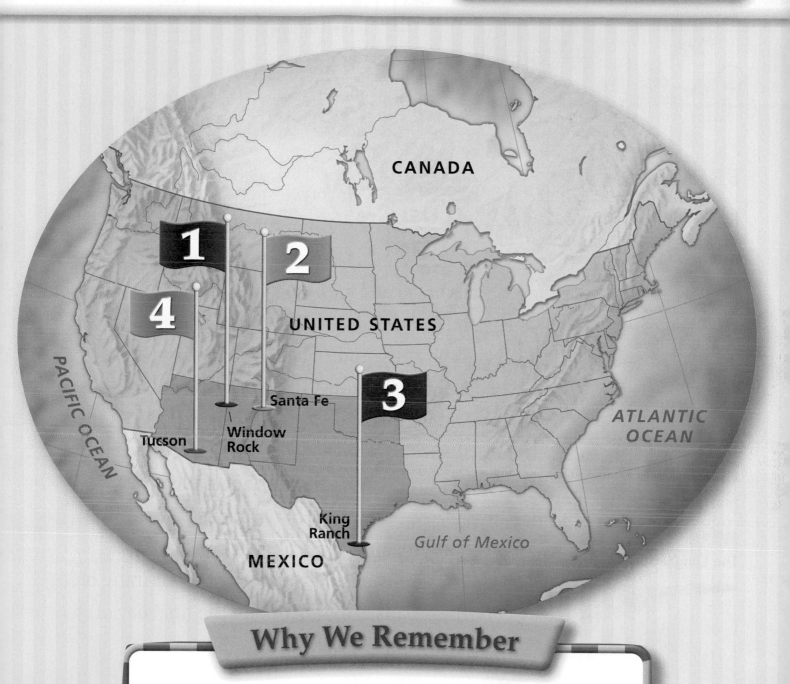

CANADA

UNITED STATES

PACIFIC OCEAN

ATLANTIC OCEAN

Santa Fe

Window Rock

Tucson

King Ranch

Gulf of Mexico

MEXICO

1

2

3

4

Why We Remember

The Southwest region has a varied and colorful history. The Navajo, the Spanish explorers, and the region's Mexican neighbors have all left their marks on the culture of the Southwest. Now, technology and space exploration are helping the region to develop even more. The Southwest remains a fine landscape for those who want to explore.

1850　　　　1900　　　　1950

1864
The Long Walk

1868
Navajo sign a treaty
with the United States
government.

1923
Navajo Tribal
Council is formed.

Window Rock

The Navajo

PREVIEW

Focus on the Main Idea
The Navajo have lived in the
Southwest for centuries.

PLACES
Fort Canby, Arizona
Bosque Redondo, New Mexico
Window Rock, Arizona

PEOPLE
Kit Carson
Henry Chee Dodge

VOCABULARY
hogan

EVENTS
The Long Walk

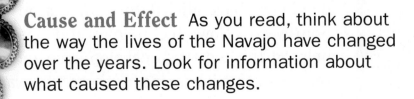

You Are There

You've spent the day wandering around the fairgrounds, sampling frybread and barbecue and watching artists make beautiful jewelry. Then you spent some time at the rodeo, cheering on the riders. Now it is evening, time for dancing. You watch the dancers make their way across the floor. Their movements are graceful and full of purpose. The Navajo dance, then the Apache. Now a Pueblo group appears. You want to know more about these dances. Perhaps you can learn about the meaning of these dances tomorrow, on the final day of the Navajo Nation Fair.

Cause and Effect As you read, think about the way the lives of the Navajo have changed over the years. Look for information about what caused these changes.

Early Culture

When European explorers came to North America, the Navajo (NAH vah hoh) lived in the hot, dry land of the Southwest. They did not call themselves *Navajo*. They called themselves *Diné* (Din NAY), which means "the people."

The Navajo were mainly hunters and gatherers, but they learned farming, pottery making, and basket weaving from the Pueblo, who lived nearby.

The Navajo lived in homes called **hogans.** Usually, a hogan had only one room. The frame of the hogan was made of logs, which were covered with a thick layer of soil. Later, hogans were made of stone, adobe, or wood. The door of a hogan would always face east, toward the rising sun.

The Navajo got sheep and horses from the Spanish colonists who settled

▶ **Navajo blankets are skillfully woven and highly prized.**

in the area. Raising sheep became very important to the Navajo. The Navajo used the sheep for food and wool.

The Navajo were organized into clans, or family groups. Each clan had a leader, but there was no main Navajo leader. When white settlers came, the U.S. government made a treaty with the Navajo, but only a few clans knew about the treaty. This led to conflict.

REVIEW What are some ways that the Navajo culture was influenced by the Pueblo?
Main Idea and Details

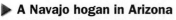
▶ **A Navajo hogan in Arizona**

The Long Walk

In 1863, a soldier named **Kit Carson** was ordered by the U.S. government to stop the conflicts between the Navajo and the white settlers in New Mexico. First, Colonel Kit Carson and his men destroyed Navajo crops and hogans. Then, they took the Navajo's animals. The Navajo were left with little food and without a safe place to live. Carson ordered the Navajo to leave their land and move to the army post at **Fort Canby,** now known as Fort Defiance, in Arizona.

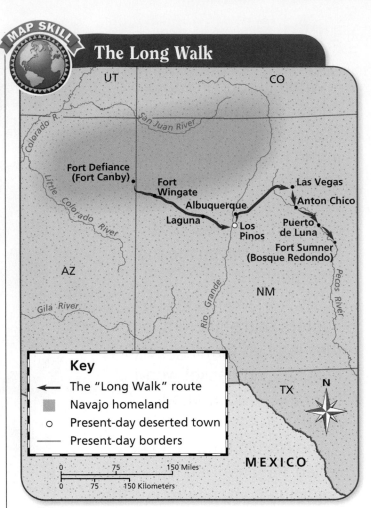

► **Kit Carson**

In 1864, many Navajo arrived at Fort Canby. The soldiers gave the Navajo food and blankets. However, in order to prevent further conflict with the Navajo, the army pushed them farther east.

MAP SKILL

The Long Walk

► The Long Walk covered almost 300 miles.

MAP SKILL Use Map Scale *About how far was Fort Canby from Los Pinos?*

The Navajo were forced to walk 300 miles to an area known as **Bosque Redondo** (BOHS kay ray DON doh).

Bosque Redondo was near Fort Sumner, in eastern New Mexico. It was a very difficult journey. Many Navajo died along the way. Their journey became known as "The Long Walk."

The soil at Bosque Redondo was poor for growing crops. The water was not safe to drink. Clothing and blankets were scarce. Many more Navajo became sick and died.

Finally, in 1868, the U.S. government decided to allow the Navajo to return home. The Navajo signed a treaty with the government. They would live on a reservation of 3.5 million acres that included their old lands. In return, the Navajo promised to end their conflict with the white settlers. The government promised to build schools for the Navajo and to give them sheep to herd. The Navajo returned to rebuild their homes and their lives.

REVIEW Why was life at Bosque Redondo difficult for the Navajo? **Main Idea and Details**

The Navajo Tribal Council

In 1923 oil and minerals were discovered on the Navajo reservation. The Navajo Tribal Council was formed to make agreements over drilling for oil and digging for minerals on Navajo land. The council made the first written system of Navajo laws. **Henry Chee Dodge** was the first chairman of the Navajo Tribal Council.

The Navajo are now officially called the Navajo Nation. The Navajo capital is in **Window Rock, Arizona.** Today, the Navajo Tribal Council is the largest tribal government body in the United States. The council members and a chairperson are elected every four years. The Council meets often in Window Rock to make decisions for its people.

REVIEW How did the discovery of oil and minerals on their land affect the Navajo? **Cause and Effect**

▶ Navajo wait to receive coupons for food at Fort Sumner after the Long Walk.

Navajo Life Today

The Navajo Nation is the largest Native American group in the United States. Many Navajo live on the reservation, which covers parts of Arizona, New Mexico, and Utah.

The Navajo continue to keep much of their traditional culture. Even though many young people speak only English, the Navajo language is taught in schools on the reservation. Many Navajo families still live in hogans and work together in agriculture. Both men and women play an important role in Navajo politics, business, and religion.

Navajo culture includes many ceremonies. Some of the ceremonies are for curing sickness. Others teach the history of the people and their responsibility to the Navajo Nation. The Navajo also respect nature and aim to "walk in beauty" always.

REVIEW What are some ways that the Navajo keep their traditional culture? **Main Idea and Details**

► **Navajo shepherds**

Summarize the Lesson

- **1864** The Navajo were forced to walk 300 miles to New Mexico.
- **1868** The Navajo were allowed to return to their land.
- **1923** The Navajo Tribal Council was formed.
- **Today** The Navajo Nation is the largest Native American group in the United States.

LESSON 1 | REVIEW

Check Facts and Main Ideas

1. **Cause and Effect** On a separate sheet of paper, make a chart like the one shown. Fill in the missing causes of the events listed.

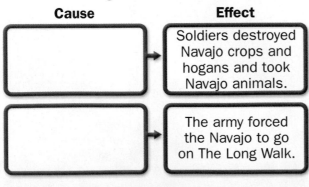

Cause	Effect
	Soldiers destroyed Navajo crops and hogans and took Navajo animals.
	The army forced the Navajo to go on The Long Walk.

2. What was the early Navajo culture like? Use the word **hogan** in your answer.

3. How is Navajo culture today similar to the early Navajo culture?

4. How are the members of the Navajo Tribal Council chosen?

5. **Critical Thinking:** *Evaluate* Do you think it is better for the Navajo people to be governed by the Navajo Tribal Council rather than by laws made by people outside the Navajo Nation? Why or why not?

Link to ∞ Art

Draw a Picture The Navajo people use materials from their land and their animals to create art. Research types of Navajo art. Tell about one type of Navajo art and draw pictures to show it.

Henry Chee Dodge 1857–1947

Henry Chee Dodge faced many hardships as a child. Both his Navajo mother and Mexican father died when Chee was very young. At age six he was forced to march with his people on The Long Walk.

After the U.S. government allowed the Navajo to return home in 1868, Chee Dodge learned to speak English. He soon began to interpret for the U.S. agents governing the Navajo. Later, he worked to keep peace between his people and the government agents. When the first Navajo Tribal Council was formed in 1923, Chee Dodge became chairman. He served until 1928. In 1942, Chee Dodge was once again elected tribal chairman. In 1945, Henry Chee Dodge was awarded the Silver Achievement Medal from the Indian Council Fire. In his acceptance speech he said,

BIOFACT

Before the U.S. government reduced Navajo livestock herds in the 1930s, Chee Dodge owned a flock of sheep so large that it took two months to shear them all.

> ***"The greatest of all Indian needs is education."***

Learn from Biographies

How do you think Henry Chee Dodge's experiences helped prepare him to be chairman of the Navajo Tribal Council?

For more information, go online to *Meet the People* at **www.sfsocialstudies.com**.

Research and Writing Skills

Identify Primary and Secondary Sources

What? A primary source is an eyewitness account or observation. Primary sources can be letters, diaries, documents, speeches, interviews, quotations, and even photographs and newspaper interviews.

A secondary source is a secondhand account of history. Writers of secondary sources collect information about a person, place, or event from different sources. Then they organize that information and present it in their own way. History textbooks and articles in encyclopedias and newspapers are examples of secondary sources.

In this primary source quotation, a Navajo Code Talker describes an experience during World War II. Navajo Code Talkers worked with the U.S. Marines from 1942 to 1945. They sent secret radio messages in Navajo. The enemy was never able to decode these messages.

> **"One experience that stands out in my memory is being on combat patrol in Okinawa in Japan. Our patrol was pinned down for two days—the antenna of my radio was shot off, but I was able to get a message through [in code] for reinforcements."**
>
> **Roy O. Hawthorne,**
> **Kin lichii'nii Clan**

The description below tells about the same event as a reporter might write in a newspaper article. The article would be a secondary source.

Those Marines were able to get themselves out of many difficult situations using their Navajo words as a code language in voice (radio and wire) transmission. For instance, a combat patrol in Okinawa got a message asking for reinforcements through in code in the middle of fighting.

Why? As you study, you can use primary and secondary sources for different purposes.

Primary sources can give you information about how real people thought, felt, or acted at a particular time and place.

Secondary sources help show how people have come to understand an event that took place in the past.

How? To tell if something is a primary source or a secondary source, consider the following:

In a primary source, the writer is a part of the action described, or an eyewitness to it. The writer may say, "I saw this," or "we did that." In the example on page 330, Roy O. Hawthorne describes his own feelings and actions. It is clear from his words that he was present.

Secondary sources are written by someone who did not see the events firsthand. The writer is not part of the events described. Instead, he or she describes what took place.

Both primary and secondary sources are useful. They can provide a different point of view of the same information.

Think and Apply

1. Suppose you wanted to read the words of a soldier in a war. Would you look for a **primary source** or a **secondary source**? Explain.

2. If you need a single source to tell you about all of the events leading up to a certain battle, what kind of source might be most helpful? Explain.

3. In which type of source is the writer also a part of the scene?

▶ **Navajo Code Talkers**

331

1500	1600	1700	1800

1540
Coronado sets off to find the "Cities of Gold."

1610
City of Santa Fe is founded.

1687
Father Kino founds missions in Arizona.

1720
Mission San José is established in San Antonio, Texas.

Spanish Influence

PREVIEW

Focus on the Main Idea
Explorers and missionaries brought a Spanish presence to the Southwest.

PLACES
San Antonio, Texas
Santa Fe, New Mexico

PEOPLE
Father Eusebio Kino

VOCABULARY
viceroy
missionary
vaquero

You Are There

It has been a long journey. It seems as if you've been walking for years, searching for gold. You haven't found any yet.

When you started this expedition, you were sure that you would find cities of gold. After all, eyewitnesses said they had seen them, glistening in the desert sun. But when you got there, every "golden city" you came upon was only a town of mud and brick. This time, though, you know there must be treasure ahead.

You're making your way toward the grand city of Quivira. Your guide has been there. He has seen its riches! You only hope it is but a few more days' walk.

▶ Spanish soldiers wore helmets similar to this one on their expeditions in North America.

 Draw Conclusions As you read, think about the effects that the Spanish had on life in the Southwest.

Coronado and His Search

One of Spain's purposes for sending explorers to the Americas was to find gold. When the **viceroy,** or governor, of Mexico heard reports of "Cities of Gold" to the north, he wanted to claim them for Spain. The cities were said to have ". . . walls of gold blocks, gates studded with precious jewels, and streets paved with silver. . . . "

In 1540, the viceroy sent Francisco Vásquez de Coronado to search for Cíbola, the golden cities.

On his journey, Coronado saw a Zuñi pueblo near the present-day border of New Mexico and Arizona. The walls that were supposed to be gold were merely adobe shining in the desert sun. But Coronado did not give up.

Coronado sent search parties in different directions. You have read about the group that went west. They became the first Europeans to see the Grand Canyon. Another group came upon the Gulf of California. A group that went east explored Pueblo villages on the Rio Grande in what is now New Mexico.

Meanwhile, Coronado's party had heard about a mythical city of riches called "Quivira." They traveled as far as present-day Kansas, but they found no gold. They found only herds of buffalo and Native American villages.

Coronado returned to Mexico and reported that there was no gold. His expedition was labeled a failure.

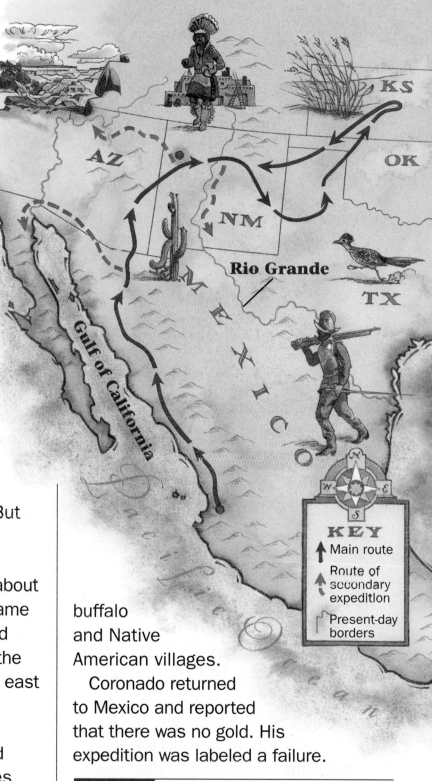

Coronado's Expedition

KS

OK

AZ

NM

Rio Grande

TX

MEXICO

Gulf of California

KEY
↑ Main route
↑ Route of secondary expedition
▯ Present-day borders

REVIEW What did Coronado and his explorers find on their journey instead of gold? **Main Idea and Details**

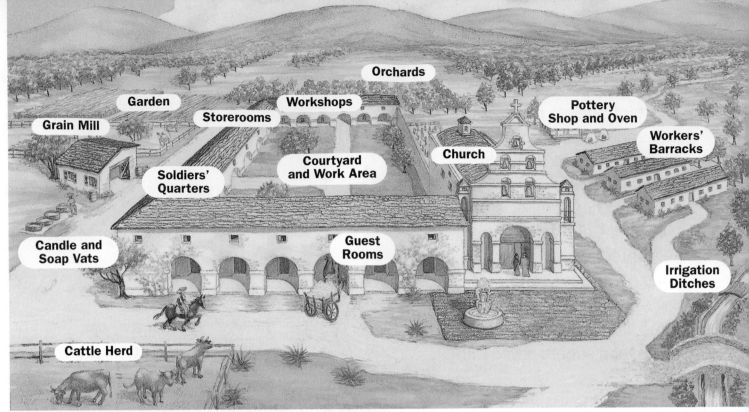

Missions had many buildings and work areas.

Labels: Orchards, Garden, Grain Mill, Workshops, Storerooms, Pottery Shop and Oven, Workers' Barracks, Church, Soldiers' Quarters, Courtyard and Work Area, Candle and Soap Vats, Guest Rooms, Irrigation Ditches, Cattle Herd

Spanish Missions

When the Spanish moved into what is now New Mexico, they brought missionaries with them. A **missionary** is a person who is sent into other parts of the world by a religious organization to spread its beliefs. Spanish missionaries in the Southwest set up missions, which were their headquarters. Each mission tried to support itself by raising cows, pigs, and sheep. Mission farms also raised crops such as corn, beans, fruit, and pumpkins.

Over time the missions spread into Texas and Arizona. In 1687, **Father Eusebio Kino** founded three missions in present-day Arizona, where he taught Native American Pima and Yuma people for 25 years. He was kind to the Native Americans and they were devoted to him. One of his missions, Mission Dolores, which was in Sonora, Mexico, had a ranch with cattle and sheep, wheat and corn fields, and orchards. It even had a water-powered mill so the people who lived there could grind their own grain.

Mission San José in **San Antonio, Texas,** was established in 1720. It was so beautiful that it was called "Queen of the Missions." Most missions were enclosed by stone and mud walls with wooden gates that could be locked. They had buildings for the missionaries, offices, and a church. Missions also had rooms for Native Americans and others who lived there.

The purposes of missions were to claim land and to make Christians of the Native Americans.

The Spanish government supported the missions because they wanted the Native Americans to become good citizens and loyal subjects of the king of Spain. The Spanish also saw the Native Americans as laborers. Most Native Americans who lived at the missions were put to work farming, making leather goods, spinning yarn, and weaving cloth.

Native Americans were persuaded to enter the mission in exchange for food and protection from enemies. Sometimes, however, they were forced to live and work at the missions. Some Spanish viceroys treated Native Americans cruelly. But some missionaries were kind to the Native Americans and protected them from people who mistreated them.

Some Native Americans who lived at the mission married and built homes near there. In time, pueblos grew up around missions. The mission priests allowed the pueblos to govern themselves with some supervision from the missionaries.

REVIEW Why were Spanish missions started in the Southwest?
🕙 **Draw Conclusions**

"Remember the Alamo!"

Then and Now

The Alamo is one of five Spanish missions in San Antonio, Texas. Its real name is Mission San Antonio de Valero. It was built in 1718, when Texas was still part of Mexico. In 1836, a band of Texas settlers used the mission as a fort to fight for independence from Mexico. All the Texas solders were killed. Soon after, Texas won its independence with the rally cry "Remember the Alamo!"

Today, the Alamo is a historical site. Other missions are part of the San Antonio Mission National Historical Park. Some, such as Mission San José, are still active places of worship.

▶ Only the chapel remains of the mission that the Texans used as a fort.

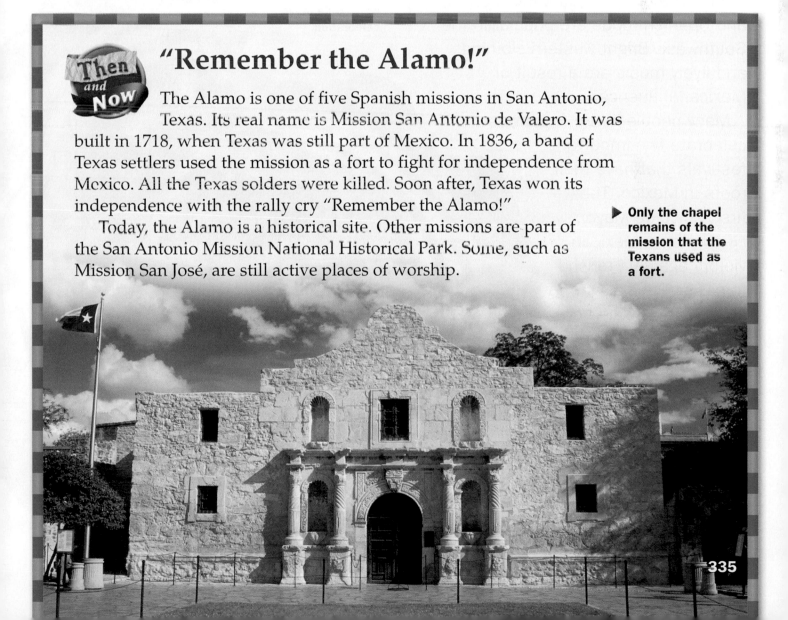

Influence of Spanish and Mexican Culture

The influence of Spanish and Mexican culture can be seen throughout the Southwest. Some of the Spanish mission churches are still standing. By 1610, the Spanish had founded **Santa Fe,** the capital of present-day New Mexico. Santa Fe is the oldest center of government in the United States. Today many Spanish-style buildings can be seen in the Southwest.

The culture of Native Americans from the Southwest and Mexico influenced the culture of the region. Mexican and Spanish foods are popular in the Southwest. Bright western clothing and lively music are a result of Mexican influence.

Many people in the Southwest celebrate two important festivals that have their roots in Mexico. The first, *Cinco de Mayo,* celebrates a Mexican victory against French forces at Puebla, Mexico, in 1862. The second, Mexican Independence Day, is also known as *Diez y Seis de Septiembre* (September 16).

The festival celebrates Mexico's independence from Spain.

Modern ranches also reflect the influence of Spanish culture. The Spanish were the first to bring cattle to the region. They started the cattle ranches of the Southwest. Spanish cowboys, called *vaqueros,* handed down the skills used by modern cowboys—herding cattle, roping, branding, rounding up herds, and riding on trail drives.

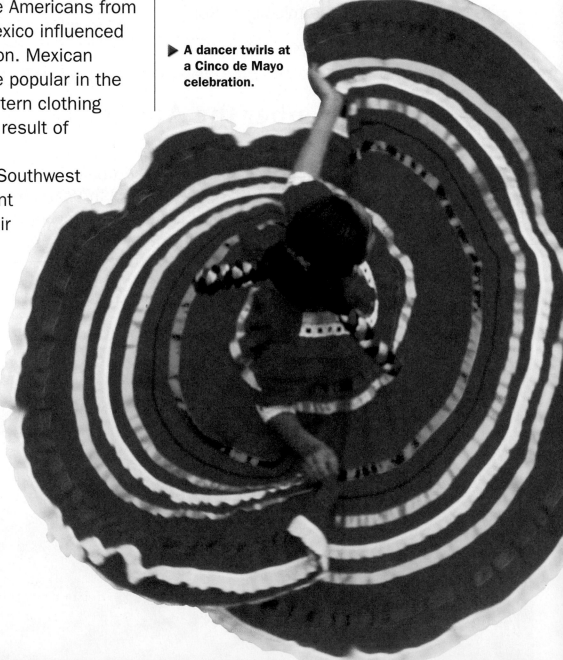

▶ **A dancer twirls at a Cinco de Mayo celebration.**

Even the language of the Southwest uses many Spanish words. The wooden pen for cattle and horses is called by the Spanish name *corral*. The ropes used to capture steers and horses are called *lassos*. *Ranch* comes from the Spanish word *rancho*. Many people in the Southwest speak both English and Spanish.

REVIEW How did Spanish settlers affect cattle ranching in the Southwest? **Cause and Effect**

Summarize the Lesson

1540 Coronado set off in search of gold.

1610 City of Santa Fe was founded.

1687 Father Kino founded missions in Arizona.

1720 Mission San José was established in San Antonio.

Today Spanish influences can be seen throughout the Southwest.

▶ **Santa Fe, New Mexico**

LESSON 2 REVIEW

Check Facts and Main Ideas

1. ↻ **Draw Conclusions** On a separate sheet of paper, fill in a conclusion about Coronado's exploration from the facts given.

Details

> Coronado came to find the "Cities of Gold."

> He did not find any gold.

> He did not find anything of value to the **viceroy**.

Conclusion

2. What parts of the Southwest did Coronado's soldiers explore?

3. How did the Spanish missions affect the settlement of the Southwest?

4. How is Spanish influence still seen in the Southwest?

5. **Critical Thinking:** *Recognize Point of View* Why did some Native Americans resist living at missions? How did their point of view differ from those who lived at missions willingly?

Link to ⌘ Writing

Write a Travel Brochure Do some research to learn about a Spanish mission in the Southwest that is still open to visitors. Write a travel brochure to tell tourists about interesting things to do and see at the mission. Be sure to draw some pictures for your brochure. Use the term **missionary** in your brochure.

1850   1875   1900

1853
King Ranch is established.

1865
Jesse Chisholm blazes a cattle trail.

1870
Philip Armour starts a meat packing industry.

1890
The open range is closed.

San Antonio

King Ranch

PREVIEW

Focus on the Main Idea
The cattle industry boomed in the Southwest in the 1800s. The cowboys who herded cattle became part of our nation's lore.

PLACES

San Antonio, Texas
King Ranch

PEOPLE

Philip Armour
Annie Oakley
Calamity Jane (Martha Canary)
Jesse Chisholm

VOCABULARY

tallow
homestead

TERMS

Chisholm Trail

▶ A cowhand's spur

Ranches and Drivers

You Are There

It is June of 1872. You and your team are driving a herd of about 3,000 cattle from Texas to Abilene, Kansas. You still have hundreds of miles to go on the dusty Chisholm Trail. You can't drive the cattle too fast or they will lose weight, so you cover only about 15 miles a day. It will take about six weeks to get to Abilene. The work is hard and the days are long. The sun beats down on your hat. The kerchief you wear over your face protects you from breathing in dust. At night you sleep on the ground in your bedroll. You can't wait to get to a hot bath and a soft bed!

Draw Conclusions As you read, draw your own conclusions about why ranching became such an important industry in the Southwest.

Cattle Country

The Spanish missionaries and soldiers brought cattle to Texas. When the missionaries withdrew, they left the cattle behind. As a result, settlers moving to Texas found thousands of wild cattle roaming the grasslands.

The early settlers raised cattle to use as meat for their families. They used cattle for other purposes too. For example, cattle hides were used for leather, and horns and hooves were made into buckles and buttons. The **tallow,** or fat, of the cattle was used for candles and soap. Some settlers sold a few cattle to people in nearby towns.

During the Civil War, **Philip Armour** sold beef to the army. Then in 1870, Armour started a meat-packing industry in Chicago. Business people in Texas thought that the market for beef would grow. The possibility of large profits attracted people from the East and overseas to invest in raising beef. Suddenly raising cattle became a booming business.

Texas farmers and ranchers coming home from the Civil War began rounding up the wild cattle. They grazed them on grasslands until they were large enough to sell. Since there was no railroad connection in Texas yet, they took cattle to railroad towns in Kansas and Missouri. There the cattle were loaded onto freight cars headed for meat-packing plants in Kansas City or Chicago.

As the market for beef grew, cattle ranching spread northward out of Texas. Before long, not only the Southwest, but also the northern plains states as far north as Montana and the Dakotas were cattle country. The northern plains that once were grazing land for buffalo were filled with cattle.

REVIEW How was cattle raising introduced into Texas?
Main Idea and Details

▶ **A cattle drive in the Southwest**

▶ Calamity Jane, 1901

Cowboys and Cowgirls

Many different types of people worked on ranches training horses and herding cattle. After the Civil War many freed slaves hired on as cowhands. Native Americans and European settlers also worked as cowhands.

In South Texas, where some ranches were owned by Mexican families, many cowboys were of Mexican descent. In fact, the Mexican vaqueros of South Texas

▶ Native American cowboy, c. 1907

taught the newer settlers how to be cowboys.

The life of the cowboy shown today in books, movies, songs, and on TV was far from real life. Cowhands rarely fought Native Americans. They worked long hours. They often spent more than twelve hours a day on horseback. On trail drives the cowhands took turns guarding the cattle throughout the night. Cowhands slept on the ground and rarely carried guns.

Cowgirls were also a part of the old West. Only a few women went on cattle drives. The most famous cowgirls took part in rodeos and wild-west shows. **Annie Oakley** was a sharpshooter who had her own show. **Calamity Jane,** whose real name was Martha Canary, was also a famous cowgirl. She performed shooting displays in wild-west shows.

REVIEW What was the life of a real cowhand like? **Main Idea and Details**

340

The Chisholm Trail

In 1865 Jesse Chisholm, (CHIZ uhm), a trader who was part Native American, blazed, or marked, a trail from San Antonio, Texas, to Abilene, Kansas. As railroad lines were extended, the trail also went to Ellsworth, Kansas, and other cities.

The Chisholm Trail went through Indian Territory (now Oklahoma). Some Native American groups charged a toll of ten cents a head for cattle driven through their land. They also charged a grazing fee for the grass the cattle ate along the way. The toll on the Chisholm Trail could be paid with a head or two of cattle. Many ranchers began using this trail.

While the rivers along the trail provided water, they were also hazards. The cattle were afraid of water and had to be forced to cross rivers. After heavy rains some cattle were swept away by swiftly running rivers. At times the cattle got stuck in mud or quicksand along the rivers. Getting the cattle across the rivers was a difficult and dangerous job for the cowboys.

REVIEW Why did ranchers like the Chisholm Trail? **Main Idea and Details**

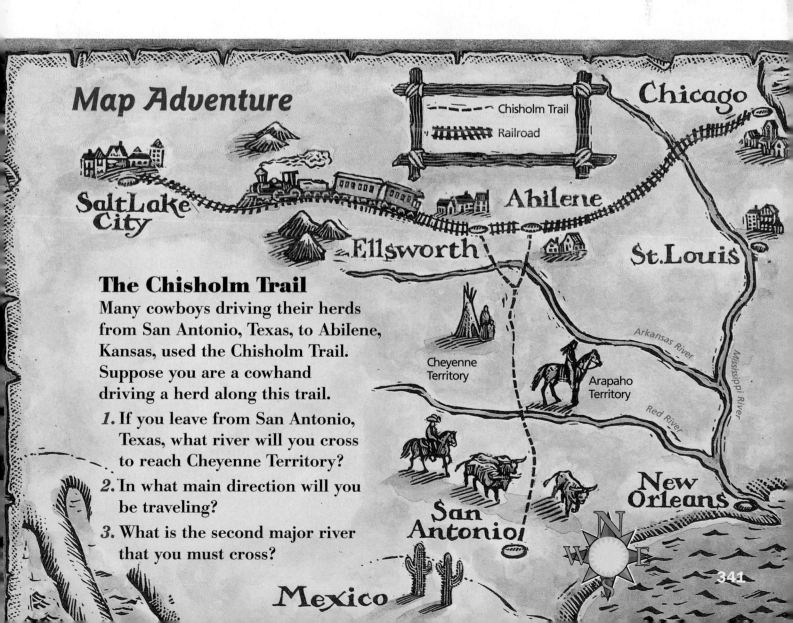

Map Adventure

Chisholm Trail
Railroad

Chicago

Salt Lake City

Abilene

Ellsworth

St. Louis

Cheyenne Territory

Arapaho Territory

Arkansas River

Mississippi River

Red River

San Antonio

New Orleans

Mexico

The Chisholm Trail

Many cowboys driving their herds from San Antonio, Texas, to Abilene, Kansas, used the Chisholm Trail. Suppose you are a cowhand driving a herd along this trail.

1. If you leave from San Antonio, Texas, what river will you cross to reach Cheyenne Territory?

2. In what main direction will you be traveling?

3. What is the second major river that you must cross?

341

▶ Some settlers to the Southwest built houses of sod on their homesteads.

How Ranching Influenced the Southwest

As more railroads were built in the Southwest, the distance from the ranches to the railroads became shorter and shorter. The days of long cattle drives were over. Cowhands now worked in different jobs on the ranches.

By 1890 ranchers could no longer graze their cattle on the open range. This was partly due to the increasing number of settlers who were moving to the Southwest. The U.S. government granted land to settlers for a few dollars if they would live on the land and raise crops. The land given to a settler was called a **homestead.** To keep animals out of their fields, homesteaders fenced their land. Cattle ranchers also began to fence their land to keep their animals from wandering off. As a result, the grasslands were no longer available for shared grazing.

Ranchers began to decrease the size of their herds to a number that could graze on their land. At the same time, they began to raise crops to feed their animals during the winter. The ranchers also began to drill water wells so their animals didn't have to travel a long way to drink.

Some large ranches still remain in the Southwest. Among them is the **King Ranch.** It was established in 1853 and it is still in business. This ranch spreads over 800,000 acres in South Texas. It is larger than the state of Rhode Island. The King Ranch is also used for scientific studies of cattle and cattle diseases.

REVIEW How did fences affect cattle ranching in the Southwest?
◑ Draw Conclusions

▶ King Ranch is about 250 square miles larger than Rhode Island.

Summarize the Lesson

— **1853** King Ranch was founded.

— **1865** Jesse Chisholm blazed a cattle trail.

— **1870** Philip Armour started a meat-packing company.

— **1890** The open range was closed.

LESSON 3 ⏵ REVIEW

Check Facts and Main Ideas

1. ◑ **Draw Conclusions** On a separate sheet of paper, fill in a conclusion that you can draw about ranching from the facts given.

Details

Cattle provided food and other necessities for early settlers.

Cowhands made their living working with cattle.

Philip Armour sold beef and started a meat-packing industry.

Conclusion

2. How did cattle raising help develop the economy of the Southwest?

3. How did ranching change when the open range was closed?

4. How have cowhands become part of the lore of our nation?

5. **Critical Thinking: *Solve Problems*** How did the Chisholm Trail solve the problem of getting cattle to the railroad towns?

Link to ⬠⬠ **Writing**

Write a Story Write a story about a day in the life of a cowboy or cowgirl. Do some research to find out more about their lives. Tell about what they wore, what they ate, and what they did. Use the words **tallow** and **homestead** in your story.

Cowboys and Cowgirls

Driving cattle to the railroads required courage and energy, and most cowboys took pride in their work. This work attracted people who were independent and who relied on themselves. During the days of the cattle trails, very few women could be called "cowgirls." Still, some women raised and sold cattle. One, Margaret Borland, even led a cattle drive. Today you can see cowgirls and cowboys as they compete in rodeos. They use roping and riding skills that were useful years ago on the cattle trails.

Flying the Texas Flag
The birthplace of American ranching, Texas was an important part of the "Wild West."

The powerful mustang—an ideal cow pony

Skillful Lady
Although very few women rode the range, in recent years women have proven that they can ride as skillfully as men. This rodeo cowgirl is competing in a demonstration of range skills.

A light touch of the rein to the horse's neck guides the horse around the barrel.

Silver concha

North American cowboy wearing batwing chaps

The Famous North American Cowboy

North American cowboys are world famous because of their role in the fabled "Wild West." The truth is that their work was hard. Cattle drives were long, and cowboys were not paid very much. The work could be boring, and it was sometimes dangerous. Modern cowboys use trucks to take cattle to pasture and special machines for branding. Riding skills are still important during round-ups and around the ranch, though.

California A-fork style saddle, c. 1870

Charros and Vaqueros

Cattle ranching in the Western Hemisphere began in Mexico. Landowners, called *charros,* and their working cowboys, the *vaqueros,* developed the skills later used by cowboys in the western United States.

Poster advertising the amazing feats of marksmanship exhibited by Annie Oakley in Buffalo Bill's Wild West show

"Little Sure Shot"

Phoebe "Annie Oakley" Moses (1860–1926) was the trick-shot star of Buffalo Bill Cody's Wild West show. She was born in Ohio. She only visited the "Wild West" as she traveled with the show!

Nat Love

Many cowboys were African Americans, Mexicans, or Native Americans. Nat Love (1854–1921) was a famous African American cowboy. He wrote a book about his life as a cowboy. In addition to driving cattle, he was a rodeo champion and a crack shot.

1900	1925	1950	1975
1911 Willis Carrier develops a useful air-conditioning system.	**1928** Air-conditioned Milam Building is completed.		**1960** California State Water Project begins.

PREVIEW

Focus on the Main Idea
High temperatures and a shortage of water can make living in the desert a challenge.

PLACES
Phoenix, Arizona
Tucson, Arizona

PEOPLE
Willis Haviland Carrier

VOCABULARY
aqueduct

Living in the Desert

You Are There
You step outside your home near Tucson, Arizona, in the Sonoran Desert. It is a warm autumn day. A lizard scurries across the stones that cover the ground. A few prickly-pear and barrel cacti grow in the yard. So do a few small mesquite trees. It can get very hot during the summer, and it doesn't rain much. Still, everywhere you look you can see beautiful mountains. Sometimes there is snow on their peaks. The sky is almost always a clear blue, with not a cloud to be seen!

◀ **Western Banded Gecko**

Cause and Effect As you read, think about what effects a dry climate has on a region.

Irrigation

The Sonoran Desert in Arizona gets only about 8 to 10 inches of rainfall a year. About half of that comes in the rainy months from July to September. In order to raise crops, people have to find other sources of water. Before Europeans came to Arizona, some Native Americans dug irrigation canals and built aqueducts to get water for their crops. An **aqueduct** is a trench or pipe used to bring water from a distance.

Today, there are dams and reservoirs in Arizona, especially in the **Phoenix** area. These reservoirs store water for various valleys and regions. In 1960, the California State Water Project was designed to bring water to Southern California. It provided funds for an aqueduct on the Colorado River. This aqueduct also carries water to the regions around Phoenix and **Tucson.**

Because of irrigation, some of the dry land of the Southwest has become rich farmland. Farms in Arizona provide fresh vegetables, citrus fruit, apples, peaches, and pecans. Another important crop is cotton. The long growing season in Arizona makes the farms very productive.

The use of irrigation has also made the desert a more inviting place to live.

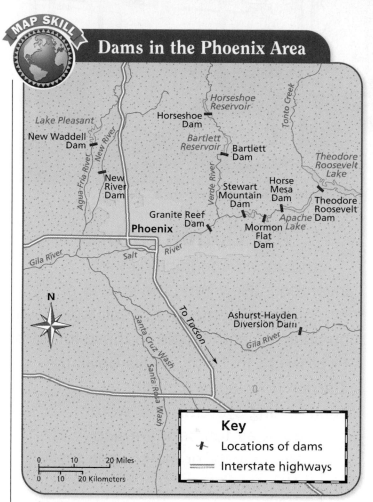

Dams in the Phoenix Area

> ► Dams control the flow of water from reservoirs.

MAP SKILL Human-Environment Interaction
How have people controlled the movement of river water in the Southwest?

Phoenix, Tucson, and other desert cities are growing communities. In the last 40 years, Arizona's population has increased almost four times over.

REVIEW Would the population of Arizona be able to grow as quickly without a good irrigation system?
◉ **Draw Conclusions**

► Irrigation helps crops grow in New Mexico.

► Carrier's air-cooling system, 1922

Air Conditioning

Although air conditioning was invented in New York, the growth of air conditioning made it possible for businesses and people to thrive in the Southwest. In 1911, **Willis Haviland Carrier** developed a useful air-conditioning system. This system cooled the air temperature and lowered humidity, or moisture in the air, at the same time.

Many factories and businesses depend on air conditioning to keep their machines and workers cool. The first high-rise air-conditioned office building, the Milam Building, was opened in San Antonio, Texas, in 1928.

Today air conditioning is common in homes and offices. It has made the heat of the Southwest easier to bear.

> **REVIEW** What effect did the invention of air conditioning have on businesses in hot climates? **Cause and Effect**

Summarize the Lesson

1911 Willis H. Carrier developed a useful air-conditioning system.

1928 The air-conditioned Milam Building was competed in San Antonio, Texas.

1960 The California State Water Project began.

LESSON 4 REVIEW

Check Facts and Main Ideas

1. Cause and Effect On a separate sheet of paper, fill in the missing causes of the effects shown below.

Cause	Effect
	Farms and cities in Arizona grew.
	People could live more comfortably in hot climates.

2. How has irrigation changed the desert in Arizona? Use the word **aqueduct** in your answer.

3. Who developed a useful air-conditioning system?

4. How have people in desert communities been able to overcome the heat and lack of plentiful water?

5. Critical Thinking: *Point of View* How might an amusement park owner and a farmer view a hot, sunny day differently?

Link to Science

Learn About Dams Find out how dams can be used to make electric power. Draw a diagram to show how this process works.

Willis Haviland Carrier *1876–1950*

Willis Haviland Carrier, "the king of cool," helped develop modern air-conditioning. Carrier studied the temperature and humidity of air. In 1911 he developed the basic equations scientists use to understand how temperature and humidity are related. He started a company to make air-conditioning systems.

Carrier also studied people. Carrier reasoned that for people to be comfortable, both temperature and humidity must be controlled. Carrier invented ways to control both temperature and humidity. People found air-conditioned air to be comfortable and refreshing!

At first, air-conditioning was used in some factories where controlling temperature and humidity was necessary. In time, theater owners began to install air-conditioners. They hoped to attract customers during hot weather. Soon more businesses got air-conditioning.

Today many homes and cars are air-conditioned. Even some schools are air-conditioned.

Learn from Biographies

Why is Carrier known as the "the king of cool"?

For more information, go online to *Meet the People* at **www.sfsocialstudies.com**.

Save "America's Main Street"?

Or remove this drive-on museum in favor of newer, safer roads?

In the early 1900s, the United States government started building a system of national highways. Route 66 stretched 2,400 miles from Chicago, Illinois, to Santa Monica, California. New businesses grew along the road. They provided places where travelers could rest, eat, and sleep.

In time, the road began to crumble. It was not repaired. A new Interstate highway system grew, and its roads went through much of the area that Route 66 covered. People traveling on these newer, faster roads did not have to go through the towns that they passed. In 1985, Route 66 was no longer a United States highway. The official road signs were removed.

Some people do not want the government to spend the money to repair old Route 66. They feel that Interstates are safer and more efficient. Other people want to preserve Route 66 as a drive-on museum.

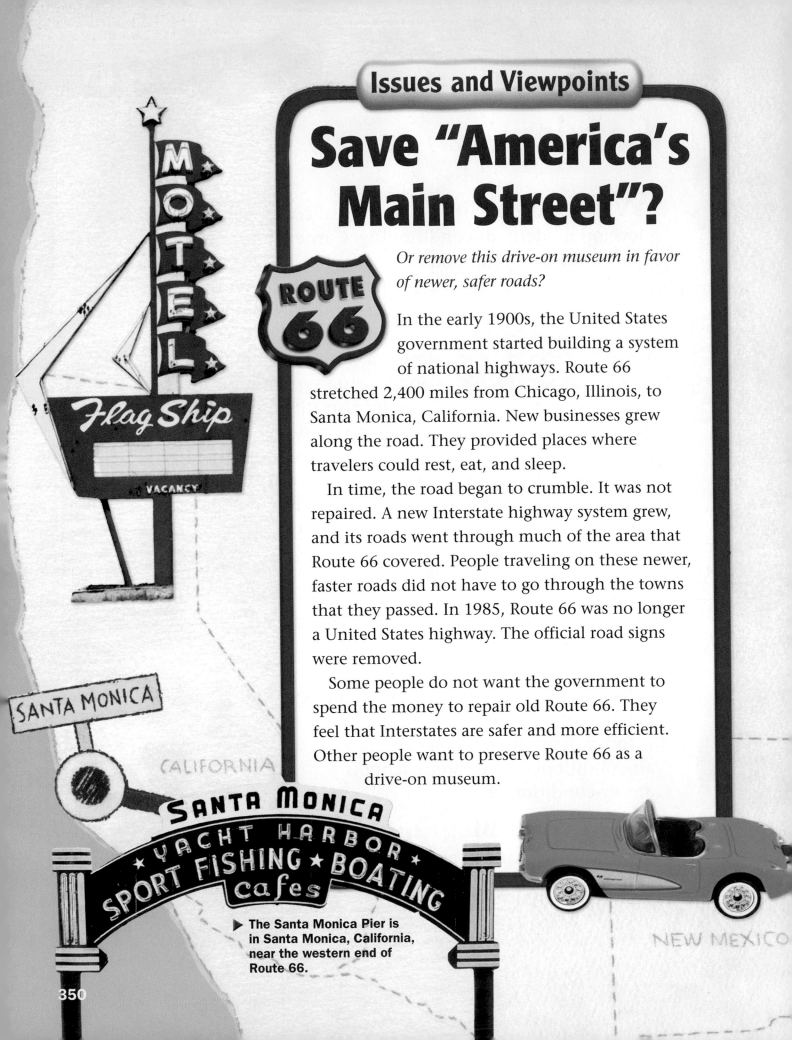

▶ The Santa Monica Pier is in Santa Monica, California, near the western end of Route 66.

350

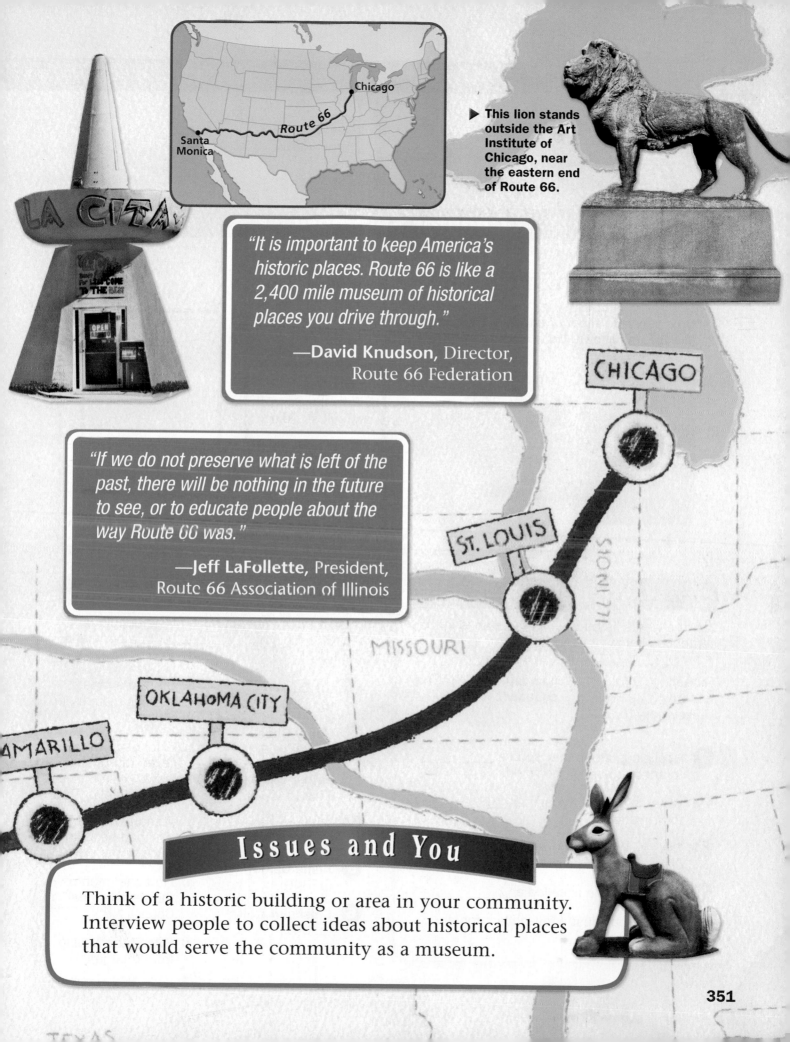

This lion stands outside the Art Institute of Chicago, near the eastern end of Route 66.

"It is important to keep America's historic places. Route 66 is like a 2,400 mile museum of historical places you drive through."

—**David Knudson**, Director, Route 66 Federation

"If we do not preserve what is left of the past, there will be nothing in the future to see, or to educate people about the way Route 66 was."

—**Jeff LaFollette**, President, Route 66 Association of Illinois

Issues and You

Think of a historic building or area in your community. Interview people to collect ideas about historical places that would serve the community as a museum.

1675   1725

1687
Father Kino
founded missions
in Arizona.

Chapter Summary

Draw Conclusions

On a separate sheet of paper, make a chart like the one shown. Draw a conclusion from the details listed.

▶ **A traditional Navajo hogan**

Details

The Navajo follow many of the same customs today as long ago.

Many missions built by the Spanish are still standing.

Modern cowboys dress and work very much like Spanish vaqueros.

Conclusion

Vocabulary

Use the words listed to fill in the blanks in the sentences below.

hogan (p. 325)   **homestead** (p. 342)
viceroy (p. 333)   **aqueduct** (p. 347)
missionary (p. 334)

1 A religious group may send a _____ to another part of the world.

2 Water is carried through an _____ for irrigation.

3 The _____ of Mexico wanted to claim land for Spain.

4 A Navajo home is called a _____.

5 Settlers paid just a few dollars for land called a _____.

People and Terms

Match the number of each of the people or terms in Column 1 with a letter of a phrase in Column 2.

1 **Kit Carson** (p. 326)

2 **Henry Chee Dodge** (p. 327)

3 **Father Eusebio Kino** (p. 334)

4 **Philip Armour** (p. 339)

5 **Annie Oakley** (p. 340)

6 **Chisholm Trail** (p. 341)

a. Started a meat-packing industry in Chicago

b. Extended from Texas to Kansas

c. A missionary

d. A sharpshooter who had her own wild-west show

e. First chairman of the Navajo Tribal Council

f. Forced the Navajo from their land

1853
King Ranch was established.

1864
The Long Walk

1865
Jesse Chisholm blazed a cattle trail.

1870
Philip Armour started a meat-packing industry.

1890
The open range was closed.

1911
Willis H. Carrier developed a useful air-conditioning system.

Facts and Main Ideas

1 How did cattle raising get started in Texas?

2 **Time Line** How many years passed between the blazing of the Chisholm Trail and the closing of the open range?

3 **Main Idea** Describe modern Navajo culture.

4 **Main Idea** How did missions help establish a Spanish presence in the Southwest?

5 **Main Idea** How have the cowboy and cowgirl been a part of our nation's lore?

6 **Main Idea** Why is the Southwest a fast-growing region today?

7 **Critical Thinking:** *Fact or Opinion* Which of the following statements are fact and which are opinion?
   a. Colonel Kit Carson captured the Navajo and held them prisoner for four years.
   b. It was not fair for Spanish missionaries to offer food and protection to Native Americans in exchange for work.
   c. Irrigation turned dry desert land into productive fields.

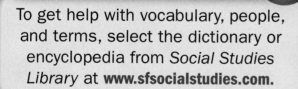

Internet Activity

To get help with vocabulary, people, and terms, select the dictionary or encyclopedia from *Social Studies Library* at **www.sfsocialstudies.com.**

Write About History

1 **Write a skit** about a day in the life of a cowboy or cowgirl.

2 **Write a TV commercial** about interesting places to visit in the Southwest.

3 **Write a magazine article** in which you tell how different the Southwest region would be without air conditioning.

Apply Skills

Identify Primary Sources

Read the primary source below. It is Coronado's description of a Native American pueblo in the Southwest from a report he made to a Spanish viceroy. Then answer the questions.

> "In this place where I am now lodged there are perhaps 200 houses, all surrounded by a wall, and it seems to me that with the other houses, which are not so surrounded, there might be altogether 500 families."

1 How do you know that this is a primary source?

2 What is the purpose of this document?

3 What is the main idea of this primary source?

End with Literature

Cowboy Country

BY ANN HERBERT SCOTT

Cowboy Country is a book that tells about the life of a cowboy, or *buckaroo*. Here is a part of the book that describes some of the things that a good buckaroo needs to learn.

Illustration by Ted Lewin

You think you'd like to learn to cowboy?
Then you'll need to watch and listen.
Most cowboys don't say much
but their eyes and ears are working all the time.
See that old cow lying on her side in the willows?
She may be asleep, but on the other hand
she could have run a thorn into her hoof.
Let's check her out. Right here by my saddle
I carry a kit for doctoring.
You don't need to be a vet
to give a sick calf a shot
or swab out a cut or treat a cow for worms.

See that bull over by the boulder?
I think he belongs to our neighbors
over beyond Lone Mountain.
Let's check his brand.

They trucked that critter all the way from Canada.
I know they wouldn't want to lose him now.

Do the cattle all look the same to you?
Well, they're just as different as people are
when you take the care to know them.
If you've seen western movies
or watched cowboys on TV,
you might guess it's bronc riding
and roping snorting steers that makes a top hand.
Well, you'd guess wrong.

Of course, any good buckaroo needs to know
how to handle a rough pony and slip a slick noose,
but it's reading cows that makes a good cowboy—
knowing what an old cow is thinking
before she knows herself. It takes years
to learn that—maybe a lifetime—
but you're starting young,
and you've got lots of time.

Main Ideas and Vocabulary

TEST PREP

Read the passage below and use it to answer the questions that follow.

Spanish explorer Francisco Vásquez de Coronado explored a large part of the Southwest in search of "Cities of Gold." He found only adobe <u>pueblos</u>. His explorations were labeled as failures.

When Spanish missionaries came to the Southwest, they brought cattle. Cattle ranching became an important part of the economy of the region. The American cowboy became a part of our nation's lore.

Later, the discovery of oil in the Southwest brought more jobs to the region. Oil brought wealth to people who came to invest in that resource.

The Navajo are one of the largest Native American groups in the United States. They also are ruled by one of the largest tribal councils. The Navajo have kept many of their old traditions.

Many people visit the Southwest to enjoy its beautiful landforms. Others come to see plants such as the saguaro cacti that grow only in the Sonoran Desert. Saguaro grow to be 60 feet tall. They are 80 years old before they begin to grow branches.

Much of the Southwest has an <u>arid</u> climate, but it is not all desert. Parts of the Southwest get a lot of rain and even have wetlands. Until the 1900s, heat and lack of water in the desert regions kept the population low. With the advances of irrigation and air conditioning, life in the desert became more comfortable. New businesses and the growth of technology have allowed desert cities to grow quickly.

1 Why did Coronado explore the Southwest?
   A He wanted to make Christians of the Navajo.
   B He was searching for the Grand Canyon.
   C He wanted to claim land.
   D He was looking for the "Cities of Gold."

2 In the passage, the word *pueblos* means—
   A Native American group
   B gold mines
   C villages
   D cattle ranches

3 According to this passage, the cactus pictured must be at least how many years old?
   A 80
   B 3
   C 25
   D 60

4 In the passage, the word *arid* means—
   A regional
   B dry
   C ranch land
   D irrigated

▶ **Saguaro cactus**

People

Choose five of the people listed below and use them in a paragraph about the Southwest Region.

García López de Cárdenas (p. 302)

John Wesley Powell (p. 302)

Theodore Roosevelt (p. 303)

Pattillo Higgins (p. 315)

Kit Carson (p. 326)

Henry Chee Dodge (p. 327)

Father Eusebio Kino (p. 334)

Philip Armour (p. 339)

Annie Oakley (p. 340)

Calamity Jane (p. 340)

Jesse Chisholm (p. 341)

Willis Haviland Carrier (p. 348)

Apply Skills

Create a Primary Source Guide About Your Community Write a three-paragraph description of a favorite community event or a favorite place in your community. With classmates, bind your descriptions into a book to create a primary source guide about your community.

Write and Share

Write and Perform a Skit With a group of classmates, write a skit about cattle ranching, cowboys, and cowgirls. Include examples that show how real lives of cowhands were different from what might be shown in a movie. Choose classmates to play each of the parts in the skit. Make costumes and perform the skit for another class.

Read on Your Own

Look for books like these in your library.

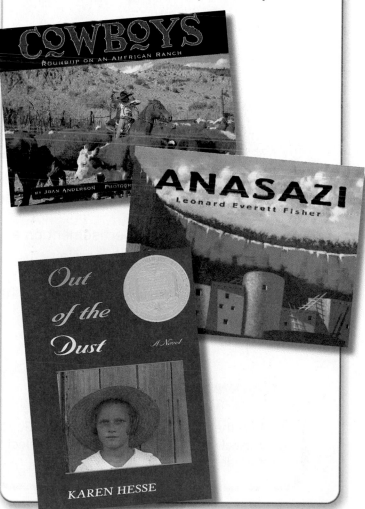

Ad Sales

Healthy businesses are good for your state's economy. Make your own infomercial about a product or a business.

1 **Form** a group. Choose a product or a business.

2 **Research** the product or business and write a list of facts about it.

3 **Write** a script for an infomercial about the product or business. Include the value and cost, as well as the history of the product or business. Give examples of its successes. Tell how it contributes to your state's economy.

4 **Make** an advertisement on a poster or banner to use in your infomercial.

5 **Present** your infomercial to the class.

Internet Activity

Explore the Southwest on the Internet. Go to **www.sfsocialstudies.com/activities** and select your grade and unit.

The West

How do the resources and people
of the West make the region unique?

"Climb the mountains. . . . Nature's peace will flow into you as sunshine flows into trees."

—John Muir, from *Our National Parks*, 1901

Thomas Moran's painting, *The Grand Canyon of the Yellowstone*, depicts one of the West's most striking landscapes.

Welcome to the West

CANADA

Key
- Pacific states
- Mountain states
- ★ State capital
- — National border

WASHINGTON
Olympia

CASCADE RANGE

Columbia River

ROCKY

MONTANA
★ Helena

Missouri River

Yellowstone River

ND

★ Salem
OREGON

SD

Boise ★
IDAHO

Snake River

WYOMING

NE

North Platte River

Cheyenne ★

SIERRA NEVADA

NEVADA

Great Salt Lake

★ Salt Lake City

UTAH

M
O
U
N
T
A
I
N
S

South Platte River

★ Denver
COLORADO

KS

Sacramento ★

Lake Tahoe

★ Carson City

GREAT BASIN

Colorado River

Arkansas River

San Joaquin River

CALIFORNIA

OK

TX

MOJAVE DESERT

Salton Sea

AZ

0   150   300 Miles
0   150   300 Kilometers

Rio Grande

NM

PACIFIC OCEAN

128°W

124°W

120°W

116°W

32°N

36°N

40°N

44°N

N

MEXICO

ARCTIC OCEAN

BROOKS RA.

ALASKA

CANADA

Juneau ★

PACIFIC OCEAN

0   300 Miles
0   300 Kilometers

70°N

60°N

50°N

160°W   150°W   140°W

PACIFIC OCEAN

HAWAII

Honolulu ★

0   100 Miles
0   100 Kilometers

160°W   155°W

20°N

▶ Sea otters live in the Pacific Ocean off the Northwest coast of the United States. Sea otters eat and sleep while floating on their backs.

▶ Most of the pineapples that are grown in the United States are grown in Hawaii.

▶ The Hoover Dam was built on the Colorado River on the border of Nevada and Arizona. Workers used more than 5 million barrels of concrete to build the dam.

▶ The Golden Gate bridge links San Francisco to Marin County, California. At 8,981 feet long, it is one of the longest suspension bridges in the world.

▶ The Rocky Mountains are the largest system of mountain ranges in North America. In the United States, the Rockies stretch across New Mexico, Colorado, Utah, Wyoming, Idaho, Montana, Washington, and Alaska.

▶ This redwood tree grows in California. Redwoods are the tallest trees in the United States. They can grow to a height of 350 feet and can live to be 2,000 years old.

363

Reading Social Studies

The West

Compare and Contrast

To **compare** is to tell how two or more things are alike. To **contrast** is to tell how two or more things are different.

Features that are alike   Features that are different

- Clue words such as *similar* and *as,* show comparisons.
- Clue words such as *different* and *but* show contrasts.
- Sometimes authors do not use clue words. Readers must make comparisons for themselves.

Read the paragraph. The sentences that **compare** and **contrast** have been highlighted.

Hawaii and southern California are alike in some ways, but are different in other ways. Both are warm and sunny much of the time. However, Hawaii has some areas that receive a great deal of rain. Unlike those places, southern California has desert areas that are very dry.

Word Exercise

Using Antonyms to Build Context An **antonym** is a word that means the opposite of another word. Learning both a word and its antonym can help you understand the word. You may be confused to read, "These volcanic mountains are also old, but many are still active." In this case, *active* means "acting or working"—active volcanoes erupt regularly. An antonym of *active* is *dormant*. *Dormant* means "asleep." A dormant volcano has not erupted in a very long time.

Not All Mountains Are the Same

There are a number of mountain ranges in the West. Two of these ranges are the Rocky Mountains and the Cascade Range. The Rocky Mountains extend more than 3,000 miles through the United States and Canada, but the Cascade Mountains cover a smaller distance, 700 miles, from northern California to British Columbia in Canada.

Most of the Rocky Mountains' peaks were formed millions of years ago during a huge shift in the Earth's crust. Over time, this shift created the mountains. Unlike most of the Rocky Mountains, many of the mountains in the Cascade Range are volcanoes. These volcanic mountains are also old, but many are still active. Mount St. Helens, one of the Cascade's most famous volcanoes, erupted in 1980.

Rainfall is heavy in the Cascade Range. Some parts get more than 100 inches of rainfall each year! The range takes its name from the cascades, or waterfalls, that can be seen in the area. Visitors to the Cascades, like those who go to the Rocky Mountains, can enjoy many different activities, including hiking and camping.

Apply it!

Use the reading strategy of comparing and contrasting to answer questions 1 and 2. Then answer the vocabulary question.

1 In what ways are the Cascade Range and the Rocky Mountains alike? Give examples from the passage that support your answer.

2 How do the two ranges of mountains differ from one another? What clue words are used in the passage to show contrast?

3 Look at the sentence that reads, "Over time, this shift created the mountains." What word is an antonym for *created*? How does the meaning of the sentence change if you replace *created* with this word?

Lesson 1

The Rocky Mountains
The Rocky Mountains are known for their majestic peaks and beautiful scenery.

1

Lesson 2

The Great Basin
The Great Basin covers many western states.

2

Lesson 3

California's Central Valley
Many fruits and vegetables come from the West.

3

ROCKY

1

CANADA

2

3

MOUNTAINS

NORTH

AMERICA

GREAT
BASIN

UNITED STATES

PACIFIC
OCEAN

CENTRAL VALLEY

MEXICO

Gulf of
Mexico

Why We Remember

The West is rich in natural resources. It has many different climates and landforms: tropics and tundra, rain forests and deserts, mountains and beaches. From the lush islands of Hawaii to the frozen lands of northern Alaska and the rugged peaks of the Rocky Mountains, the geography of the West has shaped the people who settled there. Likewise, the many cultures that have made their homes in the West have helped shape the land into a region of many contrasts.

Yellowstone
National Park

ROCKY
MOUNTAINS

PREVIEW

Focus on the Main Idea
Many parts of the West are mountainous.

PLACES

Rocky Mountains
Continental Divide
Yellowstone National Park

VOCABULARY

timberline
geyser
magma
volcano
lava

A Land of Mountains

You Are There

You have been hiking uphill for a long time. Now you are so far up the side of the mountain that there are no longer any trees growing along the trail. You know that you are not far from your goal. As you finally reach the top of the mountain, you take a look around. The peaks of other mountains rise to the north, south, and west. To the east, plains stretch as far as you can see. It is a clear day and you can see into the distance many miles away. You smile. You have hiked to the top of Pikes Peak!

Compare and Contrast
As you read, look for ways that the mountain ranges of the West are alike and different.

The Rocky Mountains

Pikes Peak, in Colorado, is one of the most famous peaks in the Rocky Mountains. The **Rocky Mountains** are the largest mountain system in North America. The "Rockies," as they are often called, are made up of a number of smaller ranges. Together, these ranges extend more than 3,000 miles from New Mexico north through Canada and into Alaska. In some places the Rockies are 350 miles wide. The highest peaks in the Rockies rise more than 14,000 feet above sea level. The Rocky Mountain states include Colorado, Utah, Wyoming, Idaho, and Montana.

The **Continental Divide** is an imaginary line that runs along the crest of the Rocky Mountains. Rivers on the east side of this line flow toward the Atlantic Ocean or the Gulf of Mexico. Rivers on the west side flow west toward the Pacific Ocean.

Most of the Rocky Mountains are covered with forests. However, most trees will not grow above a certain elevation. This line of elevation is called the **timberline.** Many Rocky Mountain peaks rise above the timberline. Most of these high peaks are covered with snow year-round.

Many animals live in the Rocky Mountains. The forests are home to black bears and grizzly bears, mountain lions, elk, mink, and many other creatures. Chipmunks, coyotes, and moose live in mountain valleys, and fish are plentiful in mountain streams. Even above the timberline, mountain goats and bighorn sheep make their homes.

The people who live in the Rocky Mountain states make use of the area's many natural resources such as minerals, ranch lands, and timber. Tourism is also important to the Rocky Mountain economy. Many people visit the Rockies every year to hike, ski, climb mountains, and enjoy the scenery.

▶ **Elk**

REVIEW What is different about the Rocky Mountains below the timberline and above the timberline?
↻ **Compare and Contrast**

Yellowstone National Park

Yellowstone National Park is the oldest national park in the world. It was established in 1872. The park covers more than 2.2 million acres of the northwest corner of Wyoming, and includes parts of Idaho and Montana. Yellowstone is famous for its many natural attractions, such as mountains, canyons, waterfalls, lakes, forests, and wildlife.

By far, Yellowstone's most popular points of interest are its geysers and hot springs. A hot spring is a pool of water heated by forces beneath Earth's surface. A **geyser** is a type of hot spring that erupts, shooting hot water into the air. There are more than 10,000 hot springs and geysers in Yellowstone. One of the most famous geysers in the park is Old Faithful, which erupts every 45 to 110 minutes.

Each time Old Faithful erupts, it sends a stream of boiling water more than a hundred feet into the air.

Why does Yellowstone have so many geysers and hot springs? Part of the park is located over a "hot spot" in Earth's crust. According to scientists, a hot spot occurs where **magma,** or molten rock, lies close to Earth's surface rather than deep underground. This magma heats groundwater that rises to the surface, causing geysers and hot springs.

Yellowstone National Park is also a place where wildlife can roam free. No one may hunt animals within the park, although fishing is allowed. As a result, many animals native to the West live within the boundaries of the park. Bison, which are also called buffalo, are plentiful in the park. Elk and moose also live within the park. Black bears, grizzly bears, and wolves are among the animals wildlife

▶ **Bison and other animals graze near hot springs during Yellowstone's winter.**

▶ **Forests in Yellowstone are still recovering from fires in 1988.**

watchers come to Yellowstone to view.

In 1988, a large portion of the park was burned in a series of wildfires. Although many acres of forests were burned, by the next year the forests were showing signs of new growth. The fires and the forests' recovery have given firefighters and scientists a chance to study the effects of wildfire in the West.

REVIEW What is the difference between a geyser and a hot spring?
◆ **Compare and Contrast**

Western Mountain Ranges

The Rocky Mountains are not the only mountains in the West. Some mountain ranges, such as the Sierra Nevada, which extends through eastern California and western Nevada, are similar to the Rockies. They are high, rugged mountains with several peaks that rise higher than 14,000 feet above sea level. Other western ranges, such as Washington's Olympic Mountains, lie along the Pacific coast.

Still other western mountain ranges, such as the Cascade Range in Washington, Oregon, and northern California, and the Aleutian Range in Alaska, have volcanoes. A **volcano** is a mountain with an opening through which ash, gas, and lava are forced. Lava, like magma, is molten rock. Magma that rises and flows on Earth's surface is called lava.

All the mountains of Hawaii are volcanoes. This chain of islands formed as volcanoes rose from the

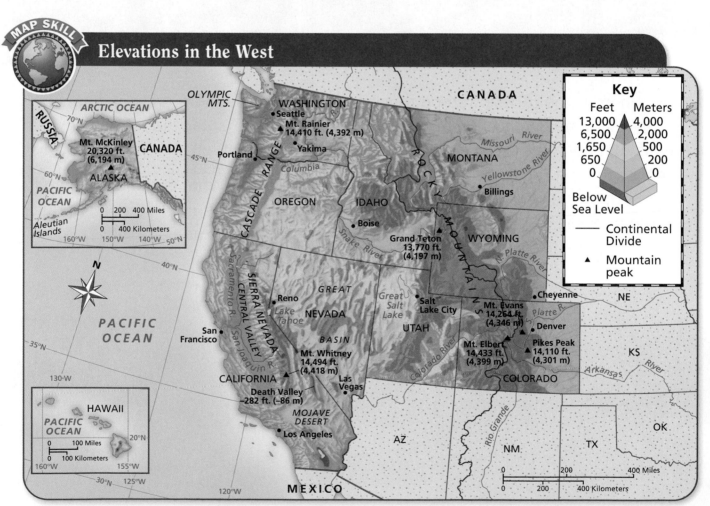

MAP SKILL
Elevations in the West

Key

Feet	Meters
13,000	4,000
6,500	2,000
1,650	500
650	200
0	0

Below Sea Level

—— Continental Divide

▲ Mountain peak

Mt. McKinley 20,320 ft. (6,194 m)

Mt. Rainier 14,410 ft. (4,392 m)

Grand Teton 13,770 ft. (4,197 m)

Mt. Evans 14,264 ft. (4,346 m)

Mt. Elbert 14,433 ft. (4,399 m)

Pikes Peak 14,110 ft. (4,301 m)

Mt. Whitney 14,494 ft. (4,418 m)

Death Valley −282 ft. (−86 m)

▶ The West has the highest and lowest elevations in North America.

MAP SKILL Use an Elevation Map *What state has the greatest difference in elevation?*

372

ocean floor. Hawaii's Mount Kilauea is one of the world's most active volcanoes.

REVIEW How are the Sierra Nevada and the Cascade Range alike? How are they different?

↷ **Compare and Contrast**

Summarize the Lesson

- The Rockies are a large system of mountains that support many kinds of plants and animals.
- Attractions at Yellowstone National Park include geysers, hot springs, and lots of wildlife.
- The West has a variety of mountain ranges.

▶ **Craggy peaks in the Sierra Nevada**

LESSON 1 REVIEW

Check Facts and Main Ideas

1. ↷ **Compare and Contrast** On a separate sheet of paper, make a chart to compare and contrast the Rocky Mountains and the Sierra Nevada. Tell how they are similar and how they are different.

Similarities	Differences

2. Which mountain system is the largest in the United States?
3. How are geysers similar to volcanoes?
4. Name some of the states in the West where mountains are located.
5. **Critical Thinking:** *Make Inferences* Why are a great many national parks located in the West?

Link to ⚭ Geography

Find the Geysers Use reference materials to learn where geysers can be found on Earth besides Yellowstone National Park. Give a report that tells what these locations have in common besides geysers.

373

When a Mountain Explodes

A volcano is a mountain that forms from material from deep inside Earth. Different kinds of volcanoes erupt in different ways. But when all volcanoes erupt, hot material from inside Earth moves to Earth's surface. This hot, melted rock material is known as magma. An active volcano is one that is erupting or might erupt. After a volcano erupts, it may remain dormant. A dormant volcano is one that has not erupted in recent times. Mount St. Helens in Washington had not erupted for 123 years. Then, in 1980, it erupted in a huge explosion. The sound of the explosion was heard 200 miles away.

Sleeping Giant
Mount St. Helens is in the Cascade mountain range. Before it erupted on May 18, 1980, Mount St. Helens was a popular vacation place. It was surrounded by peaceful forests and lakes.

Mount St. Helens Erupting
After two months of small earthquakes, the hot magma deep inside the volcano began to explode. This picture was taken 38 seconds after the first explosion started. The side of the mountain gave way, and a cloud of ash and gas blew into the sky.

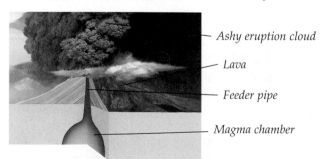

Ashy eruption cloud

Lava

Feeder pipe

Magma chamber

Inside the Volcano
Magma gathered far underground in a magma chamber. Powerful forces pushed the magma upward through the feeder pipe. Then magma, ash, and gases were pushed upward and erupted on the surface. Magma that erupts onto Earth's surface is called lava.

Four Seconds Later...
The cloud of ash grows with newly erupted material. The new material quickly rolls over the rock that had been blown from the side of the mountain.

Cascade Volcano
Mount Rainier is another volcano in the Cascade Mountains, the group that includes Mount St. Helens. Mount Rainier erupted last in the 1840s.

Mauna Loa Erupts
All the islands of Hawaii grew as volcanoes. Mauna Loa is an active volcano on the island of Hawaii. Mauna Loa erupts as a fire fountain. Lava streams down its side.

Flowing Lava
Lava like this in Hawaii erupts more slowly than at Mount St. Helens. It moves slowly down the mountain. Even so, the lava is very hot. This picture was taken at night, when you can easily see the red glow of the hot, melted rock.

Eleven Seconds Later...
The rock from the mountainside is almost completely covered by ash. Huge chunks of rock have been thrown out from the ash cloud.

375

Take Notes and Write Outlines

What? Notes are bits of information you write in your own words. An **outline** is a framework for organizing information. It lets you see main ideas and details at a glance.

Why? Taking notes helps you remember what you have read. You can use your notes to make an outline. Taking notes and making an outline are useful ways to study for a test or prepare a report.

How? Follow these steps to take notes and write an outline.

• As you read, look for main ideas and important details. Write each main idea as a heading. Use the note card on page 377 as an example.

• Write important facts and details below the heading. Use your own words. You do not need to use complete sentences. Be sure to write the title of the source, the author's name, the publication date, and the page number where you found the information.

• Sort your note cards into an order that makes sense. Then use your cards to write an outline.

• Follow the example of the outline on page 377. Write the main ideas from your cards next to Roman numerals. Then write important facts about those ideas next to a capital letter below the main idea.

Think and Apply

1 What is the source of the information on the note card on page 377?

2 What important fact can be written next to *B* under Roman numeral *I* in the outline on page 377?

3 How can taking **notes** and creating an **outline** help you prepare for a test?

Volcano A volcano is an opening in Earth's crust through which lava, hot gas, and rocks erupt. A volcano forms when melted rock from deep within Earth blasts upward through the surface. Volcanoes are often cone-shaped mountains.

The cone is caused by the buildup of lava and other materials released from inside the volcano during eruptions. It takes thousands of years to form.

Encyclopedia One

712

Description of a volcano

- a hole in Earth's surface
- lava, hot gas, and pieces of rock erupt through the hole
- volcanoes—often cone-shaped mountains

Encyclopedia One, Michael Matthews,

2002, p. 712

Volcanoes

I. Description of a volcano

A. A volcano is an opening in Earth's surface.

B. _____

C. Volcanoes are often mountains.

II. How volcanoes form

A. Melted rock deep within Earth erupts from an opening in Earth's surface.

B. Lava, hot gas, and rocks come out.

C. The buildup of these materials over thousands of years forms a cone-shaped mountain.

PREVIEW

Focus on the Main Idea
The climate in different areas
of the West varies greatly.

PLACES
Mount McKinley, Alaska
Death Valley, California
Great Basin
Mount Waialeale, Hawaii
Cascade Range

VOCABULARY
tundra
frigid
rain shadow

▶ Iditarod
teams
take 10
to 17
days to
complete
the race.

Climates in the West

You Are There It's below zero and the wind is blowing across the frozen tundra. You and your team of dogs are waiting at the starting line of the Iditarod (eye DIT uh rod). This race is the most famous dogsled race in the world. You will race for more than a thousand miles between Anchorage and Nome, Alaska.

You hear the announcer yell, "Go!" The dogs dash forward and your sled flies from the starting line. The cold air stings your face as your sled picks up speed. The crowd by the side of the trail cheers as you ride off into the Alaskan wilderness.

Compare and Contrast As you read, look for places in the West that have the same or different climates.

▶ **Mt. McKinley, also known as Denali, is the tallest mountain in North America.**

The Frosty North

Many areas of the western region of the United States have very cold winter temperatures. The tundra in Alaska, where the Iditarod is held, is one of these places. A **tundra** is a cold, flat area where trees cannot grow.

Think about these Alaskan temperatures, and you will understand how cold it really is there. In Barrow, Alaska, in the northern part of the state, the average temperature in February is −11°F. The record low temperature was recorded on January 23, 1971. On that day in Prospect Creek, Alaska, the temperature dropped to −80°F—80 degrees below zero. To understand how cold this is, remember that water freezes at 32°F *above* zero.

Not all of Alaska has these **frigid** — or very cold—temperatures. Parts of southern Alaska have temperatures that range between 28°F and 55°F during the whole year.

Some of the other states in the West also have cold winter temperatures. Idaho, Montana, Wyoming, Colorado, and parts of Washington have wintry temperatures and heavy snowfall. For example, the average temperature in January in Idaho is only 23°F.

The cold, snowy weather in parts of the West attracts thousands of tourists each year. People enjoy winter sports. They downhill ski and snowboard in the mountains. Other winter activities that people enjoy are cross-country skiing, snowshoeing, dog sledding, and ice fishing.

Tourists also enjoy the scenery, such as Alaska's majestic **Mount McKinley**. It is the highest peak in North America at 20,320 feet. Its peak is covered with snow year-round.

REVIEW How does the temperature in Alaska differ from the northern part of the state to the southern part?
⊙ **Compare and Contrast**

A Region of Many Climates

Unlike the wintry areas of the northern part of the region, parts of the West have warm weather throughout the year. Temperatures in some parts of California and Hawaii, for example, rarely drop below freezing—even in the middle of winter!

Hawaii has a tropical climate. People who live there and visitors all enjoy the warm, wet climate of Hawaii year-round. The islands have tropical rain forests, where the plants grow large and full.

▶ **A tropical rain forest in Hawaii**

California is such a large state that it has a variety of climates. Overall, though, California has two main seasons—the rainy season in the winter and the dry season in the summer. Temperatures in southern California are warm all year. Temperatures in northern California are cool in the winter, but rarely below freezing. Winter weather does come to parts of California—freezing temperatures and snow can be found in the mountains in winter.

Yet another climate can be found in California. There are deserts in southern California in the interior of the state. **Death Valley** is a desert area in southern California.

Death Valley is actually part of the **Great Basin,** a desert region in the West that includes most of Nevada and parts of Oregon, Utah, Idaho, and

▶ The Great Salt Lake is the largest inland body of salt water in the Western Hemisphere.

Wyoming. The word basin usually means "a wide, shallow bowl for holding liquids." The reason that this part of the country is called a basin is that the water from its streams drains into the area instead of into rivers that lead to an ocean. One place the water drains into in the Great Basin is the Great Salt Lake in Utah.

The Great Basin gets very hot on summer days. There are few trees. The desert shrubs that grow there need only small amounts of water to survive.

REVIEW Name one way in which Hawaii and the Great Basin are similar and one way in which they are different. ➲ **Compare and Contrast**

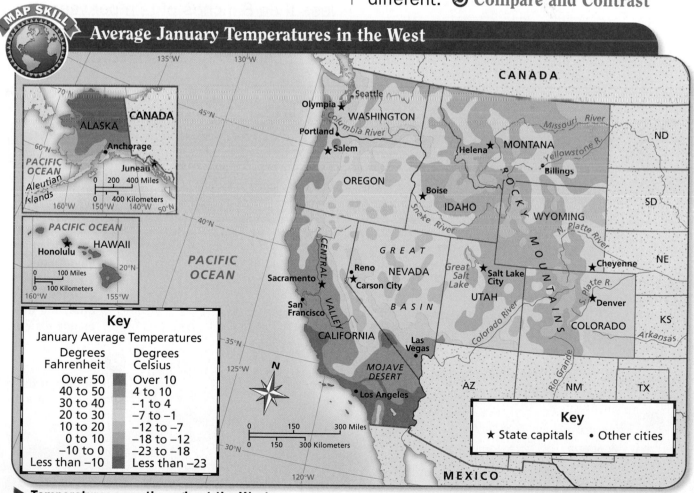

MAP SKILL **Average January Temperatures in the West**

Key
January Average Temperatures

Degrees Fahrenheit	Degrees Celsius
Over 50	Over 10
40 to 50	4 to 10
30 to 40	−1 to 4
20 to 30	−7 to −1
10 to 20	−12 to −7
0 to 10	−18 to −12
−10 to 0	−23 to −18
Less than −10	Less than −23

Key
★ State capitals • Other cities

▶ Temperatures vary throughout the West.

MAP SKILL Using Map Key *Which state has the greatest variation in temperature as shown on the map?*

Let It Rain . . . and Snow!

Precipitation in the West varies greatly. On average, fewer than two inches of rain fall each year in Death Valley, California. In fact, from October 3, 1912, to November 8, 1914, part of Death Valley had no precipitation at all. That is more than two years without rain!

However, the West is also known for record snowfalls. One of the largest snowfalls in one year was recorded at Rainier Paradise Ranger Station in Washington in the early 1970s. In one year, 1,122 inches of snow fell! Silver Lake, Colorado, has experienced one of the largest snowfalls in a 24-hour period—76 inches. That is more than six feet of snow in one day!

Some parts of the West are very rainy. The wettest place on Earth is **Mount Waialeale** (wah ya lee AH lee) in Hawaii. The average yearly rainfall on the mountain is 460 inches, or more than 38 feet of water.

Parts of Washington are also very wet. The high mountains in the **Cascade Range** greatly affect the surrounding area. West of the Cascades, in much of the Olympic Peninsula of Washington, precipitation averages more than 135 inches—or more than 11 feet—per year.

In contrast, areas east of the Cascades receive much less rain. For example, Yakima, Washington, receives less than 8 inches of rain per year.

The reason for this difference is an effect called the **rain shadow.** Winds

The Cascade Rain Shadow

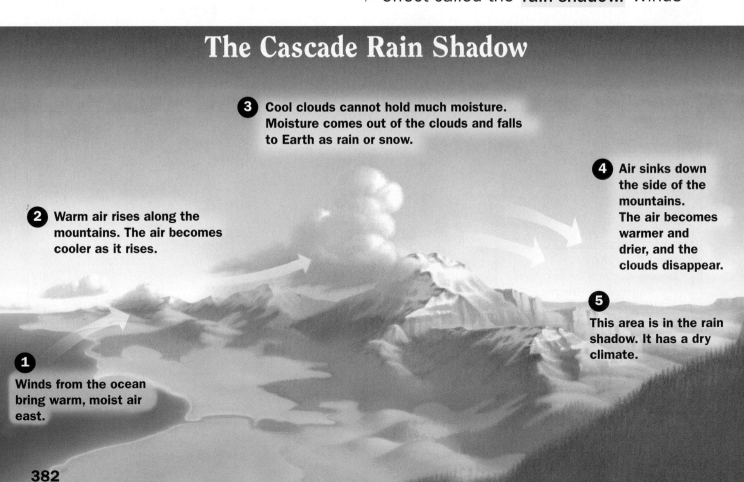

3 Cool clouds cannot hold much moisture. Moisture comes out of the clouds and falls to Earth as rain or snow.

4 Air sinks down the side of the mountains. The air becomes warmer and drier, and the clouds disappear.

2 Warm air rises along the mountains. The air becomes cooler as it rises.

5 This area is in the rain shadow. It has a dry climate.

1 Winds from the ocean bring warm, moist air east.

from the Pacific Ocean bring warm, moist air east. This warm air rises and forms clouds. The winds push the clouds up against the mountains. As the clouds rise, they become cooler. Cool air cannot hold as much moisture as warm air, so much of the water falls back to Earth as rain or snow on the western side of the mountains. By the time the clouds have passed to the eastern side of the mountains, they carry very little moisture. Therefore, the eastern side of the Cascade Range receives less rain than the western side. The land east of the Cascades lies in the rain shadow.

▶ Tropical flowers, such as this Bird of Paradise, thrive in Hawaii's warm climate.

REVIEW Why might the West be known as a region of weather contrasts? **Main Idea and Details**

Summarize the Lesson

- **Though many areas of Alaska are very cold, some parts of the state have much milder climates.**
- **The West has areas that are warm and tropical year-round.**
- **The West is home to the wettest and driest places in the nation.**

LESSON 2 ▶ REVIEW

Check Facts and Main Ideas

1. 🔄 **Compare and Contrast** On a separate sheet of paper, make a chart like the one below. List similarities and differences in the climates of Hawaii and California.

Similarities	Differences

2. Which state experienced one of the largest snowfalls in one year?

3. Explain how the **rain shadow** works.

4. Name three different climates in the West, and give an example of each.

5. **Critical Thinking:** *Point of View* Think about living in Barrow, Alaska. What do you think would be different from the way that you live now? What advantages are there to living in such a cold climate?

Link to ∞ Science

Learn About Plants With a partner, do research in the library or on the Internet to find out more about plants that live on the **tundra.** Present what you learned to the class.

WILLAMETTE VALLEY

CENTRAL VALLEY

Resources of the West

PREVIEW

Focus on the Main Idea
The West is rich in natural resources.

PLACES
Willamette Valley, Oregon
Central Valley, California

VOCABULARY
greenhouse
livestock
reforest

You Are There
The summer is over and the coolness of autumn has begun to turn the leaves gold and brown. You head for the tree that is filled with the largest apples in the orchard. You sling a canvas bag over one shoulder and climb a ladder up to the tree's branches. You reach out and pick an apple. This is just the first of many apples you'll harvest today, but this one's not going in the bag. You smile and put this apple in your pocket so that you can enjoy it later. You know it will taste wonderful. You are so lucky that your parents own this apple orchard.

Summarize As you read, think of ways to summarize what you have learned about the wide variety of resources in the West.

The Plentiful West

Apples are one of the many agricultural products of the West. Apples do not grow in all parts of the West, however. Like most crops, they grow where the climate and land are best for their growth.

The eastern part of Washington is famous for the many types of apples that are grown there. Cherries, pears, and potatoes are also grown in Washington. The biggest producer of potatoes in the United States, though, is Idaho. Oregon's **Willamette Valley** farms grow many types of berries and a wide variety of vegetables.

The state that produces the widest variety of fruits, vegetables, and nuts is California. Many farms are in the **Central Valley.** This huge area lies between the California Coastal Range to the west and the Sierra Nevada to the east. Among the fruits grown there are grapes, strawberries, peaches, plums, and melons.

Some Alaskan crops are barley, oats, hay, and potatoes. The harsh climate

▶ Apples are harvested from late August to early November.

in parts of Alaska will not support many types of plants. Some Alaskan crops are grown in greenhouses. A **greenhouse** is an enclosed structure that allows light to enter and keeps heat and moisture from escaping.

Hawaii's tropical climate is good for growing sugarcane and pineapples. Other Hawaiian crops are macadamia nuts and coffee.

REVIEW How would you compare the agricultural products of California and Alaska? ⊙ **Compare and Contrast**

Literature and Social Studies

This type of short poem is a haiku. The word *haiku* comes from Japanese words meaning "joke" and "poem."

Ripening Cherries
by Florence Vilén

Ripening cherries,
who is the first to take them,
a hand or a beak?

Not Just Fruits and Vegetables

The West produces more than just fruits, vegetables, grains, and nuts. In some western states, livestock are the main source of income from agriculture. **Livestock** are animals that are raised on farms and ranches. Cattle, sheep, and pigs are examples of livestock. Montana, Idaho, Colorado, Washington, Wyoming, Alaska, and Utah all include beef cattle as one of their main sources of income. Nevada, Utah, and Montana also produce sheep and sheep products such as wool. Milk is produced in states around the region as well.

The fishing industry is very important to the economy of some Western states. In Alaska the yearly fish catch is valued at more than a billion dollars. Workers catch cod, flounder, salmon, and halibut, among other types of fish. Shellfish, such as crab and shrimp, are also important to Alaska's economy. Hawaii also has a large fishing industry. Swordfish and tuna are caught off the coast of Hawaii.

▶ Fishing for salmon

In addition to the many food products that are grown in the West, many states grow flowers, plants, and bushes to be sold in plant and flower shops. These are often referred to as greenhouse products because they are generally grown in a greenhouse.

The West is also known for its wealth of mineral resources. Alaska and California produce oil. Coal, gold, and lead are three minerals mined in Colorado. Gold, silver, and copper, among other minerals, are mined in Nevada and Utah.

REVIEW Name one way in which Alaska and Hawaii are similar.
🔁 **Compare and Contrast**

▶ Cattle are one kind of livestock.

Agricultural Products of the West Region

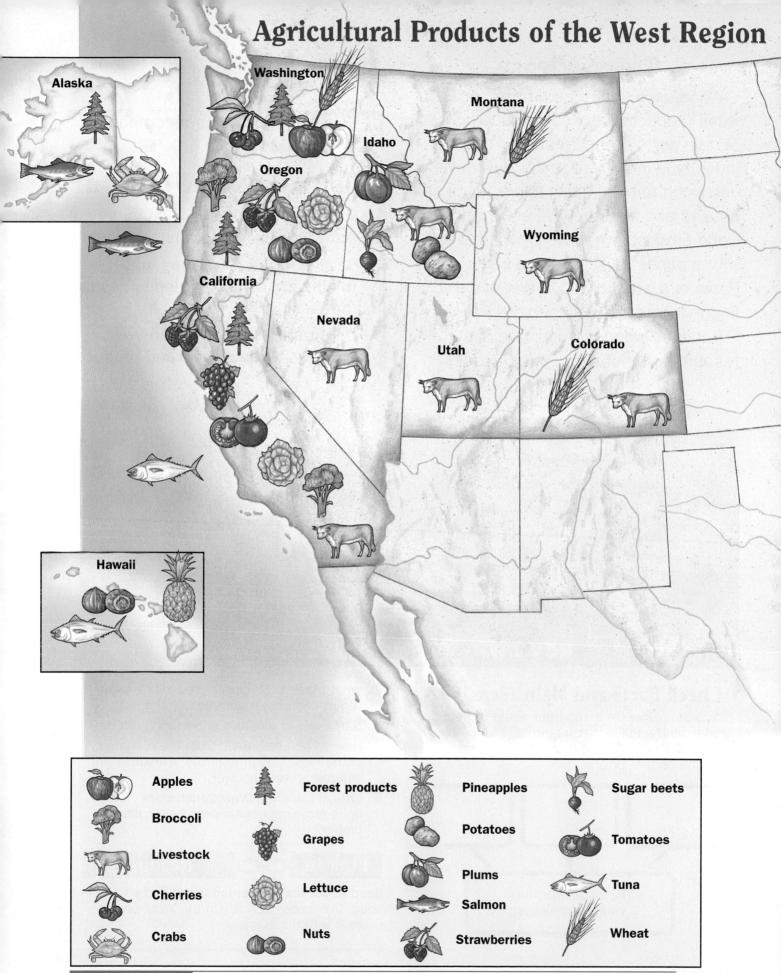

Alaska

Washington

Oregon

California

Idaho

Montana

Wyoming

Nevada

Utah

Colorado

Hawaii

Apples	Forest products	Pineapples	Sugar beets
Broccoli	Grapes	Potatoes	Tomatoes
Livestock	Lettuce	Plums	Tuna
Cherries		Salmon	Wheat
Crabs	Nuts	Strawberries	

DIAGRAM SKILL *According to this map, what states provide salmon? What states provide tuna?*
salmon: Washington, Alaska; tuna: California, Hawaii

387

Trees, Please

Wood, also known as timber, and wood products are also produced in certain parts of the West. The timber industry is important to the region. We use wood to build many things, such as houses and furniture. We also use wood products when we clean up a spill with a paper towel or read a book. Paper is a wood product. Wood is a very important part of our everyday lives.

Because wood is such a valuable resource, timber companies usually **reforest,** or plant new trees to replace the ones they have cut.

REVIEW Why do timber companies reforest? **Main Idea and Details**

Summarize the Lesson

- **The West produces a wide variety of fruits, vegetables, grains, and nuts.**
- **Raising livestock, fishing, and mining are important industries in the West.**
- **The timber industry in the West provides a variety of wood products.**

LESSON 3 REVIEW

Check Facts and Main Ideas

1. **Summarize** On a separate sheet of paper, draw the following diagram. Fill in the boxes with examples to support the summary in the bottom box.

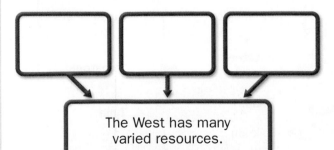

The West has many varied resources.

2. What place in California produces a wide variety of fruits, vegetables, and nuts?

3. Name one of Alaska's important industries.

4. How do people benefit from the resources of the West? Use the terms **livestock** and **reforest** in your answer.

5. **Critical Thinking: *Draw Conclusions*** How does recycling newspapers help conserve timber?

Link to ∞ Reading

Read About the Timber Industry Find an article about the timber industry in the West and share it with the class.

SETH LEWELLING

1820–1896

Seth Lewelling was born in 1820 in Randolph County, North Carolina. In 1850 Lewelling moved to Milwaukie, Oregon, and joined his brother in his plant nursery.

The Lewelling nursery was successful. Ah Bing, a farmer from China, was hired as a supervisor. He managed a team of workers. In time the nursery had 18,000 small plants to sell.

The first trees in Lewelling's nursery traveled with the family over the Oregon Trail.

BIOFACT

Lewelling and Bing became friends. Both men knew how to develop new varieties of plants. They both understood that farmers wanted to sell as much fruit as they could. Fruit that could be shipped a long way and still taste good was important.

In time, Lewelling and Bing developed a large, dark cherry that had a sweet taste. It remained crisp even when shipped a long way. Lewelling named it the Bing cherry in honor of Ah Bing. Today more people in the United States eat Bing cherries than any other variety.

Learn from Biographies

Popular varieties of apples and grapes were also developed at the Lewelling nursery. Why do you think the nursery was successful in developing new fruits?

For more information, go online to *Meet the People* at **www.sfsocialstudies.com**.

Chapter Summary

Compare and Contrast

On a separate sheet of paper, make a chart and label it like the one shown. List at least one similarity and three differences between the Rocky Mountains and desert areas of the West.

Similarities | **Differences**

▶ **Rocky Mountains**

Vocabulary

Use each word in a sentence that explains the meaning of the word.

1. **timberline** (p. 369)

2. **geyser** (p. 370)

3. **magma** (p. 370)

4. **tundra** (p. 379)

5. **rain shadow** (p. 382)

6. **livestock** (p. 386)

Places

Fill in the blanks with the place that best completes the sentence.

1. _____ form the largest system of mountains in North America. (p. 369)

2. Rivers to the east of the _____ flow toward the Atlantic Ocean. (p. 369)

3. The oldest national park in the world is _____. (p. 370)

4. A large desert region that covers many western states is _____. (p. 380)

5. _____ is the wettest place in the world. (p. 382)

Facts and Main Ideas

1. What two nations do the Rocky Mountains extend through?

2. Describe two of the landforms in Yellowstone National Park.

3. Name two valleys in the West that produce many fruits and vegetables.

4. **Main Idea** Name three mountain ranges in the West.

5. **Main Idea** Why is the land on the eastern side of the Cascade Range drier than land on the western side?

6. **Main Idea** Describe the agriculture of the West.

7. **Critical Thinking:** *Draw Conclusions* Why are greenhouses important in Alaska?

Write About Geography

1. **Write a journal entry** about a trip to Yellowstone National Park. The entry might involve an animal or a landform.

2. **Write a poem** about climbing a mountain in the Rocky Mountains. Describe what you see and how you feel.

3. **Write an advertisement** for a tour company that takes people through the West. Describe three places where you would take visitors.

Apply Skills

Write Notes and Outlines

Read the following outline. Then answer the questions.

> I. Farm products of the West
>
>   A. Fruit
>
>   B. Vegetables
>
>   C. Livestock
>
> II. Metal ores of the West
>
>   A. Copper
>
>   B. Gold
>
>   C. Silver

1. What title would you give this outline?

2. Would a note card's information about apples fit into this outline? If so, where?

3. How might you use this outline?

Internet Activity

To get help with vocabulary, people, and terms, select the dictionary or encyclopedia from *Social Studies Library* at **www.sfsocialstudies.com.**

Lesson 1

Tlingit Cultural Region
The Tlingit are part of the rich cultural history of the West.

1

Lesson 2

Sutter's Mill, California
The Gold Rush brought many new settlers to the West.

2

Lesson 3

Los Angeles, California
The film and computer industries are important to the West.

3

Tlingit
Cultural Region

CANADA

NORTH
AMERICA

UNITED STATES

Sutter's Mill

Los Angeles

PACIFIC
OCEAN

Gulf of
Mexico

MEXICO

Why We Remember

People have long been attracted to the West because of its rich resources. People have lived in the West for thousands of years. Even before the Gold Rush, Americans were traveling west for rich farmland and living space. Then the Gold Rush brought thousands of people from all over the world. Many stayed even after most of the gold was gone, and more have since arrived. All the people of the West, past and present, have aided the development of the culture and economy of the United States.

ALASKA (U.S.)
YUKON TERR.
Tlingit Cultural Region
CANADA
Juneau
PACIFIC OCEAN
BRITISH COLUMBIA

PREVIEW

Focus on the Main Idea
The Tlingit live in the northern part of the West.

PLACES
Tlingit Cultural Region
Juneau, Alaska

VOCABULARY
totem pole
potlatch

▶ **Tlingit wood carving**

The Tlingit

You Are There
Two people enter the room carrying a dish full of food that's as large as a canoe. You've never seen so much food! You are a guest at a Tlingit potlatch. Your best friend's family is celebrating the raising of their new totem pole. Your friend's grandfather rises to give a speech welcoming his guests. Soon the singing and dancing will begin. Your friend and her family help her grandfather hand out presents to the guests. Your best friend hands you a special gift. She has chosen it just for you. After the feast, the family gives the extra food to the guests—food that everyone will eat at home and remember this celebration.

Summarize As you read, think of ways to summarize what you have learned about the Tlingit.

Tlingit Traditions

The Tlingit (KLINHNG it) are Native Americans who live along the southeastern coast of Alaska and the northern coast of British Columbia in Canada. This area makes up the Tlingit cultural region. The influence of Tlingit culture is strong throughout this area.

This region is rich in natural resources. Vast forests grow there, and fish and game are plentiful. For hundreds of years the Tlingit made good use of these resources. They fished for salmon and hunted deer and seals. They used large planks of wood to build large homes. The Tlingit often carved figures into the doorways of their homes. Tlingit families often placed totem poles outside their homes as well, and some Tlingit families still follow this tradition. A totem pole is a tall post carved with the images of people and animals. These images are often brightly painted. They often represent the history of the family.

The Tlingit lived in these homes during winter. During the warmer months, they moved to smaller wooden homes near hunting and fishing grounds. They carved wooden canoes for fishing and hunting.

Because game and fish were so plentiful, the Tlingit were able to spend time making and trading goods such as canoes, blankets, copper tools and ornaments, baskets, and seal oil. They had a large trading network with other Native Americans. Sometimes they bought goods from one group to trade with another.

One of the most prized Tlingit products, even today, is the Chilkat (CHILL kat) blanket. It was traditionally woven from the dyed wool of mountain goats and sheep. These colorful blankets have detailed designs of shapes and animals. Just as a totem pole might tell the story of a family, the designs on a Chilkat blanket tell stories too.

REVIEW Whom did the Tlingit trade with, and what did they trade?
Main Idea and Details

▶ A Tlingit totem pole

▶ Guests at a potlatch often perform traditional dances.

The Potlatch

A **potlatch** is a feast held to celebrate important events such as a wedding, a birth, or a death. A potlatch also shows a family's importance to the community. Sometimes more than a hundred guests will attend a potlatch. Many northwestern Native Americans, including the Tlingit, hold potlatches. This tradition has been practiced since long before Europeans came to this region.

During a potlatch long ago, the host gave gifts such as canoes, blankets, and other goods to each of the guests. The host and honored guests made speeches. People put on carved masks and participated in traditional dances.

The host also tried to provide much more food than the guests could eat during the feast, which could last up to twelve days. Often, guests took food home so that they could share the host's generosity with others.

The potlatch is still an important part of the Tlingit culture. Speeches, dancing, feasting, and gift-giving are still important parts of a modern potlatch, although today's gifts often include money and household goods. Many modern potlatches are held during the weekend so that guests do not have to miss work or school.

REVIEW What types of events occur at a potlatch? **Summarize**

▶ Chilkat blanket

The Tlingit Today

Some Tlingit live on the same land their families have lived on for centuries. Many Tlingit make their living by logging or fishing. They live in modern villages and combine their traditions with everyday modern life.

The Tlingit and Haida (HEYE duh), another Native American group, have formed the Central Council of the Tlingit and Haida Indian Tribes of Alaska. The council governs the Tlingit and Haida people. It meets in **Juneau, Alaska.**

Also, the Tlingit and other Native Americans have formed a company called the Sealaska Corporation. This corporation builds new buildings for the Tlingit and protects Tlingit property. The corporation makes sure the Tlingit and others will have enough money and land in the future.

REVIEW What is the purpose of the Sealaska Corporation?
Main Idea and Details

Summarize the Lesson

- **The Tlingit make use of the plentiful natural resources of their region.**
- **Potlatch ceremonies involve a feast, speeches, dancing, and gift-giving.**
- **Today, the Tlingit combine tradition with everyday modern life.**

LESSON 1 REVIEW

Check Facts and Main Ideas

1. Summarize Use the details below to write a summary about the Tlingit.

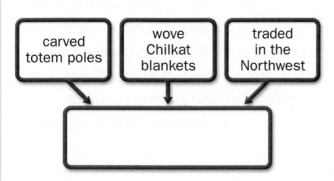

carved totem poles

wove Chilkat blankets

traded in the Northwest

2. How did the Tlingit make use of natural resources?

3. How are modern **potlatches** like potlatches long ago? How are they different?

4. Give three details about the Tlingit today.

5. Critical Thinking: *Make Inferences* Why do you think the host of a potlatch gives so many gifts?

Link to ∞ Art

Create a Sculpture You read that **totem poles** tell the history of Tlingit families. Use clay to create a sculpture that tells something about you or your family. Share its meaning with your classmates.

Masks Tell a Story

The Native Americans who lived along the Pacific Northwest Coast were expert woodcarvers. In addition to totem poles and canoes, they made masks to wear during ceremonies. Today, many groups, including the Haida, are still famous for their woodcarvings.

The Haida live on islands off the coast of Alaska and Canada.

▶ This mask represents a cat god or goddess from the Moche culture. It was made of copper and bone between A.D. 200 and A.D. 800.

Like the Haida, the Inca of South America and their ancestors also made masks. By 1500, the Inca Empire covered a large part of western South America. The Inca wore masks during festivals. They also placed masks on the deceased before they were buried. Each mask had a special meaning. Before the Inca formed their empire, many cultures existed in the area. One of the cultures, called Moche, was well-known for its crafts and artwork, including masks.

▶ This Inca warrior's mask is made of gold. It was made before Columbus came to the Americas. The Inca worked with metals such as gold, copper, and silver.

▶ This Haida mask can be worn closed
or open. When the mask is closed, it
represents an eagle, or thunderbird.
When it is open, it represents the
moon. The head in the center of the
mask has real human hair. The mask
is opened by pulling cords. The Haida
wore masks in ceremonial dances
and in performances during
potlatches. Many Haida
masks represent
spirits.

1760 1860 1960

1769
Father Serra builds the first California mission.

1848
Gold is discovered at Sutter's Mill in California.

1959
Alaska and Hawaii become states.

Sutter's Mill
San Francisco

Exploration and Growth

PREVIEW

Focus on the Main Idea
Explorers from Spain and settlers seeking gold helped shape the West.

PLACES
American River
Sutter's Mill
San Francisco, California

PEOPLE
Juan Rodríguez Cabrillo
Junípero Serra
John Sutter
James Marshall
Levi Strauss

VOCABULARY
prospector
boom town
ghost town

EVENTS
Gold Rush

> You Are There

It's 1542. Juan Rodríguez Cabrillo, a Portuguese explorer for Spain, sets sail from the west coast of New Spain, or Mexico. You're part of his crew. Cabrillo's ship is on a northerly course. He plans to explore the Pacific coast in search of riches and a water passage that connects the Pacific and Atlantic Oceans.

You don't know what to expect. You hope that the voyage will be successful. You've left your family to join Cabrillo. You have no idea what you will find. You walk the deck of the ship dreaming about finding lots of silver and gold.

▶ Statue of Juan Rodríguez Cabrillo

Draw Conclusions As you read, think about how the discovery of gold and other resources changed the West.

Exploring the West

Juan Rodríguez Cabrillo

[kah BREE oh] was probably the first European to see the coast of what is now California. The Spanish sent other explorers north along the coast of California as well. Some of these explorers suggested that Spain should send colonists to settle in the new land.

When the Spanish settled in an area, they often established Roman Catholic missions. A Franciscan priest, Father **Junípero Serra** [hoo NEE peh roh SAIR rah], decided to leave his mission to set up a mission in what is today California. Father Serra built the first California mission in 1769. That mission was the beginning of the city of San Diego.

By 1823 the Franciscans had built 21 missions in California. The missions served both Spanish settlers and Native Americans. Several California cities, such as Santa Barbara and San Francisco, began as missions.

Explorers from other lands also traveled throughout the West. In 1812 Russians built a fur-trading post at Fort Ross, north of San Francisco. Russians also claimed much of Alaska. The British built fur-trading posts along the Pacific coast in what are today Oregon and Washington.

In 1841 the first of many wagon trains brought American settlers to the

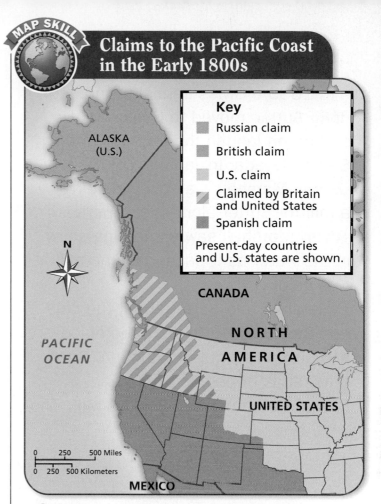

Claims to the Pacific Coast in the Early 1800s

Key
- Russian claim
- British claim
- U.S. claim
- Claimed by Britain and United States
- Spanish claim

Present-day countries and U.S. states are shown.

ALASKA (U.S.)

PACIFIC OCEAN

CANADA

NORTH AMERICA

UNITED STATES

MEXICO

0   250   500 Miles
0 250 500 Kilometers

▶ **Many countries claimed parts of the West.**

MAP SKILL Use Map Key *What modern states lie in the area claimed by both Britain and the United States?*

West. The United States wanted California to become an American territory. Mexico was now free of Spanish rule and owned the territory but refused to sell the land. In 1846 war started between Mexico and the United States over several areas of land in the West and Southwest. The United States won the war in 1848. Mexico was forced to give up California along with some of its other territories in North America.

REVIEW What brought explorers from many different countries to the West Coast? **Draw Conclusions**

Gold!

In 1839 a Swiss immigrant named **John Sutter** moved to California. He settled on land in the foothills of the Sierra Nevada. In January 1848, **James Marshall** was busy building a mill for Sutter along the **American River.** Marshall saw something shiny in the water as it passed by the mill. It was gold!

Marshall told Sutter about the gold, and they decided to keep the discovery a secret. Word got out, though. Soon thousands of people were headed toward California and **Sutter's Mill.** The California **Gold Rush** was on!

Prospectors came from all over the world hoping to find gold in California. A **prospector** is someone who searches for valuable minerals. Some came overland from the eastern United States. This was a long and dangerous trip. Some traveled by sea from the East Coast to the West Coast. At that time, the shortest sea route was a 15,000-mile journey around South America to the small port of **San Francisco** on the California coast. Prospectors even sailed across the Pacific Ocean from China. Any way the

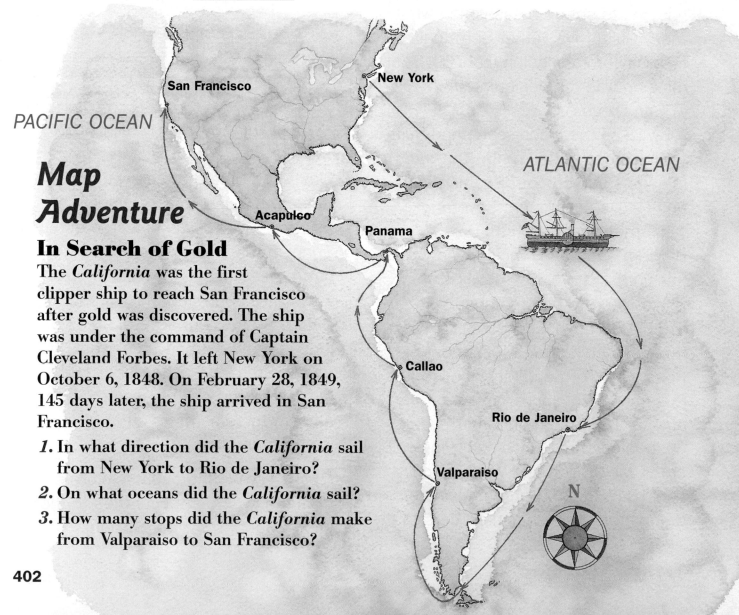

PACIFIC OCEAN

ATLANTIC OCEAN

San Francisco · New York · Acapulco · Panama · Callao · Rio de Janeiro · Valparaiso

N

Map Adventure

In Search of Gold

The *California* was the first clipper ship to reach San Francisco after gold was discovered. The ship was under the command of Captain Cleveland Forbes. It left New York on October 6, 1848. On February 28, 1849, 145 days later, the ship arrived in San Francisco.

1. In what direction did the *California* sail from New York to Rio de Janeiro?

2. On what oceans did the *California* sail?

3. How many stops did the *California* make from Valparaiso to San Francisco?

402

prospectors traveled, the journey took a long time. Most gold-seekers didn't get to California until 1849. That is how they got the name "forty-niners."

San Francisco had a good harbor. It was the closest port to the California gold fields. Many forty-niners passed through the city. By 1849 the tiny port had grown into a big city with a population of 100,000. San Francisco was not the only city that boomed because of the Gold Rush.

Wherever gold, silver, or other valuable metal ore was discovered, **boom towns** grew quickly. Miners came and so did merchants. Merchants built businesses to provide goods and services for the miners. In fact, many merchants became wealthier from the gold rush than the miners did. One of the most successful of these merchants was **Levi Strauss.** He made canvas tents for the miners until he realized that they needed sturdy pairs of pants. He made a fortune sewing and selling denim jeans.

Prospectors found valuable metal ore throughout the West. More towns, such as Denver, Colorado, and Carson City,

▶ **Panning for gold was hard work.**

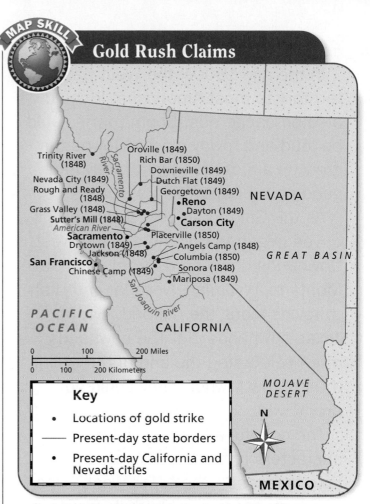

Gold Rush Claims

Trinity River (1848)
Oroville (1849)
Rich Bar (1850)
Nevada City (1849)
Downieville (1849)
Dutch Flat (1849)
Rough and Ready (1848)
Georgetown (1849)
NEVADA
Grass Valley (1848)
•Reno
Sutter's Mill (1848)
Dayton (1849)
American River
•Carson City
Sacramento
Placerville (1850)
Drytown (1849)
Angels Camp (1848)
Jackson (1848)
Columbia (1850)
GREAT BASIN
San Francisco•
Chinese Camp (1849)
Sonora (1848)
•Mariposa (1849)

PACIFIC OCEAN
San Joaquin River
CALIFORNIA

0   100   200 Miles
0   100   200 Kilometers

MOJAVE DESERT
N

Key
• Locations of gold strike
— Present-day state borders
• Present-day California and Nevada cities

MEXICO

▶ **Gold was found in many locations in the Sierra Nevada and foothills.**

MAP SKILL Use Map Scale *About how far is Mariposa from Trinity River?*

Nevada, became boom towns.

In time, a railroad was built across North America, linking the East and West Coasts. Traveling west by train was shorter and easier than sailing or traveling by wagon. More people moved to the West. Some cities, many of them along railroad lines, continued to grow. But once the metal ore was mined from an area, many boom towns were deserted. They became **ghost towns.** Today tourists can visit ghost towns throughout the West.

REVIEW Why did some merchants become wealthier than the gold miners? **Draw Conclusions**

The Wild West

In the mid-1800s, the West was new territory to most Americans. It could also be dangerous. Boom towns could be loud and rowdy places. Towns that grew up almost overnight rarely had good police departments.

As the Gold Rush ended, cattle drives began to take hold in the West. Cowhands drove herds from ranches in Montana, Wyoming, Nevada, and Utah to towns along the railroad, just as Texas cowhands did. The cowhands often celebrated the end of the trail in these "cow towns." They could get pretty wild.

The colorful and often violent characters of the West created a lasting legend—the "Wild West." One of the most famous characters was William "Buffalo Bill" Cody. In 1883 Cody formed a famous traveling show

▶ Advertisement for "Buffalo Bill's Wild West" show

called "Buffalo Bill's Wild West." It featured trick riding and rifle-shooting, western wildlife, and more.

By the 1890s, the "Wild West" had been tamed. Through songs, stories, and movies, however, the legend still lives on.

REVIEW Why was the West called the "Wild West"? **Main Idea and Details**

Then and Now · Bodie, California

Bodie, California is one of the best-preserved ghost towns in the West. A large gold and silver strike in 1877 brought mines and mills to the town. By 1880 Bodie was a boom town with more than 10,000 people and 2,000 buildings.

In only a few years, most of the gold and silver had been mined. By 1882 miners had moved on to other boom towns. In later years, fires destroyed much of Bodie. Only 170 original buildings still stand.

Today Bodie is a California State Historic Park. It is preserved much as it was when the last residents left in the mid-1900s.

▶ Bodie, California, present day

The Territories of the West Become States

State	Entry Date	Order	Flag	State	Entry Date	Order	Flag
California	Sept. 9, 1850	31st		Idaho	July 3, 1890	43rd	
Oregon	Feb. 14, 1859	33rd		Wyoming	July 10, 1890	44th	
Nevada	Oct. 31, 1864	36th		Utah	Jan. 4, 1896	45th	
Colorado	Aug. 1, 1876	38th		Alaska	Jan. 3, 1959	49th	
Montana	Nov. 8, 1889	41st		Hawaii	Aug. 21, 1959	50th	
Washington	Nov. 11, 1889	42nd					

► Some western territories were among the last territories to become states.

CHART SKILL Use a Table *Name one of the three pairs of states that gained statehood in the same years.*

Statehood for Alaska

The territories of the West became states between 1850 and 1959. Look at the chart above. You will notice that the last two territories to become states, Alaska and Hawaii, are both in the West and became states in the same year.

Alaska was once a territory claimed by the country of Russia. The Russians used the territory mainly for fur trading. In 1867 Russia sold Alaska to the United States for a little more than $7 million, or about two cents an acre. The United States hoped that fur trapping in Alaska would help the United States' economy. Alaska had even more natural resources, however.

In the 1880s and 1890s, gold was discovered in parts of Alaska and Canada. Then, just as in California, thousands of people rushed to the area. The cities of Juneau and Fairbanks grew quickly.

During World War II, military bases in Alaska were an important line of defense for the United States. Airfields and highways built during the war helped boost transportation and business development after the war. Alaska became a state in 1959. In 1968 vast oil deposits were discovered on the coast of the Arctic Ocean in Alaska. An 800-mile-long pipeline was built to bring the oil to Valdez, where it could be loaded onto ships and transported to ports around the world.

REVIEW Was the United States purchase of Alaska a good idea? Explain your answer. **Draw Conclusions**

Hawaii Becomes a State

Hawaii is a chain of islands in the Pacific Ocean. In 1900 the United States made Hawaii a territory. Hawaiian farms produced sugarcane and pineapples for export to the United States mainland.

The United States also built ports and military bases on the islands. A major base was built at Pearl Harbor. In December 1941, Japanese warplanes attacked Pearl Harbor. This brought the United States into World War II. Hawaiians had discussed statehood even before World War II. After the war ended, Hawaiians again asked for statehood. Finally, in 1959 Hawaii became the fiftieth state.

REVIEW How were the paths to statehood alike and different for Alaska and Hawaii?
⤵ **Compare and Contrast**

Summarize the Lesson

1769 Father Serra built the first California mission.

1848 Gold was discovered at Sutter's Mill in California.

1959 Alaska and Hawaii became states.

▶ A lei, or garland of flowers, is a gift of welcome in Hawaii.

LESSON 2 | REVIEW

Check Facts and Main Ideas

1. **Draw Conclusions** Copy the diagram below on a separate sheet of paper. Fill in the details that would lead to the given conclusion.

> Many changes occurred in the West during the 1800s.

2. Why did people begin to explore the West?

3. What was the California Gold Rush and how did it change the West?

4. Why did some **boomtowns** become **ghost towns?**

5. Critical Thinking: *Make Generalizations* When and how did some territories in the West become states?

Link to ∞ Music

Find a Song of the Wild West Many songs were written about life in the Wild West. Some have become famous and are still sung today. Find a song and share with your class what the song tells you about life in the Wild West.

LEVI STRAUSS
1829–1902

Levi Strauss invented modern blue jeans. He came to the United States from Germany in 1847. Six years later, during the California Gold Rush, he moved to San Francisco. There he made tents from heavy canvas and sold them at his business along with clothes, blankets, and household items. He also traveled to mining camps, selling these goods to miners.

The miners asked Strauss for tough pants, so he began to make them from canvas. Later, he used denim, a strong cotton fabric. He dyed the denim blue. Cowboys, railroad workers, and farmers bought his blue pants because the pants were comfortable and strong.

BIOFACT

The descendants of the family of Levi Strauss still own and run the company he founded, Levi Strauss & Company.

The miners wanted stronger pockets to hold tools, so Strauss added metal rivets at the corners of the pockets. Levi Strauss & Company, the business he founded, still makes blue denim pants with riveted pockets.

Strauss was very successful. His pants were inexpensive, but Strauss paid his workers a good wage. Strauss donated generously to charities and gave scholarships for students. The business he began is now about 150 years old and remains successful.

Learn from Biographies

Why was Levi Strauss successful?

For more information, go online to *Meet the People* at **www.sfsocialstudies.com.**

Understand Latitude and Longitude

What? Lines of latitude (LAT i tood) extend east and west. They are lines drawn on a map or globe that are used to determine how far north or south of the equator a place is located. Lines of latitude are also called parallels. They are always the same distance apart from one another. The globe on the left shows lines of latitude.

The equator is the imaginary line of latitude that divides Earth into the Northern Hemisphere and the Southern Hemisphere. The equator is the starting point for measuring latitude. It is labeled 0°, or zero degrees, latitude. Latitude is measured in degrees both north and south of the equator.

Find the equator on the globe on the left. Notice that the lines of latitude north of the equator are marked with an *N*. The lines that are south of the equator are marked with an *S*. The North Pole is 90°N and the South Pole is 90°S.

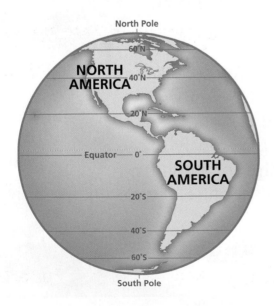

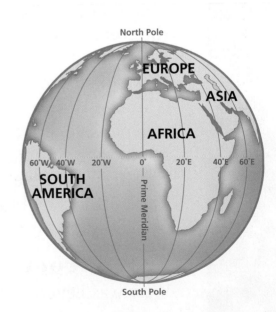

Latitude and Longitude in the West

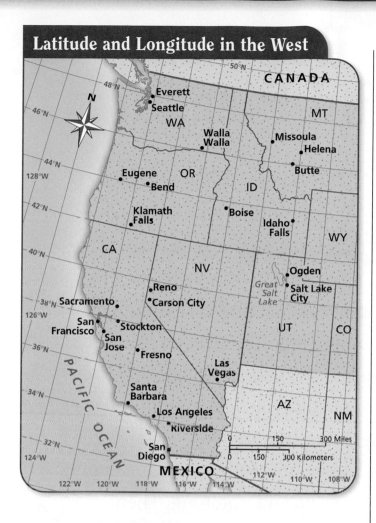

meridian are marked with an *E*. The lines west of the prime meridian are marked with a *W*. The 180th meridian is just labeled 180° without an *E* or *W*. This is because 180°E and 180°W are the same meridian.

Why? The lines of latitude and longitude together form a grid. You can see this grid on the map to the left. You can use this grid to locate places on Earth.

How? To find what city is located near 44°N, 116°W on the map at the left, first find the latitude line labeled 44°N. Then run your finger along that line until it crosses 116°W. What city is located nearest this point?

Lines of **longitude** (LON ji tood) extend north and south. They are also called meridians (muh RID ee uhns). Lines of longitude are used to determine how far east or west of the prime meridian a place is located.

The prime meridian is the starting point for measuring longitude. It is labeled 0°, or zero degrees, longitude. Longitude is measured in degrees east and west of the prime meridian.

Find the prime meridian on the globe on the right (page 408). Notice that the lines of longitude east of the prime

Think and Apply

1 What cities are located near 48°N, 122°W?

2 What city is located nearest to 34°N, 120°W?

3 What is the closest **longitude** and **latitude** for Butte, Montana?

409

Seattle
Salt Lake City
Los Angeles

PREVIEW

Focus on the Main Idea
Cities in the West have many different kinds of businesses and attractions.

PLACES
Los Angeles, California
Seattle, Washington
Salt Lake City, Utah

VOCABULARY
computer software
international trade

Business and Pleasure

You Are There

You are enjoying another beautiful, sunny day of vacation in southern California. Yesterday you went hiking in the Santa Monica Mountains near Los Angeles. Today, you just want to relax on the beach and splash in the gentle waves of the Pacific Ocean. Suddenly, you hear shouts coming from the water. It looks like a swimmer is in trouble. You wonder why people are simply standing around and watching. Then you see a person behind a big camera. A woman shouts into the megaphone, "Cut!" The swimmer laughs. It's then that you realize they are making a movie!

Compare and Contrast As you read, compare and contrast the businesses that can be found in each of the cities mentioned.

Fun in the Sun

Many movies are made in **Los Angeles, California**—and for a good reason. Because California has a sunny, pleasant climate, the area around Los Angeles is an excellent location for filming movies and television shows. Over time, the entertainment industry has grown in Los Angeles.

The pleasant climate around Los Angeles has drawn many other businesses to the area. People from across the United States and around the world come to Los Angeles to live and work. The rapid growth of Los Angeles has made it the second largest city in the United States.

People also travel to Los Angeles to visit its many attractions. Tourism is an important industry. Whether they are relaxing on the beach or riding on a roller coaster, people enjoy visiting Los Angeles.

▶ There are many amusement parks in and around Los Angeles.

REVIEW What are some reasons people come to Los Angeles?
Main Idea and Details

▶ The famous Hollywood sign has become a symbol of the movie industry in Los Angeles.

Two Western Cities

The cities of the West are as varied as the region's landscape. About a thousand miles north of Los Angeles lies the city of **Seattle, Washington.**

Seattle's economy depends on a number of different industries. Many companies that make **computer software**—programs that help computers run certain functions—have their headquarters in or near Seattle. Ships and jet airplanes are also built in the area.

Tourists to Seattle enjoy the city's historic districts and parks. Sightseers can ride the Monorail—an elevated train—through the city to the Space Needle. This tall tower has a wide view of the Seattle area and nearby mountains.

Salt Lake City, Utah, is hundreds of miles south and east of Seattle. Salt Lake City lies on the shore of the Great Salt Lake, from which the city takes its name. Like Seattle, Salt Lake City's economy depends on varied industries.

Salt is an important resource in the Salt Lake City area. The Great Salt Lake is a saltwater lake. About 2.5 million tons of salt are drawn each year from the area surrounding the lake.

Mining is also important to Salt Lake City. One of the world's largest open-pit copper mines is located near the city. Valuable minerals such as lead and silver are mined as well.

Tourists come to Salt Lake City to enjoy its rich history. Nearby mountains also attract people who enjoy skiing and other winter sports.

Seattle and Salt Lake City are very different places. Still, they are both examples of the strong, busy cities of the West.

REVIEW Name ways that Seattle and Salt Lake City are alike and different.
◗ **Compare and Contrast**

▶ **Bingham Canyon Mine, one of the world's largest open-pit copper mines, is located in the mountains west of Salt Lake City.**

FACT FILE

The bar graph shows the increase in population in the metropolitan areas of Los Angeles, California; Seattle, Washington; and Salt Lake City, Utah from 1990 to 2000. The pie chart shows the populations of these three Western cities in relation to each other.

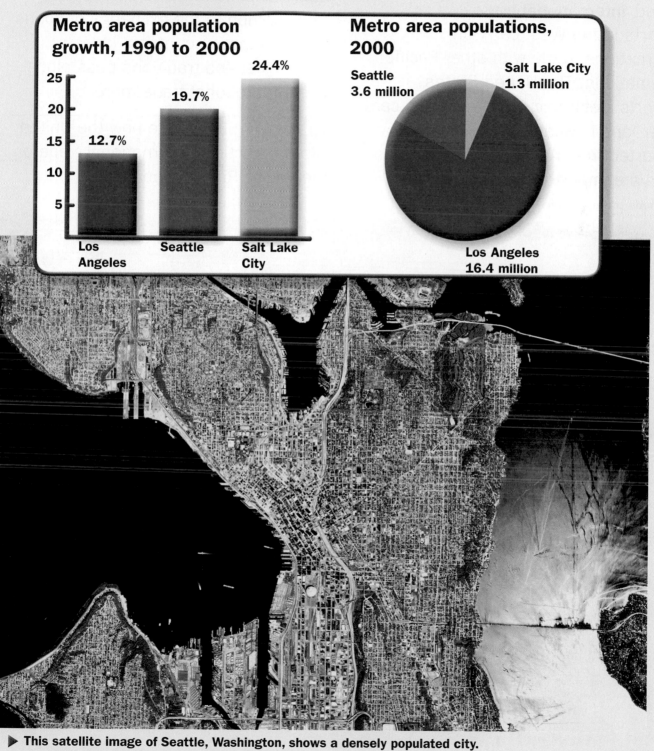

Metro area population growth, 1990 to 2000

- Los Angeles: 12.7%
- Seattle: 19.7%
- Salt Lake City: 24.4%

Metro area populations, 2000

- Seattle 3.6 million
- Salt Lake City 1.3 million
- Los Angeles 16.4 million

▶ This satellite image of Seattle, Washington, shows a densely populated city.

Trade and the Pacific Rim

Pacific Rim countries are nations that border the Pacific Ocean. The United States trades many resources, goods, and services with these countries. Trade between countries is called **international trade.**

Ports in the West carry on international trade with other Pacific Rim nations. The United States imports electronic equipment and cars from Japan. Meat and minerals are imported from Australia. Clothing and food are imported from China.

The United States also exports products to Pacific Rim countries. Movies made in Los Angeles and computer software made in Seattle are important U.S. exports. Hawaii exports agricultural products such as sugarcane, coffee, and pineapples.

In addition to the exchange of goods between these countries, ideas, languages, and traditions pass along this international trade route.

REVIEW Summarize how the United States practices international trade on the Pacific Rim. **Summarize**

▶ **Goods traded on the Pacific Rim**

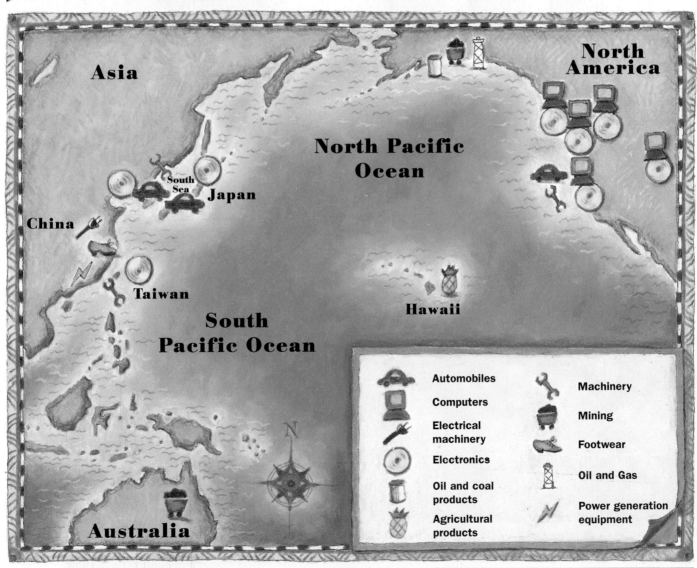

	Automobiles
	Computers
	Electrical machinery
	Electronics
	Oil and coal products
	Agricultural products
	Machinery
	Mining
	Footwear
	Oil and Gas
	Power generation equipment

DIAGRAM SKILL *According to the map, what goods and services are manufactured both in Asia and North America?*

Westward Bound

You have read many reasons why the West is a great place to live in or visit. You can enjoy viewing the region's natural beauty and wildlife. You can climb up mountains or ski down them in many Western states. You can live and work in a place with many natural resources. The West has something for everyone.

REVIEW Why is the West an interesting region to live in or visit?
Main Idea and Details

Summarize the Lesson

- The climate and industries in Los Angeles have helped it to grow in population.
- Seattle and Salt Lake City are examples of strong Western cities.
- The United States and the countries of the Pacific Rim trade many resources, goods, and services.

▶ Whale watching is an attraction on the Pacific coast.

LESSON 3 ◢ REVIEW

Check Facts and Main Ideas

1. ⟳ **Compare and Contrast** On a separate sheet of paper, compare Los Angeles and Salt Lake City. Describe similarities.

Similarities	Differences
	• Los Angeles is on the Pacific Ocean. • Salt Lake City is inland. • Los Angeles is famous for movies. • Salt Lake City is known for mining.

2. Name some of the different industries found in Los Angeles, Seattle, and Salt Lake City.

3. What is the effect of climate on the tourism industries in Los Angeles and Salt Lake City?

4. What goods does the United States import from and export to Pacific Rim countries? Use the term **international trade** in your answer.

5. **Critical Thinking:** *Point of View* Of the cities described in this lesson, which one would you most like to visit? Why?

Link to ⚬—⚬ Writing

Pen Pal Postcards Write a postcard to a person living in one of the cities from the lesson. Compare and contrast your community with theirs. Describe similarities and differences.

Building a City

Thomas Bradley "was a builder... encouraging a thriving downtown and improving mass transit. Just as important, he built bridges across the lines that divide us, uniting people of many races and backgrounds in the most diverse city in America."

—President William Jefferson Clinton

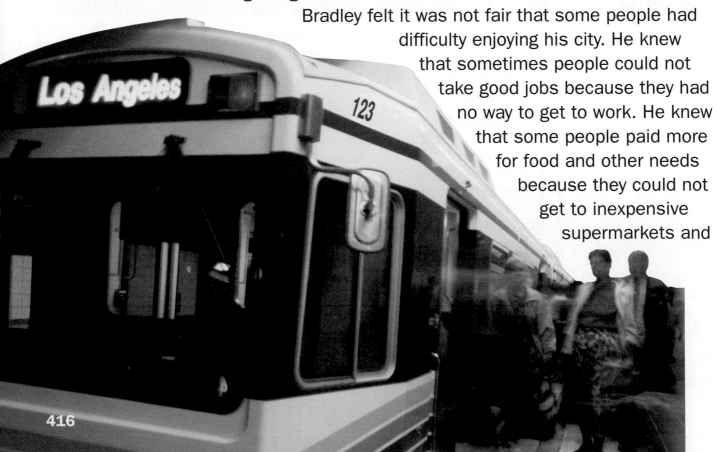

▶ **Mayor Thomas Bradley**

Thomas Bradley was mayor of Los Angeles for twenty years. He thought his city was a great place to live, and he wanted everyone to have a fair chance to enjoy it. One problem Bradley saw was his city's transportation system. Bradley knew that most people used cars for transportation. People without cars often had a hard time getting around.

Bradley felt it was not fair that some people had difficulty enjoying his city. He knew that sometimes people could not take good jobs because they had no way to get to work. He knew that some people paid more for food and other needs because they could not get to inexpensive supermarkets and

Los Angeles 123

BUILDING
CITIZENSHIP
Caring
Respect
Responsibility
Fairness
Honesty
Courage

discount stores. He worried that people had difficulty visiting museums, attending concerts, and getting to parks and beaches. Bradley decided Los Angeles needed a train system like New York's subway to help make transportation fairer.

Over many years Bradley worked to have the Metro Rail system built. Now many people ride these trains to jobs, stores, museums, parks, and other places. The Metro Rail system and other projects Bradley began have helped make Los Angeles a fairer place to live.

Thomas Bradley believed that all people should follow their dreams. He said,

> *"The only thing that can stop you is you. Dream big dreams, work hard, study hard, and listen to your teachers. Above all get along with each other. You can be anything your heart wants to be."*

Los Angeles Metro Rail System

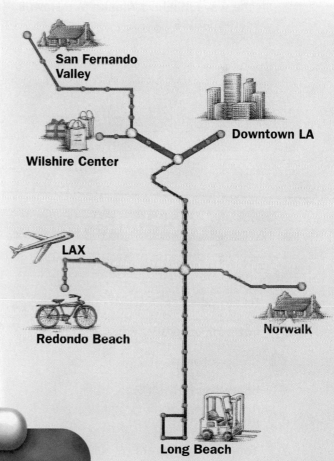

San Fernando Valley

Downtown LA

Wilshire Center

LAX

Redondo Beach

Norwalk

Long Beach

Fairness in Action

Other people in United States history have taken action when they saw people being treated unfairly. Research a person who has worked for fairness toward immigrants, workers, or people of a different race or religion. You may choose an important figure in history or someone from your own community.

1750   1800   1850

1769
Father Serra established the first California mission.

1841
Wagon trains traveled West.

1848
The United States won the territory of California from Mexico. Gold was discovered in California.

Chapter Summary

Compare and Contrast

On a separate sheet of paper, fill in the diagram to list similarities and differences in the ways in which Alaska and Hawaii became states.

Similarities	Differences

▶ **Sunset in Barrow, Alaska**

Vocabulary

Use each word in a sentence that explains the meaning of the word.

1. **totem pole** (p. 395)
2. **potlatch** (p. 396)
3. **prospector** (p. 402)
4. **boom town** (p. 403)
5. **ghost town** (p. 403)
6. **computer software** (p. 412)
7. **international trade** (p. 414)

People and Places

Write these sentences on a separate sheet of paper. Fill in the blank with the name of a person or place from this chapter.

1. The Tlingit's governing council meets in _____. (p. 397)
2. A priest, _____, built the first mission in California. (p. 401)
3. In 1848 John Marshall discovered gold in California at _____. (p. 402)
4. _____ sold sturdy pants during the Gold Rush in California. (p. 403)
5. _____ is a city in Utah that was named for a nearby body of water. (p. 412)

1900   1950   2000

1867
The United States purchased Alaska from Russia.

1883
"Buffalo Bill" Cody started his Wild West show.

1900
The United States claimed Hawaii as a territory.

1959
Alaska and Hawaii were granted statehood.

Facts and Main Ideas

1. What is the purpose of a totem pole?

2. How did some missions in California grow and change?

3. **Time Line** How many years passed between the year the United States purchased Alaska and the year the United States claimed Hawaii?

4. **Main Idea** Describe the Tlingit way of life.

5. **Main Idea** How did the discovery of gold change the West?

6. **Main Idea** What are some products that are traded among the Pacific Rim countries?

7. **Critical Thinking:** *Make Inferences* Why is the West Coast a convenient place for international trade?

Write About History

1. **Write a journal entry** describing how you might feel if you learned that gold had been discovered in your state. Would you believe it? Would you want to become a prospector?

2. **Write a newspaper report** about a local potlatch. Tell why the potlatch was held, who attended, and what kinds of gifts were given.

3. **Write a travel brochure** about a city in the West. Choose one western city to research and write about. Include information about things to see and do in and around the city.

Apply Skills

Understand Latitude and Longitude

1. What is the approximate latitude and longitude of Denver?

2. What is the approximate latitude and longitude of Pikes Peak?

3. What national monument is between 40°N, 109°W and 41°N, 109°W?

4. Name the Colorado cities that are located at about 105°W.

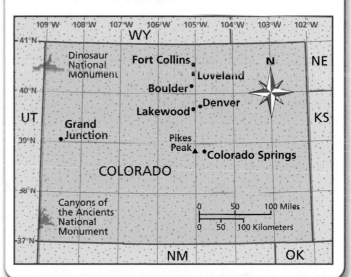

Internet Activity

To get help with vocabulary, people, and terms, select the dictionary or encyclopedia from *Social Studies Library* at **www.sfsocialstudies.com**.

End with a Song

Sweet Betsy

Sweet Betsy was a fictional woman who left Pike County, Missouri and headed for the California gold mines. This song celebrates all the hearty people who traveled westward to California after gold was found there in 1848.

Folk Song from the United States
Adapted and arranged by Lillian Wiedman

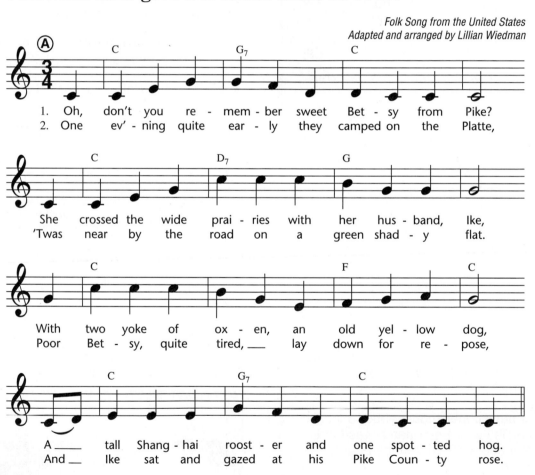

1. Oh, don't you re-mem-ber sweet Bet-sy from Pike?
2. One ev'-ning quite ear-ly they camped on the Platte,

She crossed the wide prai-ries with her hus-band, Ike,
'Twas near by the road on a green shad-y flat.

With two yoke of ox-en, an old yel-low dog,
Poor Bet-sy, quite tired, __ lay down for re-pose,

A __ tall Shang-hai roost-er and one spot-ted hog.
And __ Ike sat and gazed at his Pike Coun-ty rose.

from Pike

B Too - ra - lee, _____ too - ra - lay, _____

Too - ra - lee, too - ra - lay,

Sing-ing too - ra - lee, too - ra - lee, too - ra - lee ay.

3. They soon reached the desert where Betsy gave out.
And down on the sand she lay rolling about.
While Ike, in great tears, looked on in surprise:
Said, "Betsy, get up, you'll get sand in your eyes." *Refrain*

4. The rooster ran off and the oxen all died:
The last piece of bacon that morning was fried.
Poor Ike got discouraged and Betsy got mad:
The dog wagged his tail and looked awfully sad. *Refrain*

5. The alkali desert was burning and hot,
And Ike, he decided to leave on the spot:
"My dear old Pike County, I'll go back to you."
Said Betsy, "You'll go by yourself if you do." *Refrain*

6. They swam the wide rivers, they crossed the tall peaks,
They camped out on prairies for weeks and for weeks,
Fought hunger and rattlers and big storms of dust,
Determined to reach California or bust. *Refrain*

421

Main Ideas and Vocabulary

TEST PREP

Read the passage below and use it to answer the questions that follow.

Many people think of the West as a region of mountains. The Rocky Mountains, which are the largest system of mountain ranges in North America, are located in the West. So are the Sierra Nevada and the Cascade Range. Mount McKinley, the highest point in North America, is located in the western state of Alaska.

Yellowstone, the nation's oldest national park, is located in the mountains of Wyoming, Idaho, and Montana. It is famous for its scenery, wildlife, and hot springs. Some hot springs, such as the famous Old Faithful, are <u>geysers</u>. An eruption from Old Faithful sends boiling water more than 100 feet into the air.

The West is much more than mountains, however. The Great Basin is a desert that is often quite hot. Death Valley, California, is more than 200 feet below sea level. It is the lowest elevation in North America. Parts of the West produce lots of fruit and vegetables. California's Central Valley and Oregon's

Willamette Valley are famous for their farm products. Tropical Hawaii produces crops such as sugarcane and pineapples.

The history and culture of the West is as varied as the region's landscape. In 1848 gold was discovered at Sutter's Mill in California. This triggered the Gold Rush. Soon <u>prospectors</u> from around the world came to California to search for gold. Merchants followed, hoping to make money by selling goods to the miners. Cities throughout the West grew as gold, silver, and other valuable ores were discovered.

Today the West is home to many different cultures. Some, such as the Tlingit, have lived in southern Alaska for hundreds of years. One Tlingit tradition is the carving and displaying of totem poles. The carvings on a totem pole include symbols of a family's history. Another Tlingit tradition is the potlatch, a feast where gifts are given. Potlatches can last many days.

1 According to the passage, what is the highest place in North America?
A Death Valley
B Yellowstone
C Mount McKinley
D The Great Basin

2 In the passage, the word *geysers* means
A lakes made by humans
B very old trees
C wildlife of the West
D hot springs that erupt

3 In the passage, the word *prospectors* means
A people opening stores
B people searching for valuable ore
C people going on vacation
D people climbing mountains

4 What item below is not a part of Tlingit culture?
A a totem pole
B a potlatch
C a pineapple
D gift-giving

People and Places

Write a sentence or two explaining why each of the following people or terms is important.

1 **Yellowstone National Park** (p. 370)

2 **Death Valley, California** (p. 380)

3 **Willamette Valley, Oregon** (p. 385)

4 **Juan Rodríguez Cabrillo** (p. 401)

5 **Junípero Serra** (p. 401)

6 **John Sutter** (p. 402)

7 **Levi Strauss** (p. 403)

Write and Share

Write and Share a Story With a group of classmates, write a story about a person who comes to California seeking his or her fortune during the Gold Rush. Choose one person from the group to read the whole story, or split the story into sections and let each group member read.

Apply Skills

Write Notes and Outlines

Choose one topic covered in Unit 6, such as Yellowstone National Park, the Tlingit culture, or the Gold Rush, and do research on it. As you do your research, take notes. Then use your notes to write an outline about the topic. Illustrate the outline, if you wish.

Upper Geyser Basin
Old Faithful
Castle Geyser
Morning Glory Pool

Things to See in Yellowstone National Park
I. Upper Geyser Basin
   A. Old Faithful
   B. Castle Geyser
   C. Morning Glory Pool
II. Mammoth Hot Springs
   A. Minerva Terrace
   B. Canary Spring
   C. Elk

Read on Your Own

Look for books like these in the library.

Great State

Create a booklet that shows what's great about your state today—and what will be great in the future.

1 Form a group. Choose a current event in your state.

2 Write a paragraph about the event. Predict what will happen in the future and write several sentences.

3 Draw or find pictures that illustrate the event today and what might occur in the future.

4 Put your group's paragraphs and pictures together into a booklet. Share it with the class.

Internet Activity

Learn more about the West. Go to **www.sfsocialstudies.com/activities** and select your grade and unit.

Table of Contents

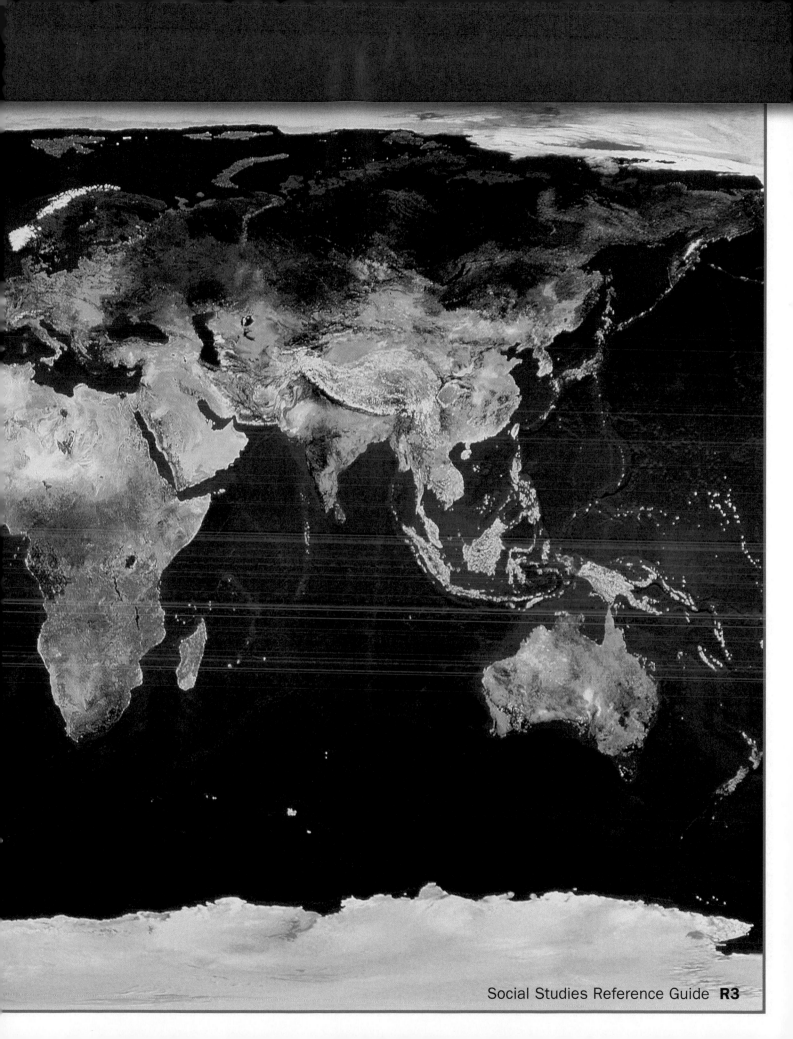

Central America and the West Indies

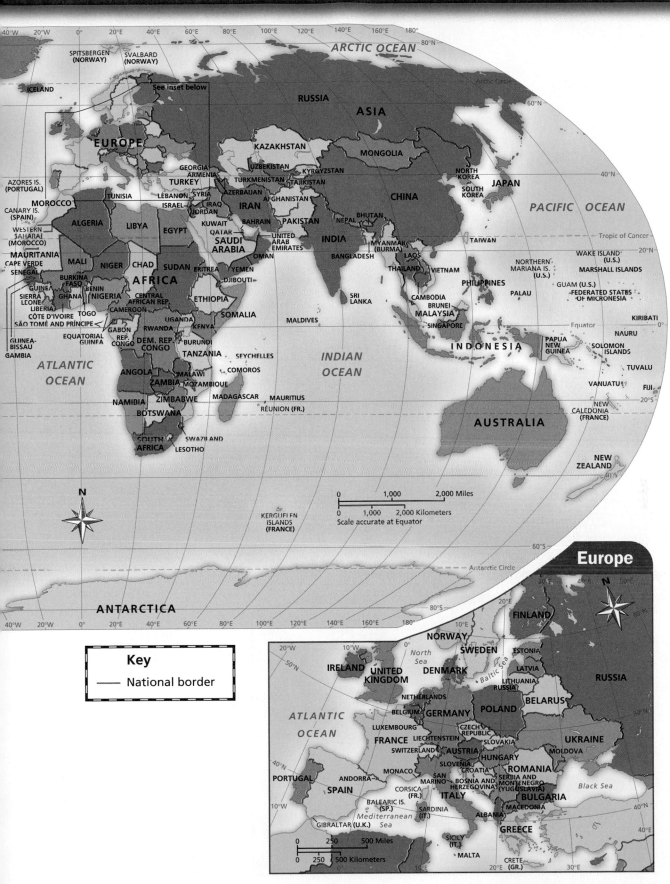

40°W 20°W 0° 20°E 40°E 60°E 80°E 100°E 120°E 140°E 160°E 180°

SPITSBERGEN
(NORWAY)   SVALBARD
           (NORWAY)

ARCTIC OCEAN   80°N

ICELAND

See inset below

RUSSIA

ASIA   60°N

EUROPE

KAZAKHSTAN
                    MONGOLIA
AZORES IS.   GEORGIA   UZBEKISTAN   KYRGYZSTAN   40°N
(PORTUGAL)   ARMENIA
           TURKEY   TURKMENISTAN TAJIKISTAN   NORTH
                                                            KOREA   JAPAN
CANARY IS.   TUNISIA   LEBANON SYRIA AZERBAIJAN   SOUTH PACIFIC OCEAN
(SPAIN)   MOROCCO   ISRAEL   IRAQ   IRAN   AFGHANISTAN CHINA   KOREA
                              JORDAN   BHUTAN
WESTERN   KUWAIT   BAHRAIN PAKISTAN NEPAL   Tropic of Cancer
SAHARA   ALGERIA LIBYA EGYPT QATAR—   TAIWAN
(MOROCCO)   UNITED   SAUDI   INDIA MYANMAR   WAKE ISLAND   20°N
CAPE VERDE MAURITANIA   ARAB   ARABIA   (BURMA)   NORTHERN   (U.S.)
                      MALI NIGER CHAD EMIRATES OMAN BANGLADESH LAOS MARIANA IS. MARSHALL ISLANDS
SENEGAL   SUDAN   ERITREA YEMEN   THAILAND VIETNAM (U.S.)
       BURKINA   AFRICA   DJIBOUTI   GUAM (U.S.)
GUINEA FASO   BENIN NIGERIA CENTRAL   SRI   PHILIPPINES FEDERATED STATES
SIERRA GHANA   AFRICAN REP. ETHIOPIA   LANKA   CAMBODIA   OF MICRONESIA
LEONE   CAMEROON   BRUNEI   PALAU
LIBERIA TOGO   SOMALIA   MALDIVES   MALAYSIA   KIRIBATI
CÔTE D'IVOIRE   GABON UGANDA KENYA   SINGAPORE   Equator   0°
SÃO TOMÉ AND PRÍNCIPE EQUATORIAL RWANDA   NAURU
GUINEA-   GUINEA REP. DEM. REP. BURUNDI   INDONESIA PAPUA   SOLOMON
BISSAU   CONGO CONGO TANZANIA SEYCHELLES   INDIAN   NEW   ISLANDS
GAMBIA   OCEAN   GUINEA   TUVALU
      ATLANTIC   ANGOLA MALAWI   COMOROS   VANUATU
      OCEAN   ZAMBIA MOZAMBIQUE   FIJI
                  ZIMBABWE   MADAGASCAR MAURITIUS   NEW   20°S
           NAMIBIA   RÉUNION (FR.)   CALEDONIA
              BOTSWANA   AUSTRALIA   (FRANCE)

                   SOUTH   SWAZILAND
                   AFRICA   LESOTHO   NEW
                                                                                    ZEALAND

           N

                                        KERGUELEN
                                        ISLANDS
                                        (FRANCE)

0   1,000   2,000 Miles
0   1,000   2,000 Kilometers
Scale accurate at Equator

ANTARCTICA

40°W 20°W 0° 20°E 40°E 60°E 80°E 100°E 120°E 140°E 160°E 180°

Arctic Circle

60°N

Tropic of Cancer

Equator

Antarctic Circle   60°S

80°S

Key
—— National border

Europe

N

20°W 10°W 0° 10°E 20°E

FINLAND

NORWAY   SWEDEN
                    ESTONIA
IRELAND UNITED DENMARK   LATVIA   RUSSIA
         KINGDOM   Baltic Sea LITHUANIA
North   RUSSIA
Sea   NETHERLANDS   BELARUS
ATLANTIC BELGIUM GERMANY POLAND
OCEAN   LUXEMBOURG   CZECH
         FRANCE LIECHTENSTEIN REPUBLIC UKRAINE
                 SWITZERLAND AUSTRIA SLOVAKIA
                         SLOVENIA HUNGARY MOLDOVA
PORTUGAL ANDORRA— MONACO CROATIA ROMANIA
         SPAIN   SAN BOSNIA AND SERBIA AND Black Sea
              BALEARIC IS. MARINO HERZEGOVINA MONTENEGRO
CORSICA (SP.)   ITALY   (YUGOSLAVIA) BULGARIA
GIBRALTAR (U.K.) (FR.)   MACEDONIA
         SARDINIA   ALBANIA
Mediterranean (IT.)   GREECE
Sea   SICILY
         (IT.)
         MALTA   CRETE
                 (GR.)

0 250 500 Miles
0 250 500 Kilometers

50°N
40°N
10°W

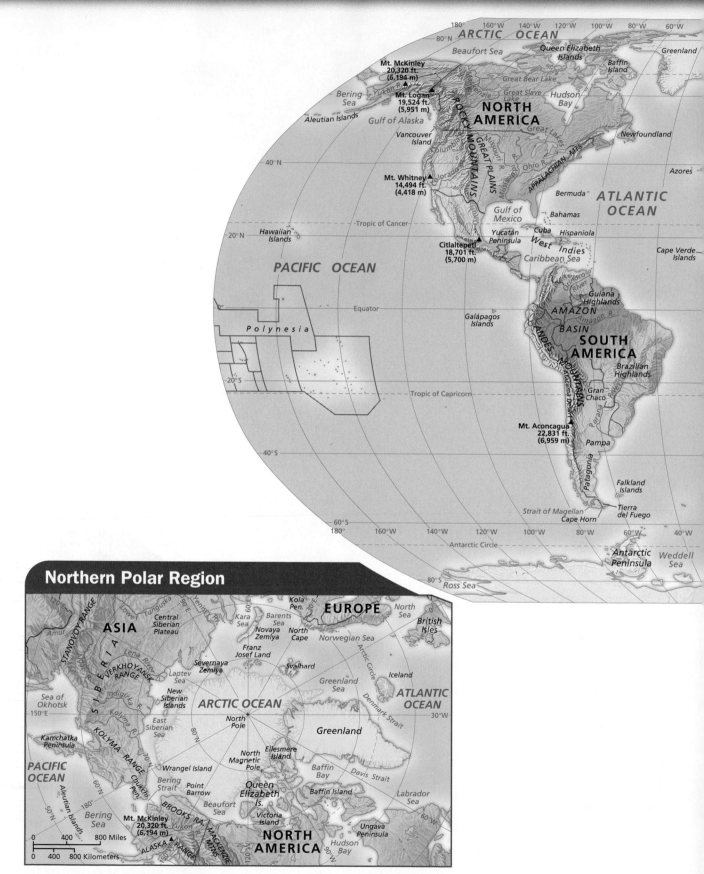

Northern Polar Region

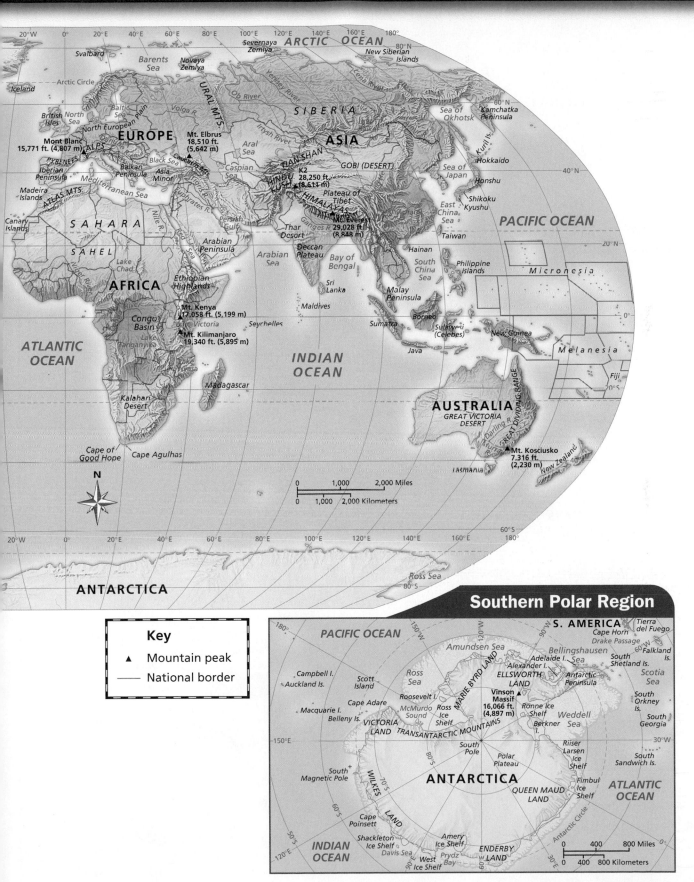

Key

▲ Mountain peak

— National border

Southern Polar Region

Atlas
Map of the Western Hemisphere: Political

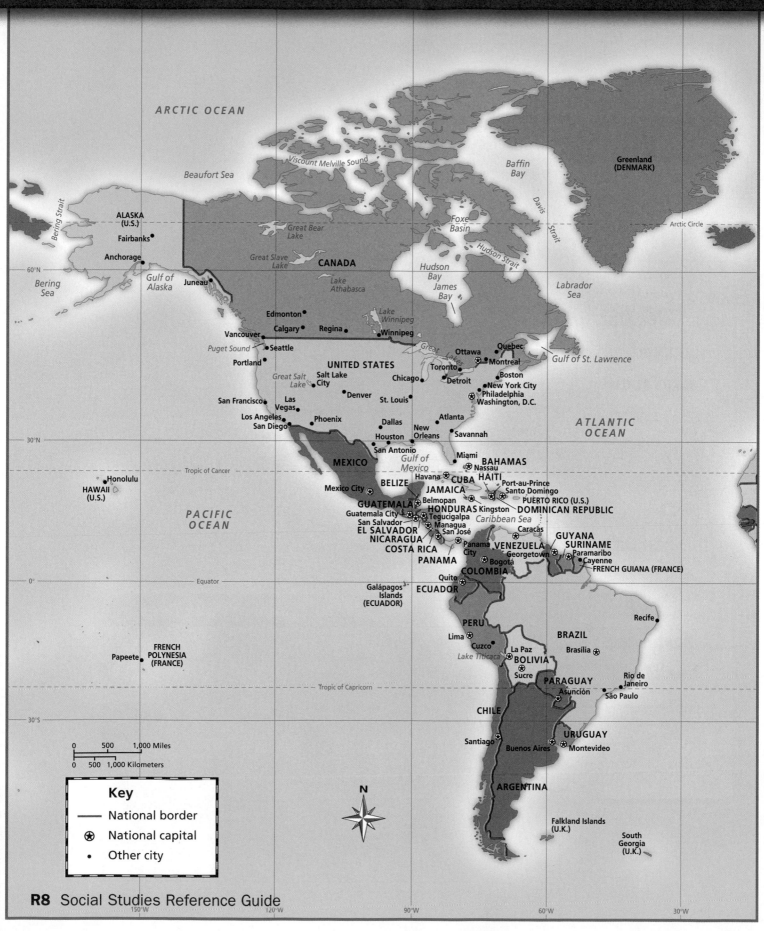

ARCTIC OCEAN

Beaufort Sea

Viscount Melville Sound

Baffin Bay

Greenland (DENMARK)

Bering Strait

ALASKA (U.S.)

Fairbanks

Anchorage

Great Bear Lake

Great Slave Lake

CANADA

Foxe Basin

Davis Strait

Arctic Circle

60°N

Bering Sea

Gulf of Alaska

Juneau

Lake Athabasca

Hudson Bay

James Bay

Labrador Sea

Edmonton

Lake Winnipeg

Calgary

Regina

Winnipeg

Great Lakes

Ottawa

Quebec

Gulf of St. Lawrence

Vancouver

Puget Sound

Seattle

Portland

UNITED STATES

Salt Lake City

Great Salt Lake

Chicago

Toronto

Detroit

Montreal

Boston

New York City

Philadelphia

Washington, D.C.

San Francisco

Denver

St. Louis

Las Vegas

Los Angeles

San Diego

Phoenix

Dallas

Atlanta

ATLANTIC OCEAN

30°N

Houston

New Orleans

Savannah

Honolulu

San Antonio

Miami

BAHAMAS

Nassau

HAWAII (U.S.)

Tropic of Cancer

MEXICO

Gulf of Mexico

BELIZE

Havana

CUBA

HAITI

Mexico City

Belmopan

JAMAICA

Port-au-Prince

Santo Domingo

PUERTO RICO (U.S.)

PACIFIC OCEAN

GUATEMALA

Guatemala City

HONDURAS

Kingston

DOMINICAN REPUBLIC

Tegucigalpa

San Salvador

Managua

Caribbean Sea

EL SALVADOR

San José

NICARAGUA

Caracas

GUYANA

COSTA RICA

Panama City

VENEZUELA

SURINAME

PANAMA

Georgetown

Paramaribo

Cayenne

COLOMBIA

Bogotá

FRENCH GUIANA (FRANCE)

0°

Equator

Quito

ECUADOR

Galápagos Islands (ECUADOR)

Recife

PERU

BRAZIL

FRENCH POLYNESIA (FRANCE)

Papeete

Lima

Cuzco

La Paz

Brasília

Lake Titicaca

BOLIVIA

Tropic of Capricorn

Sucre

PARAGUAY

Rio de Janeiro

Asunción

São Paulo

30°S

CHILE

Santiago

URUGUAY

Buenos Aires

Montevideo

0   500   1,000 Miles

0   500   1,000 Kilometers

ARGENTINA

Falkland Islands (U.K.)

South Georgia (U.K.)

N

Key
— National border
⊛ National capital
• Other city

150°W   120°W   90°W   60°W   30°W

ARCTIC OCEAN

North Magnetic Pole

Ellesmere Island

Queen Elizabeth Islands

Melville Island

Viscount Melville Sound

Devon Island

Banks Island

Baffin Bay

Greenland

Point Barrow

Beaufort Sea

Victoria Island

Baffin Island

Davis Strait

Arctic Circle

Brooks Range

Mt. McKinley 20,320 ft. (6,194 m)

Yukon River

Mackenzie Mts.

Great Bear Lake

Foxe Basin

Cape Farewell

Bering Strait

Alaska Range

Yukon Plateau

Mackenzie River

Liard R.

Great Slave Lake

CANADIAN

Hudson Strait

60°N

Bering Sea

Gulf of Alaska

Mt. Logan 19,524 ft. (5,951 m)

Coast Mountains

Peace R.

Athabasca R.

Lake River

Lake Athabasca

Saskatchewan River

SHIELD

Hudson Bay

James Bay

Labrador Sea

Kodiak Island

ROCKY

Labrador

Alaska Peninsula

Queen Charlotte Islands

Lake Winnipeg

GREAT

NORTH AMERICA

Great Lakes

St. Lawrence R.

Newfoundland

Gulf of St. Lawrence

Aleutian Islands

Vancouver Island

Puget Sound

Coast Ranges

Cascade Range

Snake R.

MOUNTAINS

Black Hills

Missouri R.

PLAINS

Mississippi R.

Ohio R.

APPALACHIAN MTS.

Nova Scotia

Bay of Fundy

Cape Cod

Long Island

Mt. Whitney 14,495 ft. (4,418 m)

Sierra Nevada

Great Salt Lake

GREAT BASIN

Platte

INTERIOR PLAINS

Arkansas R.

Ozark Plateau

Cape Hatteras

ATLANTIC OCEAN

Death Valley (lowest point in N.A.) -282 ft. (-86 m)

Colorado R.

Sonoran Desert

Sierra Madre Occidental

Rio Grande

Sierra Madre Oriental

COASTAL PLAIN

30°N

Baja California

Gulf of Mexico

Tropic of Cancer

Hawaiian Islands

Citlaltépetl 18,701 ft (5,700 m)

Yucatán Peninsula

Bahamas

Cuba

Greater Antilles

Hispaniola

Puerto Rico

Lesser Antilles

PACIFIC OCEAN

Lake Nicaragua

Caribbean Sea

Isthmus of Panama

Lake Maracaibo

Chimborazo 20,561 ft. (6,267 m)

Orinoco R.

Guiana Highlands

Galápagos Islands

Llanos

Rio Negro

Amazon R.

Cape São Roque

Equator

Line Islands

AMAZON BASIN

Tapajós R.

Xingu R.

Tocantins R.

Marquesas Islands

Huascarán 22,205 ft. (6,768 m)

Mato Grosso Plateau

Paraguay R.

São Francisco R.

Brazilian Highlands

Cook Islands

Tuamotu Archipelago

Society Islands

Lake Titicaca

ANDES

Altiplano

SOUTH AMERICA

Tropic of Capricorn

Atacama Desert

Gran Chaco

Paraná R.

Iguazú Falls

30°S

Uruguay R.

Mt. Aconcagua 22,831 ft. (6,959 m)

Pampa

N

Valdés Peninsula (lowest point in S.A.) -131 ft. (-40 m)

Patagonia

Strait of Magellan

Tierra del Fuego

Falkland Islands

South Georgia

Cape Horn

0   500   1,000 Miles
0 500 1,000 Kilometers

Key

▲ Mountain peak

▼ Below sea level

— National border

150°W   120°W   90°W   60°W   30°W

RUSSIA

ARCTIC OCEAN

160°E

AK

Arctic Circle

40°N
180°

PACIFIC OCEAN

20°N

HI

WA

OR

ID

NV

UT

CA

AZ

250   500 Miles

0   250   500 Kilometers

Key

⊛ National capital

— National border

Tropic of Cancer

160°W

140°W

120°W

Greenland
(DENMARK)

CANADA

ATLANTIC
OCEAN

Gulf of Mexico

MEXICO

BAHAMAS

CUBA

HAITI   DOM.
         REP.

JAMAICA

MT ND MN WI MI ME VT NH MA CT RI NY PA NJ
SD WY NE IA IL IN OH WV VA DE MD DC
CO KS MO KY NC TN SC OK AR MS AL GA TX LA FL 'M

N

100°W   80°W   60°W

State or area	Abbreviation
Alabama	AL
Alaska	AK
Arizona	AZ
Arkansas	AR
California	CA
Colorado	CO
Connecticut	CT
Delaware	DE
District of Columbia .	DC
Florida	FL
Georgia	GA
Hawaii	HI
Idaho	ID
Illinois	IL
Indiana	IN
Iowa	IA
Kansas	KS
Kentucky	KY
Louisiana	LA
Maine	ME
Maryland	MD
Massachusetts	MA
Michigan	MI
Minnesota	MN
Mississippi	MS
Missouri	MO
Montana	MT
Nebraska	NE
Nevada	NV
New Hampshire	NH
New Jersey	NJ
New Mexico	NM
New York	NY
North Carolina	NC
North Dakota	ND
Ohio.	OH
Oklahoma	OK
Oregon	OR
Pennsylvania	PA
Rhode Island	RI
South Carolina	SC
South Dakota	SD
Tennessee	TN
Texas	TX
Utah	UT
Vermont	VT
Virginia	VA
Washington	WA
West Virginia	WV
Wisconsin	WI
Wyoming	WY

Atlas
Map of the United States: Political

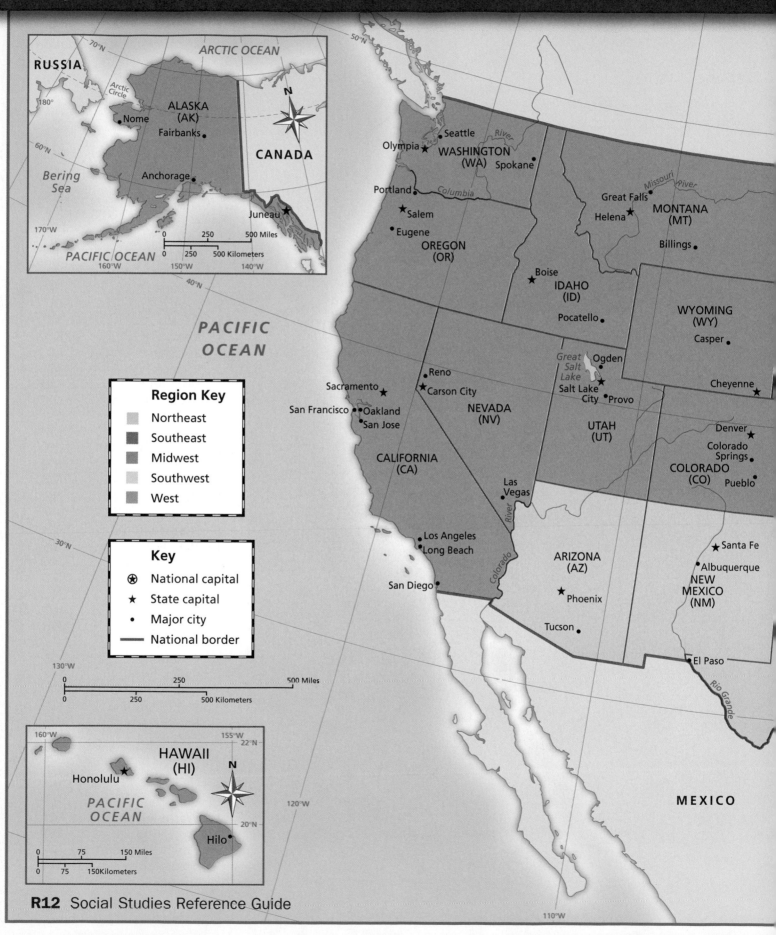

RUSSIA

ARCTIC OCEAN

70°N

Arctic Circle

180°

ALASKA (AK)

Nome

Fairbanks

N

CANADA

60°N

Bering Sea

Anchorage

170°W

Juneau

0 250 500 Miles

0 250 500 Kilometers

PACIFIC OCEAN

160°W 150°W 140°W

40°N

PACIFIC OCEAN

50°N

River

Seattle

Olympia WASHINGTON (WA)

Spokane

Portland Columbia

Salem

Eugene

OREGON (OR)

Boise

IDAHO (ID)

Pocatello

Great Falls Missouri River

Helena MONTANA (MT)

Billings

WYOMING (WY)

Casper

Great Salt Lake

Ogden

Salt Lake City Provo

Cheyenne

Region Key

Northeast
Southeast
Midwest
Southwest
West

Reno

Sacramento Carson City

San Francisco Oakland

San Jose

NEVADA (NV)

UTAH (UT)

Denver

Colorado Springs

COLORADO (CO) Pueblo

CALIFORNIA (CA)

Las Vegas

30°N

Key

⊛ National capital
★ State capital
• Major city
― National border

Los Angeles
Long Beach

San Diego

Colorado River

ARIZONA (AZ)

Phoenix

Tucson

Santa Fe

Albuquerque

NEW MEXICO (NM)

130°W

0 250 500 Miles

0 250 500 Kilometers

El Paso

Rio Grande

160°W 155°W

22°N

HAWAII (HI)

Honolulu

N

PACIFIC OCEAN

120°W

20°N

Hilo

0 75 150 Miles

0 75 150 Kilometers

MEXICO

110°W

CANADA

NORTH DAKOTA
(ND)
★ Bismarck
Grand
Forks
Fargo

SOUTH DAKOTA
(SD)
★ Pierre

MINNESOTA
(MN)
Duluth
Minneapolls ★ St. Paul

Lake Superior

Green
Bay

WISCONSIN
(WI)
Madison
Milwaukee

Lake Michigan

MICHIGAN
(MI)
Lansing ★
Grand
Rapids
Detroit

Lake Huron

Lake Ontario

Lake Erie

NEW HAMPSHIRE (NH)
VERMONT (VT)
Burlington
Montpelier ★

MAINE
(ME)
★ Augusta
Portland
★ Concord

Albany
Buffalo
NEW YORK
(NY)
Hartford ★

MASSACHUSETTS
(MA)
Boston ★
★ Providence

RHODE ISLAND
(RI)

Sioux
Falls
Missouri

NEBRASKA
(NE)
Omaha
Lincoln ★

IOWA
(IA)
Cedar
Rapids
Davenport
Des
Moines

Rockford
Chicago
Gary

Peoria

Fort
Wayne

Toledo
Cleveland

OHIO
(OH)
Columbus

Wheeling
Pittsburgh

PENNSYLVANIA
(PA)
Harrisburg ★
Newark
New York

Trenton

Philadelphia
Baltimore
Dover
Annapolis

CONNECTICUT
(CT)

NEW JERSEY (NJ)
DELAWARE (DE)

MARYLAND (MD)

Kansas
City
Kansas
City
Topeka ★
KANSAS
(KS)
Wichita

Jefferson
City
MISSOURI
(MO)

St.
Louis
Evansville
ILLINOIS
(IL)
Springfield
Indianapolis
INDIANA
(IN)
Cincinnati
Ohio
Louisville
Frankfort
KENTUCKY
(KY)

Charleston

WEST
VIRGINIA
(WV)
Richmond
VIRGINIA
(VA)
Washington, D.C.
Norfolk

Tulsa
Oklahoma
★ City
OKLAHOMA
(OK)

Fort
Smith
Little
Rock
ARKANSAS
(AR)

Nashville ★
TENNESSEE
(TN)
Memphis

Knoxville
Charlotte

Columbia

NORTH CAROLINA
(NC)
Raleigh ★

SOUTH
CAROLINA
(SC)
Charleston

ATLANTIC
OCEAN

Fort
Worth
Dallas

Shreveport
LOUISIANA
(LA)
Baton Rouge
New Orleans

MISSISSIPPI
(MS)
Jackson

Biloxi

Birmingham

ALABAMA
(AL)
Montgomery

Mobile

GEORGIA
(GA)
Atlanta
Columbus

Savannah

Jacksonville

TEXAS
(TX)
Austin ★
San
Antonio
Houston

Tallahassee ★

FLORIDA
(FL)
Tampa

Laredo
Corpus
Christi

N

Gulf of Mexico

Miami

BAHAMAS

50°N

40°N

70°W

30°N

80°W

100°W

90°W

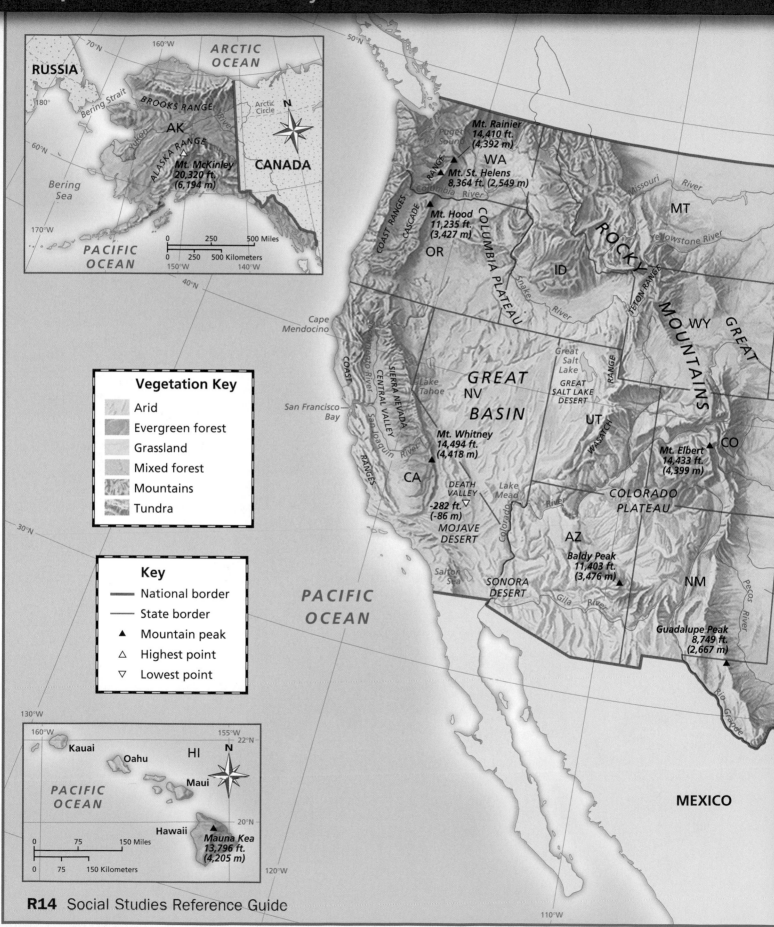

Vegetation Key
- Arid
- Evergreen forest
- Grassland
- Mixed forest
- Mountains
- Tundra

Key
- National border
- State border
- ▲ Mountain peak
- △ Highest point
- ▽ Lowest point

RUSSIA

ARCTIC OCEAN

BROOKS RANGE

AK

ALASKA RANGE

Yukon River

Mt. McKinley
20,320 ft.
(6,194 m)

Bering Strait

Bering Sea

PACIFIC OCEAN

Arctic Circle

N

CANADA

Kauai

Oahu

Maui

HI

N

PACIFIC OCEAN

Hawaii

Mauna Kea
13,796 ft.
(4,205 m)

Cape Mendocino

San Francisco Bay

COAST RANGES

COAST RANGES

CENTRAL VALLEY

Sacramento River

San Joaquin River

SIERRA NEVADA

Lake Tahoe

CA

Mt. Whitney
14,494 ft.
(4,418 m)

DEATH VALLEY
-282 ft.
(-86 m)

MOJAVE DESERT

Salton Sea

PACIFIC OCEAN

Puget Sound

CASCADE RANGE

Mt. Rainier
14,410 ft.
(4,392 m)

Mt. St. Helens
8,364 ft. (2,549 m)

WA

Mt. Hood
11,235 ft.
(3,427 m)

OR

COLUMBIA PLATEAU

Columbia River

Snake River

ID

Great Salt Lake

GREAT SALT LAKE DESERT

NV

GREAT BASIN

UT

WASATCH

Lake Mead

Colorado River

AZ

Baldy Peak
11,403 ft.
(3,476 m)

SONORA DESERT

Gila River

MT

ROCKY MOUNTAINS

Missouri River

Yellowstone River

TETON RANGE

WY

RANGE

GREAT

COLORADO PLATEAU

Mt. Elbert
14,433 ft.
(4,399 m)

CO

NM

Guadalupe Peak
8,749 ft.
(2,667 m)

Pecos River

Rio Grande

MEXICO

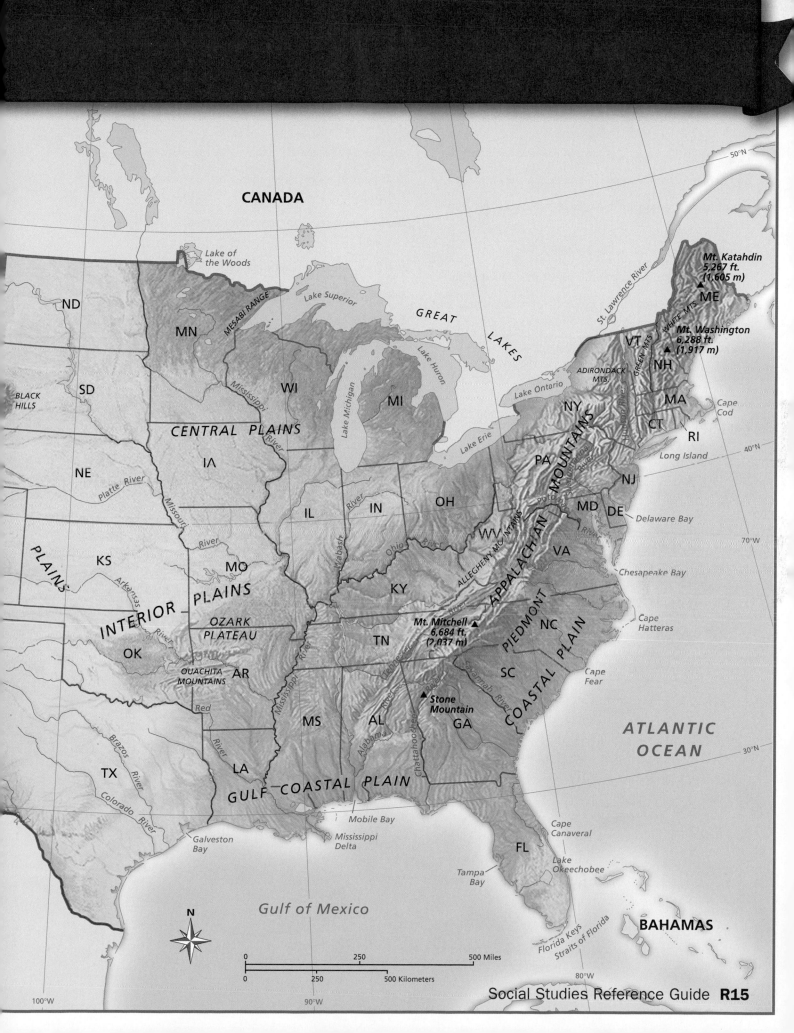

CANADA

Lake of
the Woods

ND

MN

Lake Superior

GREAT

LAKES

MESABI RANGE

Lake Huron

St. Lawrence River

Mt. Katahdin
5,267 ft.
(1,605 m)

ME

SD

BLACK
HILLS

WI

Lake Michigan

MI

VT

GREEN MTS.

WHITE MTS.

Mt. Washington
6,288 ft.
(1,917 m)

NH

CENTRAL PLAINS

Lake Ontario

ADIRONDACK
MTS.

MA

Cape
Cod

NE

IA

Mississippi

River

IL

IN

OH

NY

Hudson River

CT

RI

Lake Erie

PA

MOUNTAINS

Long Island

Platte River

Missouri

Wabash River

Ohio

River

WV

ALLEGHENY MOUNTAINS

Potomac

NJ

MD

DE

Delaware Bay

River

Susquehanna

River

VA

Chesapeake Bay

KS

MO

River

KY

APPALACHIAN

70°W

PLAINS

Arkansas

River

OZARK
PLATEAU

Mt. Mitchell
6,684 ft.
(2,037 m)

PIEDMONT

NC

Cape
Hatteras

INTERIOR

PLAINS

OK

OUACHITA
MOUNTAINS

AR

TN

Tennessee River

SC

COASTAL PLAIN

Cape
Fear

Red

River

Mississippi

River

Stone
Mountain

Savannah River

Brazos

River

TX

MS

AL

Alabama

River

Chattahoochee River

GA

ATLANTIC
OCEAN

30°N

Colorado River

LA

GULF

COASTAL

PLAIN

Galveston
Bay

Mobile Bay

Mississippi
Delta

Cape
Canaveral

FL

Lake
Okeechobee

Tampa
Bay

Gulf of Mexico

N

Florida Keys

Straits of Florida

BAHAMAS

0   250   500 Miles
0   250   500 Kilometers

50°N

40°N

100°W   90°W   80°W

Geography Terms

basin bowl-shaped area of land surrounded by higher land

bay narrower part of an ocean or lake that cuts into land

canal narrow waterway dug across land mainly for ship travel

canyon steep, narrow valley with high sides

cliff steep wall of rock or earth, sometimes called a bluff

coast land at the edge of a large body of water such as an ocean

coastal plain area of flat land along an ocean or sea

delta triangle-shaped area of land at the mouth of a river

desert very dry land

fall line area along which rivers form waterfalls or rapids as the rivers drop to lower land

forest large area of land where many trees grow

glacier giant sheet of ice that moves very slowly across land

gulf body of water, larger than most bays, with land around part of it

harbor sheltered body of water where ships safely tie up to land

hill rounded land higher than the land around it

island land with water all around it

lake large body of water with land all or nearly all around it

mesa flat-topped hill with steep sides

mountain a very tall hill; highest land on Earth

mountain range long row of mountains

mouth place where a river empties into another body of water

ocean any of the four largest bodies of water on Earth

peak pointed top of a mountain

peninsula land with water on three sides

plain very large area of flat land

plateau high, wide area of flat land, with steep sides

port place, usually in a harbor, where ships safely load and unload goods and people

prairie large area of flat land, with few or no trees, similar to a plain

river large stream of water leading to a lake, other river, or ocean

riverbank land at a river's edge

sea large body of water somewhat smaller than an ocean

sea level an ocean's surface, compared to which land can be measured either above or below

slope side of a mountain or hill

source place where a river begins

swamp very shallow water covering low land filled with trees and other plants

tributary stream or river that runs into a larger river

valley low land between mountains or hills

volcano mountain with an opening at the top, formed by violent bursts of steam and hot rock

waterfall steep falling of water from a higher to a lower place

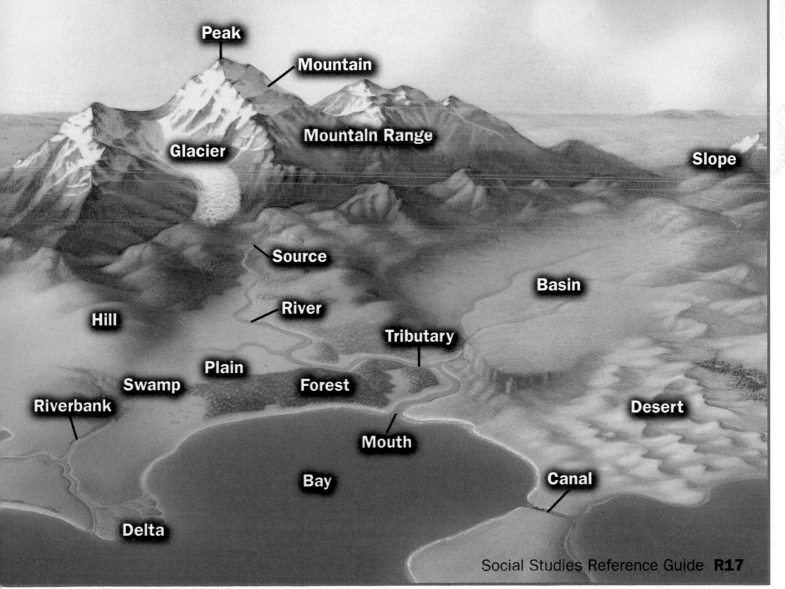

Facts About Our Fifty States

	AL — Alabama	AK — Alaska	AZ — Arizona	AR — Arkansas	CA — California	CO — Colorado
Capital	Montgomery	Juneau	Phoenix	Little Rock	Sacramento	Denver
Date and order of statehood	1819 (22)	1959 (49)	1912 (48)	1836 (25)	1850 (31)	1876 (38)
Nickname	Heart of Dixie	The Last Frontier	Grand Canyon State	Land of Opportunity	Golden State	Centennial State
Population	4,447,100	626,932	5,130,632	2,673,400	33,871,648	4,301,261
Square miles and rank in area	50,750 (28)	570,374 (1)	113,642 (6)	52,075 (27)	155,973 (3)	103,730 (8)
Region	Southeast	West	Southwest	Southeast	West	West

	IN — Indiana	IA — Iowa	KS — Kansas	KY — Kentucky	LA — Louisiana	ME — Maine
Capital	Indianapolis	Des Moines	Topeka	Frankfort	Baton Rouge	Augusta
Date and order of statehood	1816 (19)	1846 (29)	1861 (34)	1792 (15)	1812 (18)	1820 (23)
Nickname	Hoosier State	Hawkeye State	Sunflower State	Bluegrass State	Pelican State	Pine Tree State
Population	6,080,485	2,926,324	2,688,418	4,041,769	4,468,976	1,274,923
Square miles and rank in area	35,870 (38)	55,875 (23)	81,823 (13)	39,732 (36)	43,566 (33)	30,865 (39)
Region	Midwest	Midwest	Midwest	Southeast	Southeast	Northeast

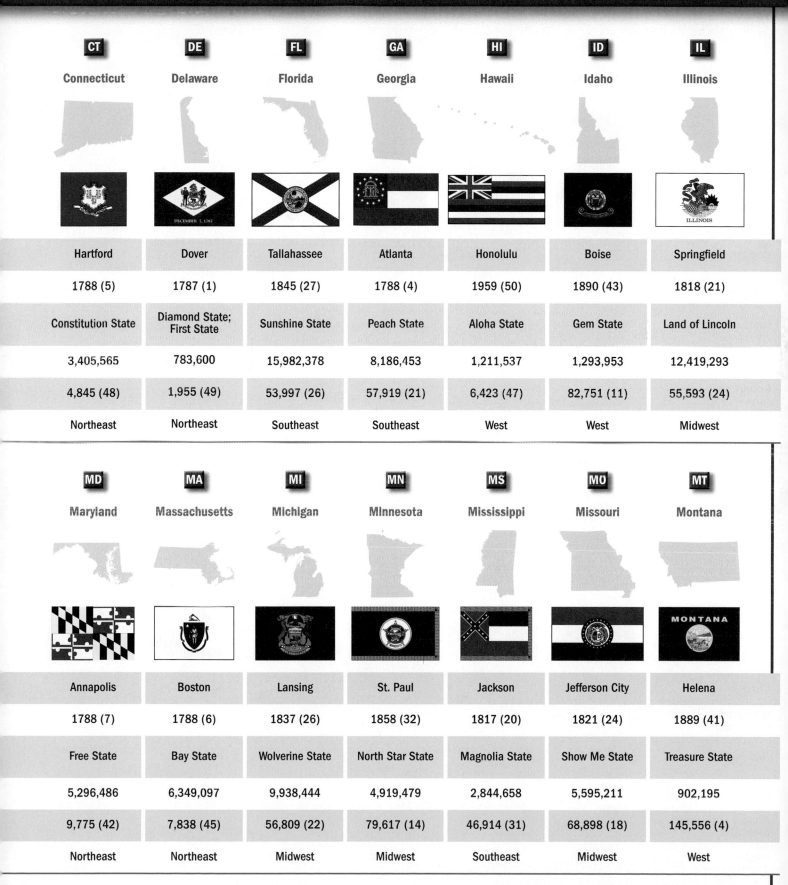

	CT	DE	FL	GA	HI	ID	IL
	Connecticut	Delaware	Florida	Georgia	Hawaii	Idaho	Illinois
Capital	Hartford	Dover	Tallahassee	Atlanta	Honolulu	Boise	Springfield
Statehood	1788 (5)	1787 (1)	1845 (27)	1788 (4)	1959 (50)	1890 (43)	1818 (21)
Nickname	Constitution State	Diamond State; First State	Sunshine State	Peach State	Aloha State	Gem State	Land of Lincoln
Population	3,405,565	783,600	15,982,378	8,186,453	1,211,537	1,293,953	12,419,293
Area	4,845 (48)	1,955 (49)	53,997 (26)	57,919 (21)	6,423 (47)	82,751 (11)	55,593 (24)
Region	Northeast	Northeast	Southeast	Southeast	West	West	Midwest

	MD	MA	MI	MN	MS	MO	MT
	Maryland	Massachusetts	Michigan	Minnesota	Mississippi	Missouri	Montana
Capital	Annapolis	Boston	Lansing	St. Paul	Jackson	Jefferson City	Helena
Statehood	1788 (7)	1788 (6)	1837 (26)	1858 (32)	1817 (20)	1821 (24)	1889 (41)
Nickname	Free State	Bay State	Wolverine State	North Star State	Magnolia State	Show Me State	Treasure State
Population	5,296,486	6,349,097	9,938,444	4,919,479	2,844,658	5,595,211	902,195
Area	9,775 (42)	7,838 (45)	56,809 (22)	79,617 (14)	46,914 (31)	68,898 (18)	145,556 (4)
Region	Northeast	Northeast	Midwest	Midwest	Southeast	Midwest	West

Facts About Our Fifty States

	NE Nebraska	NV Nevada	NH New Hampshire	NJ New Jersey	NM New Mexico	NY New York
Capital	Lincoln	Carson City	Concord	Trenton	Santa Fe	Albany
Date and order of statehood	1867 (37)	1864 (36)	1788 (9)	1787 (3)	1912 (47)	1788 (11)
Nickname	Cornhusker State	Silver State	Granite State	Garden State	Land of Enchantment	Empire State
Population	1,711,263	1,998,257	1,235,786	8,414,350	1,819,046	18,976,457
Square miles and rank in area	76,644 (15)	109,806 (7)	8,969 (44)	7,419 (46)	121,365 (5)	47,224 (30)
Region	Midwest	West	Northeast	Northeast	Southwest	Northeast

	SC South Carolina	SD South Dakota	TN Tennessee	TX Texas	UT Utah	VT Vermont
Capital	Columbia	Pierre	Nashville	Austin	Salt Lake City	Montpelier
Date and order of statehood	1788 (8)	1889 (40)	1796 (16)	1845 (28)	1896 (45)	1791 (14)
Nickname	Palmetto State	Mount Rushmore State	Volunteer State	Lone Star State	Beehive State	Green Mountain State
Population	4,012,012	754,844	5,689,283	20,851,820	2,233,169	608,827
Square miles and rank in area	30,111 (40)	75,898 (16)	41,220 (34)	261,914 (2)	82,168 (12)	9,249 (43)
Region	Southeast	Midwest	Southeast	Southwest	West	Northeast

NC	ND	OH	OK	OR	PA	RI
North Carolina	**North Dakota**	**Ohio**	**Oklahoma**	**Oregon**	**Pennsylvania**	**Rhode Island**
Raleigh	Bismarck	Columbus	Oklahoma City	Salem	Harrisburg	Providence
1789 (12)	1889 (39)	1803 (17)	1907 (46)	1859 (33)	1787 (2)	1790 (13)
Tar Heel State	Sioux State	Buckeye State	Sooner State	Beaver State	Keystone State	Ocean State
8,049,313	642,200	11,353,140	3,450,654	3,421,399	12,281,054	1,048,319
48,718 (29)	68,994 (17)	40,953 (35)	68,679 (19)	96,003 (10)	44,820 (32)	1,045 (50)
Southeast	Midwest	Midwest	Southwest	West	Northeast	Northeast

VA	WA	WV	WI	WY
Virginia	**Washington**	**West Virginia**	**Wisconsin**	**Wyoming**
Richmond	Olympia	Charleston	Madison	Cheyenne
1788 (10)	1889 (42)	1863 (35)	1848 (30)	1890 (44)
Old Dominion	Evergreen State	Mountain State	Badger State	Equality State
7,078,515	5,894,121	1,808,344	5,363,675	493,782
39,598 (37)	66,582 (20)	24,087 (41)	54,314 (25)	97,105 (9)
Southeast	West	Southeast	Midwest	West

State Names and Mottoes

Northeast

Connecticut ....From an Algonquian word meaning "beside the long river."
Motto He who transplanted still sustains

Delaware ....Named in honor of a colonial governor of Virginia, Lord De La Warr.
Motto Liberty and Independence

Maine ....May be a reference to the fact that the state's land is part of the mainland.
Motto I direct

Maryland ....Named in honor of Henrietta Maria, queen of Charles I of England.
Motto Strong deeds, gentle words

Massachusetts .....From a Massachusett word meaning "at or about the great hill."
Motto By the sword we seek peace, but peace only under liberty

New Hampshire ....Named for Hampshire, a county in England.
Motto Live free or die

New Jersey ....Named for island named Jersey off the coast of England.
Motto Liberty and Prosperity

New York ....Named in honor of England's Duke of York.
Motto Excelsior; Ever upward

Pennsylvania ....In honor of Admiral William Penn, father of the state's founder, William Penn. It means "Penn's woods."
Motto Virtue, Liberty, and Independence

Rhode Island ....Named for the Greek Island of Rhodes.
Motto Hope

Vermont ....From French *verts monts*, meaning "green mountains."
Motto Freedom and Unity

Southeast

Alabama ....Named for the Alabama, Native Americans who lived in the area.
Motto We Dare Defend Our Rights

Arkansas ....From a Lakota word meaning "downstream place."
Motto The people rule

Florida ....From the Spanish phrase "feast of flowers," meaning Easter.
Motto In God We Trust

Georgia ....Named in honor of King George II of England.
Motto Wisdom, justice, and moderation

Kentucky ....From an Iroquois word meaning "land of tomorrow."
Motto United we stand, divided we fall

Louisiana ....Named in honor of King Louis XIV of France.
Motto Union, justice, and confidence

Mississippi ....From a Native American word meaning "father of waters."
Motto By valor and arms

North Carolina ......Named in honor of England's King Charles I.
Motto To be rather than to seem

South Carolina ......Named in honor of England's King Charles I.
Mottoes While I breathe I hope

Tennessee ....From the Cherokee word *Tanasi*, meaning "villages."
Motto Agriculture and Commerce

Virginia ....From a nickname for England's Queen Elizabeth I.
Motto Thus Always to Tyrants

West Virginia ....From a nickname for England's Queen Elizabeth I.
Motto Mountaineers are always free

Midwest

Illinois . . . . From an Algonquian word meaning "superior men."
Motto State Sovereignty, National Union

Indiana . . . . Means "land of the Indians."
Motto The Crossroads of America

Iowa . . . . From a Native American word meaning "beautiful land."
Motto Our liberties we prize and our rights we will maintain

Kansas . . . . From a Lakota word meaning "people of the south wind."
Motto To the stars through difficulties

Michigan . . . . From an Ojibwa word meaning "great water" or "great lake."
Motto If you seek a pleasant peninsula, look about you.

Minnesota . . . . From a Dakota word meaning "sky-tinted water."
Motto The star of the north

Missouri . . . . Named after the Missouri, Native Americans who lived in the region and whose name means "town of the large canoes."
Motto The welfare of the people shall be the supreme law

Nebraska . . . . From an Oto word that means "flat water," referring to the Platte River.
Motto Equality before the law

North Dakota . . . . Dakota is a Native America word meaning "friend."
Motto Liberty and union, now and forever, one and inseparable

Ohio . . . . From the Iroquois word meaning "good river."
Motto With God, all things are possible

South Dakota . . . . Dakota is a Native American word meaning "friend."
Motto Under God, the people rule

Wisconsin . . . . From an Ojibwa word, *Ouisconsin,* believed to mean "grassy place."
Motto Forward

Southwest

Arizona . . . . From a Pima word meaning "little spring." **Motto** God enriches

New Mexico . . . . Named by the Spanish for lands north of Mexico.
Motto It grows as it goes

Oklahoma . . . . From Native American words meaning "red man."
Motto Work conquers all things

Texas . . . . From a Caddo word meaning "friends." **Motto** Friendship

West

Alaska . . . . From an Aleut word meaning "great land." **Motto** North to the Future

California . . . . Named for a mythical island in a Spanish story. **Motto** Eureka

Colorado . . . . From the Spanish word for "red," to describe the Colorado River.
Motto Nothing without Providence

Hawaii . . . . May be named for Hawaiki, the traditional Polynesian homeland.
Motto The life of the land is perpetuated in righteousness

Idaho . . . . An invented name the meaning of which is unknown.
Motto It is forever

Montana . . . . From the Spanish word for "mountainous."
Motto Gold and Silver

Nevada . . . . From a Spanish word meaning "snow-capped."
Motto All for our country

Oregon . . . . May have come from a river shown as "Ouaricon-sint" on a 1715 French map.
Motto She flies with her own wings

Utah . . . . Named after the Ute, Native Americans who lived in the region and whose name means "people of the mountains." **Motto** Industry

Washington . . . . Named in honor of George Washington. **Motto** Bye and Bye

Wyoming . . . . From a Native American word meaning "large prairie place."
Motto Equal Rights

Symbols of the United States

Our National Flag

The flag of the United States of America is an important symbol for our country. The flag should be shown respect at all times. When we say the Pledge of Allegiance to the flag, we are saying that we will be good citizens of the United States of America.

When saying the Pledge of Allegiance, stand, face the flag, and place your right hand over your heart.

The Pledge of Allegiance

I pledge allegiance to the flag
Of the United States of America
And to the Republic for which it stands,
One Nation under God, indivisible,
With liberty and justice for all.

Displaying the Flag

Display the flag only from sunrise to sunset, except when bad weather might damage the flag.

No other flag or pennant should be placed above the U.S. flag. If another flag is displayed on the same level, it should be to the right of the flag of the United States of America.

When the flag passes in a parade, stand and put your hand over your heart.

When singing the National Anthem, everyone should rise and stand at attention. A man should remove his hat with his right hand and place the palm of his right hand over his heart.

Flag Holidays

The flag of the United States should be flown every day, but especially on these holidays:

New Year's Day	January 1
Inauguration Day	January 20
Lincoln's Birthday	February 12
Washington's Birthday	third Monday in February
Easter Sunday	varies
Mother's Day	second Sunday in May
Armed Forces Day	third Saturday in May
Memorial Day	last Monday in May (half-staff until noon)
Flag Day	June 14
Independence Day	July 4
Labor Day	first Monday in September
Constitution Day	September 17
Columbus Day	second Monday in October
Navy Day	October 27
Veteran's Day	November 11
Thanksgiving Day	fourth Thursday in November
Christmas Day	December 25

By Executive Order, the flag flies 24 hours a day at the following locations:

The Betsy Ross House, Philadelphia, Pennsylvania

The White House, Washington, D.C.

The United States Capitol, Washington, D.C.

Iwo Jima Memorial to U.S. Marines, Arlington, Virginia

Battleground in Lexington, MA (site of the first shots in the Revolutionary War)

Winter Encampment Cabins, Valley Forge, Pennsylvania

Fort McHenry, Baltimore, Maryland (A flag flying over Fort McHenry after a battle during the War of 1812 provided the inspiration for "The Star-Spangled Banner.")

The Star-Spangled Banner Flag House, Baltimore, Maryland (This is the site where the famous flag over Fort McHenry was sewn.)

Jenny Wade House, Gettysburg, Pennsylvania (Jenny Wade was the only civilian killed at the battle of Gettysburg.)

USS *Arizona* Memorial, Pearl Harbor, Hawaii

Our National Anthem

Francis Scott Key wrote the words of "The Star-Spangled Banner" during the War of 1812. After a heavy battle, he was proud to see that the American flag was still flying over a fort that had been heavily damaged during the night. This song became the official national anthem in 1931.

The Star-Spangled Banner

Oh, say! can you see by the dawn's early light,
What so proudly we hailed at the twilight's last gleaming?
Whose broad stripes and bright stars, through the perilous fight,
O'er the ramparts we watched were so gallantly streaming?
And the rocket's red glare, the bombs bursting in air,
Gave proof through the night that our flag was still there.
Oh, say does that Star-Spangled Banner yet wave
O'er the land of the free and the home of the brave?

On the shore, dimly seen through the mists of the deep,
Where the foe's haughty host in dread silence reposes,
What is that which the breeze, o'er the towering steep,
As it fitfully blows, half conceals, half discloses?
Now it catches the gleam of the morning's first beam,
In full glory reflected now shines on the stream;
'Tis the Star-Spangled Banner! O, long may it wave
O'er the land of the free and the home of the brave!

Oh! thus be it ever, when freemen shall stand
Between their loved home and the war's desolation!
Blest with victory and peace, may the heav'n rescued land
Praise the Power that hath made and preserved us a nation.
Then conquer we must, when our cause it is just,
And this be our motto: "In God is our trust."
And the Star-Spangled Banner in triumph shall wave
O'er the land of the free and the home of the brave!

Sometimes in history it becomes necessary for a group of people to break political ties with the country that rules it. When this happens, it is proper to explain the reasons for the need to separate.

We believe that all men are created equal and given by their Creator certain rights that cannot be taken away. People have the right to live, be free, and seek happiness.

Governments are established to protect these rights. The government gets its power from the support of the people it governs. If any form of government tries to take away the basic rights, it is the right of the people to change or end the government and to establish a new government that seems most likely to result in their safety and happiness.

Wise judgment will require that long-existing governments should not be changed for unimportant or temporary reasons. History has shown that people are more willing to suffer under a bad government than to get rid of the government they are used to. But when there are so many abuses and misuses of power by the government, it is the right and duty of the people to throw off such government and form a new government to protect their basic rights.

The colonies have suffered patiently, and now it is necessary for them to change the government. The king of Great Britain has repeatedly abused his power over these states. To prove this, the following facts are given.

In Congress, July 4, 1776

When, in the course of human events, it becomes necessary for one people to dissolve the political bands which have connected them with another, and to assume, among the powers of the earth, the separate and equal station to which the laws of nature and nature's God entitle them, a decent respect to the opinions of mankind requires that they should declare the causes which impel them to the separation.

We hold these truths to be self-evident; that all men are created equal, that they are endowed by their Creator with certain unalienable rights, that among these are life, liberty, and the pursuit of happiness.

That to secure these rights, governments are instituted among men, deriving their just powers from the consent of the governed; that whenever any form of government becomes destructive of these ends, it is the right of the people to alter or to abolish it, and to institute new government, laying its foundation on such principles, and organizing its powers in such form, as to them shall seem most likely to effect their safety and happiness.

Prudence, indeed, will dictate that governments long established should not be changed for light and transient causes; and accordingly all experience hath shown that mankind are more disposed to suffer, while evils are sufferable, than to right themselves by abolishing the forms to which they are accustomed. But when a long train of abuses and usurpations, pursuing invariably the same object, evinces a design to reduce them under absolute despotism, it is their right, it is their duty, to throw off such government, and to provide new guards for their future security.

Such has been the patient sufferance of these colonies; and such is now the necessity which constrains them to alter their former systems of government. The history of the present king of Great Britain is a history of repeated injuries and usurpations, all having in direct object the establishment of an absolute tyranny over these states. To prove this, let facts be submitted to a candid world.

He has refused his assent to laws the most wholesome and necessary for the public good. He has forbidden his governors to pass laws of immediate and pressing importance, unless suspended in their operation till his assent should be obtained; and when so suspended, he has utterly neglected to attend to them.

The king has not given his approval to needed laws. He has not allowed his governors to pass laws needed immediately. The king has made the governors delay laws until they can get his permission and then he has ignored the laws.

He has refused to pass other laws for the accommodation of large districts of people, unless those people would relinquish the right of representation in the legislature, a right inestimable to them, and formidable to tyrants only.

He has refused to pass other laws to help large districts of people, unless those people would give up the right of representation in the legislature, a right priceless to them and threatening only to tyrants.

He has called together legislative bodies at places unusual, uncomfortable, and distant from the depository of their public records, for the sole purpose of fatiguing them into compliance with his measures.

He has called together legislative bodies at unusual and uncomfortable places, distant from where they store their public records, and only for the purpose of tiring them into obeying his measures.

He has dissolved representative houses repeatedly, for opposing, with manly firmness, his invasions on the rights of the people.

He has repeatedly done away with legislative groups that firmly opposed him for taking away the rights of the people.

He has refused, for a long time after such dissolutions, to cause others to be elected; whereby the legislative powers, incapable of annihilation, have returned to the people at large for their exercise; the state remaining, in the meantime, exposed to all the dangers of invasion from without and convulsions within.

After he has dissolved these representative meetings, he has refused to allow new elections. Because of this lack of legislative power, the people are exposed to the dangers of invasion from without and violence within.

He has endeavored to prevent the population of these states; for that purpose obstructing the laws for the naturalization of foreigners, refusing to pass others to encourage their migrations hither, and raising the conditions of new appropriations of lands.

He has tried to prevent people from immigrating to these states by blocking the process for foreigners to become citizens, refusing to pass laws to encourage people to travel to America, and making it harder to move to and own new lands.

He has obstructed the administration of justice, by refusing his assent to laws for establishing judiciary powers.

He has interfered with the administration of justice by refusing to approve laws for establishing courts.

He has made judges dependent on his will alone for the tenure of their offices, and the amount and payment of their salaries.

He has made judges do what he wants by controlling how long they serve and how much they are paid.

He has erected a multitude of new offices, and sent hither swarms of officers to harass our people and eat out their substance.

He has created many new government offices and sent many officials to torment our people and live off of our hard work.

He has kept among us, in times of peace, standing armies, without the consent of our legislatures.

In times of peace, he has kept soldiers among us, without the consent of our legislatures.

He has affected to render the military independent of, and superior to, the civil power.

He has tried to make the military separate from, and superior to, the civil government.

He has combined with others to subject us to a jurisdiction foreign to our constitution and unacknowledged by our laws, giving his assent to their acts of pretended legislation:

He and others have made us live under laws that are different from our laws. He has given his approval to these unfair laws that parliament has adopted:

For forcing us to feed and house many British soldiers;

For using pretend trials to protect British soldiers from punishment for murdering people in America;

For cutting off our trade with the world;

For taxing us without our consent;

For taking away, in many cases, the benefits of trial by jury;

For taking us to Great Britain to be tried for made-up offenses;

For doing away with the free system of English laws in a neighboring province and establishing a harsh government there, enlarging its boundaries as a way to introduce the same absolute rule into these colonies;

For taking away our governing documents, doing away with our most valuable laws, and changing our governments completely;

For setting aside our own legislatures and declaring that Great Britain has power to make laws for us in all cases whatsoever.

He has deserted government here, by not protecting us and by waging war against us.

He has robbed our ships on the seas, destroyed our coasts, burned our towns, and destroyed the lives of our people.

He is at this time sending large armies of foreign hired soldiers to complete the works of death, destruction, and injustice. These deeds are among the cruelest ever seen in history and are totally unworthy of the head of a civilized nation.

He has forced our fellow citizens, who were captured on the high seas, to fight against America, to kill their friends and family, or to be killed themselves.

He has stirred up civil disorder among us and has tried to cause the merciless killing of the people living on the frontiers by the American Indians, whose rule of warfare includes the deliberate killing of people regardless of age, sex, or conditions.

In every stage of these mistreatments we have asked for a solution in the most humble terms; our repeated requests have been answered only by more mistreatment. A leader who is so unfair and acts like a dictator is unfit to be the ruler of a free people.

For quartering large bodies of armed troops among us;

For protecting them, by a mock trial, from punishment for any murders which they should commit on the inhabitants of these states;

For cutting off our trade with all parts of the world;

For imposing taxes on us without our consent;

For depriving us, in many cases, of the benefits of trial by jury;

For transporting us beyond seas, to be tried for pretended offenses;

For abolishing the free system of English laws in a neighboring province, establishing therein an arbitrary government, and enlarging its boundaries, so as to render it at once an example and fit instrument for introducing the same absolute rule into these colonies;

For taking away our charters, abolishing our most valuable laws, and altering fundamentally the forms of our governments;

For suspending our own legislatures, and declaring themselves invested with power to legislate for us in all cases whatsoever.

He has abdicated government here, by declaring us out of his protection and waging war against us.

He has plundered our seas, ravaged our coasts, burned our towns, and destroyed the lives of our people.

He is at this time transporting large armies of foreign mercenaries to complete the works of death, desolation, and tyranny already begun with circumstances of cruelty and perfidy scarcely paralleled in the most barbarous ages, and totally unworthy the head of a civilized nation.

He has constrained our fellow citizens, taken captive on the high seas, to bear arms against their country, to become the executioners of their friends and brethren, or to fall themselves by their hands.

He has excited domestic insurrection among us, and has endeavored to bring on the inhabitants of our frontiers, the merciless Indian savages, whose known rule of warfare is an undistinguished destruction of all ages, sexes, and conditions.

In every stage of these oppressions we have petitioned for redress in the most humble terms; our repeated petitions have been answered only by repeated injury. A prince, whose character is thus marked by every act which may define a tyrant, is unfit to be the ruler of a free people.

Nor have we been wanting in attentions to our British brethren. We have warned them, from time to time, of attempts by their legislature to extend an unwarrantable jurisdiction over us. We have reminded them of the circumstances of our emigration and settlement here. We have appealed to their native justice and magnanimity; and we have conjured them, by the ties of our common kindred, to disavow these usurpations, which would inevitably interrupt our connections and correspondence. They, too, have been deaf to the voice of justice and consanguinity. We must, therefore, acquiesce in the necessity which denounces our separation, and hold them, as we hold the rest of mankind, enemies in war; in peace, friends.

We, therefore, the representatives of the United States of America, in General Congress assembled, appealing to the Supreme Judge of the world for the rectitude of our intentions, do, in the name and by the authority of the good people of these colonies, solemnly publish and declare that these United Colonies are, and of right ought to be, free and independent states; that they are absolved from all allegiance to the British crown, and that all political connection between them and the state of Great Britain is, and ought to be, totally dissolved; and that, as free and independent states, they have full power to levy war, conclude peace, contract alliances, establish commerce, and do all other acts and things which independent states may of right do. And, for the support of this declaration, with a firm reliance on the protection of Divine Providence, we mutually pledge to each other our lives, our fortunes, and our sacred honor.

We have also asked for help from the British people. We have warned them, from time to time, of attempts by their government to extend illegal power over us. We have reminded them why we came to America. We have appealed to their sense of justice and generosity; and we have begged them, because of all we have in common, to give up these abuses of power. They, like the king, have not listened to the voice of justice and brotherhood. We must, therefore, declare our separation. In war the British are our enemies. In peace, they are our friends.

We therefore, as the representatives of the people of the United States of America, in this General Congress assembled, appealing to God for the honesty of our purpose, do solemnly publish and declare that these United Colonies are, and rightly should be, free and independent states. The people of the United States are no longer subjects of the British crown. All political connections between the colonies and Great Britain are totally ended. These free and independent states have full power to declare war, make peace, make treaties with other countries, establish trade, and do all other acts and things which independent states have the right to do. To support this declaration, with a firm trust on the protection of God, we pledge to each other our lives, our fortunes, and our sacred honor.

Button Gwinnett (GA)	Thomas Nelson, Jr. (VA)	Richard Stockton (NJ)
Lyman Hall (GA)	Francis Lightfoot Lee (VA)	John Witherspoon (NJ)
George Walton (GA)	Carter Braxton (VA)	Francis Hopkinson (NJ)
William Hooper (NC)	Robert Morris (PA)	John Hart (NJ)
Joseph Hewes (NC)	Benjamin Rush (PA)	Abraham Clark (NJ)
John Penn (NC)	Benjamin Franklin (PA)	Josiah Bartlett (NH)
Edward Rutledge (SC)	John Morton (PA)	William Whipple (NH)
Thomas Heyward, Jr. (SC)	George Clymer (PA)	Samuel Adams (MA)
Thomas Lynch, Jr. (SC)	James Smith (PA)	John Adams (MA)
Arthur Middleton (SC)	George Taylor (PA)	Robert Treat Paine (MA)
John Hancock (MA)	James Wilson (PA)	Elbridge Gerry (MA)
Samuel Chase (MD)	George Ross (PA)	Stephen Hopkins (RI)
William Paca (MD)	Caesar Rodney (DE)	William Ellery (RI)
Thomas Stone (MD)	George Read (DE)	Roger Sherman (CT)
Charles Carroll (MD)	Thomas McKean (DE)	Samuel Huntington (CT)
George Wythe (VA)	William Floyd (NY)	William Williams (CT)
Richard Henry Lee (VA)	Philip Livingston (NY)	Oliver Wolcott (CT)
Thomas Jefferson (VA)	Francis Lewis (NY)	Matthew Thornton (NH)
Benjamin Harrison (VA)	Lewis Morris (NY)	

"Among the natural rights of the Colonists are these: First, a right to life; Secondly, to liberty; Thirdly, to property; together with the right to support and defend them in the best manner they can."

Samuel Adams, The Report of the Committee of Correspondence to the Boston Town Meeting.

"All, too, will bear in mind this sacred principle, that though the will of the majority is in all cases to prevail, that will to be rightful must be reasonable; that the minority possess their equal rights, which equal law must protect, and to violate would be oppression."

Thomas Jefferson, First Inaugural Address.

Facts About Our Presidents

	1 George Washington	**2** John Adams	**3** Thomas Jefferson	**4** James Madison	**5** James Monroe
Years in Office	1789–1797	1797–1801	1801–1809	1809–1817	1817–1825
Life Span	1732–1799	1735–1826	1743–1826	1751–1836	1758–1831
Birthplace	Westmoreland County, Virginia	Braintree County, Massachusetts	Albemarle County, Virginia	Port Conway, Virginia	Westmoreland County, Virginia
Home State	Virginia	Massachusetts	Virginia	Virginia	Virginia
Political Party	Federalist	Federalist	Democratic-Republican	Democratic-Republican	Democratic-Republican
First Lady	Martha Dandridge Washington	Abigail Smith Adams	None	Dolley Payne Madison	Elizabeth Kortright Monroe
Religion	Episcopalian	Unitarian	Deist	Episcopalian	Episcopalian

	12 Zachary Taylor	**13** Millard Fillmore	**14** Franklin Pierce	**15** James Buchanan	**16** Abraham Lincoln
Years in Office	1849–1850	1850–1853	1853–1857	1857–1861	1861–1865
Life Span	1784–1850	1800–1874	1804–1869	1791–1868	1809–1865
Birthplace	Orange County, Virginia	Cayuga County, New York	Hillsboro, New Hampshire	Mercersburg, Pennsylvania	Harden County, Kentucky
Home State	Virginia	New York	New Hampshire	Pennsylvania	Illinois
Political Party	Whig	Whig	Democratic	Democratic	Republican
First Lady	Margaret Smith Taylor	Abigail Powers Fillmore	Jane Appleton Pierce	None	Mary Todd Lincoln
Religion	Episcopalian	Unitarian	Episcopalian	Presbyterian	Attended Presbyterian services

6	7	8	9	10	11
John Quincy Adams	Andrew Jackson	Martin Van Buren	William H. Harrison	John Tyler	James K. Polk
1825–1829	1829–1837	1837–1841	1841	1841–1845	1845–1849
1767–1848	1767–1845	1782–1862	1773–1841	1790–1862	1795–1849
Braintree, Massachusetts	Waxhaw, South Carolina	Kinderhook, New York	Charles City County, Virginia	Charles City County, Virginia	Mecklenburg County, North Carolina
Massachusetts	Tennessee	New York	Ohio	Virginia	Tennessee
Democratic-Republican	Democratic	Democratic	Whig	Whig	Democratic
Louisa Johnson Adams	None	None	Anna Symmes Harrison	Letitia Christian Tyler; Julia Gardiner Tyler	Sarah Childress Polk
Unitarian	Presbyterian	Dutch Reformed	Episcopalian	Episcopalian	Presbyterian

17	18	19	20	21	22 24
Andrew Johnson	Ulysses S. Grant	Rutherford B. Hayes	James A. Garfield	Chester A. Arthur	Grover Cleveland
1865–1869	1869–1877	1877–1881	1881	1881–1885	1885–1889; 1893–1897
1808–1875	1822–1885	1822–1893	1831–1881	1829–1886	1837–1908
Raleigh, North Carolina	Point Pleasant, Ohio	Delaware, Ohio	Orange, Ohio	Fairfield, Vermont	Caldwell, New Jersey
Tennessee	Illinois	Ohio	Ohio	New York	New York
Democratic	Republican	Republican	Republican	Republican	Democratic
Eliza McCardle Johnson	Julia Dent Grant	Lucy Webb Hayes	Lucretia Rudolph Garfield	None	Frances Folsom Cleveland
No specific affiliation	Methodist	Methodist	Disciples of Christ	Episcopalian	Presbyterian

Facts About Our Presidents

	23 Benjamin Harrison	**25** William McKinley	**26** Theodore Roosevelt	**27** William H. Taft	**28** Woodrow Wilson
Years in Office	1889–1893	1897–1901	1901–1909	1909–1913	1913–1921
Life Span	1833–1901	1843–1901	1858–1919	1859–1930	1856–1924
Birthplace	North Bend, Ohio	Niles, Ohio	New York, New York	Cincinnati, Ohio	Staunton, Virginia
Home State	Indiana	Ohio	New York	Ohio	New Jersey
Political Party	Republican	Republican	Republican	Republican	Democratic
First Lady	Caroline Scott Harrison	Ida Saxton McKinley	Edith Carow Roosevelt	Helen Herron Taft	Ellen Axson Wilson; Edith Galt Wilson
Religion	Presbyterian	Methodist	Dutch Reformed	Unitarian	Presbyterian

	35 John F. Kennedy	**36** Lyndon B. Johnson	**37** Richard M. Nixon	**38** Gerald R. Ford	**39** James E. Carter
Years in Office	1961–1963	1963–1969	1969–1974	1974–1977	1977–1981
Life Span	1917–1963	1908–1973	1913–1994	1913 –	1924–
Birthplace	Brookline, Massachusetts	Stonewall, Texas	Yorba Linda, California	Omaha, Nebraska	Plains, Georgia
Home State	Massachusetts	Texas	California	Michigan	Georgia
Political Party	Democratic	Democratic	Republican	Republican	Democratic
First Lady	Jacqueline Bouvier Kennedy	Claudia "Lady Bird" Taylor Johnson	Thelma "Pat" Ryan Nixon	Elizabeth (Betty) Warren Ford	Rosalynn Smith Carter
Religion	Roman Catholic	Disciples of Christ	Quaker	Episcopalian	Southern Baptist

29	**30**	**31**	**32**	**33**	**34**
Warren G. Harding	**Calvin Coolidge**	**Herbert Hoover**	**Franklin D. Roosevelt**	**Harry S. Truman**	**Dwight D. Eisenhower**
1921–1923	1923–1929	1929–1933	1933–1945	1945–1953	1953–1961
1865–1923	1872–1933	1874–1964	1882–1945	1884–1972	1890–1969
Morrow County, Ohio	Plymouth, Vermont	West Branch, Iowa	Hyde Park, New York	Lamar, Missouri	Denison, Texas
Ohio	Massachusetts	California	New York	Missouri	Kansas
Republican	Republican	Republican	Democratic	Democratic	Republican
Florence DeWolfe Harding	Grace Goodhue Coolidge	Lou Henry Hoover	Anna Eleanor Roosevelt	Bess Wallace Truman	Marie "Mamie" Doud Eisenhower
Baptist	Congregational	Quaker	Episcopalian	Baptist	Presbyterian

40	**41**	**42**	**43**
Ronald Reagan	**George H. W. Bush**	**William J. Clinton**	**George W. Bush**
1981–1989	1989–1993	1993–2001	2001–
1911–	1924–	1946–	1946–
Tampico, Illinois	Milton, Massachusetts	Hope, Arkansas	New Haven, Connecticut
California	Texas	Arkansas	Texas
Republican	Republican	Democratic	Republican
Anne "Nancy" Davis Reagan	Barbara Pierce Bush	Hillary Rodham Clinton	Laura Welch Bush
Disciples of Christ	Episcopalian	Baptist	Methodist

Learn About Your State

You read about different regions of the United States. You read about many general things about your region. You may have found out some things about your state when you were reading about your region. Your state has its own special landforms, climate, history, economics, and culture.

Use reference materials in your classroom or library to write a guidebook about your state. What makes your state special? The skills you learned in this book will help you organize material about your state. Here are some things to include.

Your State's Geography

Find out some facts about your state's geography. In what region is your state? What is the state capital? What are the populations of some of the large cities? What states are neighbors of your state?

Make a chart with some facts about your state. Here is a chart that some students in Pennsylvania made. What special facts about your state would you add?

Facts About Pennsylvania

Region: Northeast

Large Cities: Philadelphia, Pittsburgh, Erie, Scranton, Harrisburg

State Capitol: Harrisburg

Nickname: The Keystone State

Neighbor States: New York, New Jersey, Delaware, Maryland, West Virginia, Ohio

Pennsylvania state capitol building in Harrisburg

Your State's Landforms

Use reference materials to find out about rivers and landforms in your state. Include the information in your guidebook. Do mountain ranges go through your state? Is your state on the coast of an ocean? Does your state have a desert area?

Make a physical map of your state. Use reference materials to find out about landforms and their elevations. Mark the highest point and the lowest point in your state. Include some rivers and cities. Here is a map that some students in North Carolina made.

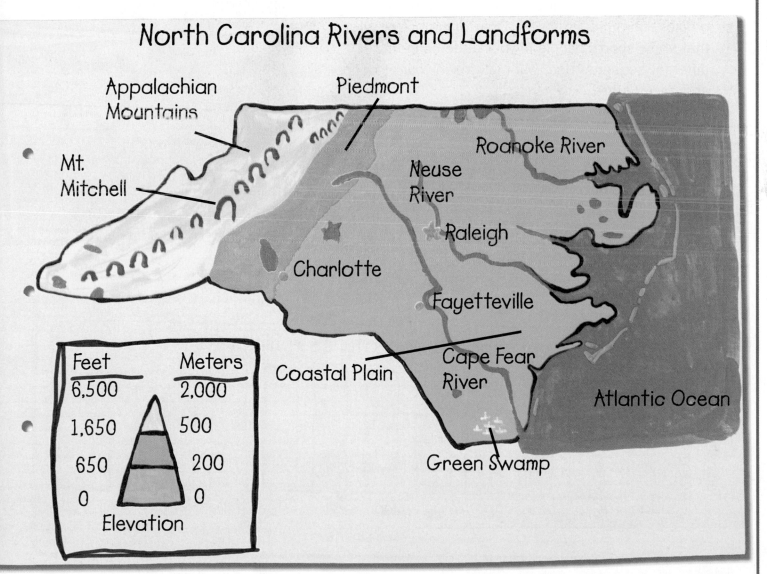

North Carolina Rivers and Landforms

Appalachian Mountains

Piedmont

Roanoke River

Mt. Mitchell

Neuse River

Raleigh

Charlotte

Fayetteville

Cape Fear River

Coastal Plain

Atlantic Ocean

Green Swamp

Feet	Meters
6,500	2,000
1,650	500
650	200
0	0

Elevation

Your State's Climate

What are some outdoor sports that people in your state can do in the winter? How can you describe the climate of your state? Does your state have very cold winters and hot summers, or is your state warm for much of the year? How much rain and snow falls in your state during the year?

Use reference materials to learn about your state's climate. Find out how the temperature changes throughout the year. How does the average precipitation change from month to month? Make a line graph or a bar graph to show your state's temperature or precipitation through a year. Draw or cut out pictures that show sports people in your state do during different seasons. Use your pictures in your guidebook about your state.

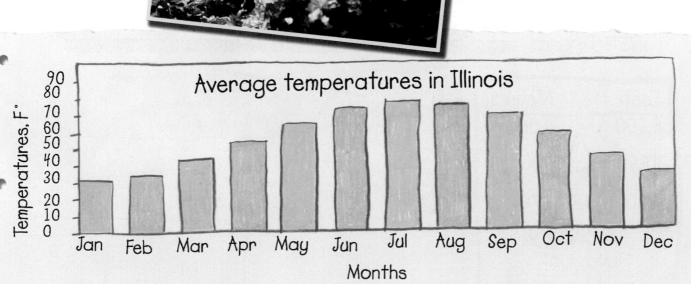

Average temperatures in Illinois

Temperatures, F°

90
80
70
60
50
40
30
20
10
0

Jan Feb Mar Apr May Jun Jul Aug Sep Oct Nov Dec

Months

Plants and Animals in Your State

Do saguaros grow near your home? If you live in the Southwest, you might see saguaros growing. But if you live in the Northeast, you would see different plants. You know that certain plants and animals are more likely to live in some regions than in others. Alligators might be swimming in wetlands of the Southeast, but it is not likely that you would see them in the rivers of the West.

What animals and plants might you see in your state? Add the plants and animals that live in your state to your guidebook. Include your official state animal, tree, and flower. Are any animals and plants in your state endangered species?

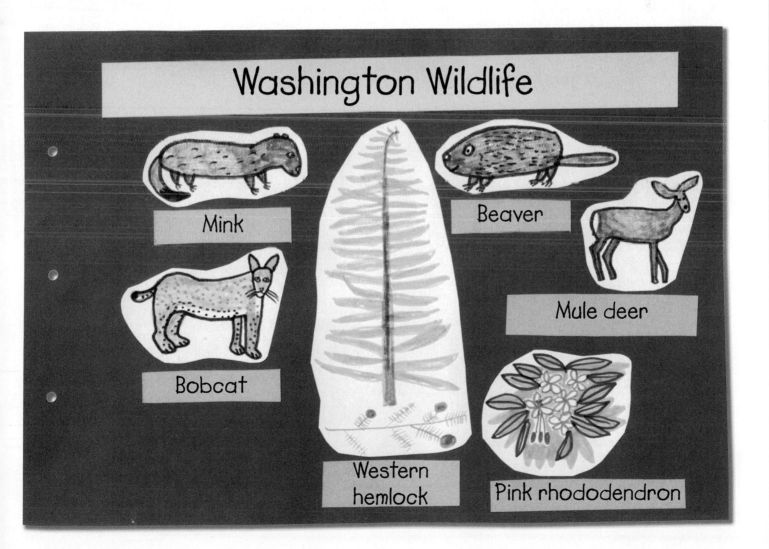

Washington Wildlife

Mink

Beaver

Mule deer

Bobcat

Western hemlock

Pink rhododendron

Your State's Resources

Some states have lots of rich farmland, others have oil or mineral resources, and still other states have thick forests. Your state might have all of these! Natural resources can be found on Earth's surface or can be mined from deep inside Earth.

Some natural resources are used within the state to make materials and products. Natural resources are also shipped to other states and countries where they can be used.

Make a list of natural resources found in your state. Choose one resource from the list. Make a diagram that shows where in your state the resource is found, and then show some ways that the resource is used. If the resource is shipped to other places, show the shipping method most often used.

Natural Resources of Minnesota
- Fertile soil for farming
- Trees
- Water in lakes and rivers
> Iron ore

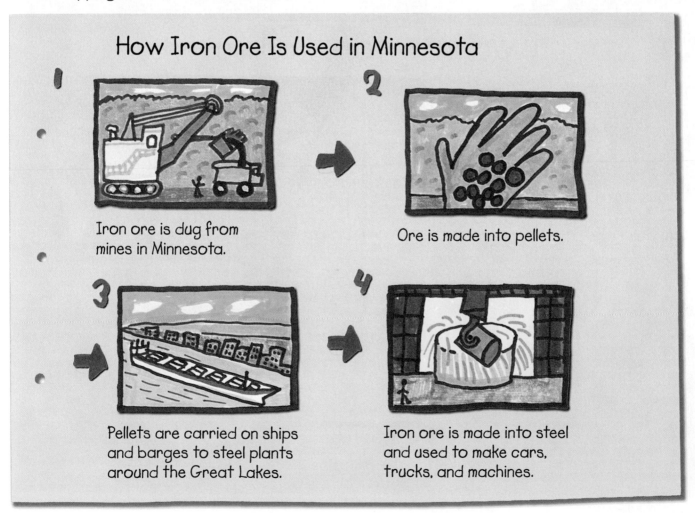

How Iron Ore Is Used in Minnesota

1 Iron ore is dug from mines in Minnesota.

2 Ore is made into pellets.

3 Pellets are carried on ships and barges to steel plants around the Great Lakes.

4 Iron ore is made into steel and used to make cars, trucks, and machines.

Your State's Economy

The natural resources of an area can help its businesses grow. A state's climate can also affect its businesses.

Find out about the main kinds of businesses in your state. How do the businesses use the natural resources of the area? Does the climate affect your state's businesses?

Do research to find out about businesses in your state. Include a section in your state guidebook that shows how one type of business depends on the resources or climate of your state. Here's a picture that some students in New Mexico made.

▶ In October, people come to the International Balloon Fiesta in Albuquerque.

▶ Tourism is a business in New Mexico

Visit New Mexico

Enjoy sight-seeing

Have fun skiing

Go on fun hikes

See historical places

Your State's History

People and events make up the history of a place. Many groups of people have come to live in each state. Native Americans, explorers, and settlers have lived throughout the country. Events have brought changes to every area.

Use reference materials to learn about the history of your state. Find out about the earliest groups of people who lived in your state. Research the explorers who visited your state. Then, find out about other people who settled in your state. What events brought major changes to your state?

Make a time line for your state. Include at least five dates in your time line. Here is a time line that some students in Alaska made.

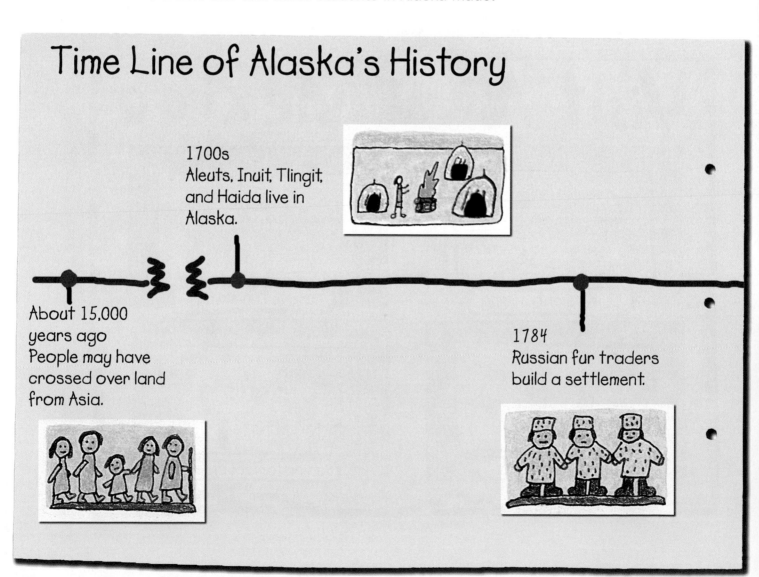

Time Line of Alaska's History

1700s
Aleuts, Inuit, Tlingit, and Haida live in Alaska.

About 15,000 years ago
People may have crossed over land from Asia.

1784
Russian fur traders build a settlement.

▶ These people in Barrow, Alaska are watching the sun setting over the Arctic Ocean.

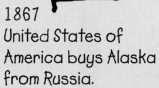

1897–1898
Alaska Gold Rush attracts thousands of people.

1959
Alaska becomes the 49th state.

1867
United States of America buys Alaska from Russia.

1939–1945
World War II brings changes to Alaska. Many people move here, and many new roads are built.

1968
Large oil deposits are discovered.

People from Your State

You can learn a lot about your state's history by reading about famous people who have lived in your state. Some famous people from your state have also made a difference in the whole country.

Do research to find out about famous people from your state. Choose one person you admire and make a picture card about him or her. On your card, list the dates and place in which the person lived. Then list some reasons why the person became well-known. Your class might display all the cards as a set of State Heroes. Students in Massachusetts made cards like these.

State Heroes of Massachusetts

Crispus Attucks
1723–1770
- Crispus Attucks was an African American who lived in Boston.
- He led a group of colonists against British soldiers.
- He was the first American to die in the Revolutionary War.

Susan B. Anthony
1820–1906
- Susan B. Anthony was born in Adams.
- She fought for women getting the right to vote.
- She worked for equal rights for women.

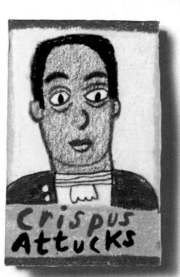

Alexander Graham Bell
1847–1922
- Alexander Graham Bell lived in Boston.
- He had a school for teachers of the deaf.
- He invented the telephone.

John F. Kennedy
1917–1963
- John F. Kennedy was born in Brookline.
- He was the 35th President of the United States of America.
- He said, "Ask what you can do for your country."

Gazetteer

This Gazetteer is a geographic dictionary that will help you locate and pronounce the names of places in this book. Latitude and longitude are given for many cities. The page numbers tell you where each place appears on a map (m) or in the text (t).

Acadia National Park (ə kā′ de ə nash′ə nəl pärk) Area in eastern Maine famous for its cliffs and rocky coastline. (t. 108)

Alabama (al′ ə bam′ ə) One of the states in the Southeast region of the United States. (m. 160)

Alaska (ə las′ kə) A West region state that lies northwest of Canada. (m. 362; t. 378, 405)

Albuquerque (al′ bə kėr′ kē) City in New Mexico where new technological products are developed; 35°N, 106°W. (m. 314, t. 316)

American River (ə mer′ ə kən riv′ ər) River in Colorado where gold was discovered in 1848. (t. 402, m. 403)

Appalachia (ap′ ə lā′ chə) Mountainous area in the eastern United States, covering parts of eleven states. (t. 169)

Appalachian Mountain Range (ap′ ə lā′ chən moun′tən rānj) Oldest range of mountains in the United States, extending from eastern Canada to Alabama. (m. 98, t. 106)

Arizona (ar′ə zo′ nə) One of the states in the Southwest region of the United States. (m. 294)

Arkansas (är′ kən sȯ) One of the states in the Southeast region of the United States. (m. 160)

Atlanta (at lan′ tə) Capital of Georgia and a major business and transportation center; 33°N, 84°W. (m. 210, t. 211)

Atlantic City (at lan′ tik sit′ ē) Vacation and resort city along the Atlantic coast in New Jersey; 39°N, 74°W. (t. 109)

Badlands National Park (bad′ landz′ nash′ ə nəl pärk) Area of South Dakota where wind and water have carved the soft rock into jagged ridges and sharp spires. (m. 242, t. 244)

Beaumont (bō′ mont) City in southeastern Texas where major oil fields are located; 30°N, 94°W. (m. 314, t. 315)

Bering Strait (bir′ ing strāt) Narrow body of water in the north Pacific Ocean that separates North America from Asia. (t. 39)

Big Springs (big springz) Town located in Nebraska around which much wheat and sunflowers are grown; 41°N, 102°W. (m. 247, t. 247)

Bosque Redondo (bos′ kā rē don′ dō) Area in New Mexico where the Long Walk by the Navajo ended in 1864. (m. 326, t. 326)

Boston (bȯ′ stən) Capital and largest city in Massachusetts and a center for culture, transportation, and commerce; 42°N, 71°W. (m. 142, t. 143)

Pronunciation Key

a in hat	ō in open	sh in she
ā in age	ȯ in all	th in thin
â in care	ô in order	ᴛʜ in then
ä in far	oi in oil	zh in measure
e in let	ou in out	ə = a in about
ē in equal	u in cup	ə = e in taken
ėr in term	u̇ in put	ə = i in pencil
i in it	ü in rule	ə = o in lemon
ī in ice	ch in child	ə = u in circus
o in hot	ng in long	

Gazetteer

Cahokia (kə hō′ kē ə) French trading post on the eastern side of the Mississippi River near St. Louis; 38°N, 90°W. (m. 276, t. 277)

California (kal′ə fôr′ nyə) One of the states in the West region of the United States. (m. 362)

Capitol (kap′ə təl) Building in Washington, D.C., where Congress meets. (t. 50)

Cascade Range (ka skād′ rānj) Pacific coast mountain range formed by volcanoes, where rainfall is heavy. (m. 372, t. 382)

Catskill Mountains (kats′ kil moun′ tənz) Smaller part of the Appalachian Mountain Range, located in eastern New York State. (m. 98, t. 107)

Central Plains (sen′ trəl plānz) Grassy region in the eastern part of the Midwest, drained by the Great Lakes and the Mississippi River basin. (m. 247, t. 247)

Central Valley (sen′ trəl val′ ē) A major fruit-growing area in California. (m. 384, t. 385)

Charleston (chärlz′ tən) Seaport in South Central South Carolina in whose harbor the Civil War began; 32°N, 80°W. (m. 202, t. 203)

Charlestown (chärlz′ toun) Native American reservation in Rhode Island where the Narragansett live today; 41°N, 71°W. (m. 126, t. 128)

Chesapeake Bay (ches′ə pēk′ bā) Bay in the Atlantic Ocean between the states of Maryland and Virginia. (m. 116, t. 117)

Colorado (kol′ə rad′ ō) One of the states in the West region of the United States. (m. 362)

Connecticut (kə net′ə kət) One of the states in the Northeast region of the United States. (m. 98)

Continental Divide (kon′ tə nen′ tl də vīd′) Ridge in the Rocky Mountains that divides streams flowing toward the Pacific Ocean from those flowing toward the Atlantic Ocean. (t. 369)

Dahlonega (dä′ lon ē′ gə) Town in mountainous area of northern Georgia near where gold was discovered in 1828; 34°N, 84°W. (m. 210, t. 211)

Death Valley (deth val′ ē) Dry valley in southern California that has the lowest elevation in North America. (m. 372, t. 382)

Delaware (del′ə wâr) One of the states in the Northeast region of the United States. (m. 98)

Delaware Bay (del′ə wâr bā) Inlet of the Atlantic Ocean between the states of Delaware and New Jersey. (m. 98, t. 119)

Duluth (də lüth′) City in Minnesota on Lake Superior near where the Ojibwa settled; 46°N, 92°W. (m. 256, t. 257)

Dust Bowl (dust bōl) Area in the Great Plains where a long drought occurred in the 1930s, causing many farmers to suffer. (t. 272)

Ellis Island (el′ is ī′ lənd) Small island in New York City harbor that served as the main point of arrival for many immigrants from 1892–1943; 41°N, 74°W. (m. 130, t. 132)

Everglades National Park (ev′ər glādz′ nash′ə nəl pärk) Large area of wetlands in southern Florida. (m. 178, t. 179)

 F

Florida (flôr′ə də) One of the states in the Southeast region of the United States. (m. 160)

Florida Keys (flôr′ə də kēz) Chain of small islands located off the southern coast of Florida between the Atlantic Ocean and the Gulf of Mexico. (m. 167, t. 173)

Fort Canby (fôrt kan′ bē) Place known today as Fort Defiance in New Mexico, where many Navajo surrendered in 1864; 35°N, 109°W. (m. 326, t. 326)

 G

Georgia (jôr′ jə) One of the states in the Southeast region of the United States. (m. 160)

Grand Canyon National Park (grand kan′ yən nash′ə nəl pärk) Deep gorge in northern Arizona formed by the Colorado River. (m. 300, t. 304)

Great Basin (grāt bā′ sn) Large desert region that covers most of the state of Nevada. (m. 378, t. 380)

Great Lakes (grāt lāks) Largest set of freshwater lakes in the world, located between the United States and Canada. (m. 233, t. 233)

Great Plains (grāt plānz) Grassy area in the western part of the Midwest region, in the rain shadow of the Rocky Mountains. (m. 247, t. 247)

Green Mountains (grēn moun′ tənz) Smaller part of the Appalachian Mountain Range that runs north and south through Vermont into Massachusetts and Connecticut. (m. 98, t. 106)

 I

Idaho (ī′ də hō) One of the states in the West region of the United States. (m. 362)

Illinois (il′ə noi′) One of the states in the Midwest region of the United States. (m. 226)

Illinois Waterway (il′ə noi′ wȯ′tər wā′) Several rivers and canals that connect Lake Michigan with the Mississippi River. (m. 234, t. 234)

Indiana (in′ dē a′nə) One of the states in the Midwest region of the United States. (m. 226)

Inner Coastal Plain (in′ər kō′ stl plān) Land area in the Southeast region lying between the Outer Coastal Plain and the Piedmont area. (m. 167, t. 167)

Iowa (ī′ə wə) One of the states in the Midwest region of the United States. (m. 226)

 J

Jamestown (jāmz′ toun) Village that was the first permanent English settlement in North America, on the James River in Virginia; 37°N, 76°W. (m. 194, t. 196)

Juneau (jü′ nō) Capital of the state of Alaska, where the Tlingit governing council meets; 58°N, 134°W. (m. 394, t. 397)

★ H ★

Hawaii (hə wī′ ē) State in the eastern part of the Pacific Ocean, made up of a group of islands. (m. 362)

Hoopeston (hüp′ stən) Town located in Illinois around which large crops of corn and soybeans are grown; 40°N, 87°W. (m. 246, t. 247)

Houston (hyü′ stən) Major city in southeastern Texas where the Johnson Space Center and the Texas Medical Center are located; 29°N, 95°W. (m. 314, t. 317)

Pronunciation Key		
a in hat	ō in open	sh in she
ā in age	ȯ in all	th in thin
â in care	ô in order	ᴛʜ in then
ä in far	oi in oil	zh in measure
e in let	ou in out	ə = a in about
ē in equal	u in cup	ə = e in taken
ėr in term	u̇ in put	ə = i in pencil
i in it	ü in rule	ə = o in lemon
ī in ice	ch in child	ə = u in circus
o in hot	ng in long	

Gazetteer

K

Kansas (kan′ zəs) One of the states in the Midwest region of the United States. (t. 21, m. 226)

Kentucky (kən tuk′ ē) One of the states in the Southeast region of the United States. (m. 160)

Key West (kē west) Island and seaport in the Florida Keys, which lie off the coast of southern Florida; 24°N, 81°W. (m. 172, t. 173)

King Ranch (king ranch) A large ranch in Texas that is also used for the scientific study of cattle. (m. 338, t. 343)

L

Lake Seneca (lāk sen′ə kə) Largest of the Finger Lakes in upstate New York, noted for its large vineyards. (t. 113)

Lexington (lek′ sing tən) Town in Massachusetts near Boston where the first shots of the American Revolution were fired; 42°N, 71°W. (m. 130, t. 131)

Los Alamos (lȯs al′ ə mōs) Town in northern New Mexico where nuclear energy is studied; 36°N, 106°W. (m. 314, t. 316)

Los Angeles (lȯs an′ jə ləs) City in southern California that is the second largest city in the United States; 34°N, 118°W. (m. 410, t. 411)

Louisiana (lü ē′ zē an′ə) One of the states in the Southeast region of the United States. (m. 160)

Louisiana Territory (lü ē′ zē an′ə ter′ə tôr′ ē) Area purchased by the United States in 1803 that included much of the land west of the Mississippi River to the Rocky Mountains. (m. 41, t. 41)

M

Mackinaw (mak′ə nȯ) City in the far northern part of the Lower Peninsula of the state of Michigan where the French colonial fort of Michilimackinac was located; 45°N, 84°W. (m. 264, t. 265)

Maine (mān) One of the states in the Northeast region of the United States. (m. 98)

Maryland (mer′ə lənd) One of the states in the Northeast region of the United States. (m. 98)

Massachusetts (mas′ə chü′ sits) One of the states in the Northeast region of the United States. (m. 98)

Massachusetts Bay (mas′ə chü′ sits bā) Bay near the city of Boston; a center for fishing and boating. (m. 98, t. 119)

Michigan (mish′ə gən) One of the states in the Midwest region of the United States. (m. 226)

Midwest Region (mid′ west′ rē′ jən) Region of the United States that has flat grassy plains and large areas of forests. (m. 4, 10; t. 12)

Milwaukee (mil wȯ′ kē) City in Wisconsin near where the Ojibwa settled; 43°N, 88°W. (m. 256, t. 257)

Minnesota (min′ə sō′ tə) One of the states in the Midwest region of the United States. (m. 226)

Mississippi (mis′ə sip′ ē) One of the states in the Southeast region of the United States. (m. 160)

Mississippi River (mis′ə sip′ ē riv′ ər) Major river in the United States that flows through the Midwest south from Minnesota to the Gulf of Mexico. (m. 38, 234; t. 41, 234)

Missouri (mə zùr′ ē) One of the states in the Midwest region of the United States. (m. 226)

Mitchell (mich′ əl) Town in South Dakota where the Corn Palace is located; 43°N, 98°W. (m. 246, t. 247)

Montana (mon tan′ ə) One of the states in the West region of the United States. (m. 362)

Monticello (mon′ tə chel′ ō) Home of Thomas Jefferson, located near Charlottesville, Virginia. (t. 197)

Mount McKinley (mount mə kin′ lē) Highest peak in North America, located in Alaska. (m. 372, t. 379)

Mount Pleasant (mount plez′ nt) Town in Michigan where some members of the Saginaw Nation of Native Americans live; 43°N, 84°W. (m. 256, t. 257)

Mount Waialeale (mount wī ə lā ä′ lē) Mountain in Hawaii that receives the heaviest annual rainfall in the United States. (t. 382)

Myrtle Beach (mèr′ tl bēch) Atlantic coast resort city in South Carolina; 33°N, 79°W. (m. 166, t. 167)

★ N ★

Nebraska (nə bras′ kə) One of the states in the Midwest region of the United States. (m. 226)

Nevada (nə vad′ ə) One of the states in the West region of the United States. (m. 362)

New Hampshire (nü hamp′ shər) One of the states in the Northeast region of the United States. (m. 98)

New Jersey (nü jėr′ zē) One of the states in the Northeast region of the United States. (m. 98)

New Mexico (nü mek′ sə ko) One of the states in the Southwest region of the United States. (m. 294)

New York (nü yôrk) One of the states in the Northeast region of the United States. (m. 98)

New York City (nü yôrk sit′ ē) Largest city in the United States, located in southeast New York; served as the first capital of the United States; 41°N, 74°W. (t. 131, 143; m. 142)

Niagara Falls (nī ag′ rə fòlz) Great waterfall on the Niagara River on the boundary between the United States and Canada; a city in the western part of New York State; 43°N, 79° W. (m. 104, 105; t. 105)

North Carolina (nôrth kar′ə li′ nə) One of the states in the Southeast region of the United States. (m. 160)

North Dakota (nôrth də kō′ tə) One of the states in the Midwest region of the United States. (m. 226)

Northeast Region (nôrth′ est′ rē′ jən) Region in the United States that contains the country's oldest mountains, the Appalachian Mountain Range. (m. 4, t. 12)

★ O ★

Ohio (ō hi′ ō) One of the states in the Midwest region of the United States. (m. 226)

Oklahoma (ō′ klə hō′ mə) One of the states in the Southwest region of the United States. (m. 294)

Oregon (ôr′ə gən) One of the states in the West region of the United States. (m. 362)

Outer Coastal Plain (ou′ tər kō′ stl plān) Land area of low elevation along the Atlantic and Gulf coasts in the Southeast region. (m. 167, t. 167)

★ P ★

Pennsylvania (pen′ səl vā′ nyə) One of the states in the Northeast region of the United States. (m. 98)

Philadelphia (fil′ə del′ fē ə) City in southeastern Pennsylvania where the Declaration of Independence was signed and which served as the second capital of the United States from 1790 to 1800; 40°N, 75°W. (m. 130; t. 131, 137, 143)

Phoenix (fē′ niks) Capital of the state of Arizona, irrigated from the California State Water Project; 33°N, 112°W. (m. 346, t. 347)

Piedmont (pēd′ mont) Upland area in the Southeast region, located between the coastal plains and the Appalachian Mountains. (m. 167, t. 168)

Pittsburgh (pits′ bėrg′) City in southwestern Pennsylvania where three major rivers meet and which became a leading iron- and steel-making center; 40°N, 80°W. (m. 142, t. 143)

Plymouth (plim′ əth) Town located in eastern Massachusetts that was one of the first English settlements in North America; 42°N, 70°W. (m. 130, t. 131)

Pronunciation Key

a in hat	ō in open	sh in she
ā in age	ò in all	th in thin
â in care	ô in order	ᴛʜ in then
ä in far	oi in oil	zh in measure
e in let	ou in out	ə = a in about
ē in equal	u in cup	ə = e in taken
ėr in term	ù in put	ə = i in pencil
i in it	ü in rule	ə = o in lemon
ī in ice	ch in child	ə = u in circus
o in hot	ng in long	

Gazetteer

Qualla Boundary (kwä′ la boun′ dər ē) An Eastern Cherokee reservation in western North Carolina. (m. 188, t. 191)

Rhode Island (rōd ī′ lənd) One of the states in the Northeast region of the United States. (m. 98)

Roanoke Island (rō′ə nōk ī′ lənd) Island in present-day North Carolina along the Outer Banks where the English tried but failed to establish a colony in 1587, which was called the "Lost Colony." (t. 196)

Rocky Mountains (rok′ ē moun′ tənz) Chief group of mountain ranges in the western part of the United States, extending from Alaska to New Mexico. (m. 368, t. 369)

Saguaro National Park (sə gwär′ ō nash′ə nəl pärk) Park outside Tucson, Arizona, where the saguaro cactus grows. (m. 308, t. 310)

Salt Lake City (sȯlt lāk sit′ ē) Capital and largest urban center in the state of Utah; 40°N, 112°W. (m. 410, t. 412)

San Antonio (san an tō′ nē ō) City in southern Texas where the San Jose Mission was built and where the first air-conditioned office building was located; 28°N, 97°W. (m. 332; t. 334, 341)

San Francisco (san frən sis′ kō) Major port city in California whose bay connects with the Pacific Ocean; 37°N, 122°W. (m. 400, t. 402)

Santa Fe (san′ tə fā) Capital of the state of New Mexico, founded by the Spanish in about 1609; 35°N, 106°W. (m. 332, t. 336)

Sault Sainte Marie (sü′ sānt mə rē′) City in Michigan that began as a French fort and later became a trading post; 46°N, 84°W. (m. 264, t. 265)

Seattle (sē at′ l) Largest city and major Pacific Ocean port in the state of Washington; 47°N, 122°W. (m. 410, t. 412)

Seneca Falls (sen′ə kə fȯlz) Village in west-central New York State where the National Women's Hall of Fame is located; 43°N, 76°W. (m. 136, t. 138)

Sonoran Desert (sə nôr′ ən dez′ərt) Dry area in Arizona where saguaro cactuses grow. (m. 309, t. 310)

South Carolina (south kar′ə li′ nə) One of the states in the Southeast region of the United States. (m. 160)

South Carver (south kär′ vər) Town in Massachusetts that is home to the annual Massachusetts Cranberry Harvest Festival; 41°N, 70°W. (m. 112, t. 113)

South Dakota (south də kō′ tə) One of the states in the Midwest region of the United States. (m. 226)

Southeast Region (south′ ēst′ rē′ jən) Region in the United States where the Appalachian Mountains gradually flatten into the Atlantic Coastal Plain. (m. 4, t. 12)

Southwest Region (south′ west′ rē′ jən) Region in the United States that is very dry, with many deserts, canyons, and plateaus. (m. 4, t. 13)

St. Albans (sānt ȯl′ bənz) Town in Vermont that hosts the Vermont Maple Festival each year; 44°N, 73°W. (m. 112, t. 114)

St. Augustine (sānt ȯ′ gə stēn′) City on the coast of eastern Florida, founded by the Spanish in 1565; 30°N, 81°W. (m. 195, t. 196)

St. Lawrence Seaway (sānt lôr′ əns sē′ wā′) Waterway that links the Great Lakes with the Atlantic Ocean. (m. 234, t. 234)

St. Louis (sānt lü′ is) City in Missouri on the Mississippi River where a French trading center was located in the 1600s and 1700s and which became the Midwest transportation hub in the early 1800s; 38°N, 90°W. (m. 72, 276; t. 73, 277)

Sutter's Mill (sut′ tərz mil) Location in California where gold was discovered in 1848. (t. 400, 402, m. 403)

Tennessee (ten′ ə sē′) One of the states in the Southeast region of the United States. (m. 160)

Texas (tek′ səs) One of the states in the Southwest region of the United States. (m. 294)

Tlingit Cultural Region (klin′ git kul′ chər əl rē′ jən) Area along the southeastern coast of Alaska and the northern part of British Columbia in Canada where the Tlingit people live. (m. 394, t. 395)

Tucson (tü′ son) City in the state of Arizona where new technological products are developed and which is watered by irrigation from the California State Water Project; 32°N, 111°W. (m. 346, t. 347)

Utah (yü′ tȯ) One of the states in the West region of the United States. (m. 362)

Vermont (vər mont′) One of the states in the Northeast region of the United States. (m. 98)

Virginia (vər jin′ yə) One of the states in the Southeast region of the United States. (m. 160)

Wapello County (wə pel′ ō koun′ tē) A part of Iowa where the first Midwest land rush took place in 1843. (m. 268, t. 269)

Washington (wäsh′ ing tən) One of the states in the West region of the United States. (m. 362)

Washington, D.C. (wäsh′ ing tən) The capital city of the United States, located in the District of Columbia; 39°N, 77°W. (t. 14, 48; m. 46)

West Region (west rē′ jən) Region in the United States that has extremes both in temperatures and landforms. (m. 4, t. 13)

West Virginia (west vər jin′ yə) One of the states in the Southeast region of the United States. (m. 160)

White Mountains (wīt moun′ tənz) Small part of the Appalachian Mountain Range that extends from the western part of Maine through New Hampshire. (m. 98, t. 106)

Willamette Valley (wil a′ met val′ ē) Area in Oregon where a variety of fruits and vegetables are grown. (m. 384, t. 385)

Window Rock (win′ dō rok) Capital of the Navajo Nation in Arizona; 35°N, 109°W. (m. 324, t. 327)

Wisconsin (wi skon′ sən) One of the states in the Midwest region of the United States. (m. 226)

Wyoming (wī ō′ ming) One of the states in the West region of the United States. (m. 362)

Yellowstone National Park (yel′ o ston′ nash′ə nəl pärk) Oldest national park in the world, located mostly in northwestern Wyoming, famous for its scenery, hot springs, and geysers. (m. 368, t. 370)

Pronunciation Key

a in hat	ō in open	sh in she
ā in age	ȯ in all	th in thin
â in care	ô in order	ŦH in then
ä in far	oi in oil	zh in measure
e in let	ou in out	ə = a in about
ē in equal	u in cup	ə = e in taken
ėr in term	u̇ in put	ə = i in pencil
i in it	ü in rule	ə = o in lemon
ī in ice	ch in child	ə = u in circus
o in hot	ng in long	

Biographical Dictionary

This Biographical Dictionary tells you about the people in this book and how to pronounce their names. The page numbers tell you where the person first appears in the text.

A

Adams, John (ad′ əmz) 1735–1826 Signer from Massachusetts of the Declaration of Independence and second President of the United States. (p. 131)

Albright, Madeleine (ȯl′ brīt) 1937– Immigrant from eastern Europe who became the first female United States Secretary of State. (p. 132)

Anthony, Susan B. (an′ thə nē) 1820–1906 Leader in the women's rights movement who helped to organize the Seneca Falls Convention. (p. 138)

Armour, Philip (är′ mər) 1832–1901 Businessman who started a meat-packing industry in Chicago. (p. 339)

B

Bell, Alexander Graham (bel) 1847–1922 Scottish immigrant who invented the telephone. (p. 132)

Bradley, Thomas (brad′ lē) 1917–1998 First African American mayor of Los Angeles. (pp. 416–417)

C

Cabrillo, Juan Rodríguez (kä brē′ yō) died in 1543 Spanish explorer who first saw the coast of present-day California. (pp. 400–401)

Calamity Jane (kə lam′ ə tē jān) 1852–1903 Nickname for Martha Canary, a famous cowgirl, who also performed shooting displays. (p. 340)

Canonicus (ka non′ ə kəs) c. 1565–1647 Native American ruler of the Narragansett who sold land to Roger Williams for the colony of Rhode Island. (p. 128)

Cárdenas, García López de (kär dä′ näs) (dates unknown) Spanish explorer who traveled near the Grand Canyon and the Colorado River in 1540. (p. 302)

Carnegie, Andrew (kär nā′ gē) 1835–1919 Business leader who developed the steel industry in Pennsylvania. (pp. 132, 147)

Carrier, Willis (kar′ ē ər) 1876–1950 Engineer responsible for reducing air moisture at his printing plant in Brooklyn, New York, in 1902, which led the way for the development of modern air conditioning. (pp. 348, 349)

Carson, Kit (kär′ sən) 1809–1868 Soldier who helped stop conflicts in 1863 between the Navajos and white settlers in New Mexico. (p. 326)

Chisholm, Jesse (chiz′ əm) c. 1806–1868 American trader who marked a trail from San Antonio, Texas, to Abilene, Kansas. (p. 341)

Clark, William (klärk) 1770–1838 Explorer who helped lead an expedition to find a water route to the Pacific Ocean through the Louisiana Territory in 1804–1805. (pp. 42, 278)

Cobb, Geraldyn (Jerri) (kob) 1931– First woman who trained as an astronaut, but who received the Nobel Peace Prize for piloting airplanes to take medicines, clothing, food, and doctors to people in the Amazon rain forest. (pp. 318–319)

Columbus, Christopher (kə lum′ bəs) c. 1451–1506 Spanish explorer who landed on North America in 1492. (pp. 38–39)

Coronado, Francisco Vásquez de (kôr′ə nä′ dō) 1510–1554 Spaniard who led an expedition through parts of the Southwest looking for the Seven Cities of Gold in the early 1540s. (p. 302)

Deere, John (dir) 1804–1886 Inventor of the steel plow in 1838, which made farming grasslands much easier in the Midwest. (pp. 273, 275)

De Soto, Hernando (di sō′ tō) c. 1500–1542 Spanish explorer who sailed around Florida in 1539 and then traveled along the southeast coast as far as the Mississippi River. (p. 195)

Dodge, Henry Chee (doj) 1857–1947 First chairman of the Navajo Tribal Council. (pp. 327, 329)

Douglass, Frederick (dug′ ləs) c. 1817–1895 Former slave who became an Abolitionist newspaper editor and who spoke in favor of women's right to vote. (p. 137)

Du Sable, Jean Baptiste Pointe (dü sa′ bəl) c. 1745–1818 Free man of African ancestry, born in Haiti, who became known as the "Father of Chicago" when he set up a successful trading post in the area in 1784. (pp. 266, 267)

Einstein, Albert (in′ stīn) 1879–1955 German immigrant who became one of the world's most important scientists. (p. 132)

Franklin, Benjamin (frang′ klən) 1706–1790 Signer of the Declaration of Independence who was from Pennsylvania; later was a member of the Constitutional Convention. (p. 131)

Garrison, William Lloyd (gar′ə sən) 1805–1879 Abolitionist who began publishing a newspaper called *The Liberator* in 1833. (p. 137)

Grimké, Angelina (grim′ kē) 1805–1879 Southern-born woman who wanted to end slavery and who wrote letters and pamphlets attacking its evils. (pp. 200–201)

Grimké, Sarah (grim′ kē) 1792–1873 Abolitionist sister of Angelina who also wrote about the evils of slavery. (pp. 200–201)

Hendrickson, Sue (hen′ drik sən) 1949– Archaeologist who discovered dinosaur bone fossils in South Dakota. (pp. 242, 243)

Higgins, Pattillo (hig′ ənz) 1863–1955 Scientist who discovered natural gas escaping from a stream near Spindletop Hill in Beaumont, Texas, in 1901, which soon led to the discovery of oil. (p. 315)

Inouye, Daniel (en′ ō wā) 1924– U.S. representative from Hawaii who was the first Japanese American to be elected to Congress. (p. 53)

Pronunciation Key

a in hat	ō in open	sh in she
ā in age	ȯ in all	th in thin
â in care	ô in order	⊬H in then
ä in far	oi in oil	zh in measure
e in let	ou in out	ə = a in about
ē in equal	u in cup	ə = e in taken
ėr in term	u̇ in put	ə = i in pencil
i in it	ü in rule	ə = o in lemon
ī in ice	ch in child	ə = u in circus
o in hot	ng in long	

Biographical Dictionary

J

Jackson, Andrew (jak′ sən) 1767–1845 Seventh President of the United States, who was born in present-day South Carolina and was very popular with the common people. (p. 197)

Jefferson, Thomas (jef′ər sən) 1743–1826 Virginian who wrote the Declaration of Independence, served as the third President of the United States, and purchased the Louisiana Territory from France in 1803. (pp. 42, 197)

Jolliet, Louis (jō′ lē et) 1645–1700 French explorer who traveled down Lake Michigan and the Illinois and Mississippi Rivers in 1673. (p. 265)

K

King, Martin Luther, Jr. (king) 1929–1968 African American leader who believed in the use of non-violent civil disobedience to gain civil rights in the 1950s and 1960s. (p. 206)

Kino, Eusebio (kē′ nō) 1645–1711 Spanish priest who founded three missions in present-day Arizona in 1687 where he taught Native Americans. (p. 334)

L

La Guardia, Fiorello (lə gwär′ dē ə) 1882–1947 United States congressman and later mayor of New York City. (p. 45)

La Salle, Robert (le sal) 1643–1687 French explorer who sailed down the Ohio and Mississippi Rivers in 1682, reaching the Gulf of Mexico. (p. 195)

Lewelling, Seth (lü wel′ ling) 1820–1896 Fruit grower from Oregon who helped to develop the Bing cherry. (p. 389)

Lewis, Meriwether (lü′ is) 1774–1809 Explorer who helped lead an expedition to find a water route to the Pacific Ocean through the Louisiana Territory in 1804–1805. (pp. 42, 278)

Lincoln, Abraham (ling′ kən) 1809–1865 Sixteenth President of the United States, from 1861 to 1865, during the Civil War. (p. 203)

Lucas, Anthony (lü′ kəs) 1855–1921 A mining engineer hired to drill for oil at Spindletop Hill in Texas in 1901. (p. 315)

M

Madison, James (mad′ə sən) 1751–1836 Important delegate at the Constitutional Convention who later served as the fourth President of the United States. (p. 197)

Marquette, Jacques (mär ket′) 1637–1675 French explorer who traveled down Lake Michigan and the Illinois and Mississippi Rivers in 1673. (p. 265)

Marshall, James (mär′ shəl) 1810–1885 Worker who discovered gold in California in 1848 while building a sawmill for John Sutter. (p. 402)

Mott, Lucretia (mot) 1793–1880 Women's rights leader who worked with Elizabeth Cady Stanton and Susan B. Anthony. (p. 138)

O

Oakley, Annie (ō′klē) 1860–1926 Famous cowgirl who took part in rodeos and Wild West shows. (p. 340)

P

Parks, Rosa (pärks) 1913– African American woman who protested bus segregation in Montgomery, Alabama, in 1955, leading to a bus boycott. (p. 207)

Podlasek, Joseph (pō la′ sek) Native American who is the executive director of the American Indian Center in Chicago. (pp. 260–261)

Ponce de León, Juan (pons də lē′ ən) c. 1460–1521 Spanish explorer who traveled through Florida in 1513 looking for the "fountain of youth." (p. 195)

Powell, John Wesley (pou′əl) 1834–1902 Explorer of the Grand Canyon and the Colorado Plateau in 1869 who wrote reports about his findings. (pp. 302, 305)

Roosevelt, Theodore (rō′ zə velt) 1858–1919 United States President who signed a law making the Grand Canyon a national monument. (p. 303)

Sequoyah (si kwoi′ə) c. 1763–1843 Cherokee who developed a written alphabet for his people in 1821. (pp. 190, 193)

Serra, Junípero (scr′ rä) 1713–1784 Spanish priest who set up missions in California beginning in 1769. (p. 401)

Stanton, Elizabeth Cady (stan′ tən) 1815–1902 Women's rights leader who helped write the "Declaration of Sentiments" at the Seneca Falls Convention. (pp. 138, 139)

Strauss, Levi (strous) 1829–1902 Inventor of sturdy blue jeans in the 1850s for miners in California. (pp. 403, 407)

Sutter, John (sut′ tər) 1803–1880 Owner of sawmill in California where gold was discovered in 1848. (p. 402)

Truth, Sojourner (trüth) 1797–1883 African American woman who addressed Abolitionist meetings and told about her early life as a slave. (p. 137)

Twain, Mark (twān) 1835–1910 Literary name of Samuel Clemens, who wrote books about life along the Mississippi River. (p. 283)

Washington, George (wäsh′ ing tən) 1732–1799 Virginian who led American troops in the Revolutionary War and who served as the first President of the United States, making him the "Father of the Country." (p. 190)

Williams, Roger (wil′ yəmz) c. 1603–1683 English colonist who bought land from the Narragansetts in 1636 for a colony which became Rhode Island. (p. 128)

Pronunciation Key

a in hat	ō in open	sh in she
ā in age	ȯ in all	th in thin
â in care	ô in order	ᴛʜ in then
ä in far	oi in oil	zh in measure
e in let	ou in out	ə = a in about
ē in equal	u in cup	ə = e in taken
ėr in term	ů in put	ə = i in pencil
i in it	ü in rule	ə = o in lemon
ī in ice	ch in child	ə = u in circus
o in hot	ng in long	

Glossary

This Glossary will help you understand the meanings and pronounce the vocabulary words in this book. The page numbers tell you where the word first appears.

abolitionist (ab′ ə lish′ ə nist) a reformer who believed that slavery should be erased from the law (p. 137)

adobe (ə dō′ bē) a kind of mud brick (p. 302)

agriculture (ag′ rə kul′ chər) the raising of crops or animals (pp. 28, 180)

amendment (ə mend′ mənt) a change to the Constitution of the United States (p. 52)

aqueduct (ak wə dukt) a pipe used to bring water from a distance (p. 347)

arid (ar′ id) dry, but not desert-like (p. 309)

backwoodsman (bak′ wùdz′ mən) a person who lives in forests or wild areas far away from towns (p. 198)

badlands (bad′ landz′) a region of dry hills and sharp cliffs (p. 243)

barge (bärj) a flat-bottomed boat that carries goods through lakes and rivers (p. 236)

barrier island (bar′ ē ər i′ lənd) a narrow island between the ocean and the mainland (p. 167)

barter (bär′ tər) trading one kind of good or service for another (p. 73)

bay (bā) part of a sea or lake that cuts into a coastline (p. 117)

bayou (bī′ ü) marshy river (p. 163)

Bill of Rights (bil əv rīts) the first ten amendments to the United States Constitution; they state the basic rights of United States citizens (p. 52)

bog (bog) an area of soft, wet, spongy ground (p. 113)

boom town (büm′ toun′) fast-growing town, usually located near where gold or silver have recently been discovered (p. 403)

boundary (boun′ dər ē) a line or natural feature that separates one area or state from another (p. 14)

boycott (boi′ kot) refusing to buy something as a form of protest (p. 207)

canal (kə nal′) a waterway that has been dug across land for ships to travel through (p. 234)

canyon (kan′ yən) a deep valley with steep rocky walls (p. 13)

capital resource (kap′ ə təl rē′ sôrs) something people make in order to produce other products (p. 28)

Capitol (kap′ ə təl) the building where the Congress of the United States meets (p. 50)

citizen (sit′ ə zən) an official member of a country (p. 47)

civil rights (siv′ əl rīts) the rights of a citizen, including the right to vote and protection under the law (p. 205)

Civil War (siv′ əl wôr) the United States Civil War, fought between Northern and Southern states from 1861 to 1865 (p. 203)

climate (klī′ mit) the weather patterns in one place over a long period of time (p. 19)

colony (kol′ ə nē) a settlement of people who come from one country to live in another land (p. 131)

commerce (kom′ ərs) the buying and selling of goods, especially in large amounts between different places (p. 141)

communication (kə myü′ nə kā′ shən) the way that people send and receive information (p. 84)

computer software (kəm pyü′ tər sôft′ wâr′) programs that help computers perform certain functions (p. 412)

confederacy (kən fed′ ər ə sē) a union of groups, countries, or states that agree to work together for a common goal (p. 129)

Confederacy (kən fed′ ər ə sē) the name of the Southern states in the United States Civil War (p. 203)

consensus (kən sen′ səs) a method of decision-making in which all come to agreement (p. 189)

conserve (kən sərv′) to use resources carefully (p. 29)

Constitution (kon stə tü′ shən) the written plan for governing the United States of America (p. 48)

consumer (kən sü′ mər) a person who buys goods and services (p. 74)

convention (kən ven′ shən) a meeting held for a certain purpose (p. 138)

cooperation (kō op′ ə rā′ shən) to work together to get things done (p. 127)

crab pot (krab pot) a large wire cage with several sections that crabs swim into but from which they cannot escape (p. 117)

crop rotation (krop rō tā′ shən) the planting of different crops in different years (p. 248)

culture (kul′ chər) a way of life followed by a group of people (p. 43)

demand (di mand′) the amount of an item that consumers are willing to buy at different prices (p. 77)

democracy (di mok′ rə sē) a system of government in which every citizen has a right to take part (p. 47)

desert (dez′ ərt) an area that receives less than ten inches of rain in one year (pp. 13, 309)

diverse (də vėrs′) varied (p. 145)

drought (drout) a long period with little or no rain (p. 274)

Dust Bowl (dust bōl) an area of the Midwest and Southwest that was struck by years of drought in the 1930s (p. 274)

economy (i kon′ ə mē) the way in which the resources of a country, state, region, or community are managed (p. 76)

elevation (el′ ə vā′ shən) how high a place is above sea level (pp. 21, 167)

endangered species (en dān′ jərd spē′ shēz) a kind of animal or plant that is in danger of becoming extinct (p. 179)

equator (i kwā′ tər) the imaginary line that circles the center of Earth from east to west (p. 21)

erosion (i rō′ zhən) the process by which wind and water wear away rock (p. 244)

executive branch (eg zek′ yə tiv branch) the part of government that enforces the laws (p. 51)

export (ek′ spôrt) an item sent from one country to be sold in another (p. 143)

extinct (ek stingkt′) no longer existing (p. 179)

Pronunciation Key

a in hat	ō in open	sh in she
ā in age	ȯ in all	th in thin
â in care	ô in order	ŦH in then
ä in far	oi in oil	zh in measure
e in let	ou in out	ə = a in about
ē in equal	u in cup	ə = e in taken
ėr in term	ù in put	ə = i in pencil
i in it	ü in rule	ə = o in lemon
ī in ice	ch in child	ə = u in circus
o in hot	ng in long	

Glossary

F

fall line (fȯl līn) a line of waterfalls that marks the boundary between the Piedmont and the coastal plains (p. 168)

federal (fed′ ər əl) a system of government in which the national and state governments share power (p. 48)

fossil fuel (fos′ əl fyü′ əl) a fuel formed in the earth from the remains of plants and animals (p. 183)

free enterprise system (frē en′ tər prīz sis′ təm) a system in which businesses have the right to produce any good or provide any service that they want (p. 76)

frigid (frij′ id) very cold (p. 379)

fur trade (fėr trād) the trading of goods for animal skins (p. 258)

G

geyser (gī′ zər) a hot spring that erupts and sends hot water from the earth into the air (p. 370)

ghost town (gōst toun) a town where all of the people have moved away (p. 403)

glacier (glā′ shər) huge sheets of ice that cover land (p. 105)

globalization (glō′ bə liz ā′ shən) the process by which a business makes something or provides a service in different places around the world (p. 82)

gold rush (gōld rush) a sudden movement of people to an area where gold has been found (p. 211)

gorge (gôrj) a deep, narrow valley (p. 105)

government (guv′ ərn mənt) the laws that are followed and the people that run a country (p. 47)

greenhouse (grēn′ hous′) an enclosed structure that allows light to enter and keeps in heat and moisture (p. 385)

gusher (gush′ ər) an oil well that produces a large amount of oil (p. 315)

H

harvest (här′vist) cut for use, as a crop (p. 27)

hogan (hō′ gän′) a one-room Navajo home with a door facing east (p. 325)

homestead (hōm′ sted′) land given to settlers by the United States government if they lived and raised crops on it (p. 342)

hub (hub) a center of activity (p. 280)

human resource (hyü′ mən rē′ sôrs) a person that makes products or provides services (p. 31)

humidity (hyü mid′ ə tē) the amount of moisture in the air (pp. 20, 348)

hurricane (hėr′ ə kān) a violent storm with high winds and heavy rain that forms over an ocean (p. 174)

hurricane season (hėr′ ə kān sē′ zn) the time of the year when hurricanes mainly occur (p. 174)

hydroelectricity (hī′ drō i lek′ tris′ ə tē) electricity produced by flowing water (p. 105)

hydropower (hī′ drō pou′ ər) power produced by capturing the energy of flowing water (p. 105)

I

immigrant (im′ ə grənt) a person who comes to live in a new land (p. 43)

import (im′ pôrt) an item brought from abroad to be offered for sale (p. 143)

industry (in′ də strē) a business that makes a product or provides a service (p. 28)

inlet (in′ let) a narrow opening in a coastline (p. 117)

interdependent (in′ tər di pen′ dənt) when regions rely on one another for goods, services, or resources (p. 81)

international trade (in′ tər nash′ ə nəl trād) trade between different countries (p. 414)

Interstate highway system (in′ tər stāt′ hī′ wā′ sis′ təm) a system of interconnected highways in the United States (p. 282)

irrigation (ir′ ə gā′ shən) the process of bringing water to crops (p. 248)

 **J**

judicial branch (jü dish⁄ əl branch) the part of government, made up of courts and judges, that interprets laws (p. 51)

jury (jùr⁄ ē) a panel of ordinary citizens who make decisions in a court of law (p. 58)

 **K**

key (kē) a low island (p. 173)

 **L**

landform (land⁄ fôrm⁄) a natural feature of the earth's surface (p. 11)

latitude (lat⁄ ə tüd) measurement of how far north or south of the equator a place is located (p. 408)

lava (lä⁄ və) molten rock (magma) that rises and flows on the surface of the earth (p. 372)

legislative branch (lej⁄ ə sla⁄ tiv branch) the part of government that makes laws (p. 50)

lighthouse (līt⁄ hous⁄) a tall tower with a very strong light used to guide ships (p. 108)

livestock (līv⁄ stok⁄) animals raised on farms and ranches for human use (p. 386)

lock (lok) a gated part of a canal or river used to raise and lower water levels (p. 234)

longitude (lon⁄ jə tüd) measurement of how far east or west of the prime meridian a place is located (p. 409)

The Long Walk (ᴛʜə lóng wok) a forced journey of hundreds of miles by the Navajo in the 1800s (pp. 326–327)

 **M**

magma (mag⁄ mə) molten rock beneath the surface of the earth (p. 370)

manufacturing (man⁄ yə fak⁄ chər ing) making things to use or sell (p. 28)

meridian (mə rid⁄ ē ən) line of longitude (p. 409)

mineral (min⁄ ər əl) metals and other resources dug from the ground (p. 115)

mission (mish⁄ ən) a settlement set up by a religious group to teach religion and help area people (p. 265)

missionary (mish⁄ ə ner⁄ ē) a person sent by a religious organization to spread its beliefs (p. 334)

mound (mound) a pile of earth or stone constructed by early Native Americans for a variety of purposes (p. 277)

mountain (moun⁄ tən) a very high landform, often with steep sides (p. 12)

Pronunciation Key

a in hat	ō in open	sh in she
ā in age	ȯ in all	th in thin
â in care	ô in order	ᴛʜ in then
ä in far	oi in oil	zh in measure
e in let	ou in out	ə = a in about
ē in equal	u in cup	ə = e in taken
ėr in term	u̇ in put	ə = i in pencil
i in it	ü in rule	ə = o in lemon
ī in ice	ch in child	ə = u in circus
o in hot	ng in long	

Glossary

natural resource (nach′ ər əl rē′ sôrs) something in the environment that can be used (p. 27)

need (nēd) something that a person must have in order to live (p. 73)

nonrenewable resource (non′ ri nü′ ə bəl rē′ sôrs) a resource that cannot be replaced (p. 29)

Northern Hemisphere (nôr′ ᴛʜərn hem′ ə sfir) the half of Earth north of the equator (p. 408)

opportunity cost (op′ ər tü′ nə tē kost) what is given up when one thing is chosen over another (p. 78)

passport (pas′ pôrt) a paper or booklet that gives a person permission to travel to other countries (p. 57)

peninsula (pə nin′ sə lə) a piece of land almost surrounded by water (p. 108)

pioneer (pī′ ə nēr′) a person who settles in a part of a country and prepares it for others (p. 198)

plain (plān) an area of flat land that often is covered with grass or trees (p. 12)

plantation (plan tā′ shən) a large farm that produces crops to sell (p. 198)

plateau (pla tō′) a large, flat, raised area of land (p. 13)

polar climate (pō′ lər klī′ mit) areas around the North and South Poles with the coldest temperatures (p. 22)

potlatch (pot′ lach′) a feast held by Native Americans of the Northwest to celebrate important events (p. 396)

powwow (pou′ wou′) a Native American festival (p. 128)

prairie (prâr′ ē) an area where grass grows well, but trees are rare (p. 245)

precipitation (pri sip′ ə tā′ shən) the amount of moisture that falls as rain or snow (p. 19)

primary source (prī′ mer′ ē sôrs) an eyewitness account or observation of an event (p. 330)

prime meridian (prīm mə rid′ ē ən) the starting point for measuring longitude (p. 409)

process (pros′ es) to change something so that people can use it (p. 27)

producer (prə dü′ sər) a person who makes goods or products to sell (p. 74)

product (prod′ əkt) something that people make or grow (p. 28)

profit (prof′ it) the money left over after costs are paid (p. 76)

prospector (pros′ pek tər) someone who searches for valuable minerals (p. 402)

public transportation system (pub′ lik tran′ spər tā′ shən sis′ təm) the trains and buses that carry people through a city (p. 212)

pueblo (pweb′ lō) a Spanish word that means "village," and which refers to some Native American groups in the Southwest (p. 302)

pulp (pulp) a combination of wood chips, water, and chemicals used to make paper (p. 182)

quarry (kwôr′ ē) a place where stone is dug, cut, or blasted out of the ground (p. 115)

★ R ★

rain shadow (rān shad′ ō) the side of a mountain chain that receives less precipitation than the other side (p. 382)

raw material (rȯ mə tir′ ē əl) something that is changed so that people can use it (p. 27)

Reconstruction (rē′ kən struk′ shən) the period of time after the United States Civil War when the South was rebuilt (p. 205)

recycle (rē sī′ kəl) to use something more than once (p. 29)

refinery (ri fī′ nər ē) a factory that separates crude oil into different groups of chemicals (p. 315)

reforest (rē fôr′ ist) to plant new trees to replace ones that have been cut down (p. 388)

region (rē′ jən) a large area in which places share similar characteristics (p. 11)

renewable resource (ri nü′ ə bəl rē′ sôrs) a natural resource that can be replaced (p. 29)

represent (rep′ ri zent′) the act of leaders making decisions for those who elected them (p. 47)

republic (ri pub′ lik) a type of government in which people elect leaders to represent them (p. 47)

reservation (rez′ ər vā′ shən) an area of land set aside by the United States for Native Americans (p. 128)

revolution (rev′ ə lü′ shən) a fight to overthrow a government (p. 131)

rural (ru̇r′ əl) in small towns or farms (p. 71)

★ S ★

sachem (sā′ chəm) a ruler over a portion of Narragansett territory (p. 127)

sap (sap) a liquid carrying water and food that circulates through a plant (p. 114)

savanna (sə van′ ə) a grassy plain with few trees (p. 310)

sea level (sē lev′ əl) the same height as the surface of the ocean (p. 170)

search engine (sėrch en′ jən) a special Web site that locates other Web sites (p. 262)

secede (si sēd′) to pull out of or separate from (p. 203)

secondary source (sek′ ən der′ ē sôrs) secondhand account of history (p. 330)

segregate (seg′ rə gāt′) to separate people according to their race (p. 205)

service (sėr′ vis) job that someone does for others (p. 31)

slave (slāv) a person who is owned as property by another person and is forced to work (pp. 137, 198)

sod (sod) the grass, roots, and dirt that form the ground's top layer (p. 272)

Southern Hemisphere (suᴛн′ ərn hem′ ə sfir) the half of Earth south of the equator (p. 408)

steamboat (stēm′ bōt′) a boat powered by a steam engine (p. 280)

subarctic climate (sub ärk′ tik klī′ mit) an area with short, warm summers and ground covered in snow for most of the rest of the year (p. 22)

supply (sə plī′) the amount of an item someone has to sell (p. 77)

Supreme Court (sə prēm′ côrt) the highest court of the United States (p. 51)

Pronunciation Key

a in hat	ō in open	sh in she
ā in age	ȯ in all	th in thin
â in care	ô in order	ᴛн in then
ä in far	oi in oil	zh in measure
e in let	ou in out	ə = a in about
ē in equal	u in cup	ə = e in taken
ėr in term	u̇ in put	ə = i in pencil
i in it	ü in rule	ə = o in lemon
ī in ice	ch in child	ə = u in circus
o in hot	ng in long	

Glossary

tallow (tal′ ō) animal fat used for making candles and soap (p. 339)

tax (taks′) money the government collects to pay for its services (p. 58)

technology (tek nol′ ə jē) the development and use of scientific knowledge to solve practical problems (p. 70)

temperate climate (tem′ pər it klī′ mit) moderate area between the tropical and subarctic climates (p. 23)

temperature (tem′ pər ə chər) a measurement telling how hot or cold something is (p. 19)

timberline (tim′ bər lin′) the elevation on a mountain above which trees cannot grow (p. 369)

totem pole (tō′ təm pōl) a tall post carved with images of people and animals to represent family history (p. 395)

trading post (trā′ ding pōst) a kind of store in which goods are traded (p. 266)

Trail of Tears (trāl əv tirz) the forced journey of the Cherokees to land set aside for them by the United States in what is now Oklahoma (p. 191)

transcontinental railroad (tran′ skon tə nen′ tl rāl′ rōd′) a rail line that crosses an entire country (p. 281)

transportation (tran′ spər tā′ shən) the moving of goods, people, or animals from one place to another (p. 81)

tropical climate (trop′ ə kəl klī′ mit) an area that is usually very warm all year (p. 22)

tundra (tun′ drə) a cold, flat area where trees cannot grow (p. 379)

Union (yü′ nyən) the name for the Northern states during the American Civil War (p. 203)

urban (ėr′ bən) in the city (p. 71)

vaquero (vä ker′ ō) Spanish word for "cowboy" (p. 336)

viceroy (vīs′ roi) an early governor of Mexico (p. 333)

vineyard (vin′ yərd) a place where grapevines are planted (p. 113)

volcano (vol kā′ nō) a type of mountain with an opening through which ash, gas, and lava are forced (p. 372)

want (wänt) something that a person would like to have but can live without (p. 73)

watermen (wȯ′ tər mən) men or women who gather different kinds of seafood and fish in different seasons (p. 117)

waterway (wȯ′ tər wā′) a system of rivers, lakes, and canals, through which ships travel (p. 234)

weather (weŦH ′ ər) the condition of the air at a certain time and place (p. 19)

wetland (wet′ land′) land that is covered with water at times (p. 167)

White House (wīt hous) the place where the President of the United States lives and works (p. 51)

wigwam (wig′ wäm) a Narragansett hut made of wooden poles covered in bark (p. 127)

Index

This Index lists the pages on which topics appear in this book. Page numbers after an *m* refer to a map. Page numbers after a *p* refer to a photograph. Page numbers after a *c* refer to a chart or graph.

Index

Index

election, 50, 51

electricity, 70, 105, 110, 111, 135, 183

electric light bulb, 135

elevation, 21, 167

elevation map, 170, 171, *m*170, *m*372

elk, 369, 370, *p*369

Ellis Island, New York, 132, *m*125

Empire State Building, 142

endangered species, 179

England, 131

entrepreneur, 273

E pluribus unum, 44

equator, 21, 22, 408, H1, *m*21, *m*408, *p*H1

Erie Canal, 143, 280

Erie, Lake, 113, 143, 233, 235, *m*226, *m*234

erosion, 244, 301

Europe, 40, 127, 128, 132, 190, 195, 196, 269, 401, *m*40, *m*133, *m*195

Everglades National Park, 179, *m*165, *m*167

executive branch, 51

exploration, 39–41, 68, 302, 332–337, 400, 401, *m*40, *m*333

export, 141, 414

extinct, 179

fact, 208, 209

fall line, 169, R16, *m*167

farm equipment, 274, 275, *p*275

farmhouse, 272, *p*272

federal government, 48

Finger Lakes Region, 113

fishing, 116–118, 386, 395

Florida, 14, 22, 40, 42, 43, 173, 179, 180, 195, 196, 212, R19, *m*160, *m*173, *p*41

Florida Keys, 173, *m*160, *m*167

flour, 248

flowers, 386

folklore, 198

forest, R16

forest products, *m*387

fort, 266

Fort Canby, Arizona, 326, *m*326

Fort Ross, 401

Fort Sumter, 202, 203, *p*203

forty-niners, 403

fossil, 242–244, *p*242, *p*243

fossil fuel, 183

fountain of youth, 194, 195

Four Corners, *p*15

France, 41, 265, 266, 278, *m*40

Franciscan missions, 401

Franklin, Benjamin, 131

Freedmen's Bureau, 205

freedoms, political. *See* specific freedoms

Freedom Trail, 142

free enterprise system, 76, 77, *c*76

freight train, 237, *p*237

French Quarter, *p*161

freshwater, 233

frigid, 379

Frost, Robert, 107

fruit, 180, 385

fuel, 29

fur trade, 258, 264–267, 278, 401, 405

Garrison, William Lloyd, 137, R53

Gateway Arch, 276, *p*227, *p*276

generalizations, make, 306, 307

generator, 111, *p*110

geography terms, R16, *p*R16

Georgia, 173, 180, 211, R19, *m*160

Georgia State Capitol, 211

Germany, 132, *m*130

geyser, 370

ghost town, 403, 404

gila monster, *p*346

glacier, 105, 167, 233, R16

globalization, 82, 83, *m*83

globe, H12, H13, *p*H12, *p*H13

gold, 333

Golden Gate Bridge, *p*363

gold rush, 69, 211, 393, 402–404, 405, 407, *m*402, *p*69

gorge, 105

government
Cherokee and, 191
free trade and, 76
Narragansett and, 127
Navajo and, 327
United States and, 47–52

Grand Canyon National Park, 13, 297, 299–307, *m*299, *p*293, *p*301, *p*303, *p*304

Grand Teton National Park, H6–H7, *m*H6, *p*H6–H7

Granite State, 115

grape, 112, 113, *m*114, *p*112 *m*387

graphs, 240, 241

grazing, 341, 342

Great Basin, 380, 381, *m*367, *m*381

Great Britain, 132, 401, *m*133

Index

Index

Niagara Falls, 101, 104, 105, 152, *m*103, *m*105, *p*101, *p*152, *p*153

Niagara River, 105, *m*105

Nineteenth Amendment, 138

Nobel Peace Prize, 319

nonrenewable resource, 29, 183, 315

nonviolence, 206

North America, 39, 68, *m*40, *m*195, *m*401, *m*408

North Carolina, 173, 191, 196, R21, *m*160, *m*173, *m*174

North Dakota, R21, *m*226

Northeast Region
   abolitionists in, 137
   boundaries of, 14
   cities in, 140–144, *m*142
   colonies in, 131
   immigration to, 132
   landforms of, 12, 106–109
   Native Americans in, 126–129
   Niagara Falls in, 104, 105, *p*105
   resources of, 28, 112–115

Northern Hemisphere, 408, H13, *p*H13

North Pole, 408, *m*408

notes, 376, 377

nuts, 180, *m*387

Nyiri Desert, 312, *m*312

Oakley, Annie, 340

ocean, 21, R16. *See also* specific oceans

Ocracoke Island, *p*174

Ohio, R21, *m*226

oil, 70, 314, 315, 327, 405, *m*414, *c*315

Ojibwa, 256–258, 264, 266, *p*257, *p*259

Oklahoma, 191, 295, 309, 317, 341, R21, *m*294, *m*309

Old Faithful, 370

Olympia National Park, *p*380

Olympic Mountains, 372, *m*372

Olympic Peninsula, 382

Ontario, Lake, 233, *m*234

On the Banks of Plum Creek, 271

opinion, 208, 209

opportunity cost, 78

Oregon, 13, 385, 401, R21, *m*362, *c*405

Oregon Territory, 42

Ottawa Indians, 259

otter, *p*363

Outer Coastal Plain, 167

outline, 376, 377

overfishing, 118

Pacific Ocean, 369, 383, 400, *m*H12, *m*11

Pacific Rim, 414, *m*414

paper, 388

parallel, 408

Parks, Rosa, 207, *p*207

peanut, 180, *p*161

Pearl Harbor, 406

peninsula, 108

Pennsylvania, 108, R21, *m*98

Philadelphia, Pennsylvania, 131, 137, 141, 142, *m*130, *m*136, *m*142

Phoenix, Arizona, 347, *m*346, *m*347

phonograph, 135

Piedmont, 168, 169, 179, *m*167, *p*168

Pikes Peak, 368, 369, *m*372

Pima Air and Space Museum, 316, *p*316

pineapple, *m*387

pioneer, 198, 271, 272

Pittsburgh, Pennsylvania, 141, 143, 145, *m*125, *m*142, *p*143

plain, 12, 28, 229

plantation, 198, 199, *p*199

plant nursery, 389

plants, 310, 311, 386, 389, *p*310, *p*311

plateau, 13

Platte River, *m*279

plow, 273–274, *p*273

plumb, *m*387

Plymouth, Massachusetts, 131, *m*130

Pocono Mountains, 107, *m*H13, *m*98

polar climate, 22

pollution, 118, 143, 145

Ponce de León, Juan, 40, 195, *m*40, *m*195, *p*194

Pony Express, 80

population, *c*240, *c*241, *c*413

port cities, 141, 143, 163, 237

Port of South Louisiana, 163

potato, 385, *m*387

Potawatomi Indians, 259

potlatch, 396, *p*396

Powell, John Wesley, 297, 302, 305, 306, *p*305

Powhatan Indians, 196

powwow, 128

prairie, 245, 272

prairie dog, 279

Index

talking stick, 256, *p*256

tallow, 339

technology, 70, 316–317

telephone, 132, 135

telescope, 316, *p*316

temperature, 13, 309, 349, 379, 380, *m*173, *m*309, *m*381

temperate climate, 23

Tennessee, 198, R20, *m*160

Texas, 41, 295, 309, 314, 315, 317, 339–341, 343, R20, *m*294, *m*309

Thailand, 250–251, *m*250

Thirteenth Amendment, 137, 204

"This Land Is Your Land," 3

Thoreau, Henry David, 97

timber, 388

timberline, 369

time line, 134, 135

time zone, 7, 54–55, *m*54

Tlingit, 394–399

Tlingit Cultural Region, 395, *m*393

tomato, *m*387

totem pole, 395, *p*395

trade

  barter as, 73, *p*73

  Cahokia and, 277

  Cherokee culture and, 190

  communication and, 84

  European explorers and, 40, 127

  free enterprise system and, 76, 77

  Jefferson and, 278

  Ojibwa and, 258, 264, 266

  Pacific Rim and, 414

  St. Louis and, 280

  Tlingit and, 395

trading post, 266, 267

Trail of Tears, 191, *p*191

train, 237, *p*237

transcontinental railroad, 281, *m*281

transportation, 81–84, 141, 212, 236, 237, 280–282

tree, 29, 182, 369, 388, *p*363

Triangle Region, 213

tropical climate, 22, 23, 380

Troy Female Seminary, 139

trucks, 236, 237

Truth, Sojourner, 137

Tucson, Arizona, 346, 347, *m*323

tugboat, *p*236

tuna, *m*387

tundra, 379

turbine, 111, *p*110

Twain, Mark, 283, *p*283

Tyrannosaurus rex, 242–243, *p*242, *p*243

Uncle Tom's Cabin, 201

Union, 203

United States

  boundaries in, 14, 15

  Cherokees and, 190

  Civil War in, 202–205, 281, *p*204

  climates of, 22, 23, *m*22

  communication in, 84

  culture and, 43

  exploration of, 39–41, 401, *m*40

  government of, 47–52, *c*50

  immigration to, 132, 133

  independence of, 131

  industry in, 70, 71

  inset maps of, 24, *m*4, *m*24, *m*25

  international trade and, 414

  landforms in, 12, 13

  money in, 74, 75, *p*75

  natural resources of, 27, 28

  regions of, 11–15, *m*4, *m*11

  slavery in, 136, 137

  time zone maps of, 54–55, *m*54

  trade in, 73, 76

  transportation in, 81–83, 281, *m*281

  women's rights in, 138, 139

urban, 71

Utah, 328, 381, 386, 412, R20, *m*362, *c*405

Index

Valdez, Alaska, 405

vaquero, 336, 340

vegetable, 385

Vermont, 43, 106, 108, 114, 115, R20, *m*98

Vermont Maple Festival, 114

vertical time line, 134, 135

Very Large Array, 316, *p*316

vice president, 51

viceroy, 333, 335

vineyard, 113

Virginia, 173, 196, R21, *m*160

volcano, 365, 372–373, 374–375, 377

vote, right to, 138, 205

Waialeale, Mount, 382

Walden, 97

want, 73

Wapello County, Iowa, 270, 271, *m*255, *m*270

War Between the States, 203

Washington, 382, 385, 386, 401, R21, *m*362, *c*405

Washington, D.C., 14, 48, 51, 131, *m*35, *m*98

Washington, George, 131, 190, 197

water, 29

waterfall, 168, *p*168

watermen, 116, 117, *p*117

waterway, 234, *m*234

weather, 18–23, 173, 174, *m*173

Web site, 262

Weld, Theodore Dwight, 201

Welland Ship Canal, 235, *m*105, *m*234

Western Australia, 120, *m*121

Western Cherokee, 191

West Region, 11, 13, 14, 28, 69
cities of, 411–413, 416, 417
climate of, 378–383
exploration and growth of, 400–406, *m*401
map of, *m*362, *m*372, *m*381
mountains in, 365, 368, 369, 372–373, 377, *m*372, *p*369, *p*373, *p*379
Native Americans of, 394–399
Pacific Rim trade and, 414
resources in, 384–389
Yellowstone National Park in, 370–371

West Virginia, R21, *m*160

wetlands, 167, 179, 310–311, *p*311

whale watching, *p*415

whaling, 118, *p*118

wheat, 27, 248, *m*387

White House, 51, *m*35

White, John, 196

White Mountains, 106, *m*H13, *m*98

wigwam, 127, *p*127

Wilderness Road, 198

wildfire, 371

wildlife, 370

Wild West, 340, 404

Willamette Valley, Oregon, 385

Williams, Roger, 128

Window Rock, Arizona, 327, *m*323, *m*324

winter, 21, 379, 380

Wisconsin, 249, R21, *m*226

women's rights movement, 138, 139, 140, 141

wood, 388

World Trade Center, 148

World War II, 53, 329, 330, 405, 406

World Wide Web, 262

Wright, Orville and Wilbur, 135

Wyoming, 370, R21, *m*362, *c*405

Yakima, Washington, 382

Yearling, The, 179

Yellowstone National Park, 370, 371, *m*368, *p*370, *p*371

zebra mussels, 238, *p*238

Credits

TEXT: **Dorling Kindersley (DK)** is an international publishing company specializing in the creation of high-quality reference content for books, CD-ROMs, online and video. The hallmark of DK content is its unique combination of educational value and strong visual style. This combination allows DK to deliver appealing, accessible and engaging educational content that delights children, parents and teachers around the world. Scott Foresman is delighted to have been able to use selected extracts of DK content within this Social Studies program.

140–141 from *First Ladies* by Amy Pastan in association with the Smithsonian Institution. Copyright © 2001 by Dorling Kindersley Limited and the Smithsonian Institution.

176–177 from *Eyewitness: Hurricane & Tornado* by Jack Challoner. Copyright © 2000 by Dorling Kindersley Limited.

374–375 from *Eyewitness: Volcano & Earthquake* by Susanna Van Rose. Copyright © 1992 by Dorling Kindersley Limited.

From *The Yearling* by Marjorie Kinnan Rawlings. Text copyright © 1938 Marjorie Kinnan Rawlings; copyright renewed © 1966 Norton Baskin. Reprinted with the permission of Atheneum Books for Young Readers, an imprint of Simon & Schuster Children's Publishing Division and Brandt & Hochman Literary Agents, Inc. p.179

"Ripening Cherries" by Florence Vilén. Reprinted by permission of the author. p.385

"Sweet Betsy from Pike" adapted and arranged by Lillian Wiedman. Reprinted by permission of Pearson Education, Inc. p.420

Text excerpt from *Cowboy Country* by Ann Herbert Scott. Text copyright © 1993 by Ann Herbert Scott. Reprinted by permission of Clarion Books/Houghton Mifflin Company. All rights reserved. p.354

Illustration from *Cowboy Country* by Ann Herbert Scott, pictures by Ted Lewin. Illustrations copyright © 1993 by Ted Lewin. Reprinted by permission of Clarion Books/Houghton Mifflin Company. All rights reserved. p.354

"Stopping by Woods on a Snowy Evening" by Robert Frost from *The Poetry of Robert Frost*, Edward Connery Lathem. Copyright © 1969 by Henry Holt and Co., copyright © 1951 by Robert Frost. Reprinted by permission of Henry Holt and Company, LLC. p.107

From *The Desert Is Theirs* by Byrd Baylor. Copyright © 1975 by Byrd Baylor. Reprinted by permission of Atheneum Books for Young Readers, an imprint of Simon & Schuster Children's Publishing. p.310

From *On the Banks of Plum Creek* by Laura Ingalls Wilder. Text copyright © 1937 by Laura Ingalls Wilder. Copyright renewed © 1965 Roger L. MacBridge. Used by permission of HarperCollins Publishers. p.273

Reprinted from *Josefina Saves the Day* by Valerie Tripp with permission from Pleasant Company. p.74

"Niagara" from *The People, Yes* by Carl Sandburg, copyright © 1936 by Harcourt Brace & Company and renewed 1964 by Carl Sandburg. Reprinted by permission. p.152

From "This Land Is Your Land" words and music by Woody Guthrie. TRO Copyright © 1956 (Renewed) 1958 (Renewed) 1970 (Renewed) Ludlow Music, Inc., New York, New York. Used by permission. p.iii, 3

MAPS: MapQuest.com, Inc.

ILLUSTRATIONS:
16, 17, 21, 382, R16, R17 Leland Klanderman; 36 Paul Bachem; 48, 50 Paul Perreault; 67 Neal Armstrong; 83 Joe LeMonnier; 110 Robert Lawson; 119, 402 Mike Reagan; 174, 181, 387, 389 Susan J. Carlson; 200, 201 Robert Gunn; 208 Julian Mulock; 235 Robert Van Nutt; 239, 303 Albert Lorenz; 279 Guy Porfirio; 286, 350 Darryl Ligasan; 354, 355 © Ted Lewin 389 Richard Waldrep; 414, 417 Peter Siu; 414 Elizabeth Wolf; 420 John Sandford

PHOTOGRAPHS:
Every effort has been made to secure permission and provide appropriate credit for photographic material. The publisher deeply regrets any omission and pledges to correct errors called to their attention in subsequent editions.

Unless otherwise acknowledged, all photographs are the property of Scott Foresman, a division of Pearson Education.

Cover: © Panoramic Images, Chicago, (BR) © F. Schussler/PhotoLink/PhotoDisc
Endsheets: Front - Left page: (BCL), (TL), (TR) Hemera Technologies, (BC) © Richard Price/Getty Images, (BL) © Reza Estakhrian/Getty Images, (BR) © Adam Woolfitt/Corbis, (CR) PhotoDisc, Front - Right page: © Panoramic Images, Chicago, (BC) © Amanda Clement/PhotoDisc, (TR) © Kunio Owaki/Corbis Stock Market, (CR) © C. Borland/PhotoLink/PhotoDisc (BR) Hemera Technologies, (BL) Superstock, (RC) © F. Schussler/PhotoLink/PhotoDisc, Back - Left page: (BL) © Joseph Sohm/Visions of America/Corbis, (TR) © Joseph Sohm/Chromosohm/Photo Researchers, Inc., (CR) Hemera Technologies, Back - Right page: (BL) Hemera Technologies, (CR) © Laurie Rubin/Getty Images, PhotoDisc
Front Matter:
E1 (TL) © Corbis, (C) © Heidi Zeiger Photography, (BCL) © Brian Post/Mount Washington Observatory, (CR, Bkgd) © Hemera Technologies, (B) © David R. Frazier Photolibrary, (BL) © Ed Pritchard/Getty Images; E2 (BCL) © Geoffrey Clements/Corbis, © eStock Photo, (TCL) © Corbis, (BCL) © MAPS.com/Corbis; E3 (BCL) © M. Gibson/Robertstock.com, (BCL) © Corbis, (BCL) © Steve Dunwell/Folio Inc., (Bkgd) © Mark E. Gibson Stock Photography, (BCL) © Bob Rowan, Progressive

Credits

Image/Corbis; E4 (BCL) © Flip Chalfant/Getty Images, © Ed Young/Corbis; E4-5 (C) © David W. Hamilton; E5 (BCL) © Terres du Sud/Sygma/Corbis, © Comstock Inc., © Getty Images; E6 (Inset) Corbis, (BCL) © Hulton-Deutsch Collection/Corbis; E6-7 (BCL) © A & L Sinibaldi/Getty Images; E7 (BCL) © G. Brad Lewis/Photo Researchers, Inc., © Galen Rowell/Corbis; E8-9 (Bkgd) © David Metsky; E9 (CC) © C.W. Biedel, M.D./Photri – Microstock, (BCL) © Christopher J. Morris/Corbis, © Brian Post/Mount Washington Observatory, © Cosmo Condina/Getty Images; E10 © B.S.P.I./Corbis; E10-11 (TCL, TR, TCR, CL) © Heidi Zeiger Photography, (Bkgd) © Getty Images; E11 (TCL) © Getty Images, (R) © Robert Holmes/Corbis, (BR) © Volker Mohrke/Corbis; E12-13 (CR) © Richard Cummins/Corbis; E13 (Inset) © Courtesy Women's Museum; E14 (BL) © Dave G. Houser/Houserstock, Inc., (CL) © James A. Sugar/Getty Images; E14-15 (BC, C, L) © David R. Frazier Photolibrary, (BL) © James Randklev/Getty Images, (BR) © David Hughes/Alamy.com; E15 (CR) © David W. Hamilton/Getty Images, (CR) © A. Witte/ C. Mahaney/Getty Images, (CR) © David Olsen/Getty Images, (BC) © Getty Images; E16 (TC) © Gary Randall/Getty Images, (CL) © Ed Pritchard/Getty Images; iv SuperStock v Art Resource, NY vi Jacquelyn Modesitt Schindehette vii (Detail) Estate of Grant Wood/Licensed by VAGA, New York, NY/Joslyn Museum, Omaha, NE/SuperStock viii Christie's Images/Corbis ix Geoffrey Clements/Corbis x (C) Julie Habel/Corbis, (T) Earth Imaging/Stone xii, xiii © Panoramic Images, Chicago H4 Colonial Williamsburg Foundation H5 Colonial Williamsburg Foundation H6 (Bkgd) Index Stock Imagery, (R) © Raymond Gehman/Corbis, (L) © David Muench/Corbis H7 (R) Greg Martin/SuperStock, (L) © Dewitt Jones/Corbis H8 Earth Imaging/Getty Images H17 © David Young-Wolff/Getty Images

Unit 1:
5 (TL) © Panoramic Images, Chicago, (BL) Laurence Parent, (BR) © Panoramic Images, Chicago, (CL) © Kathleen Brown/Corbis, (TR) © Walter Bibikow/Getty Images 8 (B) SuperStock, (C) © Julie Habel/ Corbis, (T) © Mark Wagner/Getty Images 10 Tom Burnside/Photo Researchers, Inc. 12 (B) © Bob Krist/Getty Images, (T) © Ron Thomas/Getty Images, (Bkgd) © Chris Sanders/Getty Images 13 (R) Jack Hoehn/Index Stock Imagery, (L) Larry Lefever/Grant Heilman Photography 14 (B) © Joseph Sohm/Corbis, (T) L © Kevin R. Morris/ Corbis 15 © Dave G. Houser/Corbis 18 NOAA /Weatherstock 22 Carl Purcell/Words and Pictures 23 (L) © Doug Wilson/Corbis, (R) PhotoDisc 26 Texas Department of Transportation 27 (TC) PhotoDisc, (BR) Eascott/Momatuk/Animals Animals/Earth Scenes, (TR) Artville, (BL) Steve Satushek 28 (T) PhotoDisc, (B) © Comstock Inc. 29 (B) Mark E. Gibson/Visuals Unlimited, (T) Grelad & Buff Corsi/Visuals Unlimited 30 Jim Emery/Folio Inc. 31 Mark E. Gibson/Visuals Unlimited 33 (BCC) Leonard Lee Rue/Bruce Coleman Collection,

(TL) © David W. Hamilton/Getty Images, (TCL) © Aldo Torelli/Getty Images, (BCL) René Burri/© Magnum Photos, (BL) © A. & L. Sinibaldi/Getty Images, (TCCL) © Dorling Kindersley, (TCCR) © Gary Irving/Getty Images, (TC) PhotoDisc, (TR) © Gene Ahrens, (BR) © Dorling Kindersley, (TCR) Dennis Stock/© Magnum Photos, (BCR) © Richard Hamilton Smith/Corbis 34 Patrick J. Endres/Visuals Unlimited 36 (B) © Andy Sacks/Getty Images, (C) Robert Clay/Visuals Unlimited 38 Museum of the History of Science, Oxford 39 Breck P. Kent/Animals Animals/Earth Scenes 41 Corbis 42 (T) Courtesy National Archives of the United States (from THE NATIONAL ARCHIVES OF THE UNITED STATES by Herman J. Viola, ©1984 Harry N. Abrams, Inc. New York), (B) SuperStock 43 SuperStock 44 Sandy Vanderlaan/Visuals Unlimited 45 Bettmann/Corbis 47 Mike Pattisall/Photri, Inc. 49 (B) Don Farrall/PhotoDisc, (C) Phil Martin/PhotoEdit, (T) SuperStock 51 Supreme Court Historical Society/Richard W. Strauss/Smithsonian Institution 52 Vivian Ronay 53 (Bkgd) © David Muench/Corbis, (L) Corbis, (BR) Courtesy, Senator Daniel Inouye 57 Photri, Inc. 58 (B) Jeff Cadge 59 © Andy Sacks/Getty Images 60, 61 Ruben R. Ramirez/El Paso Times 62 PhotoDisc 64 (C) Hulton Archive, (B) © Lawrence Manning/Corbis, (T) © Mike McQueen/Getty Images 66 N. Carter/North Wind Picture Archives 67 Museum of Mankind/© Dorling Kindersley 68 Culver Pictures Inc. 69 (B) The Granger Collection, New York, (T) © Mike McQueen/Getty Images 70 Detroit Industry, North Wall (Detail), 1932-1933, Diego M. Rivera, Gift of Edsel B. Ford, photograph ©2001/Detroit Institute of Arts 72 Gallo Images/Corbis 73 Hulton/Archive/Getty Images 75 British Museum/© Dorling Kindersley 77 (T) Jeff Greenberg/Visuals Unlimited, (B) Reuters/Corbis 78 (L) © Kelly-Mooney Photography/Corbis, (R) A. Ramey/PhotoEdit 79 © Tessa Codrington /Getty Images 80 St. Joseph Museum, St. Joseph, Missouri 81 (T) Bettman/Corbis, (B) © Bruce Hands/Getty Images 82 (R) © Jim Sugar/Corbis, (L) Robert Holmgren/Peter Arnold, Inc. 83 (R) Robert Holmgren/Peter Arnold, Inc., (L) © Lester Lefkowitz/Getty Images, (C) L. O'Shaughnessy/H. Armstrong Roberts 85 Siede Preis/PhotoDisc 88 PhotoDisc 90, 91 (Bkgd) © Panoramic Images, Chicago

Unit 2:
95, 96, 97 Art Resource, NY 98 (B) © Walter Bibikow/Getty Images 99 (TCL) © Bob Rowan/Corbis, (BCL) Randa Bishop, (CC) Donovan Reese/PhotoDisc, (R) © V.C.L/Getty Images 101 SuperStock 102 (T) © Cosmo Condina/Getty Images, (B) © Lynda Richardson/Corbis, (C) ©Jonathan Blair/Corbis 104 © Paul A. Souders/Corbis 106 © Raymond Gehman/Corbis 107 (T) AFP/Corbis, (B) © Susan Rosenthal/Corbis 108 © Buddy Mays/Corbis 109 Preston J. Garrison/Visuals Unlimited 112 © Kunio Owaki/Corbis Stock Market 113 Marilyn "Angel" Wynn/Nativestock 114 Ted Levin/Animals Animals/ Earth Scenes 115 © Joseph Sohm; ChromoSohm Inc/Corbis 116 © Lynda Richardson/Corbis 117

Credits

Sonda Dawes/Image Works 118 (B) SuperStock, (T) Courtesy Nantucket Historical Association 119 © Josh Reynolds/Image Works 120 (T) H. Armstrong Roberts, (Bkgd) Viesti Collection, Inc. 121 (T) James Watt/ Animals Animals/Earth Scenes, (C) Eric Kamp/ Index Stock Imagery, (B) © Paul A. Souders/ Corbis 122 © Lowell Georgia/Corbis 124 (TC) SuperStock, (BC) Hulton-Deutsch Collection Limited/Corbis, (B) SuperStock, (T) North Wind Pictures/North Wind Picture Archives 126 AP/Wide World Photos 127 (B) North Wind Pictures/North Wind Picture Archives, (T) Marilyn "Angel" Wynn/Nativestock 128 AP/Wide World 129 Marilyn "Angel" Wynn/ Nativestock 130 SuperStock 131 SuperStock 132 Bettmann-Corbis 135 (T), (CC), (CBC), (BC), (B) Stock Montage Inc., (TC) The Granger Collection, New York 136 The Granger Collection, New York 137 Bettmann/Corbis 138 Library of Congress/Corbis 139 (Bkgd) AP/Wide World, (R) Bettmann Archive/Bettmann-Corbis, (L) Corbis, (Bkgd) Hulton-Deutsch Collection/Corbis, (Bkgd) Library of Congress/Corbis, (Bkgd) Hulton/Archive/ Getty Images 140, 141 140 National Museum of American History, Behring Center/Smithsonian Institution 141 (TL, TR) National Museum of American History, Behring Center/Smithsonian Institution, (B) Library of Congress 143 Hulton/Archive/Getty Images 145 SuperStock 146 © Richard T. Nowitz/Corbis 147 (R) SuperStock, (L) © Patrick Ward/Corbis, (Bkgd) © Steven Rothfeld/Getty Images 148, 149 Ethan Moses 150 Marilyn "Angel" Wynn/Nativestock 152, 153 Brooklyn Museum of Art, New York, USA/Bridgeman Art Library International Ltd.

Unit 3:
157, 158, 159 Jacquelyn Modesitt Schindehette 160 © Panoramic Images, Chicago 161 (TL) © Ken Reid/Getty Images, (CL) Laszlo Selly/FoodPix, (BL) Cousteau Society/Getty Images, (CR) Benn Mitchell, (TR) PhotoDisc 163 George Gerster/Photo Researchers, Inc. 164 (T) © Michael T. Sedham/ Corbis, (C) SuperStock, (B) © Kevin Fleming/Corbis 166 © Randy Faris/Corbis 168 (T) ©James Carmichael/Getty Images, (B) © David Muench/Corbis 171 Laurence Parent 172 (R) © Nicole Duplaix/ Corbis, (L) © Forest Johnson/Corbis 175 Michael Brindle/ BrindlePix 176 (T) © David Toase/Travel Ink, (BL) © Dr. A. C. Waltham/Robert Harding 176 (BR) © Gary Williams/Getty Images 177 (R) © Volvox/Index Stock Imagery 178 SuperStock 179 Rick Baetsen/ Visuals Unlimited 180 SuperStock 182 (T) PhotoDisc, (B) © Ric Ergenbright/Corbis 183 (T) Breck P. Kent/Animals Animals/Earth Scenes 184 Colorstock/ Getty Images 185 Warren Faidley/ Weatherstock 186 (TC) © Karen Huntt Mason/Corbis, (B) SuperStock, (T) Marilyn "Angel" Wynn/Nativestock, (BC) Fort Sumpter/Visuals Unlimited 188 North Wind Picture Archives 189 (C), (B) Marilyn "Angel" Wynn/ Nativestock, (T) Richard A. Cooke/Corbis 190 The Granger Collection, New York 191 The Granger Collection, New York 192 Marilyn "Angel" Wynn/ Nativestock 193 (L) © Galen Rowell/Corbis, (R)

Newberry Library, Chicago/SuperStock, (Bkgd) Marilyn "Angel" Wynn/Nativestock 194 SuperStock 195 North Wind Picture Archives 196 © Karen Huntt Mason/Corbis 197 (T) Monticello/Thomas Jefferson Foundation, Inc., (B) North Wind Picture Archives 198 (L) Burstein Collection/Corbis 199 (TL) © Franz-Marc Frei/Corbis 201 AP/Wide World 202 Fort St. Joseph Museum 203 (B) North Wind Picture Archives, (T) Stock Montage Inc. 204 Photri, Inc. 205 The Granger Collection, New York 206 © Flip Schulke/Corbis 207 (B) Carlos Osorio/AP/Wide World, (Bkgd) Bettmann/ Corbis, (T) Rus Baxley Photography 210 © Joseph Sohm; ChromoSohm/ Corbis 211 Hulton/Archive/ Getty Images 212 David Sailors Photography 213 © Eric Horan 214 (BL) © Annie Griffiths Belt/Corbis, (BR) William Struhs, (TL) Margot Granitsas/Image Works 215 (TR) Wade Spees/AP/ Wide World, (C) Margot Granitsas/Image Works 216 (TR) Marilyn "Angel" Wynn/Nativestock 218, 219 (Bkgd) © Richard A. Cooke/Corbis

Unit 4:
223, 224, 225 (C) (Detail) Estate of Grant Wood/Licensed by VAGA, New York, NY/Joslyn Museum, Omaha, NE/SuperStock 226 © Panoramic Images, Chicago 227 (TL) © James L. Amos/Corbis, (TR) Larry Lefever/Grant Heilman Photography, (BL) © Vladimir Pcholkin /Getty Images, (BR) SuperStock, (CL) Joel Sartore/Grant Heilman Photography 229 Detail) Estate of Grant Wood/Licensed by VAGA, New York, NY/Joslyn Museum, Omaha, NE/SuperStock 230 B) © Patti McConville/Getty Images, (TC) © Dave G. Hauser/Corbis, (T) John Sohlden/Visuals Unlimited, (C) Tim Brown/Index Stock Imagery 232 Wendella Sightseeing Boats 233 B) © Macduff Everton/Corbis, (T) WorldSat International/ Science Source/Photo Researchers, Inc. 236 © Bruce Forster/Getty Images 237 Skip Nall/PhotoDisc 238 (T) Peter Yates/TimePix, (D) Dave Haas/The Image Finders 242 Emile Wamsteker/AP/Wide World 243 Reuters/NewMedia, Inc./Corbis 244 Tim Brown/Index Stock Imagery 245 SuperStock 246 (R) © Tom Bean/Corbis, (L) Artville 248 TL) © Wayne Eastep/Getty Images, (TR) © Charles O'Rear/Corbis, (BL) Zefa Visual Media - Germany/Index Stock Imagery, (BC) Inga Spence/Index Stock Imagery, (BR) Nigel Cattlin/H.S. Int./Photo Researchers, Inc., (TC) © Willard Clay/Getty Images 249 (T) © Macduff Everton/Corbis, (B) Judd Pilossof/FoodPix 250 (B) Getty Images, (CR) © Jim Richardson/ Corbis 251 (T) © Yann Layma/Getty Images, (BR) SuperStock 252 N. Carter/North Wind Picture Archives 254 TC) © Layne Kennedy/Corbis, (B) PhotoDisc, (T) Minnesota Historical Society, (BC) Fred Hultstrand History in Pictures Collection, NDSU-NDIRS, Fargo 256 Marilyn "Angel" Wynn/Nativestock 257 Minnesota Historical Society 258 © Peter Turnley/Corbis 259 © Phil Schermeister/Corbis 264 © Lowell Georgia/Corbis 266 © Layne Kennedy/Corbis 267 © Dallas and John Heaton/Corbis 268-269 © Colonial Williamsburg Foundation 270 Fred Hultstrand History in Pictures Collection, NDSU-NDIRS, Fargo 271 Michael Maslan

Credits

Historic Photographs/Corbis 272 Corbis 273 B) "Detail image" of John Deere Carries New Plow to Test Site by Walter Haskell Hinton, oil on canvas, 11x16 inches/Courtesy of the John Deere Art Collection, (T) Wallace Kirkland/TimePix, (Bkgd) PhotoDisc 274, 275 (B) Smithsonian Institution 276 (BL) PhotoDisc 277 Cahokia Mounds State Historic Site 278 R) North Wind Pictures/North Wind Picture Archives, (L), (C) Independence National Historical Park 280 Currier & Ives/The Granger Collection, New York 283 R) The Granger Collection, New York, (CL) Lowell Observatory/AURA/NOAO/NSF 284 Marilyn "Angel" Wynn/Nativestock

Unit 5:

291, 292, 293 Christie's Images/Corbis 294 (B) Laurence Parent 295 CL) Hal Gage/Index Stock Imagery, (CR) Corbis, (TR) Jess Alford/ PhotoDisc, (BC) © Steve Bly/Getty Images, (TL) © Dewitt Jones/Corbis 297 © Eddie Hironaka/Getty Images 298 T) © John Beatty/Getty Images, (C) © Art Wolfe/Getty Images, (B) © David Muench/Corbis 301 © John Beatty/Getty Images 302 © Buddy Mays/ Corbis 303 SuperStock 304 © Marc Romanelli/Getty Images 305 Bkgd) © Marc Romanelli/Getty Images, (L), (R) © John K. Hillers/Corbis 306 (B) R. Kord/H. Armstrong Roberts 308 T) © Frank Lane Picture Agency/Corbis, (B) © Art Wolfe/Getty Images 310 T) © Granitsas/Getty Images, (B) © Charles C. Place/Getty Images 311 R) © David Muench/Corbis, (L) Jack Ryan/Photo Researchers, Inc. 312 L) © Dallas and John Heaton/Corbis, (R) © David Muench/ Corbis 313 (B) © Papilio/Corbis, (T) © Gallo Images/ Corbis 314 Hulton/Archive/Getty Images 316 B) © Roger Ressmeyer/Corbis, (TR) Courtesy of the Pima Air & Space Museum 317 James P. Rowan Stock Photography 318 AP/Wide World Photos 319 B) Rhoda Sidney/PhotoEdit, (T) Courtesy Jerrie Cobb Foundation, Inc. 320 T) © John Beatty/Getty Images, (B) © John K. Hillers/Corbis 322 BC) King Ranch, Inc., Kingsville, Texas, (B) Bob Rowan; Progressive Image/Corbis, (T) Rachel Epstein/Image Works, (TC) Danny Lehman/Corbis 324 Tom Bean 325 B) North Wind Picture Archives, (TR) American Museum of Natural History/© Dorling Kindersley 326 B) Arthur Olivas, Detail, #38194/Museum of New Mexico, (T) Bettmann/Corbis 328 SuperStock 329 Bkgd) Corbis, (R) Arthur Olivas, Detail, #15950/Ben Wittick/Courtesy of Museum of New Mexico, (L) Edmond Van Hoorick/PhotoDisc 331 Marine Corps/Department of Defense 332 Wallace Collection, London, UK/Bridgeman Art Library International Ltd. 335 © Sandy Felsenthal/ Corbis 336 Kolvoord/Image Works 337 © Danny Lehman/Corbis 338 Mark Culbertson/Index Stock Imagery 339 Inga Spence/Visuals Unlimited 340 (T) Corbis-Bettmann, (B) Corbis 342 Archives and Manuscripts Division of the Oklahoma Historical Society 343 King Ranch, Inc., Kingsville, Texas 344, 345 Smithsonian Institution 346 (BR) © Brian Kenney 347 © Thomas Wiewandt/Getty Images 348 Carrier Corporation 349 B) Bettmann Archive/Corbis, (T) Corbis, (Bkgd)

Eddie Stangler/Index Stock Imagery 350, 351 Alan Rose 352 SuperStock 356 © Gary Randall/Getty Images 357 Arthur Olivas Detail, #15950/Ben Wittick/Courtesy of Museum of New Mexico

Unit 6:

359, 360, 361 Geoffrey Clements/Corbis 362 (B) © Kathleen Brown/Corbis 363 TL) © Stuart Westmorland/Getty Images, (TC) PhotoDisc, (BL) Eyewire, Inc., (C) © Robert Cameron/Getty Images, (TR) V.C.L./Getty Images 365 L) © Craig Aurness/Corbis, (R) L. Carstens/H. Armstrong Roberts 366 B) Carmen Northen/Index Stock Imagery, (T) Raymond K. Gehman/NGS Image Collection, (C) Neil Gilchrist/© Panoramic Images, Chicago 368 © Joseph Sohm/Corbis, (B) Richard Day/© Panoramic Images, Chicago 369 Tom J. Ulrich/Visuals Unlimited 370 (B) © Panoramic Images, Chicago 371 C) Chuck Nacke/Woodfin Camp & Associates, (T) Ken M. Johns/Photo Researchers, Inc. 373 © George D. Lepp/Corbis 374 TR) © Photri/Robert Harding, (TL), (BR) © Gary Rosenquist, 1980, (BL) © Dorling Kindersley, (CL) University of California/GSF 375 TL) Robert Harding, (TR), (C) © Lawrence Burr/Getty Images, (B) © Gary Rosenquist, 1980 378 Alaska Stock 379 © Harvey Lloyd/Getty Images 380 A&E Morris/Visuals Unlimited 381 Richard Olsenius/NGS Image Collection 383 Jeff Greenberg/Image Works 384 Burke/Triolo Productions/FoodPix 385 © Phil Degginger/Getty Images 386 T) Vanessa Vick/Photo Researchers, Inc., (B) Peter Adams/Index Stock Imagery 388 Gary C. Will/Visuals Unlimited 389 (C) Grant Symon, (Bkgd) Ross Frid/Visuals Unlimited 390 © Craig Aurness/Corbis 392 T) AK/Haines/Photri, Inc., (C) Hulton/Archive/Getty Images, (B) Mark Richards/PhotoEdit 394 Porterfield/Chickerine/Photo Researchers, Inc. 395 Jeff Greenberg/Image Works 396 B) Marilyn "Angel" Wynn/ Nativestock, (T) Lawrence Migdale/Photo Researchers, Inc. 398 BL) Adam Woolfit/Woodfin Camp & Associates, (TR) Robert Frerck/Woodfin Camp & Associates 399 Canadian Museum of Civilization 400 Chuck Place Photography 403 Hulton/Archive/Getty Images 404 T) Corbis-Bettmann, (B) Geoff Clifford/Woodfin Camp & Associates 405 One Mile Up, Inc. 406 (CL) PhotoDisc 407 L) Nancy Richmond/Image Works, (Bkgd) Corbis, (R) SuperStock 410 © James Cotier/Getty Images 411 (B) © Kurt Krieger/Corbis, (T) © Robert Landau/Corbis 412 © Scott T. Smith/Corbis 413 Stocktrek/PhotoDisc 415 © Paul Chesley/Getty Images 416 B) © Shelley Gazin/Corbis, (T) Lester Sloan/Woodfin Camp & Associates 418 © Galen Rowell/Corbis

End Matter:

R1 Earth Imaging/Getty Images R2 Earth Imaging/ Getty Images R18, R19 One Mile Up, Inc. R20, R21 One Mile Up, Inc. R24 One Mile Up, Inc. R26, R27 (Bkgd) Bettmann/Corbis R38 BR) © Sandy Felsenthal/Corbis, (TR) SuperStock, (TR) © Peter Cade/Getty Images, (L) © Julie Habel/Corbis R43 © Galen Rowell/Corbis

ROUTE US 66

LEWIS AND CLARK TRAIL